Dean D. Dauphinais

drives a 1994 Saturn SW2 station wagon. The day after he picked it up from the dealership, it was rear-ended on I-94 in downtown Detroit. (Not to worry, though. No one was hurt, insurance picked up the tab, and besides . . . it's leased!) Dean's previous cars include a 1992 Jeep Cherokee Laredo, a 1990 Volkswagen Golf GL, a 1985 Volkswagen Jetta GLI, a 1981 Dodge Omni Charger 2.2, and a 1976 Ford Maverick (thanks, mom).

Peter M. Gareffa

drives a 1995 Honda, the fourth in a series of Accords ("They're boring, but reliable transportation"), in addition to his beloved Harley-Davidson motorcycle. Previous vehicles include 1963 and 1969 Volkswagen Beetles, a 1966 Datsun roadster, a couple of Nissan pickups, a 1964 Plymouth station wagon, a 1969 Jaguar E-Type roadster, and a few other bikes.

CARcrazy

**The Official Motor City
High-Octane,
Turbocharged,
Chrome-Plated,
Back Road
Book of Car Culture**

Dean D. Dauphinais
Peter M. Gareffa

CARcrazy

The Official Motor City High-Octane, Turbocharged, Chrome-Plated, Back Road Book of Car Culture

VISIBLE INK PRESS

DETROIT • NEW YORK • TORONTO

CARcrazy

The Official Motor City High-Octane, Turbocharged, Chrome-Plated, Back Road Book of Car Culture

Published by Visible Ink Press™, a division of Gale Research
835 Penobscot Building
Detroit, MI 48226-4094

Visible Ink Press is a trademark of Gale Research.

Most Visible Ink Press books are available at special quantity discounts when purchased in bulk by corporations, organizations, or groups. Customized printings, special imprints, messages, and excerpts can be produced to meet your needs. For more information, contact Special Markets Manager, Gale Research, 835 Penobscot Bldg., Detroit, MI 48226. Or call 1-800-776-6265.

Art Director: Tracey Rowens

FRONT COVER PHOTO:
1957 DeSoto, from the collections of the Henry Ford Museum and Greenfield Village.

Library of Congress Cataloging-in-Publication Data

Dauphinais, Dean 1961-
    Car crazy : the official Motor City high-octane, turbocharged,
    chrome-plated, back road book of car culture / Dean D. Dauphinais,
    Peter M. Gareffa, Don Boyden.
        p.   cm.
    Includes index.
    ISBN 0-7876-0907-2 (alk. paper)
    1. Automobiles--United States--Miscellanea. 2. Automobiles-
    -Social aspects--United States. I. Gareffa, Peter M. (Peter
    Michael), 1952-   . II. Boyden, Donald P. III. Title.
    TL23.D38 1996
    629.222'0973--dc20   96-2729
                                                                  CIP

For Kathy, Sam, and Josh

contents

Detroit. Just the mention of that city brings visions of cars to mind. Detroit: the Motor City. Henry Ford. The assembly line. So, when a bunch of us big-shot editors were sitting around our downtown Detroit conference room trying to figure out what our next book should be about, it's no wonder that cars came up. After all, the centennial celebration of the American automobile was rapidly approaching and, as Michigan's new commemorative license plate says, Detroit is the "World's Motor Capital."

Since 1896, when Charles and Frank Duryea became the first to sell a gasoline-powered automobile in the United States, the automobile has revolutionized the way Americans live. Cars changed our country—and most of the world—forever. We now have highways, parking lots, drive-through banks and restaurants, and many other things we never would've had if it weren't for cars. (Want more? See the "Things We Can Thank the Car For" list on page 211.)

Cars have not only changed America, they've changed *Americans.* People in this country are car crazy. Some people love 'em, some people hate 'em, but the fact is that Americans are passionate about their automobiles. Just about everyone has a favorite—or least favorite—car and a favorite car-related memory. If you don't believe us, check out the "Motor City Memories" chapter, where you'll find auto-related reminiscences from real live Detroiters.

So, this is *Car Crazy,* Visible Ink's contribution to the celebration of the American automobile's 100th birthday. Cruise through the "Fast Facts," settle back and do some "Roadside Reading" (make sure you pull over first), or use it to plan a "Road Trip." For more fun and entertainment, exit at the "Makin' a List" chapter (did we forget anything?) or head for "At the Drive-In," which contains one of the biggest collections of car-related movies ever assembled between two covers. (Just watch out for those "totally flat" flicks!) In addition, if you're *really* car crazy, the three

Appendixes will guide you to more sources. Read this book at home, in your car, or, if you want, *to* your car. We're sure you'll be entertained and, heck, you might even learn something.

A lot of talented and helpful people brought *Car Crazy* to life. Among them are: My partner in crime, Peter Gareffa (whose daughter, Jennifer, in spite of growing up in a house full of *Road & Track* magazines, now drives a Saturn); Don "Car Man" Wellman, who helped so much it's scary; Don Boyden, whose knowledge and love of cars proved to be invaluable; designer Tracey Rowens, who worked tirelessly to create an attractive—and probably even aerodynamic—book; typesetter Marco Di Vita of The Graphix Group; Roger Matuz and the editors at Manitou Wordworks Inc.; Diane Dupuis; chief mechanic Rebecca Nelson; Judy Galens, the best neighbor an editor could have; Leslie Norback; Christa Brelin; Carol Schwartz; Sue Stefani, who dreams of driving the Oscar Mayer Wienermobile; Lauri Taylor, who, thanks to this project, can't stop humming songs about cars; Leonard C. Bruno; Robert Duncan;

Randy Bassett; Pam Hayes; Margaret Chamberlain; Evi Seoud; Dorothy Maki; Shanna Heilveil; Larry Baker; Kathy Marcaccio; Andy Malonis and the rest of the research staff; Mark Patrick, head of the Detroit Public Library's automotive collection; Chad Gretzema at Oscar Mayer Foods; Tom Snyder of the U.S. Route 66 Association; Tom McIntyre of the Cobra Owners Club of America; Gil and Dorothy Dauphinais; Jim and Barbara Cook; Otis (you know who you are); Dusty Gareffa; and Samuel Adams, brewer and patriot. A special thanks goes out to Dan Kirchner and Peggy Dusman of the Automobile Manufacturers Association, who allowed us into their vast libraries of publications and photos to do research. And, last but not least, a very special thank-you to Kathy, Sam, and Josh Dauphinais, who put up with several months of car craziness and lent their full support.

Dean D. Dauphinais
Detroit
April 1996

When American Honda Motor Company introduced the **Acura** line of automobiles in 1986, it revolutionized the U.S. luxury car market. Acura automobiles were the first Japanese luxury cars sold in the United States, and the Acura Automobile Division was the first division of a Japanese automaker to set up a separate dealership network. Acura automobiles were designed to be an extension of Honda's sporty image, with more attention paid to performance and luxury.

The 1990 launching of the **Acura** NSX won great praise from critics and much attention from car enthusiasts. The NSX was completely handmade except for some of the welding. The 3,000-pound car featured an all-aluminum body, the ability to reach 60 mph in under six sec-

onds, and an audio system by Bose. Though the sticker price for the NSX was $60,000, the highest of all Japanese cars, bids as high as $125,000 were made at some dealerships before customers even saw it.

The first use of **aluminum** alloy in a car came when Elwood Haynes began using metal in cars he manufactured in 1898.

A car was used as an **ambulance** for the first time in New York City in 1900.

In 1974 the average American family spent 33 percent of its **annual income** for a new car. In 1995 the figure had risen to 50 percent.

Source: Time, February 6, 1995.

1804: Oliver Evans, a Delaware native, drives a steam-powered dredge—the *Orukter Amphibolos*—1½ miles on a Philadelphia road and into the Schuylkill River. It is the first powered vehicle on a U.S. road.

All weather **antifreeze/coolant** was introduced by several manufacturers in 1960.

In a Massachusetts Institute of Technology poll, 63 percent of 1,000 Americans surveyed named the **automobile** as the one invention they couldn't live without. The car was followed by the light bulb, the telephone, the television, aspirin, the microwave oven, the blow dryer, and the personal computer.

Source: Detroit Free Press

From 1982 to 1992, the average household spent $8,910 on **auto insurance** but filed only one claim averaging $600.

Source: Consumer Reports, August, 1992.

In China there is 1 **automobile** for every 822 people; in India, 1 automobile for every 408 people; and in Yemen, 1 automobile for every 314 people. In the United States, there is 1 automobile for every 1.7 people.

Source: Motor Vehicle Manufacturing Association, MVMA Motor Vehicle Facts and Figures '91, Motor Vehicle Manufacturing Association, 1991.

Thirteenth-century English philosopher, scientist, alchemist, and teacher Roger Bacon was among the earliest to conceive of the **automobile**. One outstanding source on Bacon's beliefs is *The Name of the Rose*, an international best-selling novel by Umberto Eco, whose central character—William of Baskerville—is a medieval sleuth investigating a series of murders at a monastery. William states: "Roger Bacon teaches that the divine plan will one day encompass the science of machines, which is natural and healthy magic. And one day it will be possible, by exploiting the power of nature, to create instruments of navigation by which ships will proceed . . . and far more rapid than those propelled by sails or oars; and there will be self-propelled wagons . . ."

Introducing a new model of **automobile** generally takes three to five years from inception to assembly.

The average American takes approximately 50,000 **automobile trips** in his or her lifetime.

Source: Krantz, Les, *What the Odds Are: A to Z Odds on Everything You Hoped or Feared Could Happen*, Prentice Hall General Reference, 1992.

1844: American inventor Charles Goodyear patents "vulcanizing" rubber. While experimenting, he accidentally drops India rubber mixed with sulfur on a hot stove and discovers it becomes flexible enough for many uses.

There are more than 80 companies worldwide that produce **automotive glass**, including windshields. Major producers in the United States include PPG, Guardian Industries, and Libby-Owens Ford. According to the Department of Commerce, 25 percent of flat glass production in the U.S. is consumed by the automotive industry.

The first American **automotive mascot** was copyrighted by L. V. Aronson in 1909. The small gnome-like figure was named "Gobbo, God of Good Luck."

Ford economists predict that the **average price of a new car** will be $30,000 by the year 2002.

In 1972 automobiles traveled along Los Angeles freeways at an **average speed** of 60 mph; in 1982 they crawled along at an average of 17 mph.

Source: American Demographics, September, 1992.

What? No Rubber Baby Buggy Bumpers?

The BFGoodrich Company, in existence since 1870, did not begin producing car tires until the late 1890s, well after the death of its founder, Dr. Benjamin Franklin Goodrich. The first Goodrich brand products were fire hoses, wringer rolls, billiard cue tips, and household rubber products such as bottle stoppers and rubber rings for canning jars. Because of its reputation in the rubber business, the company was asked in 1896 to produce the first U.S.-made pneumatic (compressed air) tires for one of the first American automobiles, the Winton. This began a long association with the automobile industry.

The **Batmobile** used in the 1989 *Batman* movie sold at auction for $189,500 on February 27, 1996. The buyer chose to remain anonymous.

Source: USA TODAY, February 29, 1996.

The first storage **battery** included as standard equipment appeared in 1906.

1852: Studebaker brothers form a carriage company that becomes largest in the world by the 1890s; the family makes a successful transition to automobiles, introducing the first Studebaker car in 1904.

00003

In 1887 the **Benz** became the first automobile offered for sale to the public.

Since the introduction of its first tire in 1896, **BFGoodrich** has made many original contributions to the evolution of the automobile tire, including tires made of synthetic rubber (first sold in the United States by BFGoodrich in 1940), the first tubeless tire (produced by BFGoodrich in 1947), and the first American-made radial tire (introduced by BFGoodrich in 1965). In 1967 BFGoodrich developed the collapsible spare tire for cars (called the "Space Saver") and the first pneumatic "run flat" tire that could operate even when punctured.

The **Big Three** sold just 97,380 cars in Japan in 1995, or just 1.4 percent of all vehicles purchased by Japanese consumers.

A maker of aircraft engines since 1913, **BMW** made its first cars in 1929. The small, two-door, 15-horsepower sedan was adapted from a car that the company had acquired when it bought Fahrzeugwerke Eisenach, a struggling company that made a small car under license from Austin of the United Kingdom.

During the 1980s, **BMW** cars inadvertently gained a "yuppie" image because they were favored by young, urban professionals. The company sought to make its image more conservative in the early 1990s. In order to help change consumer perceptions, the advertising strategy emphasized that a better car made a better driver. To convey the message of superior performance, the tagline used in print ads and TV commercials was, "The ultimate driving machine."

The 1992 Best Recycling Innovation Award from the National Recycling Coalition went to **BMW** for the high proportion of recyclable materials used in its 3-series car. In addition, in 1992 the first recycling plants for scrapped BMW cars were opened in the United States as well as in several European nations. The 1993 3-series was designed to be over 80 percent recyclable by weight when scrapped. By 1993, BMW of North America had created three U.S. recycling centers at Hunts Point, New York, Santa Fe Springs, California, and Orlando, Florida. BMW owners who returned their cars to any of the centers received a

1864: Prolific Austrian inventor Siegfried Markus produces a wooden cart powered by a two-cycle gas engine based on one built by Belgian Jean-Joseph Etienne Lenoir. This is disputedly the first automobile.

$500 incentive toward the purchase of a new or approved used car.

In 1993 **BMW** became the best-selling German car in the United States.

The first rural **brick road** was built near Cleveland, Ohio, in 1894. Four miles of brick pavement were laid.

The first automobile called a **Buick** was built in 1900 by plumbing inventor and manufacturer David Dunbar Buick and an engineer named Walter L. Marr.

A Buick engine powered a race car to victory at the Indianapolis Motor Speedway in 1909, two years before the inception of the Indy 500.

The first car to travel across South America—from Buenos Aries, Argentina, to Santiago, Chile—was a **Buick**.

In the 1920s **Buick** dominated the automobile market and captured the world's attention through such events as a hill-climb in Africa, a tug-of-war with an elephant, and a jaunt through New Zealand.

The new medium of radio made waves in the 1920s, and in 1928 **Buick** created a hook-up to dealers across the country. Buick dealerships installed radio receivers, and potential car buyers could enjoy music while looking at the new line of Buick cars.

In 1939 **Buick** made headlines when it introduced turn signals as standard equipment—an industry first. The signal was a red plastic lens in the Buick emblem, which was mounted on the car's trunk.

The **Buick** sweepspear side decoration first appeared on the 1949 Roadmaster Riviera. The sweepspear, destined to become as widely recognized as the Buick logo, was a metal decoration that swept from the front fender in a downward curve, along the doors and up over the rear wheels.

1879: Enterprising lawyer George B. Selden applies for the first U.S. automobile patent, describing a carriage powered by a gasoline engine. Selden's patent is hotly contested until 1911, when its use is strictly limited.

Buicks of the 1950s were stylish and powerful.
Courtesy of American Automobile Manufacturers Association

The **Buick** cars of the 1950s were sleek, smooth, powerful machines that sported staggering amounts of chrome and satisfied affluent postwar consumers.

In 1979 **Buick** introduced its first front-wheel-drive car, the Riviera S Type. This Riviera, which had a turbocharged V6 engine, won the "Car of the Year" award from *Motor Trend* magazine.

The first front and rear **bumpers** introduced as standard equipment were on Wescott cars in 1919.

In 1989 Ocie McClure robbed a Japanese tourist on San Francisco's Market Street. A **cabbie** by the name of Holden Charles Hollom chased McClure down and pinned him against a wall with his cab. Hailed as a hero at the time, Hollom was later sued by McClure—who admitted the robbery—for using "excessive force." Three years after the incident, McClure won $24,595 for the injuries inflicted by Hollom and his cab.

Source: San Francisco Chronicle

The name **Cadillac** comes from Antoine de la Mothe Cadillac, founder of Detroit in the seventeenth century.

The first Model A **Cadillac** rolled out in Detroit in October 1902. The Model A made its major U.S. debut in 1903 at the New York Automobile Show, where Marketing Director William Metzger conducted an astonishingly successful sales drive. Accepting deposits as low as $10, he racked up orders of 2,283 cars by midweek, then announced to all other potential buyers that Cadillac had sold out. Between March 1903 and March 1904, a total of 1,895 cars were built—a considerable achievement for the era.

From 1903 to 1906, **Cadillac** was the third-largest selling car, following Oldsmobile and the newly established Ford. Of the three, Cadillac was considered the toughest and most reliable, and Cadillac owners enjoyed testing the car's limits by doing such things as driving it up the steps of the Wayne County Building in Detroit.

In 1912 **Cadillac** introduced the Delco system, an electric lighting and ignition

1885: German automobile pioneer Carl Benz builds a four-stroke gas engine and is generally acknowledged as being the first to perfect a gas-powered automobile.

system, which earned the car maker a second Dewars Trophy—the automobile industry's equivalent of the Nobel Prize—and revolutionized the industry.

In 1927 **Cadillac** introduced the LaSalle—a practically all-new model, from its engineering to its slick appearance. Designed to combat Packard's growing popularity, the LaSalle's key factor was its design by Harley Earl, the General Motors stylist who was to usher in the golden age of Cadillac cars. With Earl's input, Cadillac became known as both a designer's and an engineer's automobile. Earl's designs were dynamic, elegant, somewhat flamboyant, and impressive enough to compete with Packard, slowly stealing Packard's market share.

The styling of the **Cadillac** evolved through the 1930s, establishing the car as a permanent force in the luxury automobile market. A key year in its development was 1934, when Harley Earl created a streamlined, aerodynamic style with rounded fenders and a long, lean body. This style evolved over the years until 1941, the year the United States entered World War II. For Cadillac this was another watershed year in which Earl developed the "egg crate" style, with its horizontal emphasis, brought about through the elimination of the vertical grille.

In February of 1942, **Cadillac** discontinued car production and devoted all its resources to producing military trucks and other combat vehicles. After World War II, Cadillac immediately returned to production. Within two years, new car production had reached 97 percent of its pre-war peak. Demand was so great that one journalist exclaimed that "Cadillac fever is of epidemic proportions," and described how groups of people would pool their money for the purpose of jointly buying a Cadillac, which they would then share according to agreed-upon terms. "As far as can be discovered, only Cadillac enjoys this unusual tribute," he noted.

With the introduction of the **Cadillac** tail fin in 1948, Harley Earl once again instituted a style that would control the industry for a decade. Inspired by the twin tails on the Lockheed P 38 Lightning fighter plane of World War II, the tail fin was highly controversial among stylists. But it caught on immediately with the public.

1889: Scottish inventor John Boyd Dunlop invents the pneumatic (air-filled) rubber tire while trying to provide his son a more comfortable tricycle ride.

Over the years **Cadillac** pioneered such innovations as the electric starter and the overhead-valve engine.

A major restyling of the **Cadillac** body appeared in 1964. Gone were the famous fins, replaced by a low, long body with a broader front grille and completely new rear treatment.

In 1987 **Cadillac** launched the sleek Allante, a joint venture with the stylish Italian auto firm Pinifarina. Designed to give Cadillac a slick new image and capture some of the market from the Europeans, the Allante was a low-volume, high-tech "niche" vehicle that was intended to serve as a platform to introduce the Northstar System engine and transmission. The car sold well below expectations, however. Less than 3,800 Allantes sold in model years 1987 and 1988, and in 1993 the model was discontinued.

The **Cadillac** line was revamped in 1992 with newly designed Seville, Eldorado, and Fleetwood models. The Seville STS was named 1992 "Car of

the Year" by *Motor Trend*, "Automobile of the Year" by *Automobile* magazine, and one of *Car and Driver*'s "Ten Best."

In 1993 **Cadillac** made its Northstar System available on select Seville and Eldorado models. At the heart of the series of components that make up the integrated powertrain-suspension system is the Northstar engine. A dual-overhead cam, 32-valve, 4.60-liter, 295-horsepower V8, the computer controlled Northstar is capable of producing speeds of 160 miles per hour and only requires a tune-up (which consists of changing the platinum-tipped spark plugs) every 100,000 miles. The Northstar System met with wide critical acclaim in the automotive press, winning 15 editorial awards.

An average of 7,700 additional **cars** and trucks are crowding the roads of the United States every day.

Source: USA TODAY magazine, March, 1992.

According to a Valvoline/Automotive Service Excellence poll, auto technicians picked *Home Improvement* star Tim Allen (37 percent) as the best **celebrity** mechanic. Allen beat out *Roseanne* star

---

1895: The first recorded racing accident—dog hit by Panhard car in Paris-Bordeaux race in 1895. The race is dominated by gasoline-powered cars, as the top four finishers are propelled by Daimler engines.

Chevrolet Bowtie Ripped Off—Literally!

Legend maintains—and William Durant confirmed it—that the shape of the famous Chevrolet "bowtie" logo was inspired by a wallpaper pattern Durant saw in a Paris hotel room during 1908. Durant supposedly ripped off a small piece of the wallpaper, folded it up, and put it in his wallet, waiting for the day he'd put it to use. Durant's wife later disputed this story, saying instead that the design was noticed in a Sunday newspaper supplement while on vacation in Virginia. Whatever the source, the bowtie proved to be a recognizable winner and is still the marque of today's Chevrolet.

Source: The Chevrolet Story

John Goodman (24 percent), *Tonight Show* host Jay Leno (20 percent), and actor Tom Cruise (11 percent).

On November 13, 1899, R.A.C. Smith became the first person to drive a car through New York City's **Central Park**. The commissioner of Central Park, George C. Claussen, accompanied Smith on his journey, which took place in an electric automobile. Claussen later awarded Smith the first permit to operate an automobile in the park.

Source: Smith, Mark, and Naomi Black, America on Wheels, William Morrow, 1986.

Louis Chevrolet, a Swiss racing car driver and engineer, designed the first **Chevrolet** automobile, the Classic Six, in Detroit in 1911, with the financial backing of a founder of the General Motors Corporation, William C. Durant.

The **Chevrolet** Classic Six was a five-passenger touring sedan with an extensive list of features for its time: four doors, electric lights, a folding top, side curtains, a windshield, and a tool box. The engine, with six cylinders, had a potential top speed of 65 miles per hour and the ability to accelerate from zero to 50 miles per hour in 15 seconds. The car, with a price of $2,150, was affordable only for the wealthy. In its first production year, 1912, the Classic Six reached sales of 2,999.

The well-known bowtie-shaped **Chevrolet** logo appeared for the first time on Chevrolet cars in 1914.

Source: The Chevrolet Story

1895: First automotive magazines in the United States appear. They include *The Horseless Age, The Motorcycle,* and *Autocar.*

Road Test

WHICH OF THESE WERE REAL OPTIONS AT ONE TIME?

1. *Turntable (to play those Pat Boone 45s)*
2. *Seat belts*
3. *A passenger seat*
4. *Heater (a popular option in the Motor City)*
5. *Arm rests*
6. *Electric starter*
7. *Rumble seat*
8. *Radio*
9. *Carpeting*
10. *Rearview mirror*

(Answers: All of 'em.)

In 1918 **Chevrolet** produced its first truck, based on an expanded 490 platform.

The **Chevrolet** Superior debuted in 1923 and introduced the "body style" selling concept. The car came in the varieties of coupe, roadster, touring car, sedan, or sedanette (two-door with a small trunk). The highly original option of a radio installed in the car cost $200, or about one-fourth the total cost of the vehicle.

The practice of updating models annually was introduced by **Chevrolet**.

In 1924 **Chevrolet** added details—such as outside door handles and front and rear bumpers—that made their vehicles look less like horseless buggies. Blue, aquamarine, and green became the

1895: The first automobile ad, for Duryea Motor Wagon Company, appears in *The Horseless Age.*

The Corvette was America's first sports car.
Courtesy of American Automobile Manufacturers Association

major car colors, replacing black altogether.

The first built-in trunk on a **Chevrolet** appeared in 1934.

The **Chevrolet** Suburban debuted in 1935. Built on a truck chassis, the first Suburban was an all-steel wagon that carried eight passengers.

The first production station wagon offered by **Chevrolet** premiered in 1939.

In 1953 **Chevrolet** showcased its first Corvette at Motorama in response to the growing American taste for European sports cars. The designer, Harley Earl, used a body of reinforced fiberglass on a conventional frame. The first Corvettes featured bucket seats, a hand-operated convertible soft-top that folded into a behind-the-seat compartment, and 150 horsepower at 4,500 rpm.

Eighty percent of the first **Chevrolet** Corvettes were white.

At one time **Chevrolet** engineers considered turning the Corvette into a four-passenger car.

It was in 1954 that America first heard Dinah Shore croon "See the U.S.A. in Your **Chevrolet**."

The 1957 **Chevrolet**—with its tail fins and innovative front-end design—was later to become one of the most highly prized collectors' models Chevrolet produced.

Debuting in 1958 as an upscale version of the **Chevrolet** Bel Air, the Impala was one of Chevy's most popular models during the 1960s and 1970s. Sales of the 1967 model alone topped 600,000 and the 10 millionth Impala was sold in 1972. Chevrolet plans on reviving the Impala nameplate on a 1999 family car.

The **Chevrolet** Corvette Sting Ray, a 300-horsepower performance machine, made its splash on the sports car scene in 1963.

1895: First club of automobile enthusiasts, the American Motor League, is organized in Chicago and open to "any man or woman, 18 years of age or over, of good moral character and respectable standing, friendly to the motor vehicle and its interests."

The Chevrolet Camaro was the first new GM design produced from wind tunnel testing.

The Chevrolet Blazer debuted in 1969 and was first offered as a "sport pickup" and four-wheel-drive off-road vehicle. The first Blazers came in soft and hard-top models.

The 1970s inspired the Chevrolet Vega, Chevy's first subcompact car. Billed as "The Little Car that Does Everything Well," the Vega was produced in response to the fuel-thirsty needs of U.S. drivers.

The first front-wheel-drive car produced by Chevrolet was the Citation, which appeared in 1979.

The subcompact Chevrolet Cavalier debuted in 1982; the model became the top-selling car in the country in 1984 and 1985.

The one-millionth Chevrolet Corvette, a white convertible with red interior to match the first Corvette, was produced on July 2, 1992, at Corvette's assembly plant in Bowling Green, Kentucky.

More Chevrolet Corvettes have been built than any other single sports car in automotive history. They have been sold throughout North America, Europe, the Middle East, and Japan, and there are more than 600 Corvette owner clubs around the world. Corvette's Bowling Green assembly plant has become an international magnet for Corvette enthusiasts. More than 60,000 visitors are welcomed for tours each year.

The first American car to enter the Le Mans international automobile race was a Chrysler.

The first transcontinental experimental gas turbine car trip—from New York to Los Angeles—was made in a Chrysler car in 1956.

1895: First American automobile race, organized by the *Times-Herald* newspaper of Chicago, is won by a Duryea vehicle. A Benz car finishes second. This race captures headlines and spurs tinkerers throughout the United States.

The first day and night rearview mirror was introduced on **Chrysler** cars in 1958.

The first electroluminescent dash lighting display was introduced by **Chrysler** in 1959.

The "downsizing" challenge of the late-1970s was met by **Chrysler** with the Dodge Omni (and its Plymouth twin, the Horizon), the first small front-wheel-drive car built in the United States.

In 1981 **Chrysler** introduced the Plymouth Reliant and Dodge Aries "K-cars." The success of these cars allowed Chrysler to pay back money it borrowed from the federal government and return to profitability.

A turning point for **Chrysler** was the 1984 model year, when it launched the Dodge Caravan and Plymouth Voyager minivans. These vehicles caught the competition off-guard and created a new segment. The minivan's car-like handling combined with the carrying capacity of a van reshaped the way American families thought about their transportation needs.

When asked to name their favorite **classic car**, mechanics surveyed in a Valvoline/Automotive Service Excellence poll picked the 1963 Chevrolet Corvette Sting Ray (27 percent), followed by the 1957 Chevrolet Bel Air convertible (22 percent), and the 1965 Ford Mustang convertible (16 percent).

It started as a $50 bet. Dr. N.H. Jackson, of Burlington, Vermont, was sipping wine at a San Francisco club and listening in as several men agreed that autombiles were only good for short trips. A few more glasses and loud arguments later, Jackson accepted a $50 wager and began a **cross-country trip** in a new 1903 Winton with a mechanic named Sewall K. Crocker as his sidekick. Sixty-four days later and $8,000 less in pocket change, the doctor and the mechanic pulled up in New York City and claimed the $50. Along the way they ran a spell on bundled burlap for tires, ran out of gas and had to walk 29 miles to get fuel, and went 54 miles out of their way because of bad directions—seems a woman sent them off on a detour so the car would be sure to pass by her family's home. But, they

1896: The first stolen car was a Peugeot in Paris. A mechanic drove off with the Baron de Zuylen's car from the manufacturer's plant, where it had been taken for repairs.

The Viper helped polish the image of Chrysler's Dodge division.

made it and became the first people to make a trip across America by car. The good Dr. Jackson also had a later automobile first—first driver to be arrested for speeding in Burlington.

Safety padding on **dashboards** was introduced by some car manufacturers in 1954.

The **Dodge** nameplate was founded in 1913 by John and Horace Dodge. The Dodge brothers were among the first to set up a trial track to test each car before it was shipped from the factory. They examined speed, climbing, and descending, as well as engine and brake performance, on a circular wooden track outside the main plant. The first Dodge came off the factory line on November 10, 1914.

John and Horace **Dodge** died within eleven months of each other during the influenza epidemic of 1920.

Chrysler acquired **Dodge** in 1928 for $170 million.

In an effort to entice a younger market, **Dodge** launched its "Dodge Rebellion" and "Dodge Fever" promotions during the 1960s, but it really only succeeded in alienating the brand's traditionally older, conservative customer base.

The Viper helped boost the **Dodge** division's image by serving as the pace car at the 1991 Indianapolis 500 and starring in a 1993 network television crime drama series.

The 1996 **Dodge** Caravan won *Motor Trend* magazine's "Car of the Year" award. This marked the first time that a van had won the award as a "car." In 1990, the Ford Aerostar minivan grabbed the "Truck of the Year" title. Vans are considered trucks by the U.S. government and the automobile industry. The magazine declared minivans cars in 1996 "because that's how people feel about minivans. They're used as cars. They're the station wagons of today."

Source: USA TODAY, November 21, 1995.

The first electric **door locks** were introduced on several luxury cars in 1956.

1896: First recorded automobile accident in the United States occurs in New York as Henry Wells strikes bicyclist Evelyn Thomas with his Duryea electric.

In 1896 the **Duryea** Motor Wagon became the first production motor vehicle in the United States.

The development of the **electric automobile** will owe more to innovative solar and aeronautical engineering and advanced satellite and radar technology than to traditional automotive design and construction. The electric car has no engine, exhaust system, transmission, muffler, radiator, or spark plugs. It will require neither tune-ups nor gasoline.

The first **engine crank** was introduced by Englishman James Watt in 1782.

The first **engine temperature indicator** was introduced by Boyce Moto-Meter in 1912.

The first **explosion engine** was built by Charles Huygens—using gunpowder—in 1678.

The first full-skirted **fenders** were introduced on a Graham in 1932.

The car most people in the United States probably associate with **Ferrari** is the 12-cylinder Testarossa, which became the company's flagship model in 1984.

One of the most glamorous production cars in the world, the **Ferrari** Testarossa owed its futuristic styling to Pininfarina and the earlier Ferrari Boxers, but the name came straight from racing legend. The original Testarossa—literally "Red Head"—was a 2.0 liter, four-cylinder competition sports car introduced in 1956. It was called Testarossa because engineers at Ferrari finished off the camshaft covers with a red paint.

The first **Ferrari** Testarossas were raced on tight sports-car circuits, where brute power was not important. After 1958, when the Federation Internationale de Automobile (FIA) limited the size of competition engines, the Testarossa was fitted with a 3.0 liter V12 and became Ferrari's flagship racer, winning at Le

1896: First sale of an American-built, gasoline-powered car is made by the Duryea Motor Wagon Company.

Mans in its first outing. In 1960 Ferrari Testarossas took seven of the first eight spots at Le Mans, including first.

Automobile, truck, and tractor tires owe their evolution in large part to the founder of the **Firestone** Tire & Rubber Company, Harvey S. Firestone. Firestone tires graced the world's first mass-produced car, the Ford; advertisements and promotions for Firestone truck tires were largely responsible for the nation's de-emphasis of railroad freight hauling in favor of hauling by truck, indirectly giving impetus to highway construction and road improvements; and Firestone led the switch to rubber tires on tractors, which improved fuel efficiency and proved more durable than the ubiquitous steel tractor tire.

The first **folding car tops** were introduced in 1905.

Henry Ford set a speed record in 1904 by driving a **Ford** 999 91.37 mph over frozen Lake St. Clair, a Michigan lake.

Ferrari has the Right Formula

Ferrari is one of the most exclusive automobile marques in the world and probably the most famous brand name in Formula One racing. Fewer than 55,000 automobiles bearing the Ferrari marque were produced between 1946, when founder Enzo Ferrari built the first Type 125, and 1993, when the $122,000 Ferrari spyder made its debut. In the mid-1990s the top-of-the-line Ferrari 512 TR (Testarossa) sold for about $195,000. In racing, Ferrari's blood-red sports cars and Formula One racers, with their yellow and black prancing-horse emblem, are legendary for both their raw power and radical styling.

The first electric trunk lid release was introduced on **Ford** cars in 1958.

The first anti-theft ignition switch was introduced on **Ford** cars in 1959.

The top-selling American car throughout much of the 1980s, the Escort was **Ford** Motor Company's answer to the

1897: The first car insurance policy is purchased by Gilbert Loomis. The premium is $7.50 for $1,000 liability coverage on his one-cylinder car in Westfield, Massachusetts.

small, fuel-efficient cars of its foreign competitors. It was introduced in 1980, and over the next 10 years Ford sold more than 7 million of these subcompacts worldwide. The Escort retailed at an affordable price, and it was the most fuel-efficient car in Ford's American car line.

Large sales of the gas-conscious Escort allowed Ford to meet the U.S. government's corporate average fuel-efficiency (CAFE) standards (requiring a minimum average fuel efficiency for its entire fleet), which gave the company room to sell its more profitable, larger cars. So, even though the Escort was a modest little car, its success was crucial to Ford.

The first American automobile to feature antilock brakes as standard equipment was the 1985 Ford Granada.

The Escort represented a new direction in Ford's business. It was the company's first car designed to suit both foreign and domestic markets and to be built at sites across the globe. The Escort represented another departure for Ford when the car was redesigned in 1990,

as this was Ford's first joint venture with Japan's Mazda Motor Corporation. In 1995 the Escort was still one of the world's best-selling cars.

Mustang is one of the best-known brands in American automaking, with a recognition almost as high as the Ford name itself. Although the Mustang faced possible extinction in the late 1980s, its prospects have greatly improved. Restyling and upgraded equipment have brought the car up-to-date, and there has continued to be a band of devoted followers. More than 400 Mustang clubs, together having some 35,000 members, existed in the mid-1990s. Popularity of the car was also reflected in the many celebrity Mustang owners, including actor Kevin Costner, baseball star Reggie Jackson, and President Bill Clinton.

First sold in the 1986 model year, the Taurus is one of Ford Motor Company's most successful models. The company spent five years and $3 billion to develop the Taurus, and when it was introduced, the car's advanced engineering and aerodynamic design drew widespread praise. By 1992 the Taurus had become the best-selling car in the United States, barely beating out the

1897: First Stanley Steamer. Built by enterprising American twins, Francis and Freeling Stanley, it sells well because of its reliability and the twins' showmanship, and it matches succesfully against gasoline-powered cars.

The Explorer debuted in 1990 and quickly became a big seller for Ford.

Courtesy of American Automobile Manufacturers Association

Honda Accord, which had held that position since 1989.

The Ford Explorer sport utility vehicle was introduced nationwide by Ford Motor Company in April of 1990; it became the top-selling vehicle in its class in its first year.

The two-door Ford Explorer was planned in conjunction with Mazda. Mazda's engineers maintained only a consulting role in the process, resulting in the first American-made vehicle to be sold under the guise of being a Japanese product. The Mazda version of the two-door Explorer was sold under the Navajo moniker.

The Eddie Bauer edition of the Ford Explorer was a two-tone version with the added amenities of power rearview mirror, windows, and locks, rear window wiper, better tires, and a custom leather interior made a bit more charming by the addition of limited edition garment and duffel bags, compliments of Eddie Bauer, a maker of outdoor apparel.

One of the first automakers to use recycled materials and introduce air conditioners free of chlorofluorocarbons, Ford built cars in North America that were among the first to contain parts made from recycled plastic soft-drink bottles. In the Taurus, plastic resin was molded into various components, such as the grille-opening reinforcement that supported the grille and headlights. Ford is one of the world's largest automotive users of recycled plastic bottles in such structural applications. The 1993 Taurus became the first vehicle to use recycled plastic in its bumpers (in the taillight housings). In a 1992 pilot program—which was expanded in 1993—the Taurus became the first production vehicle in the United States to have air conditioners free of CFCs, which are believed to harm the Earth's protective ozone layer.

The first Ford car designed especially for the Japanese market was a version of the 1996 Taurus. The car—built with the steering wheel on the right—hit Japanese showrooms on February 27, 1996.

Inventor Rudolf Gunnerman of Reno, Nevada, has developed a breakthrough

---

1897: The Motor Car Company of London is credited as being the first used car dealership. Seventeen used cars, which had only been driven on Sundays, were available for 30 to 335 pounds.

fuel that is more than half tap water and could replace gasoline. Certified by Nevada in November of 1995 as a "clean alternative fuel," Gunnerman's concoction is made up of water, naptha (a clear liquid produced in the early stages of petroleum refining), and a binding agent. If successful, the alternative fuel would significantly reduce auto emissions and cut prices at the fuel pump by more than 50 percent.

Source: The Detroit News, February 11, 1996.

Advertising promoting **gas mileage** was first used by several car manufacturers in 1933.

Today almost all **gasoline** is used to fuel automobiles, with a very small percentage used to power agricultural equipment and aircraft.

The first nationwide chain of **gas stations** was established in 1925.

The **Geo** brand of automobile was launched in 1988 by General Motors' Chevrolet Motor Division, in a joint venture with United Motor Manufac-

turing (NUMMI), Isuzu Motors, and Suzuki Motor Company.

Overall, the **Geo** line of cars was successfully targeted at single young women. Market research showed that by the mid-1990s a whopping 80 percent of Geo Storm buyers were female, and in 1991 more than 70 percent of Prizms were sold to women.

The 1993 **Geo** Prizm was based on the Toyota Sprinter (a car offered in Japan but not in the United States). The Prizm's mechanics were identical to the Toyota Corolla's, but the two cars did not share a single body panel.

Frank and Charles Seiberling founded the **Goodyear** Tire and Rubber Company in 1898. Although totally unrelated to the Goodyear family, they named their tires after Charles Goodyear, the Connecticut inventor who accidentally discovered the key to vulcanizing rubber. Goodyear patented the process and tried to capitalize on the discovery, but he couldn't come up with any practical uses for the compound. When Goodyear's business failed, he was

1898: The first independent car dealership is established by William Metzger of Detroit; the first franchised U.S. car dealership is established by H.O. Koller in Reading, Pennsylvania, to sell Winton cars.

thrown into a Paris debtors' prison. He died, penniless, in New York in 1860.

In 1910 **Goodyear** unveiled the United States' first two-page, national magazine advertisement. The precedent-setting announcement touted Goodyear's recent industry coup, listing 44 automakers that had signed original equipment contracts to give the brand 36 percent of that market.

The first race to bear the title **Grand Prix** was run in Pau, France, in 1901. It was won by Maurice Farman, whose Panhard averaged 46.1 mph.

The first car **guarantee** was for 60 days, accepted by the National Association of Automobile Manufacturers in 1902.

The first kerosene **headlamps** were introduced by R.E. Dietz Company in 1900. They had 20 candle power, could cast a beam 200 feet, and produced steady light over even rough roads.

The first dual beam **headlamps** were introduced in 1924.

Car enthusiast Claude Marion Hertz of Nokomis, Illinois, had his **headstone** topped off with a stone Corvette.
Source: USA TODAY, February 13, 1996.

In 1993 the cost of **health care** for employees at the Ford Motor Company averaged $800 per automobile produced. This is double the per-vehicle cost of steel.
Source: The Detroit News and Free Press, March 21, 1993.

A car was used as a **hearse** for the first time in Buffalo in 1900.

Convinced that there are aliens living nearby at a top-secret government base, the people of Rachel, Nevada, officially renamed a 92-mile stretch of state **highway** 375 "The Extraterrestrial Highway." The cost? Around $3,300 for four official state highway signs. Only about 50 cars a day travel the desolate

1898: First American automobile show is held in Boston. Called the Motor Carriage Exposition of the Massachusetts Charitable Mechanics' Association, it has four exhibitors and holds a motor vehicle race and parade.

The first Honda to roll off a U.S. assembly line was a 1983 model Accord.

Courtesy of American Automobile Manufacturers Association

strip of road between Hiko and Warm Springs. No word on how many aliens are in those cars.

Source: Detroit Free Press

The **Honda** Accord brand was founded in 1976 in Tokyo, Japan, by the Honda Motor Company. The American Honda Motor Company, a wholly owned subsidiary, introduced the Accord to the United States as a subcompact in 1976. For the 1983 model year, the Accord was redesigned as a mid-sized sedan and became the first Japanese car manufactured in the United States. From 1989 through 1991, the Accord was the top-selling car in the United States.

In 1995 **Honda** celebrated the sale of its 10 millionth car in the U.S.

On February 19, 1996, **Honda** became the first Asian car company to build a luxury model in the United States when it started production on the 1996 Acura 2.2CL coupe at its plant in East Liberty, Ohio.

During a blizzard in 1996, Frank Meeks, an Arlington, Virginia, pizza store owner, delivered pizzas in his $65,000 **Hummer,** a four-wheel-drive, military-style vehicle. "In these conditions people are excited to see the pizza delivery guy," Meeks declared. "And they are really excited to see the pizza delivery guy in a Hummer."

Source: Detroit Free Press

The first **instrumentation backlighting** was introduced in 1919.

One out of every four cars built in America is built by **international auto manufacturers.** Overall, international manufacturers build more cars in America than Ford and three times more than Chrysler.

The international motor vehicle industry in America provides more than 542,000 American jobs in dealerships, manufacturing facilities, suppliers, and ports across the country.

The **Jaguar** name has graced many of the world's most elegant sedans and sinuous sports cars. The name has also come to symbolize unreserved speed and classic, hand-crafted British indul-

---

1899: William McKinley becomes the first U.S. President to ride in a car—a Stanley Steamer.

gence, even though the company's first production vehicle, in 1935, was a low-cost sedan sometimes referred to as a workingman's Bentley.

Perhaps the most famous **Jaguar** ever built was the two-seat E-Type (popularly known as the XKE), introduced in 1961. The designation "E" was chosen purposefully as a reminder of the Type C and Type D Jaguar racers, and the aerodynamic XKE was capable of reaching 150 mph. It quickly became the benchmark for all other production sports cars. The original E-Type came in two body styles, an open roadster and an even more sinuous hatchback coupe. More than 72,000 E-Types were sold, more than 49,000 of them in the United States.

In 1968 **Jaguar** introduced the XJ6 sedan, the first Jaguar company co-founder William Lyons had ever personally endorsed in advertising. Lyons called the XJ6—the first new full-size Jaguar in more than a decade—"the finest saloon car Jaguar has ever made and one that challenges comparison with any in the world." Car enthusiasts agreed. *Road & Track* called the Jaguar XJ6 "uncannily silent and gloriously swift." *Car and Driver* said, "The XJ6 has

to be one of the best balanced, most enjoyable cars made."

The 1960s were a time of great popularity for **Jaguar**. However, in the 1970s, quality and reliability deteriorated and the name nearly went out of existence in 1980. The Ford Motor Company purchased Jaguar in 1989 and planned to revive the brand with new product introductions.

The limited edition **Jaguar** XJ220 was the fastest production car in the world, with a top speed of 212 mph. It also carried a price tag of more than $600,000. Yet when Jaguar Sport Limited, a joint venture between Jaguar and Tom Walkinshaw Racing, announced in 1989 that it would build 350 of the sleek, 500-horsepower XJ220s, more than 1,500 potential buyers submitted applications. Those lucky enough to be chosen had to put down a $76,000 deposit to ensure delivery beginning in 1992. However, the Jaguar XJ220 fell from grace with some of its potential buyers in the early 1990s because of the worldwide recession that affected the luxury car market. In 1993, industry analysts said the value of the car had fallen by a third, and Jaguar Sport announced that about 100 buyers wanted out of their contracts. Cus-

1899: The first U.S. woman's driver's license is acquired by Mrs. John Phillips (that's what it said on the license) of Chicago.

tomers were allowed to invoke an escape clause by paying another $107,000. About 150 XJ220s had been delivered in 1993.

Branch Dividian leader **David Koresh** was a car enthusiast. His favorite car was his black 1968 Camaro. Koresh biographer Tim Madigan stated that Koresh's "passion for cars probably eclipsed his love of high-powered weaponry and musical instruments." The Branch Dividians left behind about 40 cars, trucks, and buses at their burned-out complex in Waco, Texas.

Source: Car and Driver, October, 1993.

Introduced during the fall of 1990, **Lexus**—Toyota Motor Corporation's first foray into the luxury car market—quickly proved to be a formidable contender in the highly competitive American market. Within a year, it threatened the position of Honda Motor Company's Acura as the best-selling Japanese luxury car in the United States and outsold Infiniti, Nissan Motor Company's entry into the luxury market, two to one. The combined force of Lexus, Infiniti, and Acura—all introduced within a six-year period in the later 1980s—took a large percentage of Mercedes' and BMW's American market share and severely threatened the position of American luxury cars such as Cadillac and Lincoln.

While developing their first cars, **Lexus** went to great effort to ensure that its cars would provide a quiet ride, even placing microphones in its early clay prototypes to detect and eliminate any sources of wind noise. Another industry first was an "anti-aging" study aimed at determining the materials that would best allow its cars to "age gracefully and with uniformity."

Priding themselves on customer service, **Lexus** dealers have gone so far as to buy back certain cars from unsatisfied customers or tell others who locked their keys in their Lexuses to break in through a back window; the dealership would then replace the window for free.

California claims to have started the specialty **license plate** craze. Designed to raise money for special interest groups and causes, California introduced the plates in the 1970s.

Source: The New York Times, September 17, 1995.

1899: First official U.S. automobile fatality occurs in New York City when Henry H. Bliss dies after being struck "by a horseless carriage" while stepping off a trolley.

Pope Paul VI rode in this Lincoln Continental limousine when he visited New York in 1965.

Courtesy of American Automobile Manufacturers Association

The first **Lincoln** was introduced in 1920 by Henry Martyn Leland and his associates and was named after Abraham Lincoln, the man whom Leland admired the most. Priced at $6,600, the Lincoln boasted a V8 engine, but did not have the elegant styling that one day would be associated with the Lincoln name. The early Lincolns made their debut in the midst of a declining economy, and they sold poorly. Experiencing financial difficulties, Leland's company was purchased by Ford in 1922 for $8 million.

In 1973 a **Lincoln** Town Car was presented as a gift by President Richard Nixon to Soviet Party Secretary Leonid Brezhnev during a state visit.

In 1977 **Lincoln** introduced the compact Versailles and the new Mark V, both of which were offered in Designer Edition models inspired by the leading designers of the day: Givenchy, Cartier, Blass, and Gucci.

In 1978 the Ford Motor Company celebrated its 75th anniversary with a Dia-

mond Jubilee Edition of the **Lincoln** Mark V, priced at about $8,000.

Established in 1920 as a small manufacturer of cork products, **Mazda** later diversified into a line of machinery products and tools. The company eventually phased out its cork business and adopted the name Toyo Kogyo, or East Sea Manufacturing. Jugiro Matsuda, who founded the enterprise in Hiroshima, firmly believed that Toyo Kogyo had to have a unique product to separate it from the legions of competitors. Hoping to take advantage of the growing demand for small trucks, he ordered the development of a three-wheeled model called the DA. Cheap and reliable, it gave Toyo Kogyo a successful entry into the automotive market.

The **Mazda** Miata was modeled after the British Lotus Elan—which Mazda engineers disassembled for "reference."

The first school for auto **mechanics** was established by the Detroit YMCA in 1904.

1899: Uriah Smith of Battle Creek, Michigan, crafts a life-sized horse's head to place on the front of cars—an effort to fool horses and keep them from becoming frightened by oncoming automobiles, a common problem of the time.

Forty-nine percent of the **mechanics** surveyed in a Valvoline/Automotive Service Excellence poll said that their family and friends ask them questions about auto service "all the time" when they are off duty.

The **Mercedes-Benz** passenger cars produced by Daimler-Benz between 1926 and the beginning of World War II are considered among the most magnificent automobiles ever created.

The first diesel-engine automobile offered for sale to the public was the **Mercedes-Benz** 260D in 1936.

In 1952 Daimler-Benz brought the **Mercedes-Benz** 300SL—the legendary gullwing coupe—to the international racing circuit. The 300SL was built using a lightweight tubular frame that made conventional doors impossible. Rudolph Uhlenhaut, a race car driver and engineer, solved the problem by designing doors cut into the roof. The doors opened upward, giving the car a bird-like appearance. Powered by the same six-cylinder engine used in the

A Mercedes Is Born

In 1897 Emile Jellinek, a wealthy Austrian banker, became a managing board member of Daimler-Motoren-Gesselschaft—founded in 1890 by Gottlieb Daimler—and a distributor of Daimler motor cars. It was Jellinek who convinced Daimler to position the engines at the front of the cars "because that was where the horse used to be." Jellinek also pressured Daimler to create faster, more powerful automobiles. His favorite sales technique apparently was to pass other motorists, especially on hills, and then stop to sell them the car he was driving.

In 1900 Jellinek asked Daimler to design a racer with a longer wheelbase, a lower center of gravity, and an engine capable of generating speeds of at least 30 mph. Jellinek also promised to purchase 36 of the cars—a big order in those days—in return for exclusive rights to distribute Daimler automobiles in Austria-Hungary, France, Belgium, and the United States. Jellinek had one other stipulation: he wanted the car named the "Mercedes," in honor of his one-year-old daughter, Maria de las Mercedes Adrenne Manuela Ramona. Daimler agreed. The first Mercedes was delivered to Jellinek in December of 1900. In 1902 Daimler-Motoren-Gesselschaft registered the name "Mercedes" as a trademark.

1900: First large, major American automobile show is held in Madison Square Garden, New York. Silent steam cars and elegant electrics dominate the show, making the gasoline cars seem noisy, smelly, and jerky.

Putting Michelin on the Map

World-renowned Michelin guides and maps are the only extension of the Michelin tire brand. These tourist tools have made the brand a generic term for "road map" in France. The first "Guide Michelin," published in 1900 by André Michelin, was primarily a list of places that sold gas. Mr. Bib, the company's mascot, played a starring role in the booklet, which helped promote the brand's image of reliability. Although there were only 3,000 cars in all of France and a 50-mile trip was newsworthy, André declared that the manual "was born with the century and would last as long as the century." But even he could not have anticipated the influence this traveler's primer would have on France's chefs and hoteliers.

André was known as a "bon vivant" and his guide quickly became the authoritative ranking of French, and later European, restaurants. The Michelin guide rates restaurants and hotels according to a star system. The top rating, often equated to earning France's Legion of Honor, is three stars; most sites listed in the guides don't even rate one star. By mid-century, Michelin had extended its line of "Red (food and lodging) Guides" to Benelux, Germany, Italy, Great Britain, and Spain. "Green (sightseeing) Guides" covered Germany, Austria, Switzerland, Italy, and many other countries.

Mercedes 300, 300SL racers took first place at Le Mans, the Bern Grand Prix, and the Carrera Panamericana, a rugged road race stretching the length of Mexico. In Mexico, the winning Mercedes 300SL averaged more than 100 mph for 1,993 miles. The only mishap was when the 300SL, traveling at 40 mph, collided with a low-flying condor.

At Le Mans in 1955, a gullwing **Mercedes-Benz** 300SLR driven by Pierre Levegh careened into the crowd, killing 83 people, including Levegh, in the worst accident in auto racing history. Daimler-Benz withdrew from factory-sponsored racing after the 1955 season because of the accident.

Founded in 1889 and represented by a tire-man mascot known as Mr. Bib, **Michelin** is the oldest, most recognizable, and highest-selling tire brand in the world. Unlike most of its rivals, Michelin's product line is comprised almost exclusively of tires. The only other product offered under the Michelin name, a global series of road maps and tourist guides, has upheld and reinforced the ideals of quality and reliability imbued in the tires.

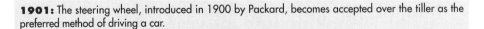

1901: The steering wheel, introduced in 1900 by Packard, becomes accepted over the tiller as the preferred method of driving a car.

The tire innovations of **Michelin** formed the foundation of its phenomenal success. From 1906 to 1937, detachable rims and spare tires, tubeless tires, treads, and low-profile tires were all introduced under the Michelin name. By 1930 Michelin became the first company to master the complicated techniques necessary to combine steel wire and rubber for use in an automotive tire. And in 1938, Michelin launched the "Metalic" tire. But the brand's most important development of the twentieth century came in 1946, when Michelin patented the radial-ply tire. Some of the basic ideas of the radial concept had first been patented in 1913 by two British men, but no one then had the capacity to build a radial without the risk of the components separating and the tire disintegrating.

The first **National Association of Retail Automobile Dealers** was formed in 1904.

More and more cars are being built to run on less polluting, less expensive **natural gas**. An average of four natural gas stations open each week in the United States.

Source: USA TODAY, November 13, 1995.

For many years **Nissan** was known mainly through its Datsun brand of automobiles. The brand was associated more with low-end economy cars, rather than the high-margin mid-size sedans and luxury automobiles Nissan intended to market. Therefore, the Datsun brand was discontinued in 1981 in favor of the corporate name.

One of the most successful **Nissan** models in the American market was the Datsun 240Z, a sports car introduced in 1969 that shared many attributes with the celebrated Ford Mustang. It was stylish, fast, fun to drive, and affordable. A small Datsun pickup truck also was very successful because it was more appropriate to many consumers' needs. It was rugged, efficient, and cheap, and its popularity encouraged many dealerships to begin carrying Datsuns.

Conoco, a subsidiary of DuPont, is developing a clear **oil** that doesn't break down as fast as regular oil. This clear oil could allow longer intervals between oil changes and should be in production by the end of 1996.

Source: The Detroit News, February 25, 1996.

1901: The beginnings of the American gas station as a place for dispensing fuel and repairing cars takes shape as one is set up in New York City.

The Oldsmobile Toronado was America's first mass-produced front-wheel-drive car.
Courtesy of American Automobile Manufacturers Association

Forever memorialized in the 1905 Gus Edwards composition "In My Merry Oldsmobile," the **Oldsmobile** division of General Motors is one of America's oldest car manufacturers.

Publicity stunts were used by **Oldsmobile** to establish the speed and durability of its early products. In 1901 Roy Chapin (later the chief executive of Hudson Motor Car Company) drove an Oldsmobile Curved Dash Runabout from Detroit to a national auto show in New York City. The trip, over dauntingly muddy roads and canal tow paths, took more than a week at 14 miles per hour. But this feat made the car the focal point of the show. Two years later, the Oldsmobile Pirate made headlines when it established a world's record of 5 miles in 6.5 minutes at Daytona Beach, Florida. And in 1905 two Olds Curved Dash Runabouts participated in the first transcontinental automobile race, traveling the 4,400 miles from New York City to Portland, Oregon, in 44 days.

In 1962 **Oldsmobile** launched America's first production car equipped with a fuel-injected, turbocharged V8 engine. Called the Jetfire, the car featured a hardtop, bucket seats, and a central console. Just two years later, Olds introduced its legendary 442 sports option, featuring a 4-barrel carburetor, 4-speed transmission, and dual exhausts. The package, available on 8-cylinder Cutlass sports coupes, hardtop coupes, convertibles, and F85 sports coupes, heralded the "muscle car" age.

An industry standard was established by **Oldsmobile** in 1965 with the introduction of the 1966 Toronado, the first mass-produced front-wheel-drive vehicle in America. The positioning of all powertrain components under the new model's hood complemented the car's front-wheel drive, giving it superior traction and handling. The innovative Toronado was widely hailed as "the most unique American automobile in many years"; it won *Motor Trend*'s "Car of the Year" and *Car Life*'s "Engineering Excellence" awards.

In 1995 the **Oldsmobile** Cutlass Supreme was the most frequently stolen car in the United States. This marked the fourth consecutive year that the Cutlass topped the list of the "hottest" cars in America. The three top positions on the most frequently stolen list belonged to Cutlass Supreme models built in the 1980s. Others in the top

---

1901: Connecticut enacts the first automobile traffic laws (speed limits—15 mph for rural roads, 12 mph for cities—and driver registration). New York State begins external car license plates, usually with the owner's initials.

10: five Honda Accord models built in the 1990s, the 1994 Toyota Camry LE, and the 1987 Chevrolet Caprice.

Source: USA TODAY

In 1955 **Packard** introduced a long-awaited luxury model designed to compete with the best Cadillacs. Despite its high-quality craftsmanship, the Packard fell short in acceleration and top speed. Soon thereafter, the Packard company folded.

Inventors of the **Papp engine** created quite a stir in 1960 by claiming a minute amount of gas could keep their engine running for 60,000 miles. But, on November 18, the Papp engine blew up during a demonstration, killing one person and injuring several others.

Source: Road & Track

One of the latest rages in **pickup trucks** is the third door. Designed to give easier access to the rear seat of full-size pickups, the third door was first marketed by Chevrolet on select extended cab CK models. The feature first appeared on a Chevrolet concept truck in 1992 and got rave reviews. Chevy engineers rolled up their sleeves and put the concept into production in 23 months, the fastest major product change in GM history. Ford quickly followed suit, offering the third door on select F150 Super Cab models. Chrysler is expected to offer a third door on its Ram pickups for the 1998 model year.

The first **Plymouth** car was introduced by Chrysler Motors in June of 1928. This first car, a four-cylinder model with a relatively modest base price of $670, offered the amenities of a more expensive car, including four-wheel hydraulic brakes and full-pressure engine lubrication. The name Plymouth, according to the company, was intended as the "symbol of the endurance and strength, the rugged honesty, enterprise and determination of achievement, and freedom from old limitations" as it is associated with the Pilgrims.

In the late 1930s, **Plymouth** made several advances in passenger safety, including the elimination of projecting knobs from the interior and the introduction of safety glass as standard equipment. In honor of its efforts, Plymouth received the Eastern Safety Conference award for the cars' design in 1939 and 1940.

1901: First American car to be manufactured in quantity is the "Curved Dash" Oldsmobile. It has a single-cylinder, seven-horsepower gas engine that gives a top speed of 18 mph, a two-speed gearbox with reverse, and sells for about $650.

Road Test

MATCH THE LOGO WITH THE APPROPRIATE VEHICLE.

1. Sailboat on the water   A. Lamborghini
2. Three-pointed star   B. Cadillac
3. Ram's head   C. Mercedes-Benz
4. Rearing stallion   D. Chevrolet
5. Bull   E. Geo
6. "Bowtie"   F. Dodge Trucks
7. Shield and wreath   G. Ferrari
8. Stylized airplane propeller   H. Chrysler
9. Five-pointed star   I. Plymouth
10. Globe   J. BMW

(Answers: 1.I 2.C 3.F 4.G 5.A 6.D 7.B 8.J 9.H 10.E)

In 1995 **Plymouth** adopted a new logo—a sailboat on the water—which was based on their original logo—an old-time masted ship on the high seas.

The **Plymouth** Prowler—a two-seat, retro-styled roadster available only in purple—began as a concept car, but Chrysler decided to start production of the vehicle in 1996. The $35,000 con-vertible will serve as an image booster for the Plymouth marque.

The origins of **Pontiac** go back to 1893. It was then that Edward M. Murphy, a manufacturer of horse-drawn buggies, established his new Pontiac Buggy Company in Pontiac, Michigan (about 20 miles north of Detroit). The buggy business had been a profitable one in the past, but as the twentieth century loomed, the businessman "read the handwriting on the wall: the horse-drawn buggy was doomed. It was the

---

1901: First long-distance, American endurance auto race is organized by the Automobile Club of America. It is planned to run 500 miles—from Cleveland to New York City—but is stopped in Buffalo by news of President McKinley's assassination.

smelly, noisy unreliable automobile that was going to prevail."

𝓢𝓸𝓾𝓻𝓬𝓮: Bosnall, Thomas E., *Pontiac: The Complete History, 1926–1986*, Bookman Publishing, 1986.

Not just a tribute to the city that housed the automotive plant, the name **Pontiac** also honors a renowned figure in American history. Chief Pontiac, of the Ottawa nation, is considered by many historians to have been one of the most important of all Native American leaders.

Product placement has frequently brought **Pontiac** into the public eye. In 1955 the company received tremendous television exposure when the popular *I Love Lucy* show used a Pontiac convertible during Lucy, Ricky, Fred, and Ethel's cross-country trip to California. In later years the most well-known Pontiac "actor" was a shining black Trans Am that played the part of KITT, superintelligent crime-fighting vehicle, on the NBC series *Knight Rider*.

In 1959 **Pontiac** introduced Wide Track. This new chassis design widened the front and rear axle width by several inches. This greatly increased a

Pontiac's "track," which contributed not only to improved handling but also to safety, since the new design enlarged the glass area enormously.

Well-received by critics (*Motor Trend* voted **Pontiac** "Car of the Year" in 1959) and public alike, Wide Track helped increase Pontiac's market share while solidifying the division's performance image. The Wide-Track Pontiacs remain valuable collectors' items to this day. The city of Pontiac, Michigan, even renamed a major thoroughfare Wide Track Drive in recognition of a design idea that paid off handsomely.

The first magnesium wheels were introduced by **Pontiac** in 1962.

To compete with the Ford Mustang, **Pontiac** introduced its Firebird in 1967.

In 1984 **Pontiac** unveiled its first mid-engine production car, the Fiero. This two-seater, with its low, angular posture and aggressive-looking details, was positioned as something of the workingman's Ferrari. Initially, the strategy

1901: Road touring signs are placed from New York City to Boston.

The Pontiac Firebird was designed to compete with Ford's Mustang.

Courtesy of American Automobile Manufacturers Association

worked: early Fiero sales were more than impressive, reaching more than 100 percent over Pontiac's predictions. But in time drivers began suspecting that the Fiero's sports-car stance was making promises that the powerplant couldn't keep. A four-cylinder engine was the only one offered, though by 1985 the car would receive a high-output V6. But continuous improvement came too late. Sales dropped off from the model's big introductory year, and by 1988 the Fiero had left the lineup—one of the best-selling, if shortest-lived, nameplates in Pontiac history.

Headquartered in Stuttgart, Germany, **Porsche** is one of the last independent sports-car makers and a legendary name in automobile road racing, with more than a dozen victories at Le Mans between 1970 and 1987. Its most popular production model is the Type 911, introduced in 1964. Although significantly redesigned over the years, the same basic car is still being sold today.

Despite more than half a century as a design engineer, Ferdinand **Porsche** never created a car that carried his name. That was left to his son Ferry, who took over management of his father's business after World War II and introduced the first Porsche in 1948.

The younger Porsche would later write: "Throughout the war I never abandoned the idea of building our sports car, one bearing the Porsche name."

The first **Porsche** was built from spare Volkswagen parts, which were plentiful in postwar Germany. It was an open two-seater with an aluminum body pounded into shape over a wooden form. It was designated the Type 356. The car was shown for the first time in Geneva in 1949, and received generally good reviews.

The **Porsche** 550 Spyder was an open two-seater with a wide collar that enclosed the headrests, giving the car a hunchbacked appearance. It was built so low to the ground that Hans Hermann was able to steer his Spyder beneath a railroad-crossing barrier during a road race in 1954, barely avoiding being hit by an oncoming train. Since his competition had to stop, Hermann easily won his class.

In 1954 **Porsche** introduced a car designed specifically for girl-watching in sunny Southern California. The idea came from John von Neumann, a Hol-

---

1901: A New York Supreme Court judge offers the opinion that owners of steam-powered automobiles should be proceeded by a runner waving a red flag to warn other wayfarers (and horses).

lywood car dealer and Porsche's U.S. importer's west coast distributor. The Speedster was based on the Type 356, but it was strictly bare bones. It was an open two-seater with a low-cut, removable windshield and side curtains instead of crank-up windows. The Speedster also had a folding top that nearly obscured visibility when it was up and did little to keep out the rain, but it still became one of Porsche's most sought-after cars. Sometimes compared to a bathtub with wheels, the Speedster was so popular in the United States that it wasn't available in Europe for the first nine months.

In 1969 **Porsche** and Volkswagen collaborated on the VW-Porsche 914, a mid-engine, two-seat sports car that came with either a Volkswagen or more expensive Porsche engine. The body design was pure Porsche and extremely popular, but the association with Volkswagen hurt Porsche's elitist image. Porsche purchased Volkswagen's interest in the venture in 1973 and discontinued the Type 914 in 1976.

In 1987 **Porsche** attempted to stimulate sales by introducing an entry-level car, the Porsche 924. Priced at less than $20,000, the 924 was a commercial failure. It was underpowered for a Porsche

The Future's So Bright, They Had to Make Shades

Since 1978 the Porsche name has also appeared on a variety of consumer products designed by Butzi Porsche. Butzi, who created the Type 911 body style, left Porsche AG in 1972 to form his own design firm in Zell-am-See, Austria. When he was unable to sell some of his more artistic designs to other manufacturers, he founded Porsche Design Produkte GmbH. in 1978 to turn his ideas into products. Hans Peter Porsche joined his brother as business manager.

Among the items to carry the Porsche name were a line of sunglasses with interchangeable lenses, men's titanium wristwatches, leather goods, and headphones that were put on display by the New York Museum of Modern Art. In 1984 Butzi Porsche told *Forbes*, "Every designer is at first happy to work on cars because they are very emotional products. But after a while cars are all the same."

and sporty cars from mass marketers like Honda and Mazda cost about as much—and were faster.

In 1989 **Porsche** launched the Type 911 Carrera 4, its first four-wheel-drive car.

1902: One of the earliest U.S. speeding violations is recorded as a man is arrested and fined $10 for driving in excess of 10 mph in Minneapolis.

Looking for a Good Sign

The development of retroreflective sheeting by the 3M Company in the 1940s changed the face of traffic signs forever. This material, with reflective elements like glass beads on or under a transparent plastic film, is designed to reflect some of the light from vehicle headlights back to the driver so that the sign will be better visible at night. Although exotic possibilities like projecting holographic traffic signs above the roadway have been suggested for the future, it is more likely that drivers will see conventional refinements of signs to make them more visible, especially at night. Internally illuminated street signs are already in use in parts of Nevada and California. Self-illuminated signs that use light-emitting diodes powered by solar-charged batteries have also been developed, but their use may be restricted because they cost roughly five times more than a traditional sign.

One popular feature of the Carrera 4 was a retractable spoiler. The spoiler, mounted just below the rear window, was triggered automatically when the car reached 50 mph and retracted into the bodywork when the car came to a stop.

The first automobile to show up on a

U.S. **postage stamp** was a Baker Brougham—an electric taxi—in 1901.

The first **radio** offered as an accessory was introduced by Springfield Body Corporation in 1923.

American car **registrations** passed the 1 million mark in 1913.

An average **rental car** is driven 2,000 to 3,000 miles each month.

Source: The Wall Street Journal, November 4, 1992.

In 1930 Charles Creighton and James Hargis made a round trip from New York to Los Angeles without stopping the engine once; it took them 43 days and they drove the whole trip in **reverse**.

Early **road signs** lacked the reflectorized technology prevalent in signs today. The first traffic sign using reflective sheeting was installed on the outskirts of Minneapolis in 1939.

1902: Packard introduces its advertising slogan, "Ask the man that owns one"—which remains in use until 1956.

The Rolls-Royce—introduced in 1904 as a joint venture between engineer Frederick Henry Royce and dealership-owner Charles Rolls—has become one of the most famous cars in the world. From hand-crafted leather and walnut interiors to "Spirit of Ecstasy" hood ornaments, Rolls-Royce automobiles represent the ultimate in motoring elegance. Other automobiles are flashier, faster, or more technologically advanced, but Rolls-Royce automobiles are considered by many to be the final word in overstated luxury.

About 1,300 Rolls-Royce cars were made in 1993. Each took from four to six months to produce.

In 1994 Rolls-Royce claimed that about two-thirds of the 117,000 Rolls-Royce automobiles made between 1904 and 1994 were still in running condition.

The first automobile to have a head-light washer-wiper system was a Saab 99.

There's No Agony with this Ecstasy

The famous Rolls-Royce radiator-cap mascot—The Spirit of Ecstasy—was created in 1911 by Charles Sykes, a sculptor and artist. He was commissioned by Rolls-Royce distributor/promoter Claude Johnson, who was unhappy with some of the ornaments that owners were affixing to their Rolls-Royce cars. Johnson suggested a figure along the lines of a classic Greek statue, but Sykes favored a more fluid sculpture. He called his figurine—a woman in a flowing, wind-swept robe—"The Spirit of Speed." However, a press release written by Johnson renamed the figurine "the Spirit of Ecstasy, who has selected road travel as her supreme delight, and has alighted on the prow of a Rolls-Royce car to revel in the freshness of the air and the musical sound of her fluttering draperies." The statuette, sometimes inaccurately referred to as a winged figure, also became known as "The Flying Lady."

Sykes supervised production of the figurines until 1928, personally signing the base of each. In 1933 Sykes sculpted a kneeling figure of a woman in flowing robes that was used on most Rolls-Royce Phantom IIIs, Wraiths, Silver Wraiths, Silver Dawns, and Phantom IVs. Over the years, Rolls-Royce figurines have been made of various metal alloys, but never, despite the mythology, of solid silver.

1902: Running boards—a long step mounted on a car's body under the doors to help passengers get in and out—appear first on a Silent Northern car built by Jonathan Maxwell and Charles King of Detroit.

Every Rolls-Royce car takes months to make.

Courtesy of American Automobile Manufacturers Association

The first mass-produced turbocharged car was introduced by **Saab** in 1977.

The first four way **seat adjustment** was introduced in 1952.

Front **seat belts** were first introduced as standard equipment in 1963.

Rear **seat belts** first became standard on most cars in 1965.

The first automobile **showroom** was opened in New York City by Percy Owen—who sold Winton cars—in 1899.

The first remote **sideview mirror** control was introduced on several cars in 1958.

Motor driven **snow removal equipment** was used nationwide for the first time in 1922.

The **Society of Automotive Engineers**— the first association of automobile engineers—was formed in 1905.

In 1860 French engineer Jean Lenoir created what most closely resembles the **spark plug** of today. He combined an insulator, electrodes, and spark gap in a single unit. As part of his patent application for the internal combustion engine that year, he devoted one sentence to describing the spark plug. He refined this spark plug in 1885.

A spark plug is under constant attack by corrosive gases at 4,500 degrees Fahrenheit, crushing pressures of 2,000 pounds per square inch, and electrical discharges of up to 18,000 volts. This unrelenting assault under the hood of a typical car occurs dozens of times per second and over a million times in a day's worth of driving.

The U.S. government enacted a nationwide 55 mph **speed limit** in 1974 after a foreign oil embargo created a serious gasoline shortage. In 1987 Congress let states raise the speed limit on

1903: First automobile used as a police car in the United States is a Stanley Steamer in Boston. It has a top speed of 10 mph.

rural interstates to 65 mph. On November 28, 1995, President Bill Clinton signed the repeal of the federal speed limit law, allowing states to set their own speed limits. Several states were considering 75 mph speed limits despite opponents' arguments that the higher speeds would mean more highway deaths and increased insurance rates. Montana planned to eliminate highway speed limits altogether during the day—drivers would be able to drive whatever speed they deem "reasonable and proper."

The first magnetic **speedometer** was introduced in 1908.

A speedometer warning buzzer was introduced in 1956.

Two French Jesuit missionaries in China are rumored to have constructed **steam-propelled vehicles** in the 1660s.

The first broken **stone road** was introduced in England by John Macadam in 1815.

Cars made by **Studebaker** set 160 endurance or speed records in 1928.

Two entrepreneurs—Harvey Lamm and Malcolm Bricklin—founded **Subaru** of America in 1968 as the exclusive U.S. sales and marketing company for Subaru automobiles, manufactured by the Japanese company Fuji Heavy Industries.

The first car **Subaru** introduced into the U.S. market was the Subaru 360 mini. Powered by a two-stroke engine and running at an impressive 66.3 miles per gallon, it sold for $1,297. It was nevertheless a failure because *Consumer Reports* pronounced it unsafe for U.S. roads.

In 1983 **Subaru** became the first carmaker to offer optional four-wheel drive on all models and introduced the first four-wheel drive with an automatic transmission.

Lear Seating Corporation of Southfield, Michigan, is developing a built-in

1903: Automobile innovations this year are all-steel car bodies and pressed-steel frames, shock absorbers, and glass windshields.

windshield **sunshade** that would install itself at the push of a button.

Source: The Detroit News, February 25, 1996.

The first **tire chains** were introduced in 1905.

In the 1970s the oil shortage sent the cost of producing **tires** soaring (one tire requires at least six gallons of oil to make).

The first U.S. **toll roads** were opened in Connecticut and Pennsylvania in 1792.

Upon her death and in accordance with her will, an Englishwoman's beautifully preserved 1932 Austin was crushed into a solid block of metal to serve as her **tombstone**.

Source: Road & Track

The Toyota Corolla, a subcompact, two-door sedan, was introduced to the United States in 1968. At that time, the Corolla and its forerunners—the Corona and the Crown—ranged in price from $1,800 to $4,000. The Corolla had already made its debut in Japan two

years earlier. The car was developed after a predecessor, the two-cylinder Publica, flopped. Shortly after its U.S. introduction, Corolla blossomed into a winner for Toyota. By 1970 the car had become the number-two best-selling import in the United States.

The Corolla was **Toyota**'s dream car. Of the automaker's 15 lines, Corolla comprised 24.3 percent of production by the end of the 1970s. Corolla had even replaced the VW Beetle as the world's top-selling small car. From 1968 to 1978, cumulative Corolla production mushroomed from 100,000 cars to 750,000 annually.

The **Toyota** Camry took its name from an Anglicized version of the Japanese "kan-muri," which means crown.

The first synchronized **traffic light system** was installed in Houston, Texas, in 1922.

The first illuminated **traffic signal** was installed in London, England, in 1868. It was manually turned and consisted of two gas lamps, one red and one

1903: Ford Motor Company is organized in Detroit with $28,000 capital put up by 12 shareholders. The Dodge Brothers—exclusive parts suppliers for Ford—invest $10,000 and are bought out a decade later for $32 million.

0 0 0 4 7

Traffic signals brought some order to the early days of driving.

Courtesy of American Automobile Manufacturers Association

green, with signal arms atop a pole. Shortly after its inauguration, however, it blew up while the lamps were being lit, killing a policeman.

The first electric **traffic signal** was installed in Cleveland, Ohio, in 1914. It consisted of a green and red light with a warning buzzer to indicate when the light was about to change.

The first **traffic signal** to use the familiar green, yellow, and red lights was installed in New York City in 1918. It was operated manually from an elevated observation post in the middle of the street.

The first three-color, four-way **traffic signal** was installed in Detroit in 1920.

The next time you feel like cutting in front of one of those big **trucks** on the freeway, remember this: at 55 mph it can take an 18-wheeler more than 100 yards to stop.

Preston Tucker formed the **Tucker** Corporation in 1946, convinced that war-weary Americans would immediately want to buy a car. The Tucker Torpedo was unveiled in July of 1947. Innovative features on the Torpedo included fuel injection, pressurized water cooling, and aerodynamic design. Other features included pop-out safety windshields, lively body colors, and a cyclops headlight that turned in the direction the car was moving. Fifty-one Tucker automobiles were built. Sale price was about $2,400. Today the 49 cars that remain are worth $250,000 to $500,000.

Amber front **turn signal** lights were first adopted in 1962.

The **Vector** M12, an exotic car made in Jacksonville, Florida, comes with a V12 engine and lamb's wool carpeting. It also goes from zero to 60 in just over three seconds. For those who don't want to pay the car's $184,000 sticker price, the Vector can be leased for $2,999 a month.

Source: CNN Interactive

1903: Barney Oldfield becomes the first driver to break the one-minute mile in a gas-powered automobile, racing to 64 mph in Henry Ford's 999.

According to a report by the International Road Federation in Geneva, the city with the highest **vehicle density** on its roads is Hong Kong, with 261 vehicles per 0.6 miles.

Source: International Herald Tribune, November 19, 1992.

In 1972 the 15,007,034th **Volkswagen** Beetle came off the production line, making it the highest produced car ever, overtaking the Ford Model T.

One of the world's best-selling cars, the **Volkswagen** Golf became known for its firm, responsive handling, good gas mileage, and the quality of its "German engineering." It was first sold in Europe in 1974 and was exported to the United States—where it was called the Rabbit through 1984—a year later. A high-performance version, the GTI, was first sold in the early 1980s.

The early **Volkswagen** Golf was so successful that its front-wheel-drive, hatchback design was copied by many competing automakers.

The first international automaker to build vehicles in the U.S. was **Volkswagen**. They opened their Westmoreland, Pennsylvania, plant for production of the Rabbit in 1978.

Total production of **Volkswagen** Golfs reached 14 million by 1993. In Germany, its home market, the Golf has consistently been the top-selling car.

Sam Marchese devised a clever solution to the problem of having VWs with good front ends but damaged rears. Sam, president of the Gus Mozart Body Works in Palo Alto, California, put them together and created a double **Volkswagen**; you couldn't tell if it was coming or going.

Source: Road & Track

The Swedish car company **Volvo** exported its first automobiles to the United States in 1956—to a less than rousing reception. The styling of the PV444 was reminiscent of the 1940s, and only a few hundred cars were sold during the first couple of years. Volvo, however, developed a marketing strategy around the car's durability—the car

1903: The first fire engine is a Stanley Steamer mounted with two handheld fire extinguishers, capable of putting out a raging barbecue.

built tough enough for the rugged Scandinavian weather and road conditions—and developed a loyal following.

In an effort to update its image, in the 1960s **Volvo** introduced cars like the stylish P1800, which was driven by Roger Moore in the British television show *The Saint.* The P1800 was also the official car at the 24-hour race at Sebring in 1963 and 1964.

The **Volvo** 144, introduced in 1966, was the first Volvo to truly catch on with U.S. car buyers. The Volvo 144 and the luxury model Volvo 164 met all proposed U.S. safety standards for the 1970s even before they were announced. The Volvos had front-seat belts for all passengers, four-wheel disc brakes, split steering columns, and energy-absorbing crumple zones in both the front and rear.

Cars made by **Volvo** have been widely recognized as leaders in durability and passenger safety. In 1976, for example, the National Highway Traffic Safety Administration, charged with setting U.S. safety standards, chose the Volvo 240 as the benchmark for testing all other passenger vehicles.

The Environmentally Friendly Volvo

In 1992 Volvo stunned the automobile industry by unveiling a sleek, experimental four-door sedan that it called the Environmental Concept Car, or ECC for short. The ECC, developed at Volvo's Monitoring and Concept Center in Camarillo, California, was powered by a hybrid electric/gas turbine engine. When running on batteries alone, the ECC had a range of about 50 miles and could qualify as a Zero Emission Vehicle under California's strict environmental pollution regulations. With the diesel-fueled gas turbine engine running to recharge, the ECC was classified as an Ultra Low Emission Vehicle—the most pollution-free class for a combustion engine.

The ECC was also designed to be environmentally friendly when it came time to recycle the car. The body was made of aluminum, which could be melted down and used again. All the plastic parts inside the car were designed for easy removal so they, too, could be recycled. Volvo said the ECC could be in production early in the twenty-first century.

Cars are not **Volvo**'s only business. The company is also a leading maker of trucks and buses worldwide.

1903: Henry Ford sells his first Model A.

Oil pressure and generator **warning lights** ("idiot lights" to some) were first introduced to replace gauges in 1953.

The first standard car **warranty** was for 90 days/4,000 miles and was issued by the National Automobile Chamber of Commerce in 1931.

The first power **windows** were introduced in 1946.

The first wrap-around **windshield** was introduced on several Kissel Kars in 1913.

The glass **windshield** first appeared around 1905 with the invention of safety glass—glass tempered (tempering is a heat treatment) to make it especially hard and resistant to shattering. This type of windshield was popular well into the middle of the century, but it

was eventually replaced by windshields made of laminated glass—a multilayer unit consisting of a plastic layer surrounded by two sheets of glass. In many countries, including the U.S., auto windshields are required by law to be made of laminated glass. Laminated glass can bend slightly under impact and is less likely to shatter than normal safety glass.

A bi-layer **windshield** has been developed that consists of one sheet of glass joined to a single sheet of polyurethane. Unique features of this windshield include ultraviolet resistance, self-healing of scratches, weight savings, more complex shapes, increased safety due to retention of glass splinters, and anti-fog capability.

Powered **windshield wipers** became standard equipment on many cars in 1923.

The first two-speed electric **windshield wipers** were introduced by Chrysler in 1940.

1904: First national inventory of roads is conducted by the U.S. Office of Public Road Inquiries (OPRI). Of the over two million miles of public roads, only 153,662 miles have any kind of surfacing.

America's First "Paper" Car

The Selden patent case was one of the most astonishing events in the history of the American automobile industry. Although George B. Selden never built a machine, the argument could be made that he invented the country's first automobile. At least on paper.

Selden, a New York patent attorney, had first seen a gasoline engine at the Philadelphia Exposition in 1876, where inventor George Brayton was demonstrating his two-cycle motor. Selden was very impressed and commissioned a gas engine to be built for him, based on the Brayton design. At the same time, he designed a road-going carriage that could be powered by this engine. Selden never built the carriage, but—undoubtedly as a result of his line of work—he did have the presence of mind to apply for a patent in 1879. As the years went by and technology advanced, Selden kept his patent current through occasional updates and revisions.

Finally, in 1895, with automobiles being produced by a number of American manufacturers, Selden decided the time was right to put his patent to work for him. He announced his intention to begin collecting royalties from every car built in America. The resulting court cases shook American industry and almost rewrote the history of the U.S. automobile. Selden's patent was pretty much airtight: On paper, he had invented a horseless carriage, and he had filed a series of carefully worded patents and amendments that appeared to prove it.

A group of automakers banded together, recognized the validity of Selden's patent, and agreed to pay him royalties in exchange for the exclusive rights to build cars under it. This group, the Association of Licensed Automobile Manufacturers (ALAM) proclaimed itself the only legitimate U.S. automobile

1904: First person to exceed 100 mph in an automobile is Frenchman Louis E. Rigolly, whose large Gobron-Brille is timed at 103.56 mph in Ostend, Belgium.

industry, then set about trying to legally prevent any other companies from producing automobiles.

Other manufacturers were outraged, and they threw their resources into fighting Selden and the ALAM. One of the leading patent-breakers was the fiercely independent Henry Ford, who actively fought Selden from 1903 to 1911, when an Appeals Court finally ruled in his favor. By that time, however, Selden's patent had almost expired anyway, and in the meantime he had become quite wealthy from the royalties.

Ford's Better Idea

The Ford Model T put America on wheels and was the single most influential car in the history of the automobile industry. Affectionately called the Tin Lizzie and the Flivver (along with other nicknames, some not as endearing), the Model T was the first dependable, widely affordable automobile: with its introduction in 1908 everyone could get car crazy. The Model T's popularity also transformed American industry, driving the boom in automobile manufacturing that resulted in the modern factory and well-paying jobs for thousands of laborers.

When the Ford Motor Company was established in 1903, Henry Ford was tinkering with the idea of producing a low-priced, dependable automobile affordable to the masses, with an engine

that could be maintained easily and adapted for a variety of farm uses (from dragging a plow to powering a butter churn). Ford confronted several challenges along the way: by standardizing parts and making them easily interchangeable and available, the Model T offered simple maintenance; by using vanadium steel, which Ford first encountered on a French racing car, the body and parts would be lighter, yet sturdier than other automobiles of the time; and by continuously improving production methods, the price and manufacturing costs could be held down while meeting great consumer demand. The Model T was a triumph of basic engineering, tough enough to handle the roads of the time throughout rural and urban America.

The Model T was rugged, simple to operate, dependable, and easy to maintain. Unlike most cars of its time, the Tin Lizzie's steering wheel and controls were on the left side of the car; its dominance on the road led all American car makers to adopt left-sided steering as a standard. The Model T had a peppy engine—winning a New York-to-Seattle race in 1909 over cars like the Acme, the Shawmutt, and the Italia, all of which cost five times as much as the Flivver. The engine was easy to maintain as well, with a standard joke being that a piece of wire, a hairpin and a screwdriver were all that was needed to keep it running. While maintaining the basic model and engine for the next

1905: First removable automobile tire rims are introduced by the Michelin Company of France. Before these, punctured or damaged tires had to be repaired while the wheels remained attached to the car.

two decades, Ford gradually introduced improvements and new features. The 1911 Model T Touring, for example, featured new fenders, wheels, axles, and engine modifications; headlights and a horn became standard equipment. A whole separate accessories industry grew quickly to supply Model T owners with more goods, despite a Ford warranty that was voided if non-factory installed accessories were added.

But the Model T could also be stubborn and noisy. It rattled and bounced and backfired. Starting in cold weather was difficult, often challenging drivers to find novel ways to heat the engine or warm the spark plugs: a favorite ploy was to remove the spark plugs, heat them inside an enclosed area, like a kitchen, and then put them back and quickly beginning the ritual for starting the Model T. Here's the starting ritual: the driver first adjusts spark and gas levers under the steering wheel; then, the driver runs to the front of the car to vigorously turn the cranky, stubborn old hand crank while praying for the engine to catch after only maybe two or three turns this time, please; then, the driver runs back to readjust the spark and gas levers before the engine stalls. Most times this ritual was successful. Assistance was always welcome.

Three colors were available on Model Ts up until 1914: red on touring models, gray on runabouts, and green on town cars and landaulets (or couplet). From 1914 until 1926 the Model T was available only in black on all models—the coupe, the 2-passenger closed car, the couplet (with an adjustable roof), the Depot wagon (a precursor to the station wagon), the sedan, the town car, the touring car, the pick-up, the runabout, and the speedster.

When it became an overnight sensation, Ford began concentrating on production methods, tinkering with the idea of having groups of workers focusing on individual components; to this he added a moving assembly line in 1913. Ford soon introduced the 8-hour day and the $5 day, paying workers twice as much as most other factories. His factories were designed by Detroit architect Albert Kahn, who created spacious work areas enclosed with glass to offer maximum natural lighting.

The first factory-made Model T appeared in 1908 and sold for $850. Over 17,000 Model Ts were sold during its first year, a phenomenal record. Just four years earlier, the world's entire automobile industry produced 22,000 cars; by 1914, the Ford Highland Park Plant alone produced almost 250,000 Model Ts, and over 700,000 were built in 1917. In 1913, a Model T was produced every 12.5 hours; after mass production and the assembly line were in place in 1914, a Model T could be produced every 1.5 hours; and during an intense day in 1925, a Model T was pro-

1905: First trucks, introduced by Packard, Mitchell, and Maxwell.

The Ford Model T was the single most influential car in the history of the automobile industry.

Courtesy of American Automobile Manufacturers Association

duced every 10 seconds! Over 9,000 cars were produced that single day. This ever-increasing efficiency was reflected in the price—an all-time low of $295 for a 1924 Model T.

But American driving tastes were changing by then. Consumers were willing to pay higher prices for better performance, power, and styling. The philosophy known as "Fordist" and "Fordism," which projects steadily declining prices through consistently improved production methods, was undermined. Ford, however, stubbornly insisted on continuing to produce only the Model T. It wasn't until 1927, after more than 15 million Flivvers had been sold, that Ford announced the end of the line was near, and the Tin Lizzie was retired to history.

Some Assembly Required

In 1908 Henry Ford began production of the Model T automobile. Based on his original Model A design first manufactured in 1903, the Model T took five years to develop. Its creation inaugurated what we know today as the mass production assembly line. This revolutionary idea was based on the concept of simply assembling interchangeable component parts. Prior to this time, coaches and buggies had been handbuilt in small numbers by specialized craftspeople who rarely duplicated any particular unit. Ford's innovative design reduced the number of parts needed as well as the number of skilled fitters who had always formed the bulk of the assembly operation, giving Ford a tremendous advantage over his competition.

Ford's first venture into automobile assembly with the Model A involved setting up assembly stands on which the whole vehicle was built, usually by a single assembler who fit an entire section of the car together in one place. This person performed the same activity over and over at his stationary assembly stand. To provide for more efficiency, Ford had parts delivered as needed to each work station. In this way each assembly fitter took about 8.5 hours to complete his assembly task. By the time the Model T was being developed Ford had decided to use multiple assembly stands with assemblers moving from stand to stand, each performing a specific function. This process reduced the assembly time for each fitter from 8.5 hours to a mere 2.5 minutes by rendering each worker completely familiar with a specific task.

Ford soon recognized that walking from stand to stand wasted time and created jam-ups in the production process as faster workers overtook slower ones. In Detroit in 1913, he solved this problem by introducing the first moving assembly line, a conveyor that moved the vehicle past a stationary assembler. By eliminating the need for workers to

1905: First reported auto theft in the U.S. occurs in St. Louis.

00057

move between stations, Ford cut the assembly task for each worker from 2.5 minutes to just under 2 minutes; the moving assembly conveyor could now pace the stationary worker. The first conveyor line consisted of metal strips to which the vehicle's wheels were attached. The metal strips were attached to a belt that rolled the length of the factory and then, beneath the floor, returned to the beginning area. This reduction in the amount of human effort required to assemble an automobile caught the attention of automobile assemblers throughout the world. Ford's mass production drove the automobile industry for nearly five decades and was eventually adopted by almost every other industrial manufacturer. Although technological advancements have enabled many improvements to modern day automobile assembly operations, the basic concept of stationary workers installing parts on a vehicle as it passes their work stations has not changed drastically over the years.

The Oscar Mayer Wienermobile: Rolling Through History

Imagine the scene back in 1936 when Carl Mayer came into his Uncle Oscar's office with a new advertising idea. Carl had a vision of a 13-foot long hot dog car that would travel the streets of

Chicago and let everyone know about Oscar Mayer's hot dogs.

It must have taken some explaining to describe his dream of the rolling frank. Luckily, Uncle Oscar was a man with vision and gave the thumbs up. Every version of the Wienermobile since has brought smiles and fun wherever it goes. From dodging Duesenbergs in the 1930s to hotdogging on highways in the 1990s, the Oscar Mayer Wienermobile is truly a piece of Americana.

Here are some Wienermobile historical highlights:

1936: Carl Mayer, nephew of the company's founder, came up with the idea of a 13-foot metal hot dog on wheels to transport the world's smallest chef, Little Oscar. General Body Company of Chicago, Illinois, designed the first Wienermobile, which featured open cockpits in the center and rear. It was a common sight on the streets of Chicago as it promoted "German Style Wieners."

1940: By 1940, a glass enclosure was added to provide protection for the driver. Little Oscar and his Wienermobile earned fame throughout the east and midwest. With the world conflict in Europe, the Wienermobile retired from the road due to gas rationing. Oscar Mayer focused efforts on canning meats for our soldiers overseas.

1950–53: The Wienermobile made a triumphant return as five new vehicles hit the streets of America. De-

1906: Automobile innovations during the year are front bumpers, asbestos brake linings (highly resistant to burning), high-voltage magnetos, and air brakes.

signed by Gerstenlager of Wooster, Ohio, and built on a Dodge chassis, the 22-foot long hot dogs were the first to have sound systems and a sunroof. A 1952 Wienermobile is currently on display at the Henry Ford Museum in Dearborn, Michigan.

1958: Brook Stevens, designer of Miller beer's first logo and clear beer bottle and inventor of the "Excalibur" car, is also credited with the 1958 Oscar Mayer Wienermobile. The futuristic, bubble-nosed "weenie on wheels" incorporated buns into the design for the first time. Built on a Willys Jeep chassis, Stevens' design had a tremendous impact on the Wienermobile. Its influence is visible in the next three generations of vehicles.

1969: Two new vehicles were introduced by Oscar Mayer mechanics at the company headquarters in Madison, Wisconsin. Using a variety of classic automotive parts, including Ford Thunderbird taillights, these vehicles carried on the Wienermobile tradition. One of these Wienermobiles was eventually relocated to Puerto Rico.

1976: The last Wienermobile to be built before the program was discontinued in 1977. This Wienermobile was mounted on a 1973 Chevy motor home chassis. It eventually debuted as the first Wienermobile ever to tour a foreign country, visiting Spain in the early 1980s.

1977: The Wienermobiles are retired from service. Thousands of miles of wear and tear and a decision to focus more heavily on television advertising brought the program to a standstill.

1986: The Wienermobile is brought out for a 50th birthday celebration. Huge crowds of people showed up for its appearances. Cards and letters came pouring in requesting to see the famed 2-ton frank. A decision was made to build a new fleet and begin touring again in 1988.

1988: Six 23-foot long fiberglass hot dogs on wheels with license plate names such as Yummy, Big Bun, Our Dog, Hot Dog, Weenr and Oscar, tour the country in style. They feature microwave ovens, refrigerators, cellular phones and stereo systems that play 21 versions of "Oh, I Wish I Were an Oscar Mayer Wiener." Four additional Wienermobiles were built and are touring Japan and Spain. From the original fleet, two Wienermobiles are currently touring in Canada.

1995: World renowned California automotive designer Harry Bradley created the concept Wienermobile to take Oscar Mayer into the next century. This 27-foot long, 10-foot high General Motors unit has a futuristic appeal with state-of-the-art video equipment, a big screen TV and a hot dog shaped dashboard. The model underwent testing in the wind tunnel at the California Institute of Technology in Pasadena and

1906: Baltimore County commissioners allow cop Noah Walker to shoot at cars that violate the speed limit. After charges are filed by a driver whose car was a speeding target, Walker is cleared and urged to keep up the good work.

The 1936 Oscar Mayer Wienermobile was a unique advertising vehicle.

Courtesy of Oscar Mayer Foods Division of Kraft Foods, Inc., Madison, Wisconsin

could really, theoretically speaking, haul buns as it reached speeds in excess of 90 miles per hour. The fleet of six is currently touring the United States.

Source: Courtesy of Oscar Mayer Foods Division of Kraft Foods, Inc., Madison, Wisonsin.

Meet the Beetles

So-called because of its unusual, bug-like shape, the Volkswagen Beetle is by far the best-selling car in history, with more than 21 million units sold since 1938. The car's success can be partially explained by its low price, exceptional durability, and distinctive appearance, as well as the elegant but simple design of its rear-mounted, four-cylinder, "air-cooled" engine. In the United States, where it developed an almost cult following, some five million were sold between 1949 and 1979.

Volkswagen AG, founded by the German government in 1938 to produce the Beetle, long manufactured only automobiles powered by air-cooled engines, including several different sedans, the Karmann Ghia, commercial vehicles, and the Station Wagon. In the 1970s, increasingly strict U.S. safety and emissions standards, as well as new competition from inexpensive, higher-powered Japanese cars, led to the phasing out of Volkswagen's air-cooled vehicles in the United States, where the last Beetle sedan was sold in 1977 and the last convertible Beetle two

Driving the Oscar Mayer Wienermobile a Job to Relish!

Traveling the country in a 4-ton orange hot dog is not the career many students anticipate upon graduation. But for a few lucky people who can really cut the mustard, June brings a unique adventure. They are the Oscar Mayer Hotdoggers, pilots of the Oscar Mayer Wienermobiles.

The Hotdoggers spend a full year traveling across the country making promotional appearances. It is their responsibility to coordinate much of their fun and hectic schedule. Attending everything from the Super Bowl and Mardi Gras to parades and grocery store grand openings keeps the Hotdoggers enthusiastic. "It was the most chaotic and fun year of my life. I loved it," said Jason Clark, former Hotdogger.

The year begins with training at Hot Dog High where they learn all about Oscar Mayer's history and products, planning special events, and how to maneuver in traffic. If they don't scratch their buns and graduate from Hot Dog High they are given their wiener keys and they hit the hot dog highway. As spokespersons for the Oscar Mayer Wienermobile, the Hotdoggers will speak at schools, auto shows, and conduct any media interviews about the "big dog."

Source: Courtesy of Oscar Mayer Foods Division of Kraft Foods, Inc., Madison, Wisconsin.

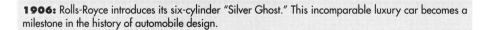

1906: Rolls-Royce introduces its six-cylinder "Silver Ghost." This incomparable luxury car becomes a milestone in the history of automobile design.

years later. By 1988 the Beetle was manufactured and sold just in Mexico, though in 1993 Beetle production resumed in Brazil.

The Beetle, developed in Germany during the Depression, owes its existence to two men—Ferdinand Porsche, a world-renowned automobile designer, and Nazi leader Adolf Hitler, who was chancellor of Germany from 1933 to 1945 and a car enthusiast. Both men were inspired by Henry Ford's low-cost Model T (1908–1927), which gave middle-class Americans their first opportunity to buy an automobile. Porsche, famous for his designs of luxury and race cars, began working on a small, inexpensive car in the 1920s, but the German automobile industry was reluctant to fund such a project, fearing the country's low-paid workers would not be able to afford even the cheapest possible car.

In 1933 Porsche and Hitler began a series of meetings to discuss the design of a new German race car, but their talks soon shifted to ideas about a cheap, reliable automobile, which Hitler called a *volkswagen,* or "people's car," a term he would use repeatedly in later speeches. Impressed by Porsche's past work and ability to discuss technical matters in layman's terms, Hitler offered him state funding to design the people's car.

After World War II a small number of Volkswagens were shipped to the United States by American servicemen, but the first officially imported Volkswagen arrived in New York on January 17, 1949. The car did not find a receptive audience. The Volkswagen seemed out of place in a U.S. market dominated by large, powerful automobiles, and the American press helped little by choosing to call it "Hitler's car." Only two were sold in the United States in 1949.

Sales in the United States, where the car was called the Beetle, would surge only after two developments: the establishment in 1955 of the company's U.S. subsidiary, Volkswagen of America, and the hiring in 1959 of Doyle Dane Bernbach (DDB) Advertising Agency. Volkswagen of American immediately set out to establish a more coordinated approach to sales and service. Dealers were given strict standards to maintain, and all were required to have clean, attractive, similar-looking showrooms. None could operate without a large parts supply and service capacity. In 1955, partially as a result of these efforts, there was a leap in U.S. sales to 32,662, and by 1959 Volkswagen, with nearly 500 dealerships, sold 96,892 Beetles and even had a long waiting list. In 1959 the Beetle accounted for some 20 percent of all U.S. imports and about 2 percent of the entire U.S. car market. U.S. manufacturers, beginning to take notice, would introduce their own line of small cars, including the Chevrolet Corvair, which also had a rear-mounted, air-cooled engine.

1906: World speed record set by a Stanley Steamer, 126 mph at Ormand Beach, Florida.

The Beetle's first U.S. advertising campaign, begun in 1959 by DDB, was a sharp departure from the traditional practice of using idealized drawings and slick, generally meaningless copy. By contrast, the Beetle campaign would come to be known for its realistic photographs; its direct, easy-to-read, factual copy, often with a humorous, self-deprecating slant; and most of all, a sense of honesty. Even perceived shortcomings of the car, especially its unusual shape, were highlighted in advertisements, one of the most famous having the caption "Ugly is only skin-deep." Among its other famous captions were "Lemon," placed under a photograph of a new Beetle, which an inspector had rejected because "the chrome strip on the glove compartment" was blemished; "Mountain Goat," which bragged about the Beetle's excellent handling in rough terrain; and "They said it couldn't be done. It couldn't," commenting on the possibility of fitting basketball star Wilt Chamberlain into the front seat of a Beetle. The DDB ads would win numerous awards and likely pushed even higher the rising curve of U.S. Beetle sales, from 127,159 in 1960 to 232,550 in 1963; 318,563 in 1966; and the 1968 peak of 423,008. So popular was the car that it even had its own Hollywood movie, *The Love Bug*, featuring a Beetle named Herbie, which was the largest grossing film in 1969 and followed by three sequels.

The subsequent decline in sales—still 371,097 in 1973 but collapsing to 243,664 the following year, 92,037 in 1975, and 27,009 in 1976—had many causes, including new competition from small, higher-powered Japanese cars. New safety and emissions standards were also becoming difficult to meet within the car's now 40-year-old design. Equally significant was the devaluation of the dollar, causing the U.S. price to jump from $1,999 in 1972 to $3,699 in 1977, the last year the Beetle sedan was sold in the United states. The convertible Beetle, with a total production of some 330,000, was last sold in 1979 at a price of $6,800.

The Beetle was phased out in most world markets as the company's production was shifted to a new line of front-engine, water-cooled cars, the most popular being the Golf (called the Rabbit in the United States until 1984). In Germany, Beetle production ended in 1978 and sales stopped in 1985. In 1992 Mexico had the honor of producing the 21 millionth Beetle.

Although not interested in reintroducing the Beetle to its major markets, Volkswagen AG is well aware of the car's enduring popularity in the United States and elsewhere. In 1993 Volkswagen chairman Ferdinand Piëch, grandson of Ferdinand Porsche, announced plans to build a new "people's car" that would be "the most affordable model in the world."

1907: Automobile taxicabs appear in New York City. The standard fare for a short ride is a "jitney"—a common term for a nickel. The term soon becomes synonymous with the service itself.

Road Test

WHICH OF THE FOLLOWING STATEMENTS ABOUT THE VW
BEETLE ARE TRUE AND WHICH ARE FALSE?

1.	Named after British rock band	T	F
2.	Brainchild of Adolf Hitler	T	F
3.	Best-selling car of all-time	T	F
4.	Never available with air-conditioning	T	F
5.	Engine was in front for one year	T	F
6.	Proven to hold 31 high school kids	T	F
7.	Original name: Insectenwagen	T	F
8.	Once available with reserve fuel tank	T	F

(Answers: 1.F 2.T 3.T 4.F 5.F 6.T 7.F 8.T)

Jeepers, Creepers, Where'd You Get that Name?

As early as 1938, with hostilities mounting in western Europe, the U.S. Army informed the nation's automobile manufacturers of its need for a light reconnaissance vehicle to replace the motorcycle and side-car used in World War I. The call launched an industry-wide competition for this valuable and prestigious military contract. Ward M. Canaday, chairman of Willys-Overland Corp. of Toledo, Ohio, set the company's vice president of engineering, Delmar "Barney" Roos, to the task of designing a light and maneuverable, yet powerful and sturdy, military vehicle.

Willys' toughest competitor in the race to design a contract-winning entry was the American Bantam Car Company, located in Pennsylvania. In fact, Bantam won the government's first request for bids in 1940 with its "Blitz Buggy." Obviously, Willys and Barney Roos did not give up; they objected to the Army's unrealistically low weight specifications and earned a second test run before Army officials in November 1940.

Willys' "Quad" car offered a choice of two- or four-wheel-drive and a pow-

1907: Speed bumps are placed in the streets of Glencoe, Illinois, to discourage speeding.

erful engine nicknamed the "Go-Devil," but it still exceeded the Army's revised weight requirements by 240 pounds. The simplest way to conform to the weight specification would have been to install a lighter, less-powerful engine, but Roos and his staff elected instead to disassemble the entire car and reevaluate the weight and composition of each part. By shortening bolts and using alternative materials, Willys' design team was able to bring the prototypical "Quad" to within seven ounces of the weight guideline.

The first production model was essentially a Willys-Overland design that incorporated features from Bantam's prototype, as well as from that of a third competitor, Ford. In 1941 Willys-Overland underbid Bantam and Ford for the 16,000-vehicles contract. As the United States became increasingly involved in the war, the contract negotiations assumed a sense of urgency; the Army required delivery of 125 per day. Later in the year, with demand running even higher than expected, Willys was compelled to turn its designs over to Ford so that the competitor could augment production. Over the course of the war, Willys supplied the Army with more than 368,000 "Quads." By that time, however, the vehicles had acquired a new name: Jeep.

Although Jeep has been a household word since World War II, the origin of the trademark has been the subject of ongoing debate. Some attribute the name to the slurring of the initials G.P.—the Army gave Willys-Overland Corporation's Quad the uninspiring designation "General Purpose vehicle." According to one Army officer, however, the term was used in Oklahoma as early as 1934 to designate a truck equipped with special equipment for drilling oil wells.

An affidavit from a Minnesota company (Minneapolis-Moline Power Implement Company) asserted that Sergeant James T. O'Brien referred to a four- or six-wheeled test vehicle as a "Jeep" in 1940. His frame of reference for the name was a character from E.C. Segar's 1930s "Popeye" comic strip. "Eugene the Jeep" was described as "a small, impish-looking animal that had the power to travel back and forth between dimensions and could solve all sorts of problems." To the soldiers who used Jeeps in World War II as litter bearers, machine-gun firing mounts, and reconnaissance vehicles, this aptly described their "G.P." as well. Most authorities credit the Segar strip as the source of the Jeep name.

The name Jeep was first used in the news media to describe the Willys vehicle in 1941, when a *Washington Daily News* photo and story told the public about the Army's new motorcar. Recognizing the marketing potential of the Jeep name, Willys-Overland registered

---

1908: Automobile innovations during the year include motor-driven horns, silent timing gear chains (the drive axle was powered by a chain running from the transmission), and baked enamel finish.

it in the United states and internationally on June 13, 1950.

The Tortoise and the Wax

Turtle Wax, packaged in a turtle-green container, is the top-selling automobile wax worldwide, maintaining a market share of 40 percent or more during the 1980s and 1990s. Continually produced since the early 1950s as Turtle Wax, the wax's predecessor, Plastone Liquid Car Polish, was first produced in 1941 by founder Ben Hirsch. He began by mixing up batches of car wax formulas in a bathtub at a small storefront in Chicago.

In the early days of the business, Ben Hirsch traveled by steetcar to introduce his automobile wax to gas station and garage owners in the city of Chicago. In a hands-on marketing tactic, Hirsch polished car fenders outside Wrigley Field, waiting for the owners to return to point out the results of his product's use.

Operating out of various storefront locations in the late 1940s and early 1950s, the young company introduced Plastone into the Canadian market by the late 1940s. It was on a sales call closer to home, however, that Hirsch was inspired to change the name of both his company and its primary product. While walking along Turtle Creek in Beloit, Wisconsin, Hirsch made a mental connection between the hard shell of a turtle and his product. Thus, according

to a 1986 company-published pamphlet, "Plastone Liquid Car Polish became Turtle Wax with the hard shell finish."

The Tucker: One Man's Dream

While the true story of Preston Tucker's struggles to produce an innovative, mass-produced sports car are clouded by legend, supposition, and Hollywood speculation, it is a certainty that the 51 Tucker automobiles he manufactured achieved his vision of a safe, stylish, innovative, reasonably priced, and fun car. The Tucker 48 sedan was much more conventional than the Tucker Torpedo sports car he originally promoted, but independent road tests and car owners consistently report excellent performance. The Tucker 48 is truly one of the most remarkable cars ever produced, and the failed heroic effort to launch this car line continues to fascinate those intrigued and inspired by visionaries. It's not surprising that the Tucker 48 is often placed front and center—as eye catching as a third headlight—in promotions for the Smithsonian Institution-sponsored commemoration of the 100th anniversary of the American automobile.

A third headlight was among the many features touted about the Tucker Torpedo in 1945, as Tucker flamboyantly promoted and attempted to raise capital for the sports car he planned to build. Some early reports indicated that the

1908: The word "pit" first enters auto racing terminology at a Grand Prix race in Dieppe, France, when a divided trench with a counter just above ground-level is provided for crews.

0 0 0 6 6

two standard headlights were to be set on fenders that turned in unison with the front wheels, thereby throwing light directly ahead of the car. The Torpedo would have an enormous 589 cubic inch displacement engine, placed in the rear, with fuel injection, hemispherical combustion chambers, and hydraulic valve actuation using columns of oil as opposed to cams and pushrods. In lieu of a conventional transmission and differential, two torque converters would drive the rear wheels. The driver would be centered in the front. Disc brakes, seat belts, a padded, crash-proof interior compartment, a speedometer located on the hood so the driver's eyes wouldn't be diverted from the road ahead, a 24-volt electrical system, electronic ignition, air-cooled brakes, a pop-out windshield, air conditioning, and doors that open to the roof were some of the additional features. With aluminum and plastic construction, the Tucker Torpedo would weigh only 2000 pounds and sell for $1,000.

Many modifications were made to these plans; some of the design elements proved impractical, while constant shortages of money, material, and time also contributed to a more conventional vehicle. The Torpedo sports car became the Tucker 48 sedan (1948 was the year the actual cars were completed). The distinctive third headlight remained; placed in the center of the front end, it moved with the steering wheel. Disc brakes, fuel injection, and electronic ignition were sacrificed; all of these features were in their embryonic stages at that time in automobile history, and Tucker's small design team did not have the time to perfect them for their model.

The Tucker 48 had a 334 cubic inch, radical six-cylinder engine capable of generating 166 horsepower and a top speed of 120 mph. It was modified into a water-cooled engine by engineer Ben Parsons. The torque converters gave way to a preselective transmission similar to that on the Cord 810. After much hesitation, the seat belts—not standard equipment on American automobiles at that time—were removed for fear that they implied inherent safety problems. As usual, the driver was placed on the left-hand side and not in the center; the speedometer was not placed on the hood; and the 24-volt electrical system was scrapped.

Most of Tucker's innovative safety features remained, including the padded, crash-proof interior compartment, a large safety steering wheel, and the pop-out windshield that ejects away from car occupants in a front end collision. Air-cooled brakes, air conditioning, a strong, steerhorn-shaped front bumper, and all independent suspension were some of the vehicle's other features. The Tucker 48 had a flat, step-down floor and a spacious interior that seats six comfortably. It reportedly got 30 miles-per-gallon at a 30 mph clip.

1908: Tire treads are invented by Frank Seiberling, who perfects a machine that cuts grooves in the tire surfaces. Up to now, tires have smooth surfaces and can give little traction when roads are bad.

The Tucker had many unique features, including a third headlight that moved with the steering wheel.

Courtesy of American Automobile Manufacturers Association

The low, aerodynamically sound, distinctive body of the Tucker 48 was designed by Alex Tremulis, who had previously worked on Duesenbergs, Auburns, and Cords. The tops of the doors curved to meet slope of the roof. Air intakes at the edges of the rear fenders fed the engine and brakes, and hot air was expelled through a rear grille. The engine provided the Tucker with the best power-to-weight ratio of any vehicle of its time, and the Tucker featured the first pressurized cooling system on an American car. The Tucker was successful in races, shattering stock car records at Indianapolis and reaching 130 mph at Bonneville. The price of the Tucker 48 listed at $2,450, generally considered a bargain. But only 51 Tuckers were built. As recently as 1986, the Tucker won rave reviews following test drives conducted by *Car and Driver* magazine.

The Tucker 48 was the largest, rear-engined passenger car ever produced. It was an innovative, futuristic automobile that staked a permanent spot in the annals of automotive history. Judged strictly on performance, safety, functional and artistic style, and fun, it was a dream come true, and the story of its dreamer—the visionary, non-conformist struggling against the system—is the stuff of American legend. How much of the story was struggle, and how much delusion, remains unanswered. The car itself is a classic, "keeping the legend alive" (the motto of the Tucker Automobile Club of America, founded in 1972).

Roving Over Land and Range

The Rover Car Company was little known outside England until it unveiled the Land Rover, its first four-wheel-drive utility vehicle—modeled after the American Motor Company (AMC) Jeep—at the Amsterdam Motor Show in 1948.

After World War II, Maurice Wilks, then chairman of Rover, purchased a surplus U.S. Army jeep to use on his farm near Coventry, England. He and his brother, Spencer—then the company's chief engineer—soon decided that Rover should build a four-wheel-drive vehicle based on the same basic design, with the idea of marketing it to other English farmers. Since there was a shortage of steel in post-war England, Rover used aluminum for the body, which was then mounted on a rigid ladder-style chassis made of steel. As a result, the vehicle—christened the Land Rover—was light, rugged, and had a low center of gravity, making it perfect for off-road use.

The Land Rover was an immediate success, with orders coming in not only from English farmers, but also police departments, the military, forestry services, and estate owners. Land Rovers also developed a foreign market, especially in Africa and the Middle East, where they were well suited for both desert and jungle terrain. Within a few years, Land Rovers were being sold in more than 30 countries, including the United States.

1908: Fisher Closed Body Company is organized by the Fisher brothers, coachbuilders who consider it unreasonable (as well as uncomfortable) to ride in an open car. Cadillac orders 150 bodies in 1910.

Under pressure to expand its market, Rover brought forth an upscale version of the Land Rover in 1970, calling it the Range Rover. The Range Rover quickly developed a following among heads of state, including Queen Elizabeth, who received a specially made Range Rover convertible for her Silver Jubilee in 1977. However, because Rover had withdrawn from the American market after 1970, Range Rovers were not available in the United States until 1987.

In 1987 the first Range Rovers built to meet U.S. safety and emission standards were delivered, and they were loaded with extras, like electric sun roofs, stereo systems, and deep-pile carpeting. Despite a $30,000 sticker price, more than 3,000 Range Rovers were sold in the first six months. Marketing surveys later showed that 68 percent of Range Rover buyers already owned three other cars and had a median household income of $200,000. Worldwide sales of Range Rover topped 20,000 in 1987. The next year, sales of Range Rover surpassed Land Rover for the first time.

Those Cars in the Little Boxes

Tiny Matchbox cars and trucks have delighted children in Europe, the United States, and Asia since the early 1950s. The brand's original parent company, Lesney Products, was at one time

Britain's largest toy company. It was the most profitable company in the country as well, and its amazing growth even earned it a place in the *Guiness Book of World Records.*

Matchbox toys began as a sideline to an already existing die-casting business. Leslie Smith and Rodney Smith, two of the company's founders, met as boys and later served together in the English Royal Navy in World War II. They went into business together once the war was over, naming their company "Lesney," a compound of their first names.

Like other small die-casting firms, Lesney experimented with making toys during lulls in their regular business. Some of the company's first toys were cars and trucks with moving wheels. The tiny, low-cost toys were an immediate hit with London children. The Smiths and a third partner, Jack Odell, soon realized that their toys could be more than just filler business. In 1951 Lesney manufactured a model Coronation Coach that sold 33,000 units. The next year the company sold more than a million of a smaller version Coronation Coach. It seemed that vehicles were their best-sellers, and the smaller they were, the better.

It was Odell who came up with the first Matchbox cars. In 1952 he made a little car for his daughter and put it in a matchbox so she could take it to school with her. Toys packaged in matchbox-

---

1908: A six-wheeled car built by the Reeves Manufacturing Company of America is named *Sex-Auto,* supposedly in innocence. The company goes out of business soon after it builds an eight-wheeled *Octo-Auto.*

style boxes had been made in Germany in the 1900s, and Lesney revived the idea for a new series of miniatures. In 1953 the company made scaled-down versions of seven of their earlier toys and put them in colorful yellow boxes with red lettering, designed after a Scandinavian brand of safety matches. The Matchbox trademark was registered that same year. The first Matchbox series included a Cement Mixer, a Caterpillar Tractor, and a Horse-drawn Milk Float, but the big hit was the London Bus.

Lesney added to its Matchbox line year by year, and by 1960 the company was making 75 different models. Matchbox cars were distinctive because of their size and packaging, but the cars were also finely crafted and extremely detailed. Some of the models depicted cars "of Yesteryear," like the 1904 Spyker touring car and the 1913 Mercer Raceabout, while others mimicked in every feature the latest Ford, Mercedes, or Ferrari. The wheels turned, the doors opened, and some sported four-wheel spring suspension. Some of the models had as many as thirteen separate parts and went through 28 different manufacturing processes. But because the cars were made in great volume, Lesney could keep the price low.

Lesney began to sell Matchbox cars in the United States beginning in 1954. The United States was Lesney's best market by far. At the height of Match-

box popularity in the 1960s, 40 percent of Lesney's production was sold in the United States, totaling approximately 100 million cars annually. The demand for Matchbox seemed unstoppable, but things changed drastically when Mattel, the largest American toy company, decided to enter the miniature car market in late 1968.

Instead of building the kind of precisely crafted models that Lesney made, Mattel introduced tiny cars that went really fast. Their Hot Wheels were race cars. Mattel's cars were built with a low-friction axle, and they were sold along with plastic race tracks so that children could pit their toys against each other and see which was the fastest. Matchbox cars had not been designed for speed, and young American consumers soon dropped the British brand for Hot Wheels. Lesney responded to Mattel's challenge by introducing the Matchbox Superfast line of racers in mid-1969, but it was too late to overcome the huge impact of the wildly successful Hot Wheels.

Matchbox cars—now a product of Tyco Toys—are still sold today. The product line is a mix of classic sellers and new products. In 1993 Tyco celebrated the 40th anniversary of Matchbox cars by recreating some of the very first Lesney Matchbox models in limited edition.

1908: Packard introduces the first rumble seat in an automobile affectionately nicknamed "the honeymoon car."

America's First True Sports Car

The Corvette, a high-performance, distinctly American sports car, has been igniting the passion of car enthusiasts since 1953. Over the years more than a million of these fiberglass two-seaters have been produced, making it the world's best-selling "true" sports car.

The father of the Corvette is generally considered to be Harley Earl, founder and head of GM's Art and Colour Section, the company's in-house styling department. Earl had been thinking seriously about a low-priced sports car as early as 1951, working privately with a personal crew on his pet project. By mid-1952 Earl's staff had completed the basic design of the car that would soon be called the Corvette. Its name came from the sleek, fast submarine chaser and convoy-escort vehicle of World War II.

Edward Cole, chief engineer of Chevrolet, reportedly jumped up and down upon seeing Earl's masterpiece for the first time. The company quickly came up with a prototype, which was unveiled to the public at the first Motorama of 1953, held at New York's Waldorf-Astoria hotel. The car was an instant success and Chevrolet was soon being barraged with inquiries from all over the country. People wanted to know when the car would be produced and how much the car would cost. Pro-

duction of the Corvette began in Flint, Michigan, on June 30, 1953. The suggested retail price was $3,513.

While the 1953 Corvette was the darling of many enthusiasts, it was not without its critics. Some thought the design—with its rocketlike rear fins, dazzling vertical grille, and sunken headlights—was too gimmicky. Others complained that true sports cars did not have automatic transmissions. The clip-in side windows were awkward to handle, and the only way to open the door from the outside was to reach inside for the release. Initial production was limited to a maximum of 300 for the balance of 1953. This policy gave Chevrolet time to address the various quality problems that surfaced, particularly as they related to the car's fiberglass-body construction.

In 1954 Corvette sales were surprisingly disappointing. Chevrolet had anticipated a sales volume of 12,000, but the year-end tally came to a mere 3,640. Rumors began circulating that the car's days were numbered. But the introduction of the Ford Thunderbird on September 23, 1954, changed all that. The Thunderbird—Ford's answer to GM's Corvette—fueled the rivalry between the two companies and helped to ensure the future of the sporty two-seater. The Thunderbird presented a big challenge for GM. It outsold Corvette for model year 1955 by a ratio of 23 to 1. This prompted a

---

1908: General Motors Corporation is founded by William C. Durant. Later the same year, GM takes over the Buick Motor Company. It adds Cadillac, Oakland, and Oldsmobile in 1909.

GM team to go to work immediately on transforming the awkward Corvette into a serious sports car.

The second-generation Corvette (1956–57) was a vast improvement over the original and is considered by many to be the epitome of Corvette styling. The 1956 model got new seats, standard roll-up windows, an optional lift-off hardtop, and distinctive body-side cavities called coves. Engineer Zora Arkus-Duntov reworked the chassis, improving steering response and handling, and added Chevrolet's powerful 265-cubic-inch V8. Designed by Cole and offered as an option on '55 models, the engine was now standard. The '56 Corvette could reach 60 mph in 7.5 seconds and a top speed of 120 mph. Corvette styling didn't change in 1957, but the engine was made even more powerful. The car could now go from 0–60 mph in 5.7 seconds and reach a maximum speed of 135 mph.

The 1958–62 Corvette has long been criticized for its gaudy, overblown design. The car sported simulated hood louvers, dummy air scoops flanking the grille, and lots of chrome. There were, however, some definite improvements in the third generation Corvette. A new dash, for example, put nearly every instrument right before the driver, and the car was a top performer, with a rerun of its '57 engine lineup.

In 1963 Chevrolet introduced an all-new Corvette—the Sting Ray. Based on GM design chief Bill Mitchell's Sting Ray Special racer, it was a huge success. Production for model year 1963 was 21,513—50 percent higher than the year before. The car—part of the fourth generation Corvette, which spanned four model years—had distinctive styling, speed, and agility. Many enthusiasts consider it to be the best Corvette ever produced. With its humped fenders, sleek hood design, and concealed headlamps, the car's design owed little to the cars that came before. In 1963 a coupe was introduced, featuring a controversial split rear window. Duntov, among others, did not like it because it hindered rear visibility. Highly prized by collectors, it lasted only one year.

For its fifth generation (1968–77) Corvette got a radical redesign based on the styling of the Mako Shark II show car. Like the 1958 Corvette that followed the highly respected second-generation design, the 1968 car was something of a disappointment to Corvette lovers.

In 1978 Corvette celebrated its 25th anniversary with the historic rollout of the Silver Anniversary 1978 models. Since Chevrolet did not have an all-new Corvette ready for the occasion, it modified the existing car with a fastback roofline and a wide, wraparound rear backlight. A silver anniversary badge replaced the traditional crossed-flags emblem, and a special Indianapolis 500 pace car replica was offered.

1908: Ford builds the Model T and makes the car affordable to great numbers of people. In the first full year of production (1909), Ford delivers 17,500 cars, twice as many as the entire industry produced five years earlier.

Car of the Stars?

From the time John Wayne took delivery of his 1953 Corvette, the car has enjoyed a star-studded existence. The long list of celebrities who've owned Corvettes includes Dinah Shore, William Shatner, all of the Beach Boys, all of the original Mercury 7 astronauts, the crew of Apollo 12, Johnny Carson, Don Johnson, Eddie Murphy, Jack Lemmon, Jill St. John, Charlton Heston, Michael Jordan, and many more.

The sixth-generation Corvette, introduced in 1984, was eagerly anticipated because it was the first truly new Corvette in 15 years. The car received rave reviews in the media. *Consumer Guide* called the '84 Corvette "a world class sports car with few rivals in performance."

Model year 1990 saw the introduction of the much-awaited RPO ZR-1, conceived by Corvette as the world's fastest production car. Originally announced for 1989, it was delayed a year because of last-minute engine problems. Available only for coupes, the ZR-1 option featured an all-aluminum, 32-valve, 5.7-liter V8 engine that developed 375 horsepower at 5,800 rpm. The all-new engine had dual overhead camshafts for each cylinder bank and a unique dual-power mode that allowed the driver to limit the power and output with a valet key in the cockpit.

In 1991 Corvette got its first major restyling since 1984, and on July 2, 1992, the one-millionth Corvette—a white convertible with red interior (to match the first Corvette)—was built at the car's assembly plant in Bowling Green, Kentucky.

While the Corvette has always been best known and revered in the United States, it has gained the respect of enthusiasts everywhere. More Corvettes have been built than any other single sports car in automotive history. They have been sold throughout North America, Europe, the Middle East, and Japan, and there are more than 600 Corvette owner clubs around the world.

Ford's Answer to the Corvette

The Thunderbird—Ford Motor Company's response to the Corvette—was introduced in 1954 as a sports car with "personal" appeal. Ford captured the public's fancy by offering a car with sporty styling, a potent V8 engine, and comfort features unavailable on most cars of its type.

The evolution of the Thunderbird grew out of the postwar buying public's desire for a different, highly efficient,

1908: First concrete pavement, laid in Detroit, is a one-mile strip on Woodward Avenue leading to the State Fair Grounds.

The 1963 Corvette Sting Ray coupe—with a split rear window—is a collector's dream.
Courtesy of American Automobile Manufacturers Association

sensitive automobile. American GIs who had spent time in Europe had grown to appreciate the European "sports car." Back home, they wanted something similar. In 1953 Chevrolet, a division of General Motors Corporation, announced its answer to the demand for an American sports car: the Corvette. Ford knew it was time to respond in kind. The result was the 1955–57 Thunderbird, one of the all-time great American automobiles.

Ford introduced the Thunderbird in prototype form in early 1954—nearly seven months before the production lines were set to roll. The Bird was an overnight success. The publicity that followed the introduction of this small, advanced-looking car caused problems for dealerships everywhere. Countless customers inquired about the car, placed orders, and complained about non-delivery.

The first production car bearing the Thunderbird name rolled off the line at Ford's Dearborn, Michigan, assembly plant on September 9, 1954. The car was 52.1 inches high, had a 102-inch wheelbase, and a curb weight of 2,833 pounds. Its standard power train was a modified V8 that put out 160 horsepower, and it was teamed with a three-speed manual transmission. An unusual feature was its separate tops—a canvas one for fair and sunny weather and a detachable plastic hardtop for foul weather. The price of the 1955 Thunder-

bird was $2,944, about $200 more than the Corvette.

The 1956 Thunderbird, rarest of all with a production total of just 15,631, incorporated Ford's new safety concept of "packaging the passengers." Standard equipment included energy-absorbing instrument panel padding, a concave safety steering wheel, safety door latches, and a shatter-resistant wheel. Distinctive portholes were added that year, as was a "continental" exterior-mount spare tire. The latter was a last-minute addition made less for safety reasons than for opening up more trunk space. The following year the Thunderbird got a shiny new bumper/grille, modest blade fins, and an extended rear deck to house the spare.

The Thunderbird has gone through many changes over the years. Perhaps the most dramatic change of all was the car's transformation from a little two-seater in its first generation to the second-generation four-seat "Squarebird"—so-called because of its squarish body style. It was a change bemoaned by sports car enthusiasts, who saw the move as a crass attempt to sell more Birds at the expense of style. In time, however, the 1958 Thunderbird has become recognized as a great car in its own right. As Richard M. Langworth noted in *The Thunderbird Story: Personal Luxury*, "All that stuff about forsaking the sports car [and] adding the hated back seat . . . misses the point. . . . The

1909: Indianapolis Speedway opens, designed by P. T. Andrews to provide a rigorous competitive testing ground for new components, systems, and designs. It is soon resurfaced with 3,200,000 bricks and is dubbed "The Brickyard."

1958 Thunderbird was [perhaps] the outstanding automotive breakthrough of the decade."

Standing 52.5 inches high and 205 inches long on a 113-inch wheelbase, the '58 Thunderbird was bigger, faster, and more plush than its predecessor. The advantages of the move to four passengers was immediately obvious. Retail deliveries of 48,482 in 1958 almost matched the number of two-seaters sold during the entire three years they were on the market. The 1958 Thunderbird was *Motor Trend* magazine's "Car of the Year."

Over the next three decades the Thunderbird would undergo equally significant changes, keeping the model in line with contemporary tastes and advancements in technology. For the 1961 model year a "projectile" look was introduced. Inside, the theme was carried out with a dual-cockpit dash panel. The standard 390-cubic-inch Sports V8 engine—equipped with a trio of twin-barreled Holley carburetors—pumped out 340 horsepower.

On the 1964 model the body partially reverted to a "square" design theme, and wall-to-wall taillamps added elegance. These were the first American cars to offer a windows-closed, flow-through ventilation system. The 1966 convertible was the last of the open air T-Birds.

A jet-aircraft-like design, featuring a long thrusting hood and a short rear deck, was introduced in 1967, as was the first four-door model. Abercrombie and Fitch, a New York store, offered a 1967 Landau-based Apollo Special, which was equipped with custom lighting, an electric sunroof, gold nameplates, and a custom interior that included a desk and television for rear-seat passengers. Only five were built.

From 1970 through 1976 Ford gave the Thunderbird a prominent sharp nose complemented by an egg-crate grille. Other distinctive features were opera windows and a stand-up hood ornament. Special among this group of Thunderbirds were several limited edition models, the rarest being a 1976 commemorative Thunderbird featuring black metal flake paint, a spare tire bulge in the trunk lid, and a "moon-roof" as standard equipment. Only 32 of these models were produced. The 1976 Thunderbird was the last of the "Big Birds."

The 1977 model year marked the first time in the history of the Thunderbird that a new model was smaller than the previous year's, mainly the result of federally mandated fuel-economy standards. The '77 car was 216 inches long, compared with 1976's overall length of 215.7 inches. But the new wheelbase was 114 inches, more than 6 inches shorter than the previous year's. Further downsizing came in 1980.

In February of 1983, the new model Thunderbird gave the public its

1909: Automobile innovations introduced during the year are electric headlights, the electric generator, four-door bodies, and oil gauges on the dashboard.

The Thunderbird that Wouldn't Rust

One unique feature of the 1958–60 Thunderbird was the use of stainless steel components, including glass moldings, wheel discs, rocker panels, and side trim. To highlight this revolutionary—and expensive—approach, Allegheny-Ludlum Steel Company made a 1960 Thunderbird entirely of stainless steel and put it in a time vault to be removed on the car's 40th anniversary.

first look at the innovative aerodynamic styling that was to become Ford's signature for the rest of the decade. For Thunderbird's 30th anniversary in 1985, a limited edition anniversary model was created with top-of-the-line features. In 1989 the Thunderbird got an even sleeker new shape—honed by more than 700 hours of wind-tunnel testing. That year the Thunderbird Super Coupe was named *Motor Trend*'s "Car of the Year." In 1990 Thunderbird celebrated its 35th anniversary with a limited edition Super Coupe.

The Thunderbird evolved from an American sports car, competing with the Corvette, to a personal luxury car, competing with the likes of the Buick Riviera and the Pontiac Grand Prix.

While the "Bird" has undergone many changes over the years, it has retained its personal luxury image and its popularity with car lovers.

Ford's Fabulous Faux Pas

In 1957, after great expense and with much fanfare, the Ford Motor Company unveiled the new Edsel as its car of the future. Two years and $250 million later the car was discontinued completely, and the Edsel became part of popular American mythology as one of the great business flops of all time.

The Edsel, while in the design stages, was referred to as the E-car (E for "Experimental"). The responsibility for the design of the car was given to Roy Brown, an industrial designer who had previously worked on Oldsmobiles for Chevrolet and Lincolns for Ford. Brown decided to create a car with both recognizable, conservative elements and novel, distinctive aspects.

For Richard E. Krafve, head of Ford's Special Products Division, the best way to achieve the optimum car design was to break down the decision-making process into a series of separate choices and then making the best choice for each; thus, choosing the shape of the headlights was separate from the choice for the hood shape, which was separate from the grill design. Krafve later calculated that there

1909: First women to drive across the United States—Alice Huyler Ramsay (leader), Nettie Powell, Margaret Atwood, and Hermaine Jahns—cruise from New York to San Francisco in a Maxwell-Briscoe in 53 days.

The 1955 Thunderbird is considered an American classic.

Courtesy of American Automobile Manufacturers Association

were more than 4,000 different design decisions made regarding the Edsel.

After the E-Car's personality had been generally defined, it needed a name. Krafve had, at the start of the E-Car's development, actually suggested the name "Edsel," in honor of president Henry Ford II's father, who had himself served as president of the Ford Motor Company from 1918 to 1943. Edsel Ford's sons, Henry, Benson, and William Clay, disliked the idea and thought their father would not have appreciated the gesture. The Special Products Division, then set out to find a name for the E-Car.

In mid-1955, Ford engaged several research companies to conduct sidewalk interviews to discover respondents' images of a series of names, including Mars, Jupiter, Ovation, Dart, Ariel, Rover, and Arrow. The results of the polling were deemed inconclusive. David Wallace, director of planning for market research, next sought the assistance of the poet Marianne Moore, whom a friend had heard speak at a university lecture, in naming the E-Car. Wallace wrote to her that "we should like this name . . . to convey, through association or other conjuration, some visceral feeling of elegance, advanced features, and design." Moore responded with such suggestions as Utopian Turtletop, Bullet Cloissoné, Pastelogram, Mongoose Civique, and Intelligent Bullet.

Unhappy with those rather unique monikers, and still without a name, the Special Products Division hired the New York-based advertising agency of Foote, Cone & Belding, which sponsored a competition among the employees in its offices in New York, Chicago, and London. The prize for the new name of the E-Car? A new E-Car naturally. The ensuing 18,000 suggestions included Henry, Benson, Apollo, Mars, Jupiter, Cavalier, Zoom, Zip, and Drof ("Ford" backward). The initial response was trimmed to 6,000, and the list was handed over to Ford. With time running short, Krafve explained that what the company needed was not 6,000 names, but *one* name—and quickly. Directors at the agency then asked its offices in New York and Chicago to each come up with a list of ten names, separately, over the coming weekend. By a profound coincidence, the two lists were found to share four names: Ranger, Corsair, Pacer, and Citation. Corsair was the favorite.

The short list was handed to the company's executive committee and Chairman of the Board Ernest Breech in early 1956. Unhappy with all of the names presented to him, Breech eventually settled on one that had been rejected a while back: Edsel. The three Ford brothers were, coincidentally, all out of town.

On November 19, 1956, Ford publicly released the new name of the

1909: Nearly 300 different makes of automobiles are available, with manufacturing operations in 24 states.

E-Car, and what had been known as the Special Products Division became the Edsel Division.

In bombastic fashion, the Edsel was introduced to 250 reporters during an extended press preview in Detroit on August 26, 27, and 28, 1957. Press dignitaries from around the country and the world were shown the 18 different models of the car from four lines (Corsair, Citation, Pacer and Ranger), treated to a hair-raising display of precision driving by a team of stunt drivers, pampered with a fashion show for their wives, and invited to a final social gala that, forebodingly, featured a former band of Glenn Miller's that still had "GM" displayed across its music stands. The spectacle cost Ford $90,000.

The car's design did elicit comment. Its most distinctive feature was its front grill; whereas the fashion of the day in car design called for a wide, horizontal front end, the Edsel's grill sat upright like a shield in the middle of more traditional grillwork. The car was filled with gadgets—levers, lights, and buttons, including push-button automatic transmission controls that sat on top of the steering columns. The cars were large, heavy, powerful, and gaudy.

If the mixed and lukewarm reviews the Edsel received from the press were the first signs of trouble, more serious was the fact that many of the Edsels that were sold and delivered failed to function properly. Close inspection and a short time on the road revealed that the cars were afflicted with inferior paint, low-grade sheet metal, and non-functioning accessories.

Within several days of its introduction, Edsel sales began to fall—and they continued to fall throughout the year. It was reported that 11,544 Edsels were delivered to dealers in September, 7,601 in October, and still fewer in November. Meanwhile, Ford had calculated that it would need to sell 200,000 Edsels a year to break even.

It was announced on January 14, 1958, that Ford was consolidating the Edsel Division with the Lincoln-Mercury Division into the Mercury-Edsel-Lincoln Division. 6,000 white-collar workers lost their jobs in the reorganization. Thereafter, the Edsel received scant attention from both the company *and* the public. In November of 1958 the Edsel's second-year models came out. The car had quickly become lighter, shorter, streamlined, less powerful, and less expensive. Sales picked up, and by mid-1959 about 4,000 Edsels were sold a month. In July of that year (one and a half years after its introduction), the total number of Edsels on the road was tallied at 83,849. By the time the third-year models were introduced in October of 1959, the Edsel looked almost nothing like its original version; it was smaller still with even leaner lines— and almost nobody bought one. The 1960 Edsel, released to showrooms just

1910: An advertising executive for Thermos designs a touring vehicle shaped like a Thermos on wheels, with the front reading "keeps hot" and the back reading "keeps cold."

The Edsel is widely regarded as one of the biggest flops in automotive history.
Courtesy of American Automobile Manufacturers Association

prior to the car's death knell, could find only 2,846 buyers.

Post-mortems were swift in coming. Many pointed to the fact that the car was designed for a different time—specifically, 1955. In that year the economy was growing, more than 7 million cars were sold (more than any other year up to that time), and Americans wanted cars that were large and powerful. As *Time* magazine summarized: "The Edsel was a classic case of the wrong car for the wrong market at the wrong time."

The Corvair: Opening the Door to Government Regulation

The Chevrolet Corvair is among the most important cars ever produced, first for the promise it offered as an American response to the rising tide of fuel-efficient, compact imports, but ultimately as the car that fueled government regulation of the automobile. It was introduced with great fanfare and praise—selling a quarter million units its first year and named *Motor Tend* magazine's "Car of the Year" in 1960. It died an agonizingly slow and ugly death, widely perceived as a safety hazard and as an example of a large corporation's insensitivity to public welfare. Had the Corvair been more successful, the history of the automotive industry

may have turned out quite differently, and the United States would likely have responded successfully much earlier to consumer demands for fuel-efficient vehicles with strong performance. But the Corvair lost out in appeal to the Mustang and other "pony cars" and became involved in the most notorious public and governmental backlash at the auto industry.

The Corvair was conceived by Edward Cole, a career GM executive who eventually became president of the corporation in 1967. Cole had been a successful engineer with Cadillac, responsible for an improved V8 engine introduced in 1949, and he designed tank engines during World War II and the Korean War. He had also participated in Cadillac experiments with rear-engine design during the late 1940s. In 1952, Cole was transferred to the struggling Chevrolet division of GM, where he developed a new V8 that helped turn Chevrolet around beginning with the 1954 model year. Cole was named General Manager of Chevrolet in 1956. While American cars were getting increasingly larger and the fin tail craze was peaking, Cole initiated development of an innovative small car that would compete against foreign compacts that were steadily gaining in popularity.

The Corvair was released in 1959 for the 1960 model year. It received substantial publicity, from road test re-

---

1910: First modern bolt-on wheels are introduced by the Sankey Company of England, replacing the old, wooden-rim/cast-iron car wheel. It can be replaced with a spare in minutes.

sults and articles speculating on its impact to praise for Cole's vision for the future and a *Time* magazine cover story on the man and the car. The Corvair was the first American mass-produced, rear-engined automobile. With its flat body and relatively flat floor, it offered roomy interior space, uncommon for small vehicles. It was GM's first car with 4-wheel independent suspension. Other distinctive features included a thin roof line that lipped over the rear window and a plane windshield (as opposed to wrap-around windshields of the time); an aerodynamically-efficient design; an air-cooled aluminum engine; and wide doors.

While the Corvair sold over a million units during the first half of the decade, news of handling problems began spreading. Even some road tests on the 1960 model noted occassional handling difficulties under normal driving conditions. Modifications to address a swing axel problem were rejected early on, primarily for cost reasons. A stabilizing bar was added instead and the 1965 model featured a redesigned rear suspension, but these changes seemed to increase public concerns about the car. Late in 1965, Ralph Nader's exposé of safety problems in American cars, *Unsafe at Any Speed: The Designed-in Dangers of the American Automobile,* focused its first chapter on the Corvair, calling it "one of the nastiest-handling cars ever built." Nader was advising a highly publicized Senate committee on automobile safety that eventually drafted legislation leading to sweeping government-mandated safety regulations. Nader's book sold briskly and President Lyndon Johnson discussed automobile safety in his 1966 State of the Union Address.

While these events helped trigger the swift decline of the Corvair and undermined consumer confidence in the automobile industry in general, the safety of the Corvair had been questioned to some extent all along, beyond occassionally critical road test evaluations. As early as 1960, a fatal, head-on collision on a curve on Highway 1 near Monterey, California, created concern about the Corvair's handling, since there was no evidence to suggest mechanical problems or driver impairment. In 1964, a woman who lost an arm in an accident was awarded $70,000 in an out-of-court settlement that was viewed by some as an indictment of the Corvair. More than 500 lawsuits were brought against GM regarding the Corvair, and though GM never lost any of the suits, many were settled out of court, some for substantial amounts of money. GM's massive legal efforts furthered negative perceptions of the Corvair, and the car attained a lasting reputation for unpredictable handling, prone to roll over even under normal driving conditions.

Over 1.8 million Corvairs were sold between 1960 and 1969, the last year of

1910: First U.S. car manufacturer to offer enclosed, weatherproof bodies as standard equipment is Cadillac. The bodies are made by Fisher.

**The Corvair was the first American mass-
produced rear-engine car.**

Courtesy of American Automobile Manufacturers Association

the Corvair Decade, but 75 percent of those sales occurred in the first five years. Sales plummeted as safety concerns mounted: just over 200,000 units sold in 1965, fewer than 90,000 units sold in 1966, and under 13,000 units sold in 1968. In all, GM lost over $8.5 million on the Corvair.

It was heralded as a car that would change automotive history, and the thousands of members of CORSA (the Corvair Society of America) as well as the father and son in the popular 1995 film *Mr. Holland's Opus* are representative of those who continue to champion the Corvair. But automotive excitement in the 1960s was driven by the sports-car, and the Corvair became linked instead with a decline in public trust and consumer confidence in the American automobile. Pat Bedard, in an article titled "Ten Cars That Made a Difference," published in the 25th Anniversary Issue of *Car and Driver* magazine (July 1980), summed up the importance of the car: "The Corvair opened the door to government regulation of the automobile . . . It changed our automaking process to such a degree that there will never be another Corvair. I don't think any other car in the last 25 years has been that significant."

M—M—Mustang

A symbol of power and performance, the Ford Mustang is one of the best-selling sports cars in the United States. More than six million have been sold since its introduction in 1964.

Although many people were involved in the Ford Mustang's development, credit usually has been given to a single man, Lee Iacocca, who in the late 1940s became an engineer at the Ford Motor Company. Soon transferred to sales, Iacocca rose quickly through the company's ranks and by 1960 became vice-president and general manager of the Ford division. Well aware of the changing car market, Iacocca insisted on "thinking young" and became preoccupied with developing a small, sporty, young-persons car—one combining the performance of a foreign car with distinctly American bodywork—which he hoped could be sold for around $2,500, or about $1,000 less than the average American car.

Ford designers began work on a two-seat sports car, and at the 1962 Grand Prix in Watkins Glen, New York, the company introduced a prototype, the Mustang I, named after the legendary P-51 Mustang fighter planes. Although its exceptional performance and small, fiberglass body were praised by car enthusiasts, Iacocca reportedly declared the prototype "not the car we want to build" because it couldn't be a "volume car." Iacocca, in fact, would insist the car have four seats, thus expanding its potential market, and before long Ford built a new prototype,

1911: First electric starter, invented by Charles F. Kettering, is installed on a Cadillac. This finally does away with the difficult and sometimes dangerous business of hand-cranking.

styled under the direction of Joe Oros, L. David Ash, and Gail Halderman. Their design—with its long front hood, short rear deck, and squared-off styling—set the classic Mustang shape.

The car's official launch was on April 17, 1964, at the New York World's Fair, though Americans were given a preview the night before, when Ford bought the 9:30 P.M. time slot on all three television networks. An estimated 27 million Americans watched the Ford program, setting off one of the greatest consumer stampedes for an automobile. Ford, which hoped to sell 100,000 of its sporty Mustangs in the first year, was swamped with 22,000 orders on the first day alone. The 100,000 mark was hit just four months later, and the 12-month total of some 417,000 set a record for a new American car. This rush, exacerbated by a shortage of Mustangs, has since become legend. In Chicago the police were called when eager Mustang customers stormed a dealership. In Garland, Texas, 15 customers wanted the same Mustang, so the dealer set up an auction; the winner, fearing the car would be sold to someone else before his check cleared the next day, refused to leave the dealership and slept that night in the Mustang. During the 1964 Christmas season, some 93,000 pedal-powered toy Mustangs were sold.

The early Mustangs came in three body styles: a two-door sedan, a con-

vertible, and a fastback (with a sloping back end). The sedan cost $2,372; the price of the convertible was $2,614. Body details would change little during the first few years, and Ford factories worked overtime to keep up with demand. By March of 1966 the one millionth Mustang was sold.

An exceptionally long list of options were available on the first Mustangs and few people selected the most economical base model, choosing instead to customize their Mustang into a higher performance or more luxurious car. The standard six-cylinder engine of the 1964 Mustang had a rating of just 101 horsepower—not much for a "sports car"—but soon the engine was modified to boost horsepower to 120. Larger eight-cylinder engines were also available, including one with a rating of 271 horsepower. Other choices included a four-speed manual and three-speed automatic transmission, styled wheels, power steering, power brakes, deluxe seat belts, air-conditioning, tinted glass, a push-button radio, a luggage rack, and special handling suspension. By choosing various options a customer could place traditional American luxuries into a car with European-style performance. The V8, in fact, transformed the Mustang into a muscle car, and the Shelby GT 350—a special Mustang developed by Carroll Shelby—was an all-out race car capable of going from 0 to 60 mph in just six seconds.

1911: Ford makes headlights and horns standard equipment on the Model T, but the company's limited warranty still becomes void if the owner adds accessories.

Buy a Mustang, Change Your Life

The Mustang was designed as a fun, affordable, young persons car, and early advertising highlighted this theme. The car even transformed lives, the ads claimed. Hyperboles knew no bounds in a 1964 *Readers Digest* ad, which stated, "Two weeks ago this man was a bashful schoolteacher in a small Midwestern city. Add Mustang. Now he has three steady girls, is on first name terms with the best head-waiter in town, is society's darling. All of the above came with his Mustang. So did buckets [seats], full wheel covers, wall-to-wall carpeting, padded dash, vinyl upholstery, and more. Join the Mustangers! Enjoy a lot of dolce vita at a low, low price."

Women, seen as an important target for the Mustang, were not excluded from the car's life-transforming miracle. "Life was just one diaper after another until Sarah got her new Mustang. Somehow Mustang's sensational sophisticated looks, its standard-equipment luxuries (bucket seats, full carpeting, vinyl interior, chiffon-smooth, floor mounted transmission) made everyday cares fade far, far into the background. Suddenly there was a new gleam in her husband's eye. (For the car? For Sarah? Both?) Now Sarah knows for sure: Mustangers have more fun!"

Despite the addition of several new models—including the Boss 302, the Mach 1, and the Grande—during the late 1960s, sales of the Mustang started to decline. Because of this, Iacocca—president of Ford from 1970 to 1978—ordered a rehaul of the car in the early 1970s. What he got was the Mustang II, introduced on September 21, 1973. Though sporty looking, the new Mustang seemed to be a small, underpowered version of the old car. Although Mustang purists would complain, the new model came at the perfect moment. Stricter U.S. government regulations on emissions, increased insurance costs, and the Middle East oil embargo had all helped deflate the high-performance car market, and customers who were worried about gas prices flocked to the Mustang II and its highway fuel efficiency of 34 miles per gallon. Sales increased, and *Motor Trend* magazine named the 1974 Mustang II its "Car of the Year."

The car was restyled again for the 1979 model year and its name reverted to Mustang (without a roman numeral). Noticeably lacking on the front grille of this model was the traditional galloping Mustang logo. Throughout the 1980s body style changed little, but mechanically the car greatly improved, and increased horsepower would return the Mustang to its reputation as a performance car. The convertible returned in 1983, boosting Mustang's reputation as a fun car. Even so, sales throughout the

1911: First use of a rearview mirror in the United States: Indianapolis 500 race driver Ray Harroun puts one on his Marmon Wasp and never looks back, winning with an average speed of nearly 75 mph.

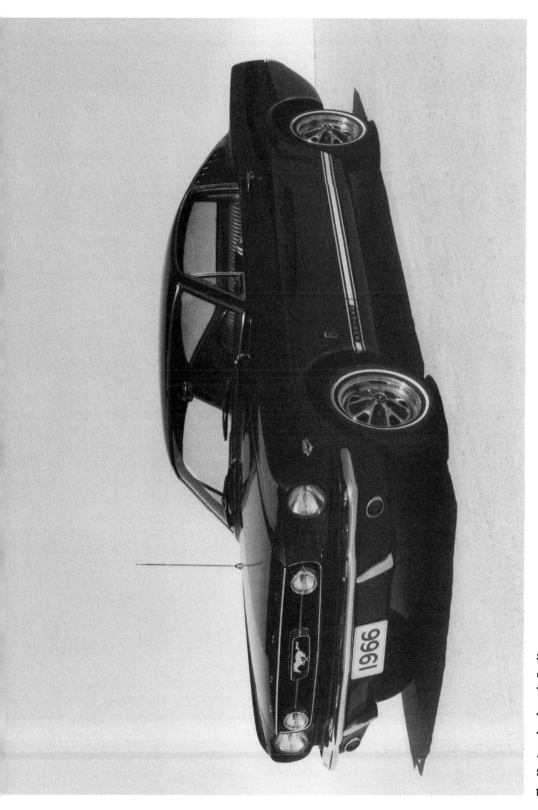

The Mustang has been in Ford's stable for more than 30 years.
Courtesy of Ford Motor Company

decade were barely enough to keep the Mustang going. At one point, in fact, Ford considered discontinuing the brand.

When Ford finally decided to go ahead with a new Mustang, it did so with the help of Mustang owners and enthusiasts. The company toyed with several designs, including those nicknamed Bruce Jenner (lean and aerodynamic) and Rambo (warriorlike). Although both were seen as suitably American, they were eventually rejected in favor of a compromise model, which came to be known as the Arnold Schwarzenegger version (rugged but cultured). The actual styling was strongly reminiscent of the 1964 Mustang, though with rounded—not squared-off—edges. Even the galloping pony returned to the front grille. And, like the original model, there was an emphasis on power. The V8 version, with a horsepower rating of 215, shot from 0 to 60 mph in just 6.9 seconds. Introduced on December 9, 1993, the newest Mustang was praised for its technological advancements, including improved handling, greater body rigidity, antilock brakes, and dual airbags. *Motor Trend* named it the 1994 "Car of the Year."

Muscle Mania

The need for speed has been a part of automotive history right from the start. The occasion of the very first automo-

bile race may have gone unrecorded, but it's a good bet that very soon after two early horseless carriages encountered each other on a dirt path, a race of sorts took place. And well before the turn of the century, organized car races had become commonplace. The phrase "racing improves the breed" was never truer than in those early days, when improved track performance was the impetus for improvements that eventually found their way to passenger vehicles, resulting in the faster, better handling, and more reliable cars that the public demanded.

So, in a sense, muscle cars have been with us from the beginning, with various manufacturers trying to outdo each other in the speed department. But it was in the years after World War II that performance began to take on special meaning. In Europe, with high fuel prices and tight, twisting roads, the desire for improved performance resulted in the growth of the sports car— MGs, Triumphs, Jaguars, Alfa Romeos, Porsches—vehicles that were most at home zipping through the curves while still delivering reasonable gas mileage.

But things were different in the United States. In the U.S. we had lower fuel costs and plenty of wide open spaces. The postwar freeway boom meant plenty of long, straight highways on which cars could cruise all day. The American automobile industry responded with a series of longer, lower,

1911: General Motors offers the first automobile securities listed on the New York Stock Exchange.

wider designs, powered by V8s of ever-increasing horsepower. Hot-rodding became a popular pastime. Backyard mechanics would lower their cars even further than the factory had, strip off non-essential parts to save weight, and increase horsepower still more. Drag-racing—sometimes at race tracks, but just as often on the main "drags" of towns across America—became the watchword of the day. Straight-line acceleration was king.

In the early 1960s, John DeLorean—the young chief engineer for GM's Pontiac Division who had developed something of a reputation as a maverick—thought he could find a niche market with a new concept: a factory hot-rod. He dropped a 389-cubic-inch, 348-horsepower V8 into Pontiac's little Tempest, transforming the average family's second car into a fire-breather. He called his creation the GTO, in honor of Ferrari's famous race-winner, the Gran Turismo Omologato. Pontiac's marketing specialists called it an interesting idea and predicted sales of 5,000 cars. In its first year, more than 60,000 GTOs were sold, and an era had begun.

Not being the types to allow a money-making trend pass unnoticed, the other American manufacturers quickly added these new "muscle cars" to their lineups. In short time, the public was awed by the Oldsmobile 442 (four barrel carb, four on the floor, dual exhausts), the Chevy Malibu SS, and

the 426 Hemi Plymouth Satellite. Later examples include the Buick Gran Sport, the Plymouth Road Runner Superbird, and the Dodge Challenger R/T Hemi.

Then there were the "pony cars," which the factories quickly found could be beefed up by shoehorning in large-block V8s. Ford's Mustang, which started out life as a pleasant little inexpensive car for the youth market, received a series of scorchers, culminating with the legendary Boss 429 V8. The Mustang was challenged by Chevy's Camaro SS and the Pontiac Firebird 400. All of these vehicles offered blinding acceleration, sporty good looks, and single-digit fuel mileage.

But, unbeknownst to the stop-light drag racers, the world had quietly begun to change. A young attorney named Ralph Nader had published a scathing indictment of the auto industry in his book *Unsafe at Any Speed,* and automobile safety was becoming an increasingly important issue. In 1966, the State of California had passed a bill requiring horsepower-robbing pollution-control devices on passenger cars. Then, a year or so later, the insurance industry announced the shocking results of a three-year study on accident levels on the nation's roads and highways, which led to drastic rate increases; not surprisingly, muscle cars were hit the hardest. Finally, in the early seventies, in the wake of turmoil in the Middle East, a series of fuel shortages resulted in sharp increas-

---

1911: First white centerline dividing a road surface is made by Edward N. Hines, road commissioner for Wayne County, Michigan. His "centerline safety stripe" is painted on River Road near Trenton, Michigan.

Road Test

MATCH THE MUSCLE CAR WITH ITS ENGINE DISPLACEMENT (IN CUBIC INCHES).

1. 1967 Buick Gran Sport		A. 400
2. 1969 Chevrolet Camaro SS		B. 340
3. 1971 Dodge Hemi Challenger		C. 429
4. 1969 Dodge Super Bee		D. 383
5. 1969 Ford Boss Mustang		E. 396
6. 1965 Ford Shelby Mustang GT350		F. 426
7. 1969 Oldsmobile Cutlass 442		G. 289
8. 1969 Plymouth Road Runner		H. 440
9. 1968 Pontiac Firebird		I. 389
10. 1964 Pontiac GTO		J. 455

(Answers: 1.B 2.E 3.F 4.H 5.C 6.G 7.J 8.D 9.A 10.I)

es in the price of gas. The muscle-car era ground to a halt.

But the cars themselves live on. And not only in our hearts and minds. Muscle cars are now among some of the most collectible of American vehicles. Enthusiasts lovingly restore them and preserve them and show them in an effort to expose new generations to these singular creations and perhaps recreate their glory days.

The SUV: Born in the USA

In the 1960s Jeeps and International Harvester Scouts were pretty much the only four-wheel-drive vehicles in the United States. These practical vehicles featured such functional options as snow plows, winches, wreckers, post-hole diggers, rotary mowers, and implement lifts. During the 1970s, however, trucks overall—and sport utility vehicles (SUVs) in particular—were restyled and repositioned to capture a more mainstream (and therefore larger) share of the U.S. auto market.

Jeep foreshadowed the movement with the 1965 introduction of its "Super Wagoneer," which combined comfort and luxury features with the practicality

1912: Edward G. Budd develops a steel-bodied car, promoting it by having elephants posing on its roof. Uni-body cars will eventually become an industry standard.

of four-wheel-drive. Automatic transmission, power/tilt steering, radios, upholstery and trim packages, power brakes and windows, and cruise control—all features on top-of-the-line cars—were incorporated in these new models. While the Super Wagoneer reached into the comfort zone, it retained the traditional Jeep versatility and on- or off-road ability.

Several external influences converged in the 1970s to create the environment in which the sport utility segment of the auto industry was born and flourished. The trend took shape in the truck market, which then encompassed anything that was not a car—vans, pickups, and open-air 4 x 4s. This segment grew more than three times faster than the auto market during the decade, the manifestation of a fundamental lifestyle change for many Americans. Some were spending more time outdoors—boating, camping, and off-road motorcycling, for example—and they needed transportation that could both haul their "toys" and negotiate the path to their often remote destinations. Other Americans got involved in the burgeoning do-it-yourself trend, building additions, making their own home improvements, or renovating historic homes. Safety became a selling factor in the North, as people began to realize that four-wheel-drive provided better handling on ice and snow. Still others who had no practical use for a truck purchased them for purely emotional rea-

sons; trucks, and especially Jeeps, represented "daring but untried adventures" for these consumers. Jeep cornered the market on this emotional appeal by virtue of its historically rugged image. The emerging sport utility market's diverse customer base reflected these varied motivations, ranging from adventurous youths to status-conscious drivers seeking "stylish utilitarianism."

By the late 1970s Jeep had already carved out a 30 percent stake in the new sport utility segment, putting it ahead of its main competitors, the Ford Bronco and Chevy Blazer. In a move that would help maintain that lead, Jeep introduced its luxurious Wagoneer Limited in 1978. The Wagoneer Limited's standard features included leather upholstery, air conditioning, and AM/FM/CB stereo. Comfort options included automatic transmission, power/tilt steering, power brakes and windows, and cruise control.

Like most American cars of its day, the Wagoneer Limited was a big, flashy vehicle. Anticipating an expansion of the compact sport utility segment, Jeep introduced a shorter, narrower, lighter model, called the Cherokee, in 1984. First launched in 1974, the Cherokee became the leader of Jeep's new XJ series and brought several design exclusives to the category. As mundane as it may seem, the vehicle's four-door design would be a key to its dominance of the sport utility segment because it

---

1912: Electric vehicles reach their high point of production and acceptance in the U.S. From now on, they will decline and virtually disappear in favor of the gasoline-powered car.

The Jeep Cherokee was a trailblazer among sport utility vehicles.

Courtesy of American Automobile Manufacturers Association

made the vehicle an alternative to the traditional family car. With a Jeep Cherokee, mommies, daddies, and even presidents could "rough it." The Cherokee XJ series was named "4 x 4 of the Year" by the three major off-road magazines in 1984, and between 1983 and 1984 Jeep sales rose an astonishing 87 percent. By then it was obvious that the sport utility segment was here to stay.

Get 'em While They're Hot!

For millions of Americans the Hot Wheels name conjures up images of the late 1960s: backyard barbecues, the Beatles, and the lunar landing. Introduced in 1968 by Mattel, Hot Wheels immediately captured the imagination of American kids. The cars were painted in flashy, psychedelic colors, and the style was undeniably cool. Hot Wheels cars sped down a bright orange track and defied gravity when they looped the loop. Even girls liked them. An instant and encompassing success, Hot Wheels cars sold so well in their first year that their sales outnumbered those of all other toy car brands combined in the year before. What's even more remarkable, however, is that Hot Wheels endured. To the kids who played with the toy when it was first introduced, it is hard to believe that Hot Wheels is now more than 25 years old and still one of the strongest brands of the giant Mattel toy company.

The concept for the Hot Wheels line of miniature cars is credited by Mattel literature to Elliot Handler, one of the original founders of Mattel. Mattel already had a huge hit in its Barbie fashion doll and was looking for a similar spearhead for its line of boy's toys. Handler is said to have been conducting research for new boy's products when he realized that almost all of the die-cast miniature vehicles currently on the market had static wheels. Handler thought that even though boys collected miniature cars for their appearance, they would be doubly enthusiastic if the cars could actually race.

Mattel's research and development department went to work to develop a prototype for a speedy, gravity-powered miniature car. They used low-friction styrene wheels hung on a thin metal torsion bar to produce minimum resistance and maximum speed. Company lore has it that Handler took one look at this new, ultra-fast car and exclaimed, "Wow, those are hot wheels," thereby coining the name for the new toy.

With the mechanical prototype in hand, Handler placed an ad in a Detroit newspaper seeking an automobile designer who could help design the body of the car. Harry Bradley, a designer with General Motors, had recently designed a new custom show car whose flashy styling convinced Handler that he was the man to work on Hot Wheels. The Mattel design team determined

1913: First free U.S. road maps are distributed by the Gulf Oil Company.

These Sizzlers were Fizzlers

In 1970, following two record-breaking years of Hot Wheels sales, Mattel introduced Hot Wheels Sizzlers, a motorized version of the popular cars. Toy store buyers pounced on the new product, ordering heavily after experiencing shortages of the Hot Wheels line in its first two years. But American parents and kids were not as enthusiastic. The higher priced motorized version of the toy had technical problems and sales stalled. On top of poor sales of the Sizzlers cars, the backlog of the new toy in retailers' stockrooms began to slow orders of other Mattel products. Mattel executives reportedly scrambled to cover up the loss with questionable accounting procedures. The debacle finally ended in the resignation of the company's founders, Ruth and Elliot Handler, and a restructuring of the entire Mattel corporation.

that the new cars should be about three inches long and would be modeled after California-style customized show cars with a scale of 1/64. All the cars would sport bright paint jobs and red-line tires. In addition, Mattel devised a system of flexible plastic track on which the Hot Wheels cars could run. The track with its famous loop was to become a symbol of the Hot Wheels brand to a generation of children.

Sixteen Hot Wheels models were introduced in 1968, including one modeled on Bradley's show car and another on the 1968 Chevrolet Corvette. Sales of the new toy cars surpassed even Mattel's expectations. Heavily advertised on network television as "the fastest metal cars in the world," the Hot Wheels line generated more than $25 million in its first year alone. Production rates for Hot Wheels reached nearly 16 million cars in 1968, and Mattel was soon making more toy cars than all the life-size automakers in the world.

The Hot Wheels cars and race sets with looping plastic track continue to be very popular and newer models of the flashy cars are introduced on an ongoing basis. By 1993, 562 different Hot Wheels had been created. Designs of Hot Wheels cars have always reflected popular culture and have changed with the fads and fashions of the times. When the cars were introduced in the late 1960s, psychedelic, wildly colored cars were all the rage. The 1980s' Reagan era saw a renewed interest in the military, with a line of camouflage vehicles, and the 1990s featured a return to California-inspired beach cars.

Over the years Hot Wheels have gone from being a toy fad to being a toy classic. There are thousands of Hot Wheels collectors around the United States who are willing to pay up to $600 for a very rare vehicle. And after two generations of children's play it seems

1913: Henry Ford sets up his first assembly line production of Model T cars and pays his workers an unheard of $5 per day. Ford revolutionizes the manufacture of automobiles and soon turns out 1,000 cars a day.

likely that Hot Wheels will remain on the toy car scene for years to come.

It's Not a Van . . . It's Not a Station Wagon . . . It's a Minivan!

The Dodge Caravan and Plymouth Voyager minivans were introduced in November of 1983 by the Chrysler Corporation. At the time of their debut Chrysler Chairman Lee Iacocca predicted that "the Voyager and Caravan will be to the 80s what the Mustang was to the 60s—vehicles that create extraordinary excitement and buyer interest and force other manufacturers to come up with copycat versions." While Iacocca has since retired, the Caravan and Voyager have more than lived up to his advance billing and continue into the 1990s as jewels in Chrysler's crown.

The minivan's story began in 1977, when the people at Chrysler wondered how they might capitalize on the industry-leading performance of their full-sized Dodge Ram Van. Father of all the minivans that would follow, the Dodge Ram controlled 45 percent of the full-size passenger van market at that time, leading both Ford and General Motors. Chrysler executives attributed this success to their strategy of providing car-like amenities in large vans, and they guessed correctly that a smaller, more economical version might appeal to a younger segment of the market.

Featuring power windows and locks, rear window defrosters, power seats, and superior audio systems, the Ram Van became the starting point for a fuel- and space-efficient alternative in the traditional station wagon market. The fuel crisis of the late 1970s, coupled with a general economic downturn, had initiated a trend towards more compact and inexpensive vehicles, and Chrysler believed consumers who missed the space and comfort of their previous autos would see a solution in minivans.

Research indicated the continued attractiveness of the comforts a station wagon could offer, but it seemed too stodgy for the younger market. With the minivans, Chrysler envisioned being the first one on the block to attract the younger buyer. Joseph Campana, then Chrysler's Vice-President of Marketing, said "There's no question in my mind that it's the station wagon of the future."

In moving from the full-size van to the minivan, the first and most important consideration was the downsizing of the vehicle. The popularity of large vans had always been limited because they did not fit in the average garage; drawing on extensive market research, Chrysler officials realized that a vehicle that could both accommodate a family and offer space for cargo was a sure winner. Setting their sights on a "garageable" product, the engineers went to work, and by 1978 Chrysler had

1913: Installment plan is first used in San Francisco to sell automobiles, allowing the buyer to purchase a car "on time" by making specified payment amounts over a certain period.

`00097`

When Chrysler's minivans were unveiled in 1983, a new automobile market was created.
Courtesy of American Automobile Manufacturers Association

earmarked the minivan as an "Investigate" item in its long-range product plan. It would be five more years before the minivans appeared, however; Chrysler's widely publicized financial problems in the late 1970s and early 1980s stalled development on the new line, while its commitment to the K-car program—which resulted in the Dodge Aries and Plymouth Reliant—monopolized what cash reserves there were.

One important boost for the minivan program was the arrival at Chrysler of Iacocca, who came over from Ford in 1978. Ironically, Iacocca and others at Ford had been the first people to realize the immense sales potential in a minivan, and for several years during the mid-1970s they had presented plans for what they called a "Mini/max" to Henry Ford, the company's chairman. Not wanting to "experiment," Ford turned the idea down.

Ford's missed opportunity became Chrysler's windfall when Iacocca and Hal Sperlich, another Ford exile, put their weight behind the minivan when they arrived at Chrysler and got it off the ground. Soon after his arrival, Iacocca procured $500 million for the vehicle's completion, an enormous commitment for a company in financial crisis. And although the final bill would come to $700 million, this commitment was the turning point in the minivan's fortunes. Another crucial event in the ongoing development of the minivan line was the approval in the spring of 1980 of $1.5 billion in guaranteed loans from the federal government. This allowed the cash-poor company to forge ahead with its future product plans.

Widely advertised and featured in the media in the months before they arrived, the Chrysler minivans were finally unveiled in November of 1983. They were hailed in *Car and Driver* as "a wonderful addition to the automotive firmament" and in *Road & Track* as "the most innovative vehicles to come out of Detroit in decades." The minivans created a new market, and the new vehicles soon justified the years of planning and development with impressive financial returns.

Priced at around $10,000, the minivans gained a solid foothold in their first full year. One year later, sales passed the 100,000 mark for the first time, and by 1988 over 200,000 were being sold per year. In 1993 Chrysler sold 262,838 of the vehicles and commanded a market share of 24.5 percent. In 1995 sales of Chrysler minivans topped 496,000, about 40 percent of the market. Chrysler totally redesigned its minivans for the 1996 model year, introducing the new vehicles in the spring of 1995.

A Different Kind of Car

General Motors created the Saturn brand of small cars as a high-quality, distinctly American import-fighter, an iden-

---

1914: First American high-speed V8 automobile engine is the water-cooled powerplant offered by the Cadillac Company. It is rated at 60 horsepower and is considered by many of its time to be the ultimate engine.

The Customer is King

In 1993 Saturn proved just how important it considered quality customer service to its long-term success. The company ignored pressure by financially troubled GM to reach profitability that year and spent an estimated $8 million to $35 million on an intense customer relations effort during a voluntary recall of 350,000 cars.

tity each car wears proudly with its very name: the namesake of Saturn is the Saturn rocket, a rocket that symbolically carried the United States ahead of the Soviet Union in the space race. This goal of carrying American automakers ahead of the Japanese in the small-car race was so crucial to GM that it initially promised an investment of $5 billion in the project (later reduced to an estimated $3.5 billion) when it founded the subsidiary, the Saturn Corporation, in 1985.

Saturn concentrated on building a high-quality and high-volume car designed to take business away from Japanese top-sellers like the Honda Accord and Toyota Celica, without doing the same damage to GM's other cars. In 1990 Saturn launched a sedan and a coupe (a station wagon was added in 1993). The success of Saturn did not disappoint: Saturn cars rocketed to third place in the subcompact car market in just three years after their retail introduction.

This success certainly owed something to Saturn's efforts to create high-quality cars by empowering every employee to be a partner in the constant process of improving production efforts. But absolutely crucial to Saturn's success was its marketing strategy of selling the car through enthusiasm for the company—a strategy masterfully created and conducted by Saturn's ad agency, Hal Riney & Partners of San Francisco. This was an advertising strategy repeatedly summed up by Saturn's understated marketing tag line, "A different kind of company. A different kind of car." A perfect example of the intense brand loyalty of Saturn owners came on June 24 and 25, 1994, when Saturn held a "Homecoming" for its customers at its plant in Spring Hill, Tennessee. Approximately 44,000 Saturn owners and their friends—from as far away as Taiwan—attended the event.

Saturn cars underwent their first major redesign for the 1996 model year. In early 1996 it was announced that Saturn dealers in southern California and Arizona would be the exclusive retailers for GM's new electric car, the EV1.

The Man of Steel (–Belted Radials)

Known in the United States as the

1914: The first wage and work benefits package is announced by Henry Ford for employees over 22 years of age. They included profit sharing and an 8-hour work day.

The Saturn line of automobiles hit the streets in 1990.
Courtesy of American Automobile Manufacturers Association

Michelin Tire Man, Bibendum (or, Mr. Bib) is one of the world's oldest and most recognized trademarks. The man made of tires emerged virtually fully formed from the imaginations of the original Michelin brothers.

While attending France's Lyon Exhibition in 1898, Edouard Michelin remarked to his brother, André, that a display of stacked tires curiously resembled the outline of a man. Around that time, André was involved in the development of a new advertising campaign for the company's bicycle and automotive tires. The Michelin man's first appearance mimicked a contemporary beer advertisement. The ad featured a plump beer drinker raising an overflowing mug. The copy read "Nunc est bibendum," a Latin phrase meaning "Now is the time to drink."

Working with Marius Roussillon, an artist who went by the pseudonym O'Galop, André co-opted the entire concept, but with an interesting twist: he replaced the beer drinker with a man made of tires and the stein of beer with a champagne glass full of nails and broken glass. Surrounding the Michelin tire man were other, presumably inferior, tire men, deflating and gasping. The headline still read "Nunc est bibendum," but in this context, it represented an unmet challenge to competitors. Coy continued, "To Your health—The Michelin Tire Swallows Obstacles."

The ad was an instant success. A few months later Thery, a famous turn-of-the-century race car driver, saw André Michelin passing by one day and shouted, "I say, there goes Bibendum." The Michelin Tire Man was christened.

The changing images of Bib have reflected changing tire shapes, artistic styles, and even cultural mores. In his early years, Bib wore pince-nez glasses and smoked a cigar. The tires he was composed of were narrower, just like turn-of-the-century bicycle and auto tires. As tire technology progressed and balloon tires replaced narrow tires, Mr. Bib changed shape to wider and more round tires in his body and head. Around 1930, as smoking and drinking (especially while driving) went out of style, Mr. Bib lost those props, too.

As health-consciousness in general spread, Bibendum slimmed down—presumably through all the bicycling, walking, running, jumping, and even flying he has done over the decades. The "running Bib" has been popular with Michelin marketers in the 1990s because he projects a forward-moving image of the company and its products.

Bib has promoted Michelin products in many different cultures around the world. The mascot can be found in many different sizes, from the huge 50-foot inflatable Bib to the tiniest Bib figurines used as desk ornaments and key rings. He has been depicted as a pilot,

1914: First use of a STOP sign is in Detroit.

leader, sportsman, gladiator, race driver, and in many other roles.

Michelin is justifiably proud and protective of its emissary, and only a very limited number of artists are au-thorized to draw Bib, so that he looks the same all over the world and projects Michelin's corporate ideals of strength, solidarity, quality and reliability.

1914: Innovations for the year include headlights built into fenders and an adjustable driver's seat (introduced by Maxwell).

0 0 1 0 3

TIM ALLEN

One of the best-known, hard-core car nuts, comedian Tim Allen has created a television character that epitomizes the obsessed male of American car culture. On his number-one-rated sitcom, *Home Improvement,* Allen's TV alter-ego, Tim Taylor, host of a cable home-improvement show, grunts his way between carpentry misadventures and hot-rod lunacy, always searching for the elusive "more power." In real life, Allen owns one of the most powerful, highly modified Mustangs available, while, on the show, Taylor is inclined to install a big-block V8 in a dishwasher or graft a jet helicopter engine onto a riding lawn-mower.

Allen was born Tim Allen Dick in Denver, Colorado, on June 13, 1953. He inherited his love of automotive things from his father, a "car guy" who loved to tinker—installing dual exhausts, bigger carburetors, and modified intake manifolds in his own quest for more power. Allen has fond memories of bonding with his father and brothers at various car-related events. Unfortunately, Allen's father was killed by a drunk driver, and soon after this tragedy, his mother moved the family to her hometown, Birmingham, Michigan, where Allen completed high school. He later attended Central Michigan University and Western Michigan University, from which he earned a B.A. in television production.

Allen spent some time working in a sporting-goods store, eventually making his way into the store's in-house advertising department. Then, after a now-famous brush with the law, for which he served some time in a correctional facility, he began a successful career in standup comedy. His stage show centered around a uniquely masculine brand of humor, combining a passion for cars with the universal male

1915: Automobile innovations include aluminum pistons, torsional vibration dampers, a spare tire placed in the trunk (introduced by Franklin), and tilt-beam headlights (introduced by Cadillac).

penchant for power tools, home-repair projects, and mayhem. Punctuating the act was his trademark sound, a grunting "AH, AH, AH" noise somewhere between that of a Neanderthal and a baboon. He picked up this twist by listening to his audiences and recalling the sounds he and his brothers used to make around the dinner table.

This successful comedy formula led to an offer from the Disney Company, in 1990, to appear on one of two sitcoms, which had already been written. Allen turned them down and, instead, pitched his own concept to Disney executives. *Home Improvement* was born.

MARIO ANDRETTI

A fan favorite, Mario Andretti was intense on the track and a charismatic emissary for auto racing in public. The "Arrivederci, Mario" tour in 1993, when Andretti received special honors and standing ovations at each event he raced, was a tribute to his success, longevity, and popularity. His achievement spans a wide variety of racing events: he won the Indianapolis 500, the Daytona 500, and the 12 hours of Sebring, as well as a Formula One World Championship and four USAC Indy Car championships. Film of his excitement at winning the Indianapolis

500 in 1969 and getting hugged by Andy Granatelli, his big-as-a-bear race team leader, became a popular clip in race highlights, documentaries, and television commercials as a moment of pure triumph.

Andretti was born on February 28, 1940, in Montona, Italy, soon after the outbreak of World War II. During the war, the Andretti family was interred in a displaced person's camp. Andretti had been racing in Italy by the time his family immigrated to the United States in 1955. In 1959, he and his brother, Aldo, began competing secretly, against their father's wishes, with a 1948 Hudson they adapted for racing. An accident involving Aldo exposed their activities, but Andretti's insistence on continuing to race gradually won over his father. Andretti won 20 sprint and midget races during the next three years. He drove in his first Indianapolis 500 in 1965, finishing third, an excellent rookie performance that led to talk-show appearances. The fact that he won the USAC National Championship that year and was named rookie of the year solidified his reputation. Two years later he won the Daytona 500, stunning experienced stock car drivers. By the time he won the Indianapolis 500, he had a large following among fans and the media. For the next two decades, which featured consistent achievement and an opportunity to race with his sons, Michael and Jeff, Mario Andretti was

1915: The Packard Twin Six feaures the first American 12-cylinder engine, built by Jesse Vincent. Showrooms remain open 24 hours a day to accommodate crowds, and Czar Nicholas II and the Maharajah of India are purchasers.

the most internationally recognizable name in all of racing.

Although many unrelated, independent developments contributed to the development of the automobile—from the invention of the wheel to the first steam-powered vehicles to the various improvements on the internal-combustion engine—Carl Benz is generally credited with being the first to install a gasoline engine in a vehicle and drive it. In 1885, he cruised his three-wheeled carriage, powered by a two-stroke gas engine, through the streets of Munich, Germany, leading the way for future automotive pioneers, including Gottlieb Daimler, who also claimed to have invented the automobile.

In 1872, Benz had started a small factory in Mannheim, Germany. Although it failed, he had become interested in mechanical devices and decided to reform the company to build engines. In 1879, he produced his first stationary, two-stroke, gasoline engine with electric ignition. It sold quite well (large, stationary engines were used at the time for a variety of purposes, including farm work and powering factory tools), and Benz began experiment-

ing on a smaller engine that could be used to power a vehicle.

The two-stroke engine proved too loud and cumbersome, so Benz concentrated on a four-stroke design. In 1885 he fitted his new engine to a tubular-framed tricycle, which is the machine considered to be the forerunner of the modern automobile. Emile Roger, the French agent for Benz's stationary engines, bought this vehicle and immediately signed on as the sole agent for Benz cars in France. The automobile industry was born.

Sales grew, and in 1893 Benz produced his first four-wheeled car, the Victoria. By 1899, his firm had 400 employees, and in 1900 the Benz plant was the largest car factory in the world, with an output of about 600 cars. But competition was heating up, especially from fellow German Gottlieb Daimler, whose own fortunes had soared with his line of Daimler and Mercedes automobiles. After World War I, with a depression debilitating Germany, both the Benz and Daimler companies were struggling to sell cars. Finally, recognizing the advantages of consolidating operations, rather than competing with each other, the two firms merged in 1926. At the time Benz employed about 5,000 people, while Daimler employees numbered about 4,500.

Daimler had died in 1900, many years before the mergers; the two automotive pioneers had never met. Carl

---

1915: Work begins in Oregon on the first major highway tunnel in the United States. Called Mitchell's Point Tunnel or Storm Cliff Tunnel, it has a rounded ceiling and five side openings, each 16 feet wide, making a magnificent scenic drive.

C A R   C R A Z Y

Benz died in 1929, but the company that bears his name has gone on to become a long-standing institution in the world of automobile manufacturing.

ETTORE BUGATTI

Ettore Bugatti, an Italian who lived most of his life in France, trained to be an artist, but while still in his teens he decided that his brother had more talent and—unwilling to be second-best in anything—settled on a different course for his life. Bugatti had become interested in motor vehicles, modifying and racing a motor tricycle. Giving up art in 1898, he designed and built a four-wheeled automobile with a four-cylinder engine. In 1901, one of his cars won a gold medal at the International Sport Exhibition in Milan, and by 1902 he was working full-time as a racer and designer for the de Dietrich company.

With financing from a banker friend, Bugatti founded his own company and in 1910 produced five cars at a factory in what was then Alsace-Lorraine. In 1911, a Bugatti won its class at the Grand Prix du Mans, beating larger, more powerful competitors, and Bugatti was instantly famous. His smaller, lighter, quicker cars established themselves as the best handling vehi-

cles of their day, and demand increased dramatically.

Bugatti gained a reputation for stubbornness and eccentricity. When hydraulic brake systems began to become popular, Bugatti stuck with cables, reportedly saying, "I make my cars to go, not to stop." When the local electric company sent an overdue notice to his factory, Bugatti ordered a power-plant constructed on the grounds. Then he invited the head of the electric company to tour the immaculate new facility, declaring, "I did not like the tone of your letter, and as you see, I shall have no further need of your services."

Eventually, the Bugatti works built about 50 different models of cars, from the small, lightweight racers to some of the biggest passenger cars ever constructed—the massive and elegant Type 41 Royales. These majestic vehicles were available from the Bugatti factory for $20,000 as a rolling chassis—that is, complete except for the body, which the owner would have custom-made by a coach builder. Only seven Royales were built, making appearances as everything from sporty runabouts to huge limousines.

Like many other luxury car makers, Bugatti's story essentially ends with the Great Depression. As demand dwindled, Ettore Bugatti spent more and more time at his Paris office, leaving the running of the factory to associates. After World War II, the complex was

1915: First reasonably priced, high quality V8 is introduced in the Cadillac V8 Touring Car, engineered by D. McCall White. The engine became the base model for American engines after World War II.

seized by the French government, since Bugatti was still an Italian citizen. He fought the case in court and won, but the plant turned out no more cars. Bugatti spent the remainder of his life working on boats and other projects. In all, he registered 350 patents.

Ettore Bugatti died on August 21, 1947, but he left behind an incredible automotive legacy: of the 7,500 cars that bore his name, 1,200 survive (including all of the Royales). This is an extraordinarily high percentage, especially considering that two World Wars took place around his factory. And it is an indication of the esteem in which Bugatti cars have always been held.

LOUIS CHEVROLET

In the annals of automobile manufacturing, few names are more recognizable than Chevrolet. The line of Chevy cars and trucks, for many years a part of the giant General Motors Corporation, has long symbolized affordability and dependability in mass-produced vehicles. But the ties between automobiles and the Chevrolet name lie not in basic transportation but in the more exciting—and considerably more expensive—world of automobile racing.

Louis Chevrolet was born on Christmas Day, 1878, in Switzerland,

the second son of clockmaker Joseph Chevrolet and his wife, Angelena Marie. Six years later the family moved to France, where Louis began to develop a love of machinery by working with his father. After finishing school, Louis began building and selling bicycles. His interest gradually shifted to the automobiles that were becoming more commonplace, and in 1898 he began working as a mechanic.

Louis emigrated to Canada in 1900, settling for a time in Montreal before moving to Brooklyn, New York, where he worked as a mechanic and engineer, eventually developing an interest in automobile racing. He drove Fiats for a time, winning a number of races, and even beating the famous Barney Oldfield three times. In 1906 Chevrolet was invited, by William C. Durant, to join the Buick racing team, for which he would drive and design engines. From 1907 to 1910, Louis and his brother Arthur enjoyed considerable success at Buick.

In 1911, with General Motors beginning to phase out racing support for Buick, Durant and Chevrolet founded the Chevrolet Motor Car Company. The firm produced a series of four- and six-cylinder cars in Detroit and Flint, Michigan. But in 1913 Chevrolet left the company, probably because he had little interest in affordable, mass-market automobiles. He had spent little time in the manufacturing end of the business,

1916: First mechanical (hand-operated) windshield wipers and the first slanted windshield are introduced.

0 0 1 0 9

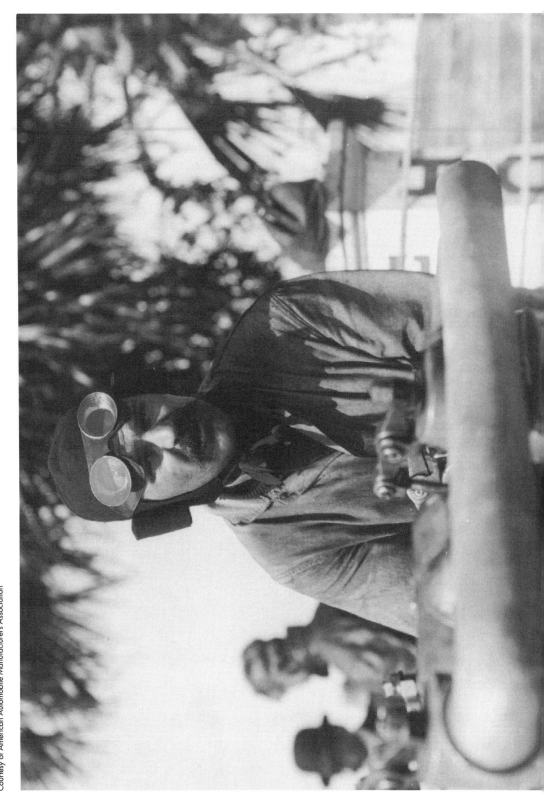

Louis Chevrolet founded the Chevrolet Motor Car Company with William Durant.

Courtesy of American Automobile Manufacturers Association

anyway. The Indianapolis Motor Speedway had opened in 1911, and it was here that Chevrolet was inevitably drawn.

The Chevrolet brothers founded the Frontenac Motor Company in 1916 to produce racing cars. While working as an engineer and continuing his winning ways on the track, Louis Chevrolet also invested in a number of profitable related ventures, including straight-8 engines, V8 engines, and aircraft engines. Although one of these businesses almost left him broke, in 1923 Louis, along with his brother, built an improved eight-valve pushrod cylinder head for the Ford Model T, dramatically improving that engine's output; racers, too, were enthusiastic about new hot-rod cylinder head.

In 1926, the Chevrolets designed a small-aircraft engine called the Chevrolair 333 and founded the Chevrolet Aircraft Corporation to build and market it. The venture was not a success, and Chevrolet spent the later years of his life in poor financial circumstances. He returned to Detroit in 1933 and worked as a mechanic for the Chevrolet Division of General Motors. But his health began to decline. He died on June 6, 1941, and he is buried not in the city where passenger cars bearing his name were produced, but in Indianapolis, near the famous Speedway that was the sight of many of his racing victories.

WALTER P. CHRYSLER

It was a fairly typical man meets car story. At an auto show in Chicago in 1908, Walter P. Chrysler, a locomotive engine mechanic and supervisor for the Chicago & Great Western Railroad, saw the future. Inspired by a Locomobile Phaeton, he combined his meager savings with a $4,300 loan to purchase the vehicle. Instead of cruising, especially since he had no previous driving experience, Chrysler spent his spare time taking the automobile apart, studying it, and rebuilding it. He was hooked. Chrysler took a 50 percent pay cut in 1912 to break into the automobile industry. A decade and a half after encountering the Locomobile Phaeton, he launched the Chrysler Corporation in spectacular fashion during the New York Auto Show. The Chrysler Six Phaeton made the most stunning debut in automotive history at that time— selling 32,000 units its first year.

Chrysler was born on April 2, 1875, in Winnebago, Kansas, a railway town where his father worked as an engineer with the Union Pacific Railroad. A few years later, the Chrysler family moved to Ellis, another Kansas railway town, where Walter spent his spare time in locomotive shops watching repairmen at work and occasionally working with them. At 18 he constructed a fully de-

---

1916: In an attempt to appeal to female customers, cars at the New York Auto Show feature vanity cases, crystal flower vases, and smelling salts.

Heartbreak Hotel . . . NOT!

The 1924 American Auto Show in New York City was one of the most famous. It was there that Chrysler Corporation first went public and introduced its first car, the Chrysler Six Phaeton, which went on to become the highest first-year seller in automotive history at that time.

Walter Chrysler had planned to introduce the new car at the annual New York Auto Show, but was denied a spot because the car and corporation had no previous production records. Instead, Chrysler rented the lobby of the nearby Commodore Hotel for a private showing. He was soon joined by other manufacturers who couldn't get spots. The Chrysler Six stole the show, and the hotel faced an overflow crowd. *The New York Times* reported that "the most important new car of the year is on exhibition at the Commodore Hotel." That was the legendary beginning of the Chrysler Six.

tailed, miniature steam locomotive and ran it on a rail track he constructed. He left home at 20 to pursue work as a journeyman machinist. Chrysler became a master mechanic and in 1908 a Superintendent of 10,000 workers at Chicago & Great Western Railroad.

Chrysler moved to the American Locomotive Company in 1910, where his outstanding work was noticed by James J. Storrow, a director of the corporation and board member of General Motors, who recommended him to Charles W. Nash, President of the Buick Motor Company. Chrysler took a pay cut (from $12,000 to $6,000) to join Buick in 1912 and quickly instituted sweeping changes in production and accounting practices. He became president of Buick in 1916 with a salary of $500,000 after making it GM's most profitable division. Chrysler resigned in 1920 when his autonomy was superseded by GM President William C. Durant. He was an unemployed millionaire at 45 who frequently entertained guests for car talk, but his wife tired of having him around the house and suggested that he go back to work. Chrysler headed the failing Willys-Overland Company (liquidated in 1921) and the failing Maxwell-Chalmers Auto Company (liquidated in 1925). He formed Chrysler Corporation in 1923; by 1927 it was the fourth largest U.S. auto firm. In 1928 he introduced Plymouth (with Amelia Earhart as its spokesperson) and DeSoto (the DeSoto Six sold 80,000 units its first year) and purchased Dodge Brothers Motor Company, which made Chrysler Corporation one of the Big Three automakers. Chrysler Corporation was the second largest U.S. automaker during the 1930s, but Chrysler began turn-

1917: Heaters are introduced as an option on many models.

Walter Chrysler introduced the Chrysler Corporation's first car in 1924.

Courtesy of American Automobile Manufacturers Association

ing his attention to other activities, including financing and helping design the Chrysler Building in New York City. He resigned from the Chrysler Corporation in 1935, at age 60, and died August 18, 1940.

ERRET LOBBAN CORD

E.L. Cord was associated with some of the most innovative and beautiful car designs of his time, including those that carried his own name. Cord was born July 20, 1894, in Warrensburg, Missouri. After attending high school in Los Angeles, he became involved in a series of auto-related enterprises, including managing garages, dirt-track racing, and selling new and used cars. In the early 1920s, he moved to Chicago to work as a salesman for the Moon Motor Car Company. In four years at Moon, he managed to save $100,000.

Cord, looking for an automotive investment of some kind, became interested in the Auburn Automobile Company. This Indiana firm was in bad financial shape, having produced only 175 cars in 1923. Cord struck a deal with Auburn's owners: they would make him general manager, with no pay. If Cord succeeded in making the company a success, he would be allowed to acquire controlling interest in the company. By 1926, Cord had become president of Auburn. He purchased the Duesenberg Company, makers of high-quality luxury vehicles, to add to Auburn's line. He also acquired suppliers like Lycoming Motors and the Kalamazoo Limousine body Company to ensure a ready source of parts. By 1929, Auburn sales hit 22,000 units.

In that year, Cord founded the Cord Corporation, a holding company that consolidated the various firms that had come under his control. By investing in his own companies, rather than playing the stock market, he initially avoided the ravages of the Depression. Cord began diversifying beyond automotive interests by acquiring aircraft and shipbuilding interests.

The first car carrying the Cord name, the Cord L-29, appeared in 1929. It was a significant engineering achievement, sporting, among other innovations, front-wheel drive. Unfortunately, the depression hit the market, and the L-29 failed to achieve the success it deserved. At the same time, Duesenberg had introduced its famous Model J, priced at almost $20,000. This now classic car, too, never saw much success. In response, Cord attempted to regroup with a single eight-cylinder model for the 1931 model year, but by 1933 the company's sales had dropped off to only 6,000 units.

1918: Car factories aid the war effort by producing aircraft engines, tanks, tractors, military vehicles, anti-aircraft guns, and shell casings, among other war materials.

Cord was also being plagued with trouble in other business areas. The government was investigating airmail contracts being handled by Cord Aviation; there was a Congressional probe of his shipbuilding operations; and the Internal Revenue Service had begun taking an interest in his activities. In 1937, the Securities and Exchange Commission charged Cord with having manipulated Auburn stock in 1935 and 1936. He was ordered to cease violation of the Securities Exchange Act.

At the age of 43, Cord sold his interest in the Cord Corporation for more than $2.6 million. He moved his family to Nevada, where he became very successful in real estate. By the 1950s he was a prominent figure in Democratic politics, serving as a representative in the Nevada state senate. Cord died in Reno on January 2, 1974.

GOTTLIEB DAIMLER

Although Carl Benz receives credit for being the first to install a gasoline engine in a vehicle and taking it for a drive (in 1885), Gottlieb Daimler quickly overtook him and is considered by many to be the founder of the automobile industry. His designs were thorough and practical, and during his lifetime he was awarded patents for many innovations that helped turn the horseless carriage into the car as we know it.

Daimler, the son of a baker, was born on March 17, 1834, in a small German village. After finishing school he became a gunmaker's apprentice and began displaying the mechanical brilliance that would determine the course of his life. He abandoned this promising career at the age of 19 to study engineering, which he pursued in Germany and abroad. After completing his education, he became the foreman at an engineering factory in Reutlingen, where he and a friend, Wilhelm Maybach, pursued their interest in internal-combustion engines.

Daimler attracted the attention of inventor and businessman Nikolaus Otto, often credited with the invention of the four-cycle engine, who hired him as technical director of his factory. Daimler hired Maybach, and the two quickly outpaced their employer in their vision for the engine and for powered vehicles. They left Otto and set about developing a practical, lightweight, high-speed, four-cycle powerplant. In 1885 they successfully installed their engine in a boat and subsequently sold several of these vessels, including one to the Shah of Persia.

After proving the viability of their engine, Daimler and Maybach started work on a four-wheel vehicle in 1886. They purchased a carriage from a local dealer and modified it for their one-

1918: Rene Thomas is the first racer to average 100 mph in an Indianapolis 500.

Mercedes-Benz Star is Elemental

The Daimler—and later Mercedes-Benz—star apparently originated with Gottlieb Daimler's sons, who recalled that their father had once sketched a star to symbolize his rising fortunes. In 1909, Daimler-Motoren-Gesselschaft registered both a three-pointed star and a four-pointed star as trademarks, but only the three-pointed star was ever used. Daimler-Motoren-Gesselschaft later said the star stood for air, sea, and land—the elements dominated by Daimler engines. The star became the radiator emblem in 1921.

and-a-half horsepower engine. It has never been established exactly when this horseless carriage first took the road, but it is generally accepted that test runs were conducted in early March of 1887. A second engine, this one water cooled and with two speeds, was installed in the carriage, and it is said to have reached a speed of 12 miles per hour.

Design improved steadily and, with capital from several investors, the Daimler-Motoren-Gesellschaft was formed on November 28, 1890. Business thrived, and the Daimler influence spread. A

subsidiary corporation was founded in England to sell cars there, but the British firm soon broke away from the parent company and negotiated for the right to produce its own cars under patent; for many years Daimler cars were produced in both countries. In 1926, in the midst of a growing depression in Germany, Daimler and its primary competitor, Benz, merged to form Daimler-Benz. The company went on to become one of the most outstanding success stories in automotive history. Unfortunately, Gottlieb Daimler died in 1900, having seen only the beginning of the impact his firm was to have, and—ironically—never meeting Carl Benz, the man whose name would forever be linked with his own.

JOHN DELOREAN

John DeLorean introduced a series of road burners for 1960s youths seeking cars with sleek lines and powerful engines. He designed the "wide-track look"—low-lying, streamlined cars set on wide wheelbases and featuring a DeLorean-patented overhead-cam engine—and devised the first "muscle car," the 1965 GTO. In many ways DeLorean, too, was fueled by style and speed, racing to tremendous accomplishments, including a share of five *Motor Trend* "Car of the Year" awards in 10 years, and spectacular crashes. He careened against the entrenched conservative culture at General Motors, then lost it all in an attempt to launch his own sports car, the DeLorean—one of the most anticipated releases of the last 20 years.

DeLorean was born on January 6, 1925, in Detroit. He served two years in the army at the end of World War II and then held several jobs, including draftsman and dance-band director, while completing a degree at Lawrence Institute of Technology. After stints selling life insurance and auto supplies, DeLorean was admitted to the Chrysler Institute, where he earned his M.A. in industrial engineering. Quickly establishing a strong reputation with the Packard Motor Company, DeLorean was recruited by Pontiac. With Peter Estes, later President of GM, and S. E. "Bunkie" Knudson, son of a former General Motors president, DeLorean transformed Pontiac from a weak-selling maker of "old lady cars" into GM's fastest-growing division. The wide-track look modernized and saved the Bonneville and Catalina models. The 1960 Pontiac Tempest, with the DeLorean-patented Tempest power train, won *Motor Trend*'s "Car of the Year" award. DeLorean became regarded as the industry's leading designer for these models and the Grand Prix, the GTO, and the Firebird. The 1965 *Motor Trend* "Car of the Year" award, in fact, went to the Pontiac group for "styling and engineering leadership."

While Pontiac was flourishing, Chevrolet—GM's largest division—was floundering, and DeLorean was appointed General Manager in 1969 to shore it up. But DeLorean, who had thrived in Pontiac's creative, quick-moving environment, met with resistance and bureaucracy at Chevrolet. He returned Chevrolet to strength and was promoted to Group Executive for North American Truck and Car Operations in 1972. But continued clashes over his plans and even his dress—colored Italian suits at first, then a tieless, blazer-and-blue-jean combo—his long hair and sideburns, and his highly-publicized engagement to model Christina Ferrare, further alienated him from GM executives. He resigned in April of 1973, and the next year he founded the DeLorean Motor Corporation. He began soliciting investments to finance the DeLorean—a powerful, stainless steel sports car that would compete with the Corvette—and was wooed by the government of Great Britain to build a plant in strife-torn Northern Ireland. The DeLorean was released after numerous delays in 1981, but sold poorly because of its high price and quality problems with the design and the bare stainless steel body (a joke circulated that he should offer free Brillo pads for polishing). His financial problems were allegedly so desperate that he turned to drug trafficking, for which he was arrested and charged in 1982. DeLorean was freed in 1985 because

---

1920: First long underwater tunnel in the United States designed specifically for automobiles, the Holland Tunnel, is begun. It is finished in 1927 after ventilation problems concerning carbon monoxide are solved.

Road Test

MATCH THE CAR WITH ITS "FATHER."

1.	John DeLorean	A.	Jaguar XK-120
2.	Harley Earl	B.	Volkswagen Beetle
3.	Henry Ford	C.	AC Cobra
4.	Lee Iaccoca	D.	Pontiac GTO
5.	William Lyons	E.	Chevrolet Corvette
6.	Ferdinand Porsche	F.	Model T
7.	Carroll Shelby	G.	Chevrolet Corvair
8.	Edward Cole	H.	Ford Mustang

(Answers: 1.D 2.E 3.F 4.H 5.A 6.B 7.C 8.G)

the FBI operation that implicated him was judged as entrapment. DeLorean was soon divorced by Ferrare and left the public eye.

JOHN AND HORACE DODGE

The Dodge Brothers—John and Horace—played significant roles in the development of the automobile industry. The first major auto suppliers, they supplied parts for the first popular American car—the 1901 Curved Dash Oldsmobile—and the monster-selling Ford Model T. John was the visionary businessman, Horace the mechanic who could make it work. With the money they made as suppliers they formed Dodge Brothers Motor Company in 1914, which quickly emerged as an industry leader. They produced an instant hit (and now a classic) with the 1914 Dodge Touring Car, introducing an "L-head" engine, an electric starter/ignition system, and an all-steel body.

John Francis Dodge (on October 25, 1864) and Horace Elgin Dodge (on

1920: A doozy—the Duesenberg—is introduced. It has an eight-cylinder engine and is the first car to use four-wheel hydraulic brakes. And it inspired the phrase, "it's a doozy."

John DeLorean was the man behind the Pontiac GTO.

Courtesy of American Automobile Manufacturers Association

John and Horace Dodge were the first major auto suppliers.

Courtesy of American Automobile Manufacturers Association

May 17, 1868) were born in Niles, Michigan. Their father owned a foundry and machine shop that never showed much profit. The family moved to Uptonville, north of Detroit, in 1882, and settled in Detroit in 1886. Horace invented an improved bicycle ball bearing, and in 1897 the brothers formed Evans & Dodge Bicycle Company with a third partner. They started their own machine shop in 1900, an excellent example of being in the right place at the right time, for Ransom Olds needed plenty of parts for his hot-selling Oldsmobile. In 1903 the Dodge Brothers signed on with Ford, becoming shareholders as well as exclusive suppliers for the emerging automaker. Their initial $10,000 investment in Ford Motor Company eventually became a $32 million payoff. John Dodge was a key business advisor to Ford, and Horace made dramatic improvements to the engine and rear axle design on Ford's Model A as well as designing machinery for production of automobile parts. They resigned from Ford in 1913 to begin their own auto manufacturing firm, prospering until their deaths, 11 months apart, in 1920. The Dodge family was influential in Detroit politics and arts and built several mansions and other Detroit landmarks. The firm was sold to the Chrysler Corporation in 1928.

FREDERICK AND AUGUST DUESENBERG

It's a Doozy!" There was no higher compliment. The expression comes from a line of high-powered, American luxury touring cars designed and built by brothers Frederick and August Duesenberg, German immigrants whose name has been elevated to the ranks of such automakers as Rolls-Royce, Bugatti, and Hispano-Suiza. For a brief period of time in the late 1920s and early 1930s, the Doozy was the car of choice for film stars, politicians, and even a few of the flashier gangsters.

The Duesenberg brothers were born in Lippe, Germany, and moved to the United States following their father's death in 1885. In 1897, Frederick, a champion bicycle racer, started a bicycle manufacturing business. At the same time, he had become intrigued with motorcycles, and in 1899 he built a gasoline engine that could be used to power a motor bike. As his interest in motor vehicles increased, Frederick decided to sell his bicycle business in 1905 to take a job with the Rambler Motor Car Company in Kenosha, Wisconsin, where he got an education in automobile manufacturing and developed an interest in race cars.

In 1905, Frederick, with his brother August, designed a racing engine and

---

1921: First recorded instance of a radio receiver in a private car occurs when the Cardiff and South Wales Wireless Society installs a set. American car manufacturers begin to offer car radios in 1928.

founded the Mason Motor Car Company to produce it. They sold this firm a year later but continued to work there until 1913, when they opened a new company in St. Paul, Minnesota, where they built engines for racing cars and boats. In 1916, the Duesenbergs, along with a group of investors, founded the Duesenberg Motors Corporation, with a factory in Elizabeth, New Jersey. Their initial product was a straight-eight engine for luxury cars. In 1920, a Duesenberg-powered racer set a land speed record at Daytona: 156 miles per hour. That same year, Duesenberg introduced its first production automobile, the Model A, which was powered by the straight-eight engine and sported radical hydraulic front-wheel brakes.

This first Duesenberg company failed. But a new firm, the Duesenberg Motor Company, took its place in 1925. They continued building the Model A but lacked capital to develop new models. In 1926, Duesenberg was acquired for $1 million by E.L. Cord, whose Cords and Auburns were produced by the Auburn Automobile Company. Cord gave the Duesenbergs free rein to embark on new product development. The result was the famous Model J, the most powerful car in the world at the time of its introduction in 1928, with a claimed 265 horsepower; it was followed by the Model SJ, an even more powerful supercharged version. Unfortunately, sales of these extremely expensive (more than $20,000) luxury

tourers were devastated by the Great Depression. Only 480 Model Js were built, while just 36 of the Model SJ ever reached the market.

Frederick Duesenberg's death in 1932 ended the Duesenberg Motor Company and its line of innovative, fast, luxurious touring automobiles. And, although a total of only 650 Duesenbergs had been built, the name had come to symbolize affluence, quality, and mechanical perfection in a way that would never be equaled in American automobile manufacturing.

ZORA ARKUS-DUNTOV

Sometimes the person most closely associated with a car isn't the designer or the builder. Sometimes it's the person who finally got it right. Such a man is Zora Arkus-Duntov, often referred to as "the father of the Corvette," but occasionally—and perhaps more appropriately—called, "the savior of the Corvette."

Chevrolet introduced its Corvette sports car in 1953, intending to provide some competition for the European sports models that had started becoming popular in the U.S. after World War II. That first Corvette was powered by a 150-horsepower, inline-six-cylinder engine and sold for $3,000. First-year sales reached 4,000 units but dropped off to

700 by the 1955 model year. The fact that an Oldsmobile sedan with a V8 was faster was one of the problems. And after the Corvette's debut year, when the public was wowed by its flashy appearance, it finally dawned on customers that it was just too slow and its handling wasn't up to that of the European cars. An eight-cylinder engine was installed in the Corvette for 1955, but by then the damage was done.

The Belgian-born Duntov was working as an engineer for Fairchild Aviation in New York in January of 1953 when he first saw the Corvette at its introduction at the Waldorf-Astoria Hotel. At the time, he wrote a letter to Ed Cole, Chevy's chief designer, asking why such a beautiful car was saddled with such a poor drive-train. He also offered a few suggestions for improvements. Cole responded by hiring him as a research engineer.

After the dismal sales year in 1955, General Motors almost abandoned the sports-car market, but in 1956 Duntov was promoted to director of high-performance vehicles and took over the Corvette project. He added disc brakes, independent rear suspension, and a limited-slip differential, improving the car's performance dramatically. He also pioneered the now-famous Rochester fuel-injection system that was offered as an option in 1957.

Duntov enjoyed a long career as chief engineer of Corvette and retired

from Chevrolet in 1975. As a result of his efforts the Corvette was not only saved, but went on to become one of the all-time great automotive success stories. For many years it was America's only home-grown sports car. It became the star of a television series (*Route 66*), competed respectably on the race track, and served as an object of lust for several generations of American teenagers.

WILLIAM C. DURANT

Perhaps no single name—with the possible exception of Henry Ford—is so identified with American automobile manufacturing as that of William C. Durant. He was not an engineer or an inventor. Durant was the financial and marketing genius who helped fuel the growth of the infant American auto industry and was instrumental in making the automobile a fact of life in this country.

Durant was born on December 8, 1861, in Boston to William Clark (a bank clerk and stockbroker) and Rebecca Crapo Durant. When the senior Durant, suffering from a series of business failures, left the family in 1872, Rebecca and her son moved back to her family home in Flint, Michigan. William Durant left school in his senior year and went to work at a series of sales and

1921: The back-up lamp is introduced on the Willys St. Claire.

clerical jobs. He got into the carriage business in 1886 when a friend impressed him with his design for a lightweight two-wheeled cart. Durant financed this venture with a bank loan, and the Flint Road Cart Company was born. Two weeks after signing their incorporation papers, Durant secured 600 orders for the vehicle. The carriage company was reorganized several times, eventually producing as many as 56,000 horse-drawn carriages per year.

By 1904, Durant was a millionaire living in New York and dabbling in the stock market. His enjoyment had come from building a successful business, not managing it. Although his new lifestyle, away from manufacturing, had kept him insulated from new developments in the carriage business—namely the installation of internal-combustion engines—he was called upon in that year by some friends from Flint to help them in a related venture. Their Buick Motor Company was failing, and they needed an organization expert to help them revive it. Thus was Durant caught up in the world of automobiles.

He reorganized the firm and, in 1905, came back from the New York Automobile Show with orders for more than 1,100 Buicks. He had immediately grasped the concept of building and selling cars. He saw that models must be positioned properly for the market, that they must be converted from a luxury into a necessity, and that they had to become reliable enough for non-mechanics to own. Durant hired talented engineers and designers. As a result of increased quality and Durant's marketing and sales efforts, 1,400 Buicks were sold in 1908 and 4,600 in 1909. Sales continued to rise. Only a few years after taking over Buick, Durant became known as one of the major players in this new industry.

In 1908, Durant purchased the Oldsmobile Company and added it to his Buick line. Then, on September 16, 1908, he surprised the automotive world by incorporating the General Motors Corporation in New Jersey, with himself as a member of the board of directors. General Motors immediately bought Buick and Oldsmobile. GM soon purchased the Oakland Motor Company (renaming it Pontiac) and, to round out the high-end line, the Cadillac Motor Company. Durant also added a number of less well-known companies to the GM stable. In 1909, he almost bought the Ford Motor Company, for $8 million, but was unable to raise enough capital to make the cash deal Henry Ford demanded.

By 1910, General Motors encompassed 25 individual companies, worth more than $50 million. These firms had been acquired at a cost of $33 million—only $6 million of it in cash. Still, all was not perfect in the burgeoning giant. Durant was often at odds with his bankers. His rapid expansion frequently

1922: First chrome-plated automobile bumpers and grills are on the Cadillac Sport touring car. This hard, shiny coating plated onto a metal surface is a mixture of chromium and other chemical elements, including nickel and copper.

left the corporation cash-poor; as quickly as money came in, Durant would engineer another acquisition, increasing the company's debt. The bankers tightened the reins and, in 1910, Durant was forced to agree to their terms in order to save General Motors.

Although his freedom within GM was restricted, he was free to do as he pleased outside of the corporate boardroom. In 1911, Durant, with some Flint backers, approached Louis Chevrolet (then an engineer and race driver for Buick) and offered to back him in a new automotive venture. He also backed several other fledgling designers and builders. Eventually, Durant's shotgun-style approach paid off. Although the Chevrolet venture failed, with Louis Chevrolet leaving shortly thereafter, Durant retained the right to use the Chevrolet name on automobiles. He folded a number of other manufacturing firms into Chevrolet, resulting in a highly successful new company. By the end of 1916, more than 70,000 Chevys had been sold.

Prior to the annual GM board of directors meeting in September of 1915, Durant had begun lobbying for votes among shareholders. At the meeting, he had enough to deadlock a vote for a new board. A compromise left Durant and two others in charge of GM. Within six months, he had achieved a virtual takeover of the giant General Motors by

his own sleeper, Chevrolet. (The Chevrolet corporation ended up owning or controlling 450,000 of GM's 825,000 shares of stock.)

Durant, now the major stockholder in General Motors, engineered the transformation of GM from a holding company into an operating company by reincorporating it in Delaware in 1916. In the move, with the exception of Chevrolet, all the various automobile and parts companies (including AC, Delco, Remy Electric, etc.) held by GM became "divisions" of the parent firm.

Although Durant was able to exert tremendous influence over General Motors, he had conflicts with other members of the board of directors. Gradually other, more conservative, factions began to structure their own changes. Finance came under control of a new committee. With Pierre Du Pont serving as GM's chairman of the board, the Du Pont Company of Wilmington, Delaware, acquired $25 million in GM and Chevrolet stock, making it the second-largest holder of GM stock.

Through the rest of the decade, Durant continued to buy GM stock with his personal funds. He believed in the company, and it was definitely on the rise. Despite occasional cash shortages and minor setbacks, GM had continued to grow dramatically. But in the early 1920s, for the first time, Durant made an offer to sell some GM stock. This greatly alarmed other directors.

1922: First "million year" ever is achieved by Ford Motor Company, which delivers 1,216,792 units of its Model T.

Durant was president of GM at the time, and the sales offer was a startling development. It was subsequently learned that he owed a large sum of money, as much as $27 million, to stockbrokers. This sum was secured by more than 4 million shares of GM stock. Other GM investors, including Du Pont and J.P. Morgan & Co., were forced to bail out Durant. In exchange for a deal that left him solvent, he agreed to give up power in GM.

At the age of 59, Durant could have easily retired comfortably, but he attempted one more automotive venture. In 1921, he founded Durant Motors. Over the next two years, he purchased factories and began making plans to introduce a line of low-cost cars to compete with Henry Ford's Model T. By 1923, he had ten factories and 4,000 dealers lined up. Although the firm did well at first, its stock peaked in 1923 and then began a decline. Throughout the 1920s, Durant Motors struggled along, well behind the new "Big Three" powers in the auto industry, Ford, General Motors, and the new Chrysler Motor Corporation, which together accounted for 70 percent of car sales. Durant Motors closed its doors in 1931.

The stock-market crash of 1929 ruined Durant. His fortune always depended heavily on stocks and bonds, rather than cash. On February 8, 1936, Durant declared bankruptcy. With his little remaining cash, and his still fa-

mous name, he dabbled in several smaller business ventures, including real estate, a shopping center, and a bowling alley. In 1942 Durant suffered a stroke in Flint, Michigan, which began a steady decline in his health. He died March 18, 1947, in New York City.

CHARLES AND FRANK DURYEA

In 1996, the celebratory year of the 100th anniversary of the founding of the U.S. automobile industry, the debate was renewed as to exactly who was the first American to build an internal-combustion vehicle. Charles Duryea was certainly one of the first to *lay claim* to being first. Duryea, born in 1861, near Peoria, Illinois, claimed that as a child he had predicted the advent of the practical horseless carriage. And, indeed, it was Charles Duryea's name that appeared on an 1895 patent for "improvements in Road Vehicles." But these and other claims have been the subject of controversy for the last 100 years.

Duryea and his brother Frank moved to Springfield, Massachusetts, to begin manufacturing bicycles. In the late 1880s, Charles became fascinated with the new internal-combustion engine, which, he had read, was being used in Europe to power road-going

1922: Introductions for the year include the air cleaner, the gas gauge, and balloon tires.

00127

vehicles. In 1891, Duryea later claimed, he had begun development of his own horseless carriage with the help of Frank, a skilled bicycle mechanic. But, in September of 1892, Charles moved the bicycle business back to Illinois, leaving Frank to continue development of the powered carriage. Many experts now feel that in Charles's absence, Frank was the one who actually made the vehicle operational. Although Charles would later lay claim to a successful test-run on April 19, 1892, it was, by objective accounts, September 20, 1893, when the experimental Duryea vehicle actually first ran on the streets of Springfield.

Although many other Americans were testing vehicles powered by internal-combustion engines, most experts give the nod to the Duryeas as the builders of the first successful gasoline automobile. They were, clearly, the first to offer a production model for sale to the public. In 1896 they founded the Duryea Motor Wagon Company and, with the backing of several Springfield investors, began manufacturing vehicles with two-cylinder, four-cycle gasoline engines.

How much each brother contributed to the venture is the subject of ongoing debate. Although they had an equal number of shares of company stock, Frank was the mechanic and engineer in charge of production. Charles, the front-man, was featured promi-

nently in the company's promotional literature, and it was Charles who applied for and got his name on the patent. Because of these and other controversies, a lifelong rift developed between the two brothers, and the Duryea Motor Wagon Company went out of business in 1898. It had produced 13 cars in 1896 and only three in 1897.

Frank Duryea continued his work as a designer and engineer, enjoying considerable success with the Stevens-Duryea Motor Car Company of Chicopee Falls, Massachusetts, from 1901 to 1909. Charles, on the other hand, fell on hard times. He continued to work in the business world, heading companies in Pennsylvania and Michigan, but saw little success. His main occupation became the writing of articles defending his claim to having developed America's first internal-combustion-powered vehicle. Charles Duryea died in 1938, Frank in 1967. The debate about their relative achievements and contributions lives on.

HARLEY EARL

One of the most famous of automobile designers, Harley Earl was born in 1893 in Hollywood. His family was involved in manufacturing: The Earl Automobile Works, founded by his grandfather,

1923: MG is introduced in England. A sporty car with wire wheels, a hand brake, and no windshield, it can reach 80 mph. MG stands for "Morris Garages," the name of William R. Morris's original retail and repair business in Oxford.

Designer Harley Earl at the wheel of GM's first concept car, the 1938 Buick "Y-Job."

Courtesy of American Automobile Manufacturers Association

began as a maker of accessories, but quickly turned to the production of custom bodywork. Harley Earl dropped out of Stanford University to join the family business, and by 1918 he had taken over as manager.

The company produced cars to be used as props for motion pictures. From there, it branched out to building custom-bodied vehicles for some of the stars. Eventually Earl's work—particularly his customized Cadillacs—came to the attention of General Motors executives. Lawrence P. Fisher, then head of Cadillac, persuaded Earl to move to Detroit in 1926 to work on a new car. GM officials had decided they needed a vehicle priced above the average Buick, but below the top-of-the-line Cadillacs. To fill the bill, Earl designed the first La Salle, a graceful 1927 model that is recognized as the beginning of the trend toward lower and wider designs throughout the automotive industry.

Earl's work so impressed GM's president, Alfred P. Sloan, Jr., that Sloan made him director of a new department that was charged with overseeing the styling of all the corporation's products, the Art and Colour Section. Earl ran with this new assignment, applying his unique perspective to all GM cars and, ultimately, dominating the Detroit styling scene for several decades.

In the postwar years, he continued designing longer, lower, and wider vehicles, with the other American manufacturers following suit. The 1948 Cadillac featured a new Earl invention: tail fins, inspired by World War II fighter planes. This idea caught on immediately, and soon fins were all the rage. The trend culminated with the 1959 Cadillac Eldorado, one of the largest cars ever to come out of Detroit (more than 20 feet in length), with lethal-looking tailfins that towered over the trunk lid and sported twin bullet taillights

Earl retired from General Motors in 1959 after 32 years in the corporation's styling division as director, vice-president, and then president. He continued working in the design field with his Harley Earl Associates, a firm he had founded in 1945. Earl died in 1969.

ENZO FERRARI

The name Ferrari conjures up visions of blood-red sports cars emblazoned with the famous prancing black horse logo. Over the course of 40 years, *Il Commendatore*—as Enzo Ferrari was reverentially known—created such legendary exotic cars as the GTO, Berlinetta Lusso, Testarossa, Daytona, and Berlinetta Boxer, and earned for himself a level of celebrity that, in his native Italy, placed him on a par with the pope.

1923: First Le Mans Grand Prix d'Endurance is run in France and won by Lagache and Leonard, who average 57.21 mph in a Chenard et Walcker. The race is formed to test a touring car's endurance, rather than its speed.

Interested in things mechanical from an early age, Ferrari trained in automotive mechanics at a repair shop owned by his father, a businessman in Modena. He began racing in 1919 and had begun earning a reputation for himself when poor health forced his retirement in 1931. He formed his own racing team and continued as manager, running the highly successful Alfa Romeo cars under his own Scuderia Ferrari banner.

During World War II, Ferrari turned to war production. His Modena shops were damaged by Allied bombs, and he moved his equipment to Maranello, where the factory and headquarters are still located. After the war, the first car carrying the Ferrari name was built, and Ferraris began to dominate the racing world in the 1950s. Alberto Ascari won back-to-back World Championships for Ferrari in 1952–53, and Argentinian great Juan Manuel Fangio claimed the crown in 1956. British driver Mike Hawthorn won in 1958, as did American Phil Hill in 1961 and Briton John Surtees in 1964.

That racing tradition continues today, of course, but the Ferrari factory had also begun to produce a series of extraordinary touring cars, for which it has become equally famous. One of the most beautiful Ferraris, the incredible 250 GTO, bowed in the late 1950s, followed in the next decade by the 275 GTB and 300GTC; the 1970s brought

A (Fast) Moving Tribute to a Son

Ferrari produced more than 4,000 Dino 246 GT and Dino 246 GTS Spyders between 1969 and 1974. The Dino was named for company founder Enzo Ferrari's son Alfredo, who designed the car and who died of leukemia shortly before it was introduced. As a tribute, the name Ferrari did not appear on the Dino except on a metal tag on the doorpost, where it was required by law. Instead, "Dino" was inscribed on a yellow disk in the center of the steering wheel and on each hub. Dino also appeared on all official factory literature.

the awesome 365/GTB-4 Daytona and the Berlinetta Boxer. Later road cars included the Testarossa and truly amazing F-40, capable of 200-miles-per-hour speeds with the handling of a Formula One car.

Ferrari's death in 1988 at the age of 90 marked the departure of one of the few remaining auto giants left in the business. And it placed the last of Europe's great automotive marques under the complete stewardship of Fiat, the giant Italian conglomerate that had acquired a majority interest in Ferrari in 1968. But nothing can erase the memories of more than 50 years of racing

1924: Price of a Ford automobile hits its lowest point ever at $290 (without a self-starter), reflecting Fordist philosophy of steadily decreasing prices as quality is mastered.

dominance and exotic road-car development and production under the personal direction of *Il Commendatore.*

HENRY FORD

Henry Ford is likely the most significant American industrialist, revolutionizing automobile production with the assembly line, creating decent-paying jobs for thousands of workers, and producing affordable cars for the masses. He succeeded through his own creativeness and hard work—an idealistic pioneer viewed by many as a hero. He was a natural mechanic, an excellent automobile racer, and a visionary businessman. He also had a stubborn streak that nearly cost him everything he built: slow to change car styles and engineering, Ford car sales floundered during the late-1920s, and his violent hostility toward organized labor nearly led to a government intervention and takeover of Ford Motor Company.

Ford was born July 30, 1863, on a farm in Greenfield Village (now Dearborn), Michigan. He had an instinct for machinery and spent more time repairing clocks, pumps, and farm equipment than farming, a continuing source of dispute with his father. He ran away to Detroit at 16, becoming a fully qualified mechanic. He married at 24 and re-turned to the farm, but soon accepted a job in Detroit at the Edison Illuminating Company. Inspired by the Duryea automobile, Ford built a workshop and produced his first automobile, the Quadricycle, in 1896. By 1899, Ford had constructed three automobiles and become chief engineer for the Detroit Automobile Company and then the Ford Automobile Company, both of which failed. Meanwhile, Ford, who was preoccupied with racing, built the 999, a large and powerful race car. The 999 was driven by Barney Oldfield, a bicycle racer whose first victory was also the first time he had driven a car. Racing success brought in investors, and the Ford Motor Company was founded. The 1903 Ford Model A was an instant success. Sales and investments were further propelled when Ford set a land speed record (more than 90 mph) with the 999 on a track of cinder and ash laid on frozen Lake St. Clair. The successful Model N was introduced in 1906, but Ford turned his attention to building a car affordable to the masses. His solution to this problem—the Model T—changed American industry. Ford introduced standardized parts and the assembly line to automobile production with astounding results.

Ford prospered with the Model T until the mid-1920s, but the Ford line was rapidly losing appeal to better engineered and more powerful vehicles. The 1932 introduction of the Ford V8, an excellent performance vehicle and

1924: For the first time, no electric or steam cars are displayed at the annual auto show in New York.

the first mass-produced, affordable V8, saved the company. The remainder of the 1930s was marked by ugly labor troubles for the man who had introduced the $5 day and provided well-paying jobs and good working conditions for thousands of laborers. Ford hired a large security force to disrupt worker attempts to form a union, leading to a 1932 confrontation where four demonstrators were killed and the famous 1937 "Battle of the Overpass," where unionists (including Walter Reuther, first President of the United Auto Workers) and some journalists and photographers were beaten. Ford held out on government pressures to recognize the union, but his wife, tired of the bloodshed and the prospect of having the company closed, offered him the choice of continuing their marriage or continuing his losing battle. Ford finally allowed a union vote in 1941. Ford's health was deteriorating, and he relinquished control of the company to his grandson, Henry Ford II, in 1945. Ford's funeral in 1947 was attended by over 100,000 people.

A. J. FOYT

A.J. Foyt is widely considered the greatest American race car driver, winning with Indy, stock, sports, dirt, midget, and sprint cars. A rugged individualist, Foyt has the image of a tough, hot-tempered, brash Texan with a red bandana slung around his neck —a guy who built and raced his own cars. But

Someone's in the Kitchen with Henry

Henry Ford was working as supervisor of generators at the Edison Illuminating Company and, in his spare time, attempting to build a practical gasoline engine that could be installed in an automobile. One evening he came into the house with the small engine and clamped it to the kitchen sink. It had a spark plug of sorts, which could be plugged into one of the house's electrical outlets. Unfortunately, it lacked a carburetor.

Ford hooked up his spark plug and, as he gave the flywheel a healthy spin, asked his wife to drip gasoline into the fuel intake while he adjusted a valve. He spun, she adjusted and dripped, the kitchen lights flickered. After several attempts, the engine coughed a few times and then finally caught. Clara Ford continued dripping as the engine roared to life, belching flames and smoke and almost tearing the sink from its moorings. History does not record whether little Edsel, then four months old and asleep in the next room, was awakened by the din.

Source: Lacey, Robert, Ford: The Men and the Machines, Ballantine, 1986.

Henry Ford with his first car, the 1896 Quadricycle.
Courtesy of American Automobile Manufacturers Association

his driving style was cool and precise with daring, well timed-charges—"he just never made mistakes," observed racing commentator and publisher Chris Economaki. Foyt's skills and sportsmanship are widely admired by other greats of the sport, and his legendary exploits include having helped rescue Johnny Rutherford and Roger McClusky from crashed and burning race cars. His intense competitiveness also alienated racers and mechanics; driving great Parnelli Jones once stood in the middle of California's Ascot dirt track as cars sped by so that Foyt would be sure to see his angry gesture. Foyt won prestigious, high-profile races—four Indianapolis 500s, two Daytona 500s, the 24 Hours of Le Mans, the 24 Hours of Daytona , the 12 Hours of Sebring—and championships on the lesser publicized dirt and midget circuits.

Born January 16, 1935, in Houston, Foyt was the son of a garage owner and racer of midget cars. From the time he could walk, Foyt was learning about engines and racing from his father. He drove a small red racer equipped with an engine around the yard when he was three, followed soon after by a midget-type racer that could reach 50 mph. At age five, Foyt raced an established midget car driver—and beat him—in a three-lap exhibition. He was the finest dirt car driver and midget racer by the time he reached 20. Foyt entered his first Indianapolis 500 in 1958 at age 23; he won his first 500

three years later, became the first four-time winner of the race in 1977, and set new Indy 500 speed records in 1964 and 1967. Foyt continued to race successfully in just about every other type of major competitive racing, winning seven USAC championships. "He could drive anything, anywhere, anytime," said NASCAR legend Junior Johnson. "Won in about everything he ever sat down in."

TOM GALE

A renaissance in American automobile design began during the mid-1980s. After the rush to compete with import compacts during the 1970s and the advent of practical, box-like designs exemplified in Chrysler's K-cars—the Dodge Aries and the Plymouth Reliant—styling for improved aerodynamics and pure commercial appeal made a comeback. Curvaceousness is in now, and one of its leading exponents is Tom Gale, known for his "cab-forward" designs on Chrysler's LH sedans, those lovely headlights on the Dodge Viper, and other eye-catching flourishes, like the jutting grille of the 1996 Dodge Ram pickup.

Gale was born on June 18, 1943, in Flint, Michigan. As a child he loved drawing cars, which he continued to do

1925: The first rental car—the "Hertz Drive-Ur-Self"—is introduced at the New York Auto Show. Hertz will become the world's largest rental car company.

Tom Gale was the designer behind Chrysler's LH sedans.
Courtesy of American Automobile Manufacturers Association

at Michigan State University and then as a body engineer and designer at Chrysler, where he started after graduation in 1967. It took 25 years, through some of the darkest times of the American auto industry, for Gale to be set free to play with design elements, and the curving of the American car and truck that began in the mid-1980s is a reflection of his influence. Bringing style to the minivan was a start; the audacious, powerful Dodge Viper in 1989 went beyond the lines with its V10 engine, rounded features, and sleek headlights that even Bugatti requested permission to replicate.

Gale has had a hand in designing some of the most distinctive and popular vehicles of the 1990s. Chrysler's LH sedans—the Eagle Vision, Dodge Intrepid, and Chrysler Concorde—are smoothed-out, roomy, and sporty. The Neon offers an appealing look, fun variety of colors, and the type of small-car performance that proved so elusive to American car manufacturers 20 years earlier, when oil shortages and dependable imports squeezed the industry. The Jeep Grand Cherokee and the rounded Dodge Ram pickup are major contributors to the dramatic rise in popularity of sport utility vehicles and trucks. This emphasis on styling, which Gale maintains is a major part of consumers' purchasing decisions—despite the fact that surveys suggest otherwise—makes him a throwback to design-emphasis that began fading in the late 1960s. Not sur-

prisingly, Gale views that era as a time when "American design was incredibly strong in all consumer products." He goes on to say, "I think there's an opportunity for it to happen again . . . I really see an awakening." It's been a long time since car design—for sheer pleasure and art's sake— has been taken so seriously.

DON GARLITS

In the late 1950s, "Big Daddy" Don Garlits brought his plain dragsters from Tampa, Florida, to Southern California to compete with expensive, glossy colored and chrome-plated models in the hotbed of drag racing. His drab-looking racers led experienced competitors to call him Don Garbage. But when the quarter-mile heats ended, Garlits' "Swamp Rats" had won every race, and the career of the most dominant of drag racers was underway. Garlits won the National Hot Road Association (NHRA) Nationals three times, and he developed and drove the first dragster to go 170, 180, and then 200 mph.

Born Donald Glenn Garlits in Tampa, Garlits hung around garages and worked with mechanics as a scrawny kid whom mechanics playfully called "Big Daddy." He began building his own engines as a teenager and

1925: Uniform road signs are adopted: route names and numbers (odd for north-south, even for east-west) and particular shapes and color schemes are among the standards.

00137

would test them in midnight races that often ended with a speeding ticket. But he established a reputation as a drag racer in Florida before taking California by storm. As a racer, mechanic, and officer with the NHRA, Garlits helped establish drag racing as a more exciting and financially rewarding motor sport. He suffered as well, incurring both internal and external burns in 1960 when an engine exploded; his two-month recovery included a bout with pneumonia and constant pain that was alleviated by morphine, to which he became briefly addicted. Another burn injury sidelined him for six months, and he also suffered three cracked vertebrae in an accident. While overcoming these setbacks and contemplating retirement, Garlits designed a safer, rear-engine dragster where the driver sat in front of the motor, away from facing potentially explosive vapors. He won the 1970 Winternationals and 1971 Springnationals with the model, culminating a career in which he contributed greatly as a mechanic, racer, administrator, and promoter of drag racing. Garlits opened the Museum of Drag Racing in Ocala, Florida, following his retirement.

JANET GUTHRIE

Considering that she learned to fly at 13, rebuilt a car for racing in her early twenties, and applied to NASA to become the first female astronaut, it's not surprising that Janet Guthrie broke the gender barrier at the Indianapolis 500. Along with a sense of daring, Guthrie brought a physics background to her pioneering efforts as well as a determination to succeed. A sense of humor helped, too, as reflected in her standard reply to whether or not a woman racer can compete physically with a man: "I *drive* the car. I don't carry it."

Guthrie was born in Iowa City in 1938. Her father was an airline pilot, and the family moved to New York City and Atlanta before settling in Miami. Guthrie developed an early passion for aviation and began flying under her father's tutelage at age 13. After graduating with a degree in physics from the University of Michigan, Guthrie took a position in the Aerospace Division of Republic Aviation. She bought an XK-120 Jaguar for the work commute and eventually began racing it in hill climbs and field trails. Guthrie began racing on tracks in the early 1960s. After an attempt to become an astronaut (she didn't meet all of NASA's educational and experience requirements), she devoted herself more to mechanics, stripping down and rebuilding a Jaguar to compete in the 1964 Watkins Glen 500, finishing sixth overall. Between 1964 and 1970, she competed in Daytona and Sebring endurance races while attempting and failing to gain a sponsorship for the Indianapolis 500. She be-

1925: Crank window lifts, one-piece windshields, and mohair upholstery become common.

came the first woman to compete in a NASCAR superspeedway race in 1976, finishing fifteenth. In 1977, she became the first woman to compete in the Indianapolis 500, but her car experienced mechanical problems and she did not finish the race. Guthrie continued to compete in NASCAR events in her Kelly Girl Chevrolet, and she finished ninth in the 1978 Indianapolis 500. The question of whether a woman could compete in auto racing had been answered, and Guthrie went on to other challenges.

PHIL HILL

In the year 1961, Grand Prix racing barely existed as far as most Americans were concerned. In much of the rest of the world, Grand Prix races drew huge crowds, rivalling even soccer matches. But in the United States, Formula One results were only occasionally listed on the back pages of the sports sections. But this changed dramatically when, in September of that year, Phil Hill became the first American to win the Formula One world drivers championship.

Hill was born in Miami on April 20, 1927, to Philip Toll and Lela Hill. The elder Philip became the postmaster in Santa Monica, California, and it was here, amid the Southern California car

culture, that the son developed his love of automobiles. His first car was a Ford Model T, which he raced on the streets of Santa Monica before he even had a driver's license. Hill dropped out of the University of Southern California and supported himself as a mechanic at the largest imported-car dealership in Los Angeles. He furthered his knowledge of things mechanical at various British motor works, including Rolls-Royce, beginning in 1949. While living in England, he developed a love for British cars, racing, among others, a supercharged MG TC. Upon his return to the United States, he continued his racing career with his own sports cars, including a Jaguar XK-120, an Alfa Romeo 8C 2900, an Aston Martin DB-2, and series of Ferraris.

Word of Hill's racing prowess spread, and he began driving for some well-known racing teams. He first competed at Le Mans in 1953 and, in 1955, became a Ferrari factory sports-car driver. Since Ferrari also ran the leading Grand Prix team, it was natural that Hill would want to move up to this highest level of competition. He began his Grand Prix career with the last two races of 1958.

He raced full seasons in 1959 and 1960, garnering his first win at the 1960 Italian Grand Prix. In 1961, Ferrari introduced its first mid-engine Formula One car, which obviously suited Hill perfectly. In the hotly contested 1961

1925: Closed-car bodies outsell open-car bodies for the first time.

season, Hill finished first in two races, second in two, third in one, and ninth in one. He secured the championship with his victory at the Italian Grand Prix on September 10.

After one more season with the Ferrari team, Hill drove for two other Formula One teams, then, from 1965 to 1967, he had campaigned an impressive array of sports cars, including Aston Martins, Carroll Shelby's Ford Cobras, and Jim Hall's Chaparral. Hill's last race was a victory in the Chaparral at Brands Hatch in 1967.

Since his retirement from racing, Phil Hill has never strayed from his love of cars. He spent some time as a television broadcaster on racing telecasts and is the co-founder of a highly regarded classic auto restoration shop. He also loves driving classic cars in vintage-race events and lends his expertise to evaluating various cars as a contributing editor for *Road & Track* magazine.

SOICHIRO HONDA

Many years ago, in a small village some 140 miles southwest of Tokyo, a fascinated young boy watched as an automobile passed through his village of Iwata Gun. Even after the auto had gone, the boy could still smell traces of oil on the road. Eight-year-old Soichiro

Honda has just had his first glimpse of an automobile. The experience started turning wheels in his own mind that eventually resulted in the Honda Motor Company, the world's leading manufacturer of motorcycles and a company that produces some of the best-selling cars in the world.

Soichiro Honda was born November 17, 1906, in Iwata Gun, Japan. His father, a blacksmith and bicycle repairman, instilled in his son a love and a penchant for mechanical things, as well as an impatience and dislike of formal education. He left school at 16 to work in Tokyo as an apprentice in an auto-repair shop. This disdain for education helped make Honda Motor Company different from all others in Japan by its shunning of the old-boy network of university graduates that enmeshes most of that country's business communities.

Honda returned to his home town in 1928 as a master mechanic and opened his own repair shop, a venture that proved extremely lucrative. Eventually he reinvested some of the profits in a new business, manufacturing piston rings, and found customers in such large companies as Toyota. During World War II, American bombers destroyed his livelihood. But after the war, with $3,300 in capital, he formed the Honda Motor Company and began manufacturing motorcycles, just the cheap, economical form of transporta-

1926: Car heaters that use the heat obtained from the engine's cooling system first appear in the United States. Foot-warmers similarly operated were found on pre-1900 Cannstatt-Daimlers in Germany.

tion needed by his recovering country. Gradually, the firm expanded into new markets, including the United States, where the famous ad slogan, "You meet the nicest people on a Honda," helped win over the American public.

The wheeled vehicles making news for Honda today are not so much its motorcycles (although those still retain a huge share of the worldwide motorcycle market), but its line of attractive, well-made, practical cars. In addition to the popular Accord, Civic, and Prelude models, which carry the Honda badge, the firm, in 1986, became the first Japanese car company to enter the high-end luxury market with the formation of its Acura Division. These cars—the sporty Integra and luxurious Legend—were designed to compete with such well-established, upscale European makes as Audi, BMW, and Mercedes. That this venture was a success is demonstrated by the quick response from Honda's competition. Toyota and Nissan quickly followed suit with their own successful luxury lines: Infiniti and Lexus, respectively.

LEE IACOCCA

To his supporters, Lee Iacocca is a miracle worker, the genius behind the original Ford Mustang in the 1960s and the executive who wrested Chrysler from the jaws of death in the late 1970s. To his critics, he is a businessman who lost sight of his business and a leader who became so caught up in the trappings of his own celebrity that he forgot how to lead.

Lido Anthony Iacocca was born October 15, 1924, in Allentown, Pennsylvania. After earning a B.S. from Lehigh University and then an M.E. from Princeton, he went to work for Ford as an engineer, but he soon developed an interest in the faster-paced world of sales and marketing and got himself assigned to Ford's Pennsylvania fleet sales office. In 1956, he attracted the attention of corporate brass with an ingenious marketing plan that catapulted his sales district to number one in the nation. Iacocca was transferred to Ford headquarters in Dearborn, Michigan, where he continued his rise to the top.

In 1960, at the age of 35, he ascended to vice-president and general manager of the Ford Division. Recognizing that Ford needed to penetrate new markets, Iacocca decided to concentrate on the young generation that he believed was primed for a car with great styling, strong performance, and a reasonable price. His instincts were right on target. The Mustang set an auto industry sales record for a first-year model.

Iacocca served as president of Ford from 1970 to 1978, but eventually his

---

1926: First car with safety glass windows as standard equipment is offered by Cadillac. This new ceramic glazing material prevents a car's windows from shattering apart when broken.

How Lee Iacocca Financed His Future

Lee Iacocca first impressed Ford's executive circle in 1956. As assistant sales manager for the Philadelphia district, he came up with a unique marketing plan to boost his district from its sorry last-place ranking in sales across the country. Tapping the appeal of car financing—a relatively new idea at the time—Iacocca mounted the "56 for 56" campaign, through which new 1956 Ford cars were offered for 20 percent down and $56 a month over three years. The plan made the Philadelphia district number one in Ford sales. Ford decided to implement the "56 for 56" campaign nationwide, resulting in the sale of an additional 75,000 cars. Iacocca was on the road to a fabulous future in the auto industry.

flamboyant nature and status as an outsider at the family-controlled company became too much for his boss, Henry Ford II. Iacocca was fired on July 13, 1978. He was offered executive positions at a number of major U.S. corporations, but his love of cars led him to accept the position of chief operating officer of the ailing Chrysler Corporation.

Here, he took charge of the U.S. automaker that was hardest hit by the energy crises of the 1970s. Its cars were considered second-rate, and its organizational structure offered a glaring case of waste and mismanagement. While a bailout by the Federal Government kept Chrysler afloat temporarily, wholesale changes were necessary.

Iacocca responded to the challenge with two major new products: the K-car and the minivan. The K-car provided a fuel-efficient, front-wheel-drive sedan that could finally stand up to the competition. And the minivan was snapped up by young families looking for spacious vehicles with more appeal than the station wagons of their parents' generation. On the strength of these and other innovations, Chrysler paid back its government loan seven years early.

But by the late 1980s, some critics felt that Iacocca's business judgment had begun to falter, leading to unwise investments and vehicles that were, once again, considered inferior to the competition. Chrysler earnings began to fall and Iacocca's star continued to decline, leading to his retirement in 1992.

YUTAKA KATAYAMA

Yutaka Katayama almost singlehandedly built Nissan Motor Company's fledgling U.S. operation into a major import power during the 1960s and 1970s.

1926: German automobile manufacturing company Mercedes-Benz is formed as the result of the merger of the separate Daimler (Mercedes) and Benz companies that had been cooperating increasingly since 1923.

Lee Iacocca is credited with saving Chrysler from financial ruin in the early 1980s.
AP/Wide World Photos

The forerunner of Nissan had actually been founded in 1911 in Tokyo as the Kwaishinsha Motor Car Works by Masujiro Hashimoto, an American-trained engineer. He named his car DAT, after the initials of his three principal financial backers. In 1928, the firm was renamed the DAT Motor Car Company, and when it unveiled an innovative new prototype in 1931, the model became known as the Datson (son of DAT); then, a year later, the name was changed again, this time to Datsun, to take advantage of Japan's rising sun emblem.

Katayama was born September 15, 1909, in Tokyo, the son of Seishi Asoh and Satoko Katayama. He earned a B.A. in economics from Keio University in Tokyo in 1935 and went to work for Nissan later that year. Throughout the 1930s, and after World War II, he held a variety of sales promotion and advertising jobs. While serving in this capacity, he had begun surveying the U.S. market and its potential, and in 1958 he displayed the company's vehicles for the first time at the Los Angeles Imported Motor Car Show. That year, he sold 58 Datsuns in the United States, and in 1960 he became vice-president of the newly established Nissan Motor Corporation in the United States.

Katayama believed racing could help promote his vehicles by demonstrating their ruggedness, so he established an active program to encourage sports-car racers; Datsuns quickly gained a reputation for quickness and durability on the track. In addition, he believed in staying very close to his dealers, and Nissan's loyal dealer network was soon setting new industry standards for service. Katayama, in 1965, was made president of the company's U.S. operation.

Katayama became famous for his adoption of American culture. He loved fishing, mountain-climbing, and American football; also opening new dealerships with huge parties and showing up for Texas barbecues in a ten-gallon hat. But the growing publicity surrounding Katayama and his flamboyant ways became increasingly disturbing to the home office. He had headed the U.S. operation for 10 years, during which time the company's annual American sales increased to 263,000 units. But in January 1975, Nissan named Hiroshi Majima to succeed "Mr. K" as president of U.S. operations, with Katayama assuming the largely honorary title of chairman. Two years later, the man who had opened the U.S. market for Nissan—and, some would argue, for the entire Japanese auto industry—was unceremoniously recalled to Japan and told he had "resigned."

WILLIAM LYONS

In England at the dawn of the motor age, all the dashing young men-about-

1927: Ford announces plans to stop production of the Model T. Over 15 million Model Ts were produced.

town rode those sporty new motorcycles—with sidecars, of course, in order to escort the young ladies about town. The only problem was that sidecars in those days left much to be desired in the area of comfort. In 1922, William Lyons, then 21, and his friend Bill Walmsley thought they could build a better version, and they set up a company to manufacture what they called the Swallow Sidecar. They were quite successful and eventually expanded their business to include the manufacturer of automobile bodies. But Lyons had greater ambitions. He wanted to build automobiles.

Lyons arranged for the Standard Motor Company to supply him with engines and chassis to fit a body that he designed. The final product, assembled at Lyons's plant, was a sporty little touring machine known as the SS-1. Lyons continued to improve his designs and, by 1935, had developed a beautiful, sleek sports model that he called the SS-Jaguar. Its successor, with a bigger engine and capable of 100 mph, was named the SS-100. It would eventually become one of the most desirable of British collector cars.

Through the years, the company expanded its line, producing a series of sedans and sports models that competed favorably with the best in the world. Following World War II, with memories of Hitler's dreaded SS Storm Troopers still fresh in the minds of the public,

Lyons changed the name of his firm to Jaguar Car Ltd. In 1948, he introduced the car that would make Jaguar a legend around the world: the XK-120. This fast, low-slung sports car quickly became the darling of the Hollywood set. Powered by the powerful, double-overhead-cam, inline-six XK engine, it also won Le Mans in 1951, the first British victory in 16 years. The 120 and its successors, the similarly styled 140 and 150, won their class at Le Mans from 1953 through 1957.

But by the end of the decade, the design had become somewhat dated. Lyons set his designers and engineers to work on a brand-new sports model. The result was the E-Type, perhaps the most famous Jaguar of all. At its introduction in 1961, the E-Type stood the world on end. No one had ever seen anything like it before on public roads. It was low. It was long, with virtually all of its length being carried ahead of the windshield. It had an interior that looked like the cockpit of a fighter plane. It was ungodly fast. And it handled better than almost anything on the road. The sinewy, sensuous E-Type was to become one of the greatest successes in automotive history.

Although Jaguar Cars Ltd. was a highly profitable enterprise, by the mid-1960s Lyons had begun to express concern for the future of the company. His children were more interested in farming than manufacturing, and there

1927: First man to exceed 200 mph on land is Englishman Henry Seagrave. He drives his twin-engine 1,000-hp Sunbeam at a top speed of 207 mph in a race in Daytona Beach, Florida.

was no one to whom he could turn over the reins of power. In 1966, he merged with the British Motor Corporation, parent company of the Austin Morris Group. Lyons attempted to keep Jaguar as independent as possible, but inevitably it became involved with BMC's losses and decline. Still, as a member of the BMC board, Lyons introduced the XJ sedan series, which is still Jaguar's mainstay today. He retired in 1972 and died in 1985. Since Lyons's retirement, Jaguar has gone through many corporate changes, including going private again in 1984 then, later, becoming part of the Ford empire. But whatever its organizational status, Jaguar cars have, since the 1930s, been a symbol of speed, handling, and quality, ranking them among the finest and most prestigious vehicles in the world.

TOM AND RAY MAGLIOZZI

To a growing audience of fans, the Magliozzi brothers are the last word in car-repair advice. With their weekly *Car Talk* show on National Public Radio a certified success, these former full-time mechanics dispense wisdom on almost any auto ailment listeners can lob their way.

Tom Magliozzi was born in 1938, his brother Ray in 1950. They both graduated from Massachusetts Institute of Technology, with Tom going on to earn a Ph.D. He worked as a marketing and engineering expert for a manufacturing company for 12 years, while Ray worked as a VISTA volunteer in San Antonio, Texas, and as a junior-high school teacher in Vermont. In 1971, the brothers opened Hacker's Haven, a do-it-yourself car-repair shop in Cambridge, Massachusetts, which reopened as a professional repair service under the name Good News Garage. They made their radio debut with a car-repair advice show on public station WBUR in Boston in 1976. *Car Talk* premiered on National Public Radio in 1987. Ray still works at Good News Garage, and Tom has become a marketing instructor at Suffolk University in Boston. They also now write a syndicated advice column that appears in more than 70 newspapers.

The brothers' wacky, shoot-from-the-hip style has endeared them to an audience that might not really be looking for car-care tips. The NPR brass have not classified *Car Talk* as news or information, but as an arts and performance broadcast. As one radio exec told *Rolling Stone,* "A lot of [our] listeners don't even own cars. Even our classical stations are picking [the show] up. . . . Like most hit things, it's just a phenomenon."

The Magliozzis often get questions on how to buy a car. To that end, they suggest never paying more than $5 a

1927: Henry Ford spends $1.5 million on one week's worth of print ads touting the new Ford Model A.

pound and (for safety purposes) never buying a car that weighs less than 3,000 pounds. When asked about squealing brake pads, they explain that this is dolphin language for, "replace me, replace me." And they maintain that if you own a standard transmission and you don't stall out at least once a day, you're wearing out the clutch.

MICHAEL MOORE

He's been called everything from a Cinderella story to a modern-day incarnation of Mark Twain to a hypocrite who abuses his privileges. Michael Moore is a muckraking journalist-turned-filmmaker and the creative spark behind one of the most popular and controversial documentaries ever, *Roger & Me*. The film follows writer/director/narrator Moore as he attempts to confront Roger Smith, then chairman of General Motors, on the effect that a series of layoffs in the 1980s had on Moore's native Flint, Michigan. Moore's goal: to take Smith on a tour of Flint, or at least get him to comment on the layoffs.

Moore was born c. 1954, in Flint, Michigan, the son of Frank (an assembly-line worker) and Veronica (a secretary) Moore. He attended the University of Michigan, Flint, and in 1976 founded a newspaper, the *Flint Voice*

(later called the *Michigan Voice*), which he edited until 1985. That year, he began working as a commentator on the *All Things Considered* program on National Public Radio. He moved to San Francisco in 1986, where he became editor of *Mother Jones* magazine. It was also in 1986 that he became an independent filmmaker, which led to the *Roger & Me* project.

Without studio funding, Moore was forced to rely on creative financing to produce his film. He held garage sales, then sold his house. He also ran bingo games. Filming over several months took Moore from Flint to GM headquarters in Detroit to New York City. And, although Moore knew less than nothing about filmmaking, he was able to rely on Kevin Rafferty, of *Atomic Cafe* fame, and Anne Bohlen, director of the Oscar-nominated *With Babies and Banners*, for technical support.

When the documentary was released in late 1989, *Roger & Me* quickly appeared on many movie critics' top-ten lists. Throughout the film runs the thread of a "plot" that has Moore trying to gain an audience with Smith. The filmmaker showed up at GM corporate offices (being turned away after showing a pizza-parlor discount card as I.D.) and haunted the neighborhoods and clubs Smith was known to frequent.

At the same time, the film depicts bleak Flint scenes, showing the results of the plant closings. One man regular-

1927: Commemorating the 10 millionth Model T, the Boston Symphony records "Flivver Ten Million," which includes rattles, bangs, honks, and explosions.

ly sells his blood; a woman raises rabbits for "pets or meat." The only Flint resident portrayed with a steady job is a sheriff's deputy who presides over evictions—on Christmas Eve.

As the film ends, Moore is shown finally gaining entry into a GM shareholders' meeting where the elusive Smith was holding forth. When Moore rises and identifies himself, Smith abruptly calls the meeting to a close.

SHIRLEY MULDOWNEY

Few other sports stars of her caliber have ever been as little known to the general public as Shirley "Cha Cha" Muldowney. She was a pioneer woman who bucked the male dominance of drag racing, went on to excel in that sport, and became the first racer—male or female—to win the National Hot Rod Association's top-fuel world championship three times. Her lifestyle and accomplishments were featured in a Hollywood film, *Heart Like a Wheel.* But despite more than a quarter century of success in her field, Muldowney failed to achieve superstar status. As she once told *The New York Times,* "The most I ever got noticed was from an English Leather commercial I did in 1975. I'm the best at what I do, but I

can still go shopping without being recognized."

Muldowney was born in 1940 in Burlington, Vermont. Her interest in cars began when her father, Belgium Benedict Rocque (a taxi driver and professional boxer) taught her to drive at the age of 12. Her first hot rod, a 1951 Mercury, built for her by her boyfriend, Jack Muldowney, provided the means for her to begin drag racing on the streets of Schenectady, New York. She dropped out of school at the age of 16 to marry Muldowney (they were divorced in 1972).

In 1959 they began racing professionally. Jack, with superior mechanical skills, built the cars and headed the pit crew, while Shirley, the more daring of the two, drove. In the early days, she was frequently booed by spectators who saw no room for a woman in the macho world of hot-rod racing. But in 1965, Muldowney became the first woman to be licensed by the National Hot Rod Association (NHRA) to operate a top-gas dragster. Although she was initially considered mainly a curiosity and gate attraction on the dragster circuit, Muldowney quickly proved she had the talent and guts to excel. She won several regional titles in the early 1970s and, after surviving several crashes and a divorce, she moved up to top-fuel dragsters, once again becoming the first woman licensed at this level of competition.

1928: Chrysler Corporation buys the Dodge Brothers Motor Company and also introduces the Plymouth and DeSoto lines, with rousing success, the same year. Chrysler becomes the third largest U.S. automaker.

Top-fuel dragsters are stiletto-shaped, 24-foot cars that rocket down quarter-mile strips in less than six seconds, reaching speeds in excess of 250 miles per hour. They boast 2,500-horsepower engines and require a great deal of strength and quick reflexes to control, as well as a parachute to slow down. Muldowney gained a reputation as the fastest racer off the line in these monsters.

Altogether, Muldowney won almost 20 NHRA titles, more than any driver except Don Garlits. And she made more quarter-mile runs in less than six seconds, and more at 250 miles per hour, than any other driver at that time. Along the way, she took top-fuel world championships in 1977, 1980, and 1982.

RALPH NADER

Ralph Nader became America's best known consumer activist through his struggle to improve automobile safety. He was an advisor to a Senate subcommittee on automobile safety that attracted large media coverage, especially when it was revealed that General Motors made a $1.7 billion dollar profit in 1964 but spent only $1.25 million in safety research. In his report to the subcommittee and in his book, *Unsafe at any Speed: The Designed-in Dangers of the American Automobile* (1966), Nader focused on design flaws in the Chevrolet Corvair that made it susceptible to rollover accidents.

By 1966, Congress passed the National Traffic and Motor Vehicle Safety Act, which required automakers to offer 17 safety features—including seat belts, padded instrument columns, side-mounted reflectors, and collapsible steering columns—as standard equipment on all American cars. Meanwhile, Nader's book, which had been selling modestly, became a bestseller after media disclosures that employees of General Motors had Nader followed and tapped his telephone in an effort to find information that could discredit him. General Motors President James M. Roche issued a public apology. Nader sued General Motors for invasion of privacy and used the out-of-court settlement to fund several consumer agencies, including the Center for Auto Safety.

Nader was born February 27, 1934, in Winsted, Connecticut, youngest of four children. The family was intensely activist, and Nader's early reading included books and articles by muckrakers—journalists who exposed political corruption and manufacturing dangers during the early part of the twentieth century. After graduating with a degree in Public and International Affairs from Princeton, Nader entered Harvard Law School and began researching automo-

1929: First station wagon offered as a private car is a version of the Ford Model A.

00149

bile safety. He had witnessed several horrible accidents while hitchhiking around the country, and in 1961 a close friend of his was paralyzed in an automobile accident. An article he wrote on automobile safety caught the attention of New York Senator Daniel Patrick Moynihan, and when Moynihan became an official in the Kennedy administration he commissioned Nader to conduct a study for the Department of Labor. This study was utilized by the Senate subcommittee and was expanded into Nader's best-selling book.

PAUL NEWMAN

All right, so he's a great actor. He's been in some of the most popular movies of all time, and he's won all kinds of awards and praise for his work in films. He's also politically active and a great humanitarian, having founded a business empire mainly to raise money for charity. But Paul Newman has also made a name for himself driving race cars.

In 1972, Newman needed to learn some basic racing moves for his role in the film *Winning*. He was hooked. At first racing sports cars was simply his means of escaping the pressures of Hollywood, and he was seen as something of an oddity by the other drivers. But four years later he drove a Triumph

TR-6 to a national championship and was awarded the President's Cup, the highest amateur award given by the Sports Car Club of America.

He turned professional in 1977, and his team ended up taking fifth place that year at the Daytona 24-hour race. By 1979 he had honed his skills enough to come in second at Le Mans, the most prestigious sports-car race of them all. He was averaging 25 races per year, and some film critics even thought his passion for driving was having an influence on his other career: after a few clinkers, he starred in a steady stream of hits.

In addition to racing, Newman has delved into the equally demanding world of team ownership. He was co-owner of an Indy car driven by Mario and Michael Andretti. But he admits he was never a very active team manager, preferring to leave the day-to-day work to the professionals, freeing him to worry about his own driving—among other things. As Newman, then 65, once said of his co-driver, 22-year-old Scott Sharp: "He's worried about winning the race. I'm worried about having a pulse."

BARNEY OLDFIELD

It's impossible to say who was the best or most famous racing driver of all

---

1930: Automobile oil cooling systems and the automotive use of stainless steel are introduced.

time. There are too many drivers and too many different types of racing for those kinds of comparisons. But when it comes to well-known and influential—not to mention colorful—American drivers, it's hard to top Barney Oldfield.

Born June 3, 1878, in Wauseon, Ohio, Oldfield left school at the age of 12. He liked to tell reporters that his first driving job was in the elevator of the Monticello Hotel in Toledo. By 1894 he had made a name for himself as a bicycle racer. In 1902 he was living in Salt Lake City and racing a gas-powered English racing bike when he learned from a friend that a man named Henry Ford was building a couple of race cars. Oldfield moved to Detroit to get in on the action.

He arrived just as Ford was getting ready to do some tests at a track in Grosse Pointe, Michigan. But neither of Ford's two cars would start, and the disgusted Ford sold them both to Oldfield and his friend. They did further work on the cars and eventually got one of them running; they named it "999" after a famous railroad train. Once Ford saw that the car performed well enough, he regained interest and the trio began preparing for a run at the mile speed record. On October 25, 1902, they towed the car to frozen Lake St. Clair (the unsprung car needed the smooth surface), where Oldfield broke the record, driving the mile in 1:01.2.

Unfortunately, the newly formed AAA disallowed the new record for obscure technical reasons, beginning a lifelong hate on the part of Oldfield for all sport organizing bodies.

But Oldfield lowered the record with further runs in Old 999, broadening his reputation in the process. With exhibitions around the country, he undoubtedly did more than anyone else to establish the sport of motor racing in the United States. He became a familiar figure at country fairs, driving wildly around dirt tracks, cigar clamped in his teeth, arms sawing madly at the huge steering wheel.

Unfortunately, he was less successful in organized racing, mainly because repeated suspensions by the AAA often kept him from competing. But during his active periods, Oldfield made appearances at all the famous races, including Indianapolis, where he drove to fifth-place finishes in 1914 and 1916. He drove for all the top teams of the day: Mercer, Stutz, Maxwell, Delage, and Peugeot, and he helped make a name for the Firestone Tire and Rubber Company with his slogan, "Firestone tires are my only life insurance."

Oldfield retired in 1918. His investment in Firestone paid off very well, and he was quite wealthy until the Depression hit in 1929. After that, he appeared in a movie, spent time writing his memoirs, and ended up working at a California country club. In 1946 he

1930: Police cars are equipped with dispatch radios.

was honored by the auto industry and by the city of Detroit for his contributions to racing. He died later that year in Beverly Hills.

Ranse thinks he can put an engine in a buggy and make the contraption carry him over the roads. If he doesn't get killed at his fool undertaking, I will be satisfied." So stated Ransom Olds' father in 1886 about his son's experiments with steam engines. Among the pioneers of the American automobile industry, Ransom Eli Olds had the longest track record with motor vehicles, produced the first inexpensive, dependable American automobile—the 1901 "Curved Dash" Oldsmobile—and founded two prosperous car companies, Oldsmobile and REO.

Olds was born in Geneva, Ohio, on June 3, 1864, the youngest of five children. His father was a blacksmith at the time, later working as a superintendent at an iron works firm, and then as a farmer. In 1880 the elder Olds opened a machine shop in Lansing, Michigan, under the name P.F. Olds & Son (the "son" was Ransom's older brother, Wallace). At 21, Ransom bought out his brother's share and quickly asserted himself as the firm's leader, developing

a steam engine that greatly increased the company's revenue. As early as 1892, Olds' steam engines in horseless carriages were receiving attention in newspapers and magazines, and an 1893 steamer carriage was among the first American-made motor vehicles to be sold. (An early Olds also became one of the first American-made cars to be exported when it was sold to an Englishman who had it shipped to India; the man was never heard from again, but the car presumably was a "first ever" on some subcontinental road.) Olds also experimented with electric motors, but he turned his full attention to gas engines after viewing several on display at the Chicago World's Fair in 1893. Olds constructed a powerful gasoline engine in 1896 and obtained a patent to produce "a road vehicle that will meet most of the requirements for the ordinary uses on the road." The Olds Motor Vehicle Company, founded in 1897, quickly produced its first car and established its presence. The terms of the patent were realized in the 1901 Olds Curved Dash Runabout.

After tiring over disputes with fellow Olds executives about building more expensive models, Olds left Olds in 1904 and founded REO, another eponymous company. The REO touring car, released in 1905, is a classic American automobile. REO soon surpassed Olds Motor Works in revenue and ranked among the top five companies in the country. But Olds began losing

---

1931: Japanese automobile manufacturing company Mazda begins making cars as the Toyo Kogyo Company Ltd.

From Ashes to Riches

Like 60 percent of the automotive ventures that were established at the turn of the century, the first Olds venture failed. In 1899 the Olds Motor Vehicle Company was reorganized into the Olds Motor Works with $500,000 in capital from Detroit investors, and a new plant was built on that city's riverfront. The company soon began producing a light, compact vehicle—the Curved Dash Runabout. Just when it appeared that Oldsmobile would take off, tragedy struck: the Olds factory burned down in March of 1901; salvaged was one completed model of the Curved Dash Runabout, along with plans, drawings, and automobile patterns for both electric and gasoline-driven vehicles.

Oldsmobile got help from the Dodge brothers—John and Horace, later manufacturers of their own cars—and other outside suppliers, who agreed to manufacture parts for the Curved Dash Olds. This helped avoid a production delay that threatened another business failure. The company was able to produce 425 cars in 1901, and 2,500 in 1902. This then phenomenal rate helped rank Michigan as the source of almost half the United States' motor vehicles.

interest in the automobile industry in 1908 and increasingly turned his attention elsewhere—to leisure activities,

aviation, boating, diesel engines, and designing and manufacturing the first practical gas-powered lawnmower.

NIKOLAUS OTTO

Okay, he never built a car. But what distinguished the early automobile from other forms of self-powered transportation, like steam wagons, was the internal-combustion engine. And it was Nikolaus Otto who developed the first practical, efficient engines using combustible gas and who paved the way for the later installation of such engines in land, sea, and air vehicles.

Otto was born on June 14, 1832, in the little town of Holzhausen, Germany. After attending the local schools, he began a commercial career in Cologne. The turning point in his life came when his attention was captured by the early gas engines, especially those built by French inventor Jean Lenoir in the mid-1800s. Lenoir's engines were an improvement over earlier models, but they still consumed fuel at an extravagant rate, making them even less efficient than steam engines.

Otto began experimenting. From 1861 to 1864, he was awarded patents in several countries for his design for a "vertical atmospheric gas engine," in which the piston was driven to the top

1932: U.S. Route 66 opens and links Chicago with Los Angeles. It later becomes popularized in song, literature, and on television.

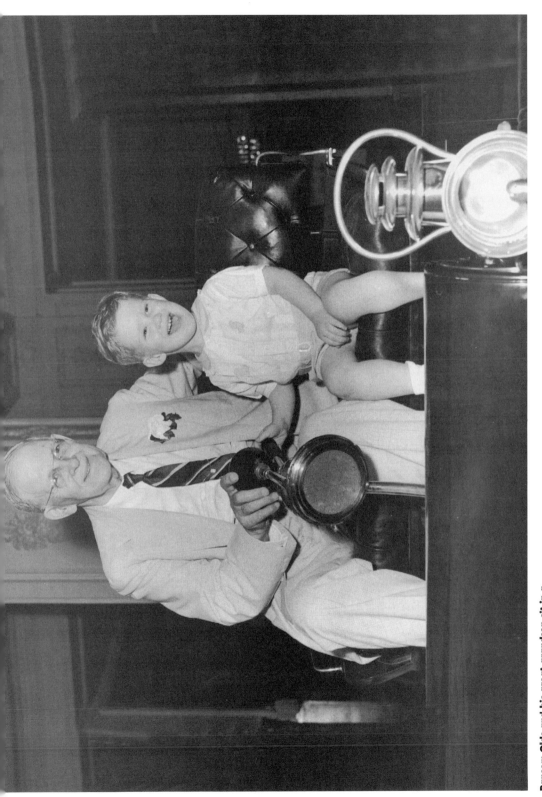

Ransom Olds and his great-grandson sit in a "Curved Dash" Oldsmobile.

Courtesy of American Automobile Manufacturers Association

of a cylinder by an explosion, and then descended by its own weight and the pressure of the atmosphere. In 1864, Otto teamed up with engineer Eugen Langren and founded the firm N.A. Otto and Company.

Their next important development was the application of the four-stroke concept to gasoline engines. They secured a patent for a new horizontal, four-stroke engine in 1876. The four-stroke principle (intake, compression, combustion, exhaust) had been described in 1862 by a French inventor, but he had never built a successful working model. Otto and Langren exhibited their four-stroke engine at the Paris Exhibition of 1878, where it created as big a stir as Otto's vertical engine a decade earlier.

From 1878 until his death in 1891, Otto continued to improve the efficiency of his engines. His high-speed, "silent" gas engine, as manufactured by several firms throughout the world, became recognized as one of the most efficient machines of its day, and for certain types of work (all stationary applications) it began to take over for the firmly established steam engine. Although the modern internal-combustion engine is the result of more than 100 years of work by numerous inventors and engineers, it may be said that the work of Nikolaus Otto served as the bridge from experimentation to practical machine.

ROGER PENSKE

Although he got his start racing motorcycles, dragsters, and sports cars, for more than 20 years now, Roger Penske has been the man whose name is synonymous with the Indianapolis 500. This independent auto executive and founder of the hugely successful Penske Corporation—which includes such ventures as car dealerships, truck leasing operations, and diesel engine manufacturing—has also spawned the most successful Indy-car racing team in history.

The tall, silver-haired Penske has been associated with some of the top names in motorsports: Mark Donahue, Mario Andretti, Al Unser, Rick Mears, and Danny Sullivan. With such talent behind the wheels, Penske Racing has won more than 50 Indy-car races, including seven Indianapolis 500 championships.

Penske was born in 1937 in Shaker Heights, Ohio. While in high school, he began racing motorcycles and dragsters and then moved on to sports cars while attending Lehigh University, from which he earned a B.S. in business administration. After graduation in 1959 he went to work as a sales engineer for Alcoa. At the same time, he continued his racing career, becoming Sports Car Club of America (SCCA) national dri-

---

1932: First fully modern highway system, the German autobahn ("automobile road") network, opens to traffic.

Roger Penske talks to driver Rick Mears during an Indy 500 practice session.
AP/Wide World Photos

ving champion in 1960 and 1961. He went to work as general manager of a Chevrolet dealership in Philadelphia in 1964 and became the owner of the dealership a year later. In 1966 he founded Penske Racing, from which would grow the Penske Corporation, the empire for which he is now famous.

Overall, Penske's businesses are among the most successful in the country. The parent firm itself spurted from annual revenues of $75 million in 1977 to more than $1 billion a decade later. The Retail Automotive Group sells cars and trucks through a number of dealerships throughout the country. The Transportation Services Group includes Hertz Penske Truck Leasing, a joint venture with Hertz Corporation, which operates fleets of lease vehicles from coast to coast. And Detroit Diesel Corporation, a joint venture between Penske and General Motors, designs, builds, and sells diesel engines around the world. The chief executive officer of this automotive empire has established a reputation as a hard-working, savvy, hands-on executive.

RICHARD PETTY

He is affectionately called King Richard, a tribute for having won more than 200 stock car races and for drawing legions of fans who came especially to watch him race. During his 34-year career, which ended with a celebrated retirement tour in 1992, Richard Petty was an ambassador for stock car racing, readily available for autographs and interviews, and a charismatic presence with his feathered cowboy hat, dark glasses, and long lean look. He was also the greatest stock car driver, winning seven NASCAR championships, seven Daytona 500s, and more than $7 million in earnings. He dominated the sport through the 1960s and 1970s; in 1967 alone, Petty won 27 of 48 races, including an unprecedented 10 wins in a row.

Petty was born July 2, 1937, in Randleman, North Carolina. His father, Lee, started racing in 1947, and Richard began working as a mechanic on his father's racing cars during his spare time. Lee Petty was a three-time NASCAR Grand National Champion. Richard began racing in 1958. Both Richard and Lee Petty competed in the first Daytona 500 in 1959, which Lee won. The 1960 Daytona, won by Junior Johnson, was the first time Petty finished ahead of his dad; Richard passed the finish line first in an earlier race that year, but his father charged past him during the "victory lap." Lee protested that scorers had missed a lap in their count and was proven correct. After a serious accident in 1961, Lee Petty concentrated on managing the family racing team, and Richard began to amass victory after victory, becoming the King of Stock Car

1932: Visors move inside cars and fender skirts are introduced.

00158

Racing and part of a family dynasty continued by his son, Kyle. Memorabilia from Richard Petty's career, including his three most successful race cars, is on display at the family-operated Richard Petty Museum in Randleman.

FERDINAND PORSCHE

From an innovative electric car in the 1890s to the highly efficient and sporty Porsche, Ferdinand Porsche had a career unparalleled for longevity in automobile innovation and refinement. He was involved in the design of more significant automobiles and components than any other engineer. Porsche developed classic models for Panhard, Austro-Daimler, Mercedes-Benz, Auto-Union, Volkswagen, Renault, and Cisitalia. Substantial improvements in torsion-bar suspension, swing axles, the opposed-cylinder engine, and the rear engine are among his many other contributions to automobile design. He designed luxury models, Grand Prix cars, touring cars that won Grand Prix races, and the "car of the people"—the Volkswagen Beetle (as it was called in the United States).

Porsche was born on September 3, 1875, in Maffersdorf, then part of Bohemia. He was the third child of a prosperous tinsmith who objected to young Ferdinand's obsession with electricity, at least until the precocious teenager installed electrical lighting in the family home in 1890. Porsche built an electric car in the 1890s and in 1897 patented the Mixte transmission, in which gas generates electric power that is transmitted to motors mounted in the wheels. In 1905 he was named Managing Director of Austro-Daimler, succeeding Paul Daimler; the 1909 and 1910 Austro-Daimler touring cars were among the finest of the time. During World War I Porsche engines were used in planes and trains. After the war Porsche joined Daimler-Benz (which became Mercedes-Benz in 1926), where he won international fame for touring cars of exceptional quality and speed, excellent for cruising and racing. In 1930, Porsche formed his own company, where he was joined by his son, Ferry. The Porsche Buro contributed designs to several manufacturers, patented an improved torsion bar, and perfected Porsche's vision of a car for the masses—which became the Volkswagen after Hitler assumed power and the state seized control of manufacturing operations.

After the war, Porsche was interred by Allied forces for having assisted the German war effort, although there was no evidence that Porsche had Nazi sympathies. While held captive in France, Porsche was consulted on the design of an improved Renault. After two years, he was freed on bond by the

1933: First drive-in movie opens in Camden, New Jersey. Although few now remain, these "passion pits" catered to the American teenagers' love of (and in) the automobile.

head of the Cisitalia firm in order to design a race car, and Porsche obliged with an innovative four-wheel-drive model. The first Porsche, which was designed primarily by Ferry based on modifications to the Volkswagen and other Porsche Buro plans, was released in 1947. Two years later, Ferdinand Porsche's 75th birthday celebration was held at a rally of Porsche owners. He died a year later. Meanwhile, the Porsche quickly established a reputation for excellent performance, a true reflection on the Porsche name.

CHARLES STEWART ROLLS AND FREDERICK HENRY ROYCE

Question: What could make a car worth more than an average three-bedroom suburban home? Answer: If you have to ask, you wouldn't understand. But Rolls-Royce has established a loyal following of customers who gladly pay such prices for the privilege of driving the car that for decades has symbolized quality, elegance, and opulence in motor vehicles.

Charles Stewart Rolls was the first Englishman to fly with Wilbur Wright, a founding member of the Royal Aero Club, and the first aviator to complete a double crossing of the English Channel. In 1902, with the backing of his father,

Lord Llangattock, he had gone into the business of selling Panhard automobiles—without much success. But in 1904, he met Frederick Henry Royce, a pioneering British automotive inventor, who had just tested the first of three experimental vehicles that he intended to begin offering for sale. Royce's insistence on the highest standards of workmanship greatly impressed Rolls, who immediately offered to sell all the cars Royce could build. Thus was formed one of the great partnerships in automotive history.

The two worked tirelessly at their respective ends of the business, and they did quite well, producing and distributing a line of two-, four-, and six-cylinder vehicles that sold respectably and proved competitive on the racing circuits. Then, in 1906, they introduced the model that would make their cars the darlings of the rich and famous—the Silver Ghost. As the British magazine *The Autocar* exclaimed in April of 1907: "At whatever speed this car is being driven . . . there is *no* engine so far as sensation goes, nor are one's auditory nerves troubled driving or standing by a fuller sound than emanates from an eight-day clock." In addition to establishing Rolls-Royce's reputation for smoothness and solidity, the Silver Ghost proved extraordinarily durable; one of these cars set a world's record in a reliability trial: 8,854 miles, non-stop. The legend was born.

1933: President Franklin D. Roosevelt and Chicago Mayor Anton Cermak are riding in a Buick Touring Car as Guiseppe Zangara attempts to assassinate Roosevelt.

Charles Stewart Rolls was killed at Bournemouth, England, on July 12, 1910, in the crash of a plane he was flying. Royce continued on as head of the firm until his death in 1933 at the age of 70. During World War I, Rolls-Royce produced a line of armored cars for the British Army, some of which saw use in World War II, almost 30 years later. Beginning in 1914, the company went into the business of manufacturing aircraft engines, which saw service in both World Wars and became famous in their own right.

But, of course, it was the cars that built the Rolls-Royce reputation. And through the years, up to the present day, those cars have been among the most highly prized vehicles ever produced, occupying a place in the garages of royalty, business magnates, Hollywood celebrities, and others who don't need to ask the price or what makes the cars worth it.

Lyn St. James alters any stereotypes one might have about classical musicians. The racing driver, writer, teacher, businesswoman, and pianist is not shy and retiring. Rather, she breaks speed records. In her forties she drove in her first Indianapolis 500, only the second woman to compete in the 81-year history of that prestigious and grueling event, finishing 11th in a starting field of 33 professional drivers.

In the 1960s, the teenage Evelyn Cornwall (she is said to have taken her last name from that of television actress Susan Saint James) began to take an interest in the muscle cars and hot rods being built by her male friends. She got serious about driving fast and, in 1976, became the Sports Car Club of America Florida Region class champion in Showroom Stock. She repeated the performance in 1977, and in 1981 was recruited by Ford Motor Company to join its motorsports program, a role she continues to fill.

St. James spent 16 years preparing the groundwork for her debut at the Indy 500 in 1992. Along the way, she became the first woman to average more than 200 mph on an oval track and the first woman to win the North American professional road race driving solo in the GTO class. She won the GTO class at the famed Daytona 24 Hours in 1987 and 1990, and set several speed records. Finally, she was able to convince sponsors like J.C. Penney, Agency Rent-a-Car, Goodyear, and Danskin to back her million-dollar car, owned by Dick Simon, at Indianapolis.

Named Rookie of the Year at the 1992 Indy 500, St. James was the first woman to capture that honor. A longtime advocate of greater opportunities

1933: Nash offers an automobile color called "Eleanor Blue" in honor of Eleanor Roosevelt, the president's wife.

for women in sports, she has been involved with the Women's Sports Foundation for many years. She has also served as director of consumer relations for the Car Care Council, a trade group that addresses safety and maintenance concerns on behalf of vehicle owners. In addition, St. James has become a successful writer, with the publication of a book, *Lyn St. James' Car Owner's Manual,* and a regular newspaper column in which she answers readers' questions about cars.

CARROLL SHELBY

Even people who don't particularly follow sports car racing know the name Carroll Shelby. Perhaps no single individual had more influence than Shelby on post-World War II American sports car design and racing.

Shelby, the son of a mail clerk, was born January 11, 1923, in Leesburg, Texas. His interest in cars began during his childhood in Dallas, where he went on to own a series of old Fords, Dodges, and a host of other vehicles. After military service as a pilot, he got involved in a variety of business enterprises and started racing cars in his spare time. He competed in his first road-race in 1952, driving an MG TC, and winning not only his own class but also beating a

much faster Jaguar XK-120. He began making a name for himself.

Shelby continued racing, competing in Jaguars, Ferraris, Austin-Healeys, Allards, Maseratis, and Aston Martins. His reputation spread rapidly, and in 1954 he drove at Le Mans for the first time. He made his first appearance in Formula One in 1955, at the Italian Grand Prix. In 1957 he had what is probably his finest year as a driver, winning 19 straight races and capturing his second SCCA championship. Unfortunately recurring pain from a back injury suffered in a crash in 1957, coupled with ongoing bouts of heart trouble, forced him to retire from racing after the 1960 season.

But Shelby had long dreamed of building a sports racer that could take on the European cars and beat them at their own game. In 1961 he learned that the Bristol engine company, which supplied motors for the British-built AC Bristol sports car, had gone out of business. He arranged for AC to supply the cars and Ford to provide high-performance V8 engines. The resulting car was the Shelby AC Cobra, one of the most potent, fire-breathing vehicles ever to be built in America. They cost $5,995—not cheap but certainly competitive with the Ferraris, Maseratis, and Corvettes they were built to compete with.

Following the success of the AC Cobra, Shelby was enlisted by Ford to develop a special edition of its popular

1934: First coil-spring independent front suspension is introduced by Cadillac. These heavy spring steel rods are shaped in a spiral and are used to provide support between the front wheels and the car body.

Carroll Shelby's AC Cobra is highly prized among collectors.
Courtesy of Lynn Park

Mustang. The Shelby GT-350 Mustang made its debut in January of 1965 (the GT-500 would follow), sporting a unique body-trim package, sports suspension, and a special edition of the Ford V8 engine. Meanwhile, Shelby's firm, Shelby-American, continued its winning ways with the Cobra, until—finally overshadowed by the more comfortable muscle-cars being built by all of the big-three—production ceased on the tireless little Ferrari-eater.

But Shelby continued working on a variety of Ford projects and managing race teams, leaving his mark on TransAm, CanAm, and, of course, Le Mans. Gradually his active racing days tapered off. But the cowboy-hatted Texan with no formal engineering background had left a racing and manufacturing heritage that has become legend among legions of sports-car enthusiasts.

ALFRED P. SLOAN, JR.

Good timing is essential for engine performance and, as Alfred P. Sloan, Jr., demonstrated, this general motor truism applies to business as well. Almost all of the giants of automotive history are visionary and quirky inventors and/or aggressive, flamboyant promoters. Sloan was a methodical businessman and manager who proved as influential as anyone in the industry's

success. General Motors became the world's largest corporation under Sloan's leadership; he devised the GM corporate structure, which became the most frequently adopted business organizational method in the twentieth century; and he established the annual emphasis on new car styles and features so vital to car crazy culture.

Alfred Pritchard Sloan, Jr., was born on May 23, 1875, in New Haven, Connecticut, the oldest of five children. His father was part owner of a wholesale tea, cigar, and coffee business—Bennett-Sloan & Company—and the business and family moved to New York City in 1895, where Sloan acquired a Brooklyn accent (which he nevah qwite lost). Sloan graduated with a bachelor's degree in electrical engineering from the Massachusetts Institute of Technology in 1895 and became a draftsman for the Hyatt Roller Bearing Company. The firm's owner was an eccentric inventor, John Wesley Hyatt, whose successful creations include a tapered roller bearing and celluloid, but who didn't have much business sense. Sloan rounded up some investors and became the firm's business manager. Good timing: the company soon became the largest manufacturer of roller bearings in the United States, feeding the suddenly booming auto industry. Sloan assumed control of the company and made frequent visits to Detroit. Since the company was geared for mass production, its profitability became utterly depen-

1934: Built-in radios are introduced in some automobiles.

dent on the automobile industry, so Sloan sought ways to assure the stability of this relationship. Good timing: the firm was one of several, including Charles F. Kettering's Dayton Engineering Laboratories Company (Delco), purchased by quickly expanding General Motors in 1916 to form the United Motors Corporation division.

This was a period of great confusion and power struggles at GM, led by its aggressive founder William C. Durant, who had regained control of the company through ingenious political and financial moves—GM was actually owned by one of its subsidiaries, Durant's Chevrolet Motor Car Company. In 1918, GM was reorganized and reincorporated and Sloan was made a vice-president. He submitted a plan for a large scale corporate restructuring (good timing), which was implemented during the 1920s and became the dominant model for corporate organizational structure in the twentieth century. The system promotes autonomous divisions with chains-of-command similar to military units and a central office that oversees the divisions and distinguishes whether decisions are made at corporate or division level. The organizational principle brought order and efficiency to GM's vast holdings, and the company prospered remarkably. Sloan became president of GM in 1923 and by the middle of the decade GM surpassed Ford as the world's largest automaker.

As president of GM, Sloan was able to balance authority and autonomy. He wooed William S. Knudson away from Ford Motor Company and placed him in charge of Chevrolet. Good timing: this came at a critical period when Henry Ford stubbornly stuck with the Model T; through improved production methods and savvy advertising campaigns, Chevrolet surpassed Ford as the top producer of low-priced cars. Sloan institutionalized the concept of introducing new styles and features annually to induce consumers to "trade up" and to ensure continually increasing sales. The first design department was created during this time with free rein to introduce style changes regardless of whether or not they improved function. Sloan vigorously pursued his objective of having GM cars "for every purse and every purpose." The Oakland Division of GM built a new six-cylinder car, the Pontiac, in 1926. Additional growth for GM occurred through other timely decisions: Sloan expanded GM's foreign influence just prior to the Great Depression and established a strong and lasting foothold; GM entered aviation in a big way at about the time of Charles Lindbergh's New York-to-Paris flight (1927); Sloan placed Charles Kettering in charge of improving the diesel engine (GM became the largest producer of these engines during the 1930s, when diesel locomotives replaced steam engines on American railroads and diesels became the favored motor for trucks

1934: "Cat's eyes," the rubber-mounted reflectors that "line" traffic lanes at night or in fog, are invented by Englishman Percy Shaw.

General Motors became the world's largest corporation under the leadership of Alfred P. Sloan, Jr.
Courtesy of American Automobile Manufacturers Association

and busses); GM, though grudgingly, became the first of the Big Three automakers to recognize the UAW; and, after Sloan retired as president in 1937 to become chairman of GM, he organized the company's contribution to the war effort—GM produced $12 billion in material for World War II.

Following the war, Sloan served GM primarily in an advisory capacity, though his influence was felt until 1956, when he effectively retired at age 81. Along with his legacy of having transformed General Motors into the world's largest and most profitable corporation, he established the Alfred P. Sloan Foundation, which promotes the study of science and technology in relation to economic and social improvement; the Sloan-Kettering Foundation for Cancer Research; and the Sloan School of Industrial Management at his alma mater, MIT. Through sound management principles and planning, not to mention good timing, Sloan became as vital as any other person to the phenomenal growth of the automotive industry. The title of Sloan's biography—*My Years with General Motors*—aptly captures the story of his life. He died in 1966.

JACKIE STEWART

One of a handful of personalities who helped transform Grand Prix racing from a somewhat obscure, elitist, pastime into an international spectator sport, Jackie Stewart developed an early interest in motor sports. His father owned a garage in Stewart's native Dumbarton, Scotland. The elder Stewart had raced motorcycles as a young man, and Jackie's older brother raced sports cars, making an appearance at Le Mans in the early 1950s.

Jackie was not a very good student (it was later concluded that he suffered from dyslexia), but he excelled at sports. And prior to beginning his racing career, he was an extremely gifted trap and skeet shooter, almost making the British Olympic Team.

Stewart began racing sports cars in 1961, competing in Porsches, AC Bristols, and Jaguars. He met team manager Ken Tyrrell of the Cooper Team, who was impressed enough with the young racer to give him his first chance to drive a single-seater, the Cooper Formula Three car. Stewart dominated the British F3 scene and, in the process, met the great car builder and team manager Colin Chapman, who offered him his first Formula One ride in the Lotus-Climax, which Stewart first drove in 1964. In an unusual display of skill for a rookie driver, on September 12, 1965, he won the Italian Grand Prix.

The offers were soon coming fast and furious. He drove his first Indianapolis 500 in 1966, unfortunately being forced to retire when his car's oil

1935: First car to offer windshield washers is the British Triumph.

Road Test

MATCH THE DRIVER WITH THE TYPE OF RACING FOR WHICH
HE/SHE IS BEST KNOWN. (YES, YOU CAN USE THE ANSWERS
MORE THAN ONCE!)

1. Jackie Stewart
2. Al Unser
3. Shirley "Cha Cha" Muldowney
4. Cale Yarborough
5. Danny Sullivan
6. Juan Manuel Fangio
7. Richard Petty
8. A.J. Foyt

A. Stock cars
B. Indy cars
C. Formula One
D. Drag racing

(Answers: 1.C 2.B 3.D 4.A 5.B 6.C 7.A 8.B)

pressure suddenly dropped. He was in the lead at the time, with only 20 miles left in the race.

For the 1968 season, Stewart joined Tyrrell's Matra team. At the end of that year, he trailed Graham Hill by only two points for the drivers' championship with only the Mexican Grand Prix left. For 38 laps the lead alternated between the two. But the Matra's fuel system gave out, leaving Stewart in second place for the year. But he came back in 1969, clinching the championship with three races still remaining on the schedule. For 1970, Tyrrell had prepared his

own car, and Stewart stuck with his old friend, abandoning the Matra with which he had just won a championship. It was an ingenious move. After winning championships in 1971 and 1973, Stewart would forever be associated with the beautiful blue Ford-powered Tyrells, not to mention the signature Scottish tartan band around his helmet. And, in addition to winning three championships, he topped Jim Clark's record of total Grand Prix wins by two, with a total of 27—a record that would stand for 14 years.

Jackie Stewart, perhaps the classi-

1935: U.S. automobile manufacturers change their annual New York Auto Show from January to November to spur demand through the usually slack winter months.

est of all Grand Prix champions, used his influence for the good of his sport and his fellow drivers. He campaigned tirelessly for improved safety in car and track design. And he proved to be a personable PR man, serving as television broadcaster and goodwill ambassador, explaining Formula One racing to audiences around the world, and working on behalf of many charitable organizations.

EIJI TOYODA

The chairman of one of the most powerful industrial clans in modern Japan, Eiji Toyoda has an almost Western flair as a go-getter and empire builder that belies his reputation in his own country as a staunch political and economic conservative. What Toyoda accomplished for his family business, Toyota Motors, was dazzling success at a time when Detroit automakers were struggling to stay profitable. Toyota, Japan's number-one automaker, spearheaded the tidal wave of small, low-priced cars that swept the United States during successive energy crises in the mid-to-late 1970s and helped change the face of American transportation.

Toyoda's uncle, Sakichi, inventor of Japan's first power-loom, founded the original family business, Toyoda Auto

matic Loom Works, in 1926 in Nagoya, about 200 miles west of Tokyo. Sakichi's son, Kiichiro, established Toyota Motor Company in 1937 as an affiliate of the Loom Works. (There are conflicting stories about why the spelling was changed when the firm was named, none of them officially confirmed.) The family was so involved in the business that Eiji's father, Heikich—younger brother of Sakichi—even made his home inside the factory. Eiji joined the firm in 1936 with a degree in mechanical engineering and was put to work on the company's first production automobile, a six-cylinder sedan.

After World War II, with Japan's industry in a shambles, the automaker began rebuilding its production facilities from scratch. Having been made director of the firm's manufacturing division, Eiji Toyoda took an extended trip to the United States to study American methodology. Upon returning to Japan, he radically redesigned his company's plants and processes based on what he had learned.

By 1967, he had become president of Toyota Motor company, and the firm continued to refine its products and its manufacturing techniques. When the energy crisis hit in the 1970s, Toyota was able to step up production to meet increased demand in the United States and around the world for smaller, more fuel-efficient transportation. Shortly thereafter, Toyota took its place as the

---

1935: World's first parking meter is installed in Oklahoma City. It looks like today's meters, only shorter.

0 0 1 6 9

world's third-largest automaker, behind GM and Ford.

PRESTON TUCKER

Preston Tucker was a throwback to the visionary tinkerers and flamboyant promoters who thrived in the free-market frontier of the automobile industry's pioneering days. The halt in car production during World War II and the prospect of a huge open market following the war made the mid-1940s seem as ripe for innovation and showmanship as the early days of the automobile. Tucker seized the day, touting a fast, stylish, safe, and revolutionary new car—the Tucker Torpedo. The thrilling attempt and agonizing failure to fulfill this dream reflects an idealist stalled by the status quo—as portrayed in the acclaimed 1986 film *Tucker: The Man and His Dream*—or the tale of a huckster whose great claims proved impractical.

Tucker was born on September 21, 1903, in Capac, Michigan. His father, Shirl, died when Tucker was two, and the family moved to a Detroit suburb now called Lincoln Park. While attending high school Tucker became car crazy and worked as an office boy at Cadillac for D. McCall White, whom he hired 25 years later to work at the Tucker Corporation. After high school, Tucker held

numerous jobs—car salesman, policeman, and mechanic for the famed Harry A. Miller, whose race cars dominated the Indianapolis 500 during the mid-1930s. He formed the Tucker Aviation Corporation in 1940 to manufacture a high-speed combat vehicle he designed. The vehicle was turned down because it was much faster than the army needed, but Tucker received a contract to produce a powered gun turret he had designed. Differences with his business partner led Tucker to leave this operation. He formed the Ypsilanti Machine and Tool Company in Ypsilanti, Michigan, the town where he settled with his wife, Vera, and five children.

In 1945 Tucker began releasing reports about a revolutionary new sports car—the Tucker Torpedo—he planned to build, and he formed the Tucker Corporation in 1946. Among the Torpedo's special features were three headlights, a powerful 589 cubic inch rear engine, numerous safety features—including a crash-proof interior compartment and standard safety belts—and aluminum and plastic construction. But Tucker struggled through three years of funding and design emergencies and disappointments. Mounting troubles culminated with bankruptcy and a federal indictment following a grand-jury probe of Tucker Corporation activities. Tucker and seven associates were charged with mail fraud conspiracies and false advertising. Despite presenting no defense witnesses—Tucker's at-

1936: The Oscar Mayer Wienermobile is born. Designed as a vehicle to transport the company's mascot—"Little Oscar, the world's smallest chef"—from store to store, the first Wienermobile rolls off the assembly line at a cost of $5,000.

torneys contended it was not necessary to defend something when there had been no offense—to counter a methodical presentation by Federal Prosecutors, Tucker and all his associates were acquitted late in 1949. Only about 50 Tuckers—renamed the Tucker 48—were actually built, and though they were impressively styled, quality automobiles, they were more conventional than originally planned. Tucker went out of business. New schemes for building a powerful and safe automobile were scrapped when he was diagnosed with cancer. He died in Ypsilanti on December 26, 1956.

1936: First pop-up headlights are offered on the innovative Cord Model 810 automobile. The lights are raised by manual winding. This classic car features a V8 engine, 125 hp, front-wheel drive, and a four-speed transmission.

Auburn-Cord-Duesenberg Museum

Auburn, Indiana

They were American classics. They roared out of the 1920s, with their low, sleek lines and their massive engines. The Auburn, the Cord, and the Duesenberg were the preferred vehicles of international playboys and rakish movie stars, tearing up the racing competition and the highways. And for a few years, just before their extinction in the Depression economy of the 1930s, the cars were all made in this northeastern Indiana town.

The first clutch-driven car with electrical ignition was built in Indiana and during the early days of the auto industry, the state was a leading manufacturing center. Studebaker remained a major player until the 1950s. But it was a young auto executive in Auburn, Indiana, E. L. Cord, who captured the country's heart: Joining the Auburn Company as a salesman, in 1926, at the age of 31, Cord became the head of the company. Almost immediately he acquired Duesenberg, the Indianapolis-based car company. Its cars were so glamorous and fast that they contributed a slang phrase to the language: "It's a doozy."

Cord was famous for driving around the country and stopping at service stations and garages, asking mechanics and motorists what they wanted in a car and how they thought a great car should look. By 1929, Auburn's line of luxury sedans had become a force in the industry. His stock car model was the first American machine to exceed 100 mph by stop watch.

But Cord was after something more, an ultimate driving machine. He teamed with a young designer, Gordon M. Buehrig, and in 1935 they brought forth the Cord 810. It had front-wheel drive, retractable headlights, a supercharged V8 engine that was capable of 115 mph. A total of 37 engineering firsts were in the car, 27 of which were adopted in standard production by the industry.

1936: San Francisco-Oakland Bay Bridge is opened to automobile traffic. Before this six-lane bridge was built, 35 million ferry boat commuters passed over the bay annually in trips that averaged one hour.

Cars of the past come alive at the Auburn-Cord-Duesenberg Museum.
Courtesy of Auburn-Cord-Duesenberg Museum

But with a selling price of $2,700, the Cord 810 was $800 more expensive than the Cadillac, the luxury car standard. In 1937, very few people were in a position to spend that kind of money for a car. It went out of production after two years and 2,320 models. A few months later the Auburn and Duesenberg lines shut down, too.

The country never forgot, though. Thirty years later, companies attempted—unsuccessfully—to build modern versions of the design. Among collectors, no American-made cars are more highly prized. At his 1965 retirement, Buehrig (who had subsequently gone on to Ford and helped design the Continental) said the comment about the Cord that pleased him most was: "It looks as if it was born on the road."

The museum is located in a former company showroom, built in 1930, and displays 140 classic cars, with special emphasis on those assembled in Auburn.

Location: Auburn is located off Interstate 69, about 20 miles north of Fort Wayne. The museum is off the Indiana 8 exit, at 1600 South Wayne Street.

Hours: Daily, 9–5.

Admission: $7 for adults, $4.50 for students.

Telephone: (219) 925-1444

Cadillac Ranch

Amarillo, Texas

Don't let 'em take me to the Cadillac Ranch," sang Bruce Springsteen, for ve-

Just Like the Good Ol' Days

The Auburn-Cord-Duesenberg Museum is the first automobile museum to inhabit an auto builder's original factory showroom building. When it opened its doors to the public on July 6, 1974, every remarkable characteristic of the 12,000-square-foot main display room had been revitalized: the elaborate, hand-painted ceiling friezes, ornate Italian three-tiered chandeliers, geometric terrazzo floor, 72 etched glass side lights, gracefully curving central grand staircase, Philippine walnut woodwork, and soaring plate glass windows carrying "AUBURN," "CORD," and "DUESENBERG" in blazing gold letters. The entire environment enjoyed by showroom visitors in the 1930s was recreated with successful authenticity. Today the museum is listed in the National Register of Historic Places and attracts 80,000 visitors a year.

hicles not yet ready for car heaven. But glory days will pass you by. What more fitting tribute for a car line synonmous with excellent performance and comfort than to be honored with a thoughtful final resting place. In tribute to all Cadillacs, 10 of the cars (symbolizing the 10 body presses of Cadillacs between 1948 and 1964) are buried out in

1936: A survey reveals that 54 percent of Americans now own cars.

The World's Largest Lemon Farm

Cadillac Ranch it ain't, but the largest collection of Edsels is owned by farmer Hugh Lesley of Oxford, Pennsylvania, who has 170 of the Ford models scattered around his farm.

the Texas panhandle, just off Route 66, west of Amarillo. They are buried with their proud fins up, nose into the ground up to the dashboard, at a mean lean of 52 degrees—the angle of the pyramids of Egypt.

"They're out there on the plains headed west on U.S. 66, just like the covered wagons," notes Stanley Marsh 3, the Texan who commissioned the project. "In my time," he states, "people went west in air-conditioned, hydromatic Cadillacs with six-way seats and radios that would seek their own channels."

Cadillac Ranch, one of the most popular roadside attractions in America, had its 20th birthday in 1994. That birthday was celebrated in the spirit of the Ranch. Marsh, sporting a six-inch pink Cadillac on his top hat, led a band of spray painters to express themselves on the previously pure white monuments. "I think graffiti shows that

Americans know how to treat their sculpture. It's like a message place."

Cadillac Ranch is open year 'round. Since part of the fun is finding it, get your kicks on Route 66 by heading west from Amarillo, a road so many Americans have traveled. "People were going to Las Vegas to break the bank, to the beach seeking blondes, to Hollywood to become a movie star," says Marsh. "[Cadillac Ranch] is a monument to the American Dream."

Location: Cadillac Ranch is just west of Amarillo on Route 66 (now I-40).

Carhenge

Alliance, Nebraska

Americans seem to have always held the conviction that anything Europeans could do, we could do better. Many U.S. cities pride themselves on their reproductions of famed European landmarks, from the elaborate to the cheesy. There is a strong impulse in our popular culture to improve upon the Old World's handiwork. That is one possible explanation for Carhenge.

Another explanation is that James Reinders simply liked to bury old cars in the ground. The Alliance resident planted 26 of them, back end first, in a grouping reminiscent of Stonehenge, the Neolithic monument on England's Salisbury Plain. Seven more vehicles

1936: Defrosters start to appear on automobiles.

Jim Reinders configured cars to the dimensions and specifications of England's Stonehenge.
Worley Studio

are fastened crosswise, to simulate the arches in the original. The surrounding treeless plain of western Nebraska even resemble the English moors. Well, kind of.

Scholars feel that Stonehenge was used as a solar observatory for religious rituals. Many people in Alliance feel that Carhenge has no use whatsoever except as a nuisance. Nevertheless, in 1989 the city council defeated an effort to have it dismantled, and granted it a zoning variance as a tourist attraction.

Location: Carhenge is located north of town, on U.S. 385.

Hours: Daily, dawn to dusk.

Admission: Free

Telephone: (308) 762-1520

Corvette Plant

Bowling Green, Kentucky

There probably has never been another American-made automobile that inspires the emotions a Corvette does in its owners. It is a different kind of car.

"To many men, their Corvette is their most precious possession," said one Michigan automobile restorer, who specializes in this car. "To some, it even comes before their wives." He quickly added, however, that about 5 percent of his business came from women and "they were the sort of people who were liberated long before women's lib became a movement."

Chevrolet was hoping for something like this when it first showed off the Vette at the 1953 General Motors Motorama. It was the pet project of GM's legendary design chief, Harley Earl. But only 300 were produced in the first year and, according to its engineer, Zora Arkus-Dontov, "it was really a dog. It was supposed to be a boulevard car in the mind of GM, but we turned it into a sports car." That's what it has remained, the quintessential American sports car.

While Ford also introduced a two-seater, its Thunderbird, in 1954 it soon became a standard passenger vehicle. But the Corvette, throughout its 29-year production history in St. Louis and since its move to Kentucky in 1983, has always been a car for serious drivers.

"The Corvette ranks just one notch below immortality on America's list of mechanical achievements," said a 1968 tribute in *Car and Driver* magazine. "Like barbed wire and the cotton gin, it borrows from no one. The Corvette is exciting, it's lusty, it stimulates all of the base emotion lurking deep in modern man."

These emotions run so deep that lawsuits are filed over the car. One Texas man sued GM in 1986 for making it a convertible again, claiming that when he bought his Corvette convertible in 1975 he was given certified as-

---

1936: The United Automobile, Aerospace, and Agricultural Implement Workers of America (UAW) is formed as a distinct union, after having been affiliated with the American Federation of Labor.

surance that it would be the last such model. The 35th anniversary model in 1988 backed up orders to such an extent that disappointed customers had to wait up to a year for delivery.

Still, the Corvette continues to be made slowly, and publicly. Despite the deliberate pace of its assembly line, about one-quarter the speed of standard production models, the company opens its plant to tour groups. Chevy managers feel it enhances the bonding process between the public and the car.

Location: The plant is off Interstate 65, exit 28, at Louisville Road and Corvette Drive.

Hours: Tours are given Monday through Friday, at 9 and 1. Closed for a month in summer. Dates vary, so call in advance.

Admission: Free

Telephone: (502) 745-8000

Crystal Cathedral

Garden Grove, California

The Reverend Robert Schuller saw the world was changing. Big city churches were fragmenting because of the move to the suburbs. Life was moving at a faster pace. People wanted to know how to use their religion to get ahead in life. The result was the *Hour of Power,* one of the longest running religious programs on television, in which Schuller talked about "possibility thinking."

So the ministry that began in 1955 in a parking lot with a congregation of 12 families and $86.87 in the first col-

lection plate, grew into the Crystal Cathedral. This star-shaped church of 10,000 windows, designed by Philip Johnson, is a religious landmark, and a monument to the persuasiveness of Schuller's message.

From the start, he unabashedly declared that a church is a business, "a shopping center for God, part of the service industry." He was among the first to encourage drive-in worship, in which people parked out in the lot and tuned in the service on the radio. Schuller always stressed the importance of a big parking lot. "You can be the greatest preacher in the world, but if people can't find a place to park they won't stop to hear your message," he said in a 1976 interview.

He differed from other televangelists in that his message was pitched more toward personal success rather than religious passion. But while his denomination, the Reformed Church in America, was declining in numbers, his congregation quadrupled in a decade. Traditional theologians criticized his message as "shallow." But Schuller insisted that people did not want to attend church to hear "one-sided bigoted statements." They wanted an optimistic message to apply to their daily lives.

"When faced by a mountain, I will not quit," runs his credo. "I will keep on striving until I climb over, find a pass through, tunnel underneath or simply stay and turn the mountain into a gold

1937: First American car to offer windshield washers is the Studebaker.

mine, with God's help." Or if not gold, then crystal.

Location: The Crystal Cathedral is off the Santa Ana Freeway (Interstate 5), at Chapman Avenue and Lewis Street.

Hours: Monday through Saturday, 9–3:30; Sunday, 1:30–3:30.

Telephone: (714) 971-4013

Daytona Beach

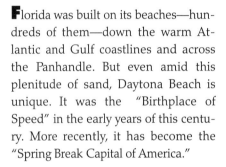

Daytona Beach, Florida

Florida was built on its beaches—hundreds of them—down the warm Atlantic and Gulf coastlines and across the Panhandle. But even amid this plenitude of sand, Daytona Beach is unique. It was the "Birthplace of Speed" in the early years of this century. More recently, it has become the "Spring Break Capital of America."

The railroad arrived here in 1888, pushing steadily south down the Florida coast. With it came the first swarm of sun-seekers, the first tourists to discover the hard-packed sand that turned this beach into a Florida landmark.

Fourteen years later, two pioneer automakers were vacationing in the area. Ransom Olds was proud of the cars he built in Michigan, but he met his match in Alexander Winton of Cleveland. A winter-long argument about the merits of their vehicles ended in an agreement to race the following year. In 1903, a one-mile track was laid out on the beach. The two cars finished in a dead heat and the drivers agreed on a rematch.

Winton showed up with Barney Oldfield, the first professional race car driver. Oldfield got the Winton up to 68.19 mph, a new speed record, and so Daytona's legendary races began. The next year, Henry Ford got into the act and several European manufacturers sent race teams, too. The track was extended to 12 miles, using the beach and a blacktop road behind it. In 1928, Malcolm Campbell raced across the sand at 206.95 mph, a land speed record. The racers eventually left for the Bonneville Salt Flats, in Utah, where the sand is just as hard and there is no high tide.

The last auto race on the sand was held in 1958: The crowds had become unmanageable and it was decided to build a permanent oval track inland. The Daytona International Speedway, opened in 1959, has become one of stock car racing's top venues and has kept Daytona at the center of the speed world.

In 1962, the spring break invasion hit the beach. For many years the greatest concentration had been in Fort Lauderdale, the setting for the early fun-in-the-sun flick *Where the Boys Are*. In the 1980s, south Florida decided to change its image and began discouraging the students from showing up. So Daytona became the preferred destination. But the crush of young bodies and their semi-riotous party atmosphere led

1937: The first drive-in bank opens in Los Angeles. In the 1990s, drive-in (or drive-through) fast food establishments will outnumber drive-in banks in the U.S.

Road Test

MATCH THE ROAD TRIP DESTINATION WITH ITS HIGHWAY
MILEAGE FROM DOWNTOWN MOTOWN.

1.	Cadillac Ranch	A.	0
2.	Carhenge	B.	2,218
3.	Corvette Plant	C.	1,132
4.	Daytona Beach	D.	714
5.	GM Building	E.	1,200
6.	Henry Ford Museum	F.	1,273
7.	Indianapolis Motor Speedway	G.	474
8.	National Automobile Museum	H.	1,063
9.	Richard Petty Museum	I.	10
10.	Wall Drug Store	J.	277

(Answers: 1.F 2.C 3.G 4.H 5.A 6.I 7.J 8.B 9.D 10.E)

local residents to complain, especially in 1989 when the annual visitation reached 400,000 students. Panama City has taken up much of the slack and Daytona has scaled back to more manageable numbers, although it remains the preferred spring break spot among Canadian students.

Cars are allowed on the beach at Daytona, although the speed limit is 10 mph. That may not be the most pleasing arrangement, but it keeps Daytona in touch with its past.

Location: Daytona Beach runs for about 23 miles, and driving is permitted between Ormond Beach and Ponce de Leon Inlet.

Admission: The daily toll is $3.

Don Garlits Museum of Drag Racing
Ocala, Florida

From James Dean to Jan and Dean, drag racing was one of the touchstones of the California youth culture of the 1950s. Restless young men, fast cars, and macho challenges on a deserted highway. It was an activity that seemed to symbolize the estrangement between that decade's cautious adult generation and their brooding offspring.

1937: The automatic transmission—as we now know it—is introduced by Oldsmobile

But it was a young man from Florida who took drag racing to new levels as a sport. Don Garlits was born in Tampa and hung around garages in his hometown, picking up invaluable information about cars and what makes them go fast. He was slight, almost sickly as a youth, so the nickname that was hung on him, "Big Daddy," was an inside joke.

When he first went to California to challenge the top dragsters on their own turf they called him Don Garbage. "They were used to those glittering, chrome-plated, technically perfect dragsters of wealthy guys," he recalled in a 1964 interview. "They took one look at my nightmare and they like to roll over laughing. Actually, they didn't get much of a laugh out of it. I cleaned up on them out there, and they went home shaking their heads."

He dominated drag racing throughout the 1960s and 1970s, just as thoroughly as Richard Petty ruled stock cars. Garlits became the first man to break the 200-mph barrier in 1972. To prove it was no fluke he went out the following weekend and broke it twice more in one day.

During the peak of his career Garlits moved to Detroit to be near his automotive sponsors. But after his retirement he moved home to Florida. The museum he opened near Ocala is filled with racing memorabilia and examples of car design and engine developments during the last 30 years of the sport.

Location: The museum is south of Ocala, just off exit 67 of Interstate 75, then south on county road 475A to 13700 Southwest 16th Avenue.

Hours: Daily, 9–5:30.

Admission: $6

Telephone: (904) 245-8661

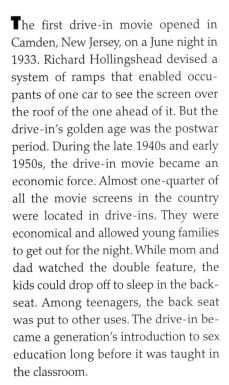

Drive-In Movie-Motel

Monte Vista, Colorado

The first drive-in movie opened in Camden, New Jersey, on a June night in 1933. Richard Hollingshead devised a system of ramps that enabled occupants of one car to see the screen over the roof of the one ahead of it. But the drive-in's golden age was the postwar period. During the late 1940s and early 1950s, the drive-in movie became an economic force. Almost one-quarter of all the movie screens in the country were located in drive-ins. They were economical and allowed young families to get out for the night. While mom and dad watched the double feature, the kids could drop off to sleep in the backseat. Among teenagers, the back seat was put to other uses. The drive-in became a generation's introduction to sex education long before it was taught in the classroom.

At about the same time, the motel was changing America's habits in overnight accommodations. People liked the convenience of driving right to their door without having to go to

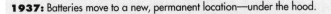
1937: Batteries move to a new, permanent location—under the hood.

the bother of parking and carrying their bags through a hotel lobby. Because of this ability to avoid the fish eye of the clerk at the front desk, the motel also became a part of the sexual revolution.

Time passed. By the 1980s, the drive-in was an endangered species. Built in formerly far-flung suburbs in the 1950s, their land value escalated as the city rushed out to surround them. It made more sense for owners to shut them down and sell the property to developers. By 1991, drive-ins made up less than 4 percent of the country's movies. And while the motel fared a little better, many of them had grown into motor hotels, with full service and a lobby entry. But in this Colorado town, two of the 1950s cultural icons live on.

The Movie Manor Motor Inn, part of the Best Western chain, allows patrons to sit in their rooms and watch movies on an outdoor screen. George Kelloff, who operates the facility, started off with the drive-in in 1955 and opened the motel with a view nine years later. The adjacent restaurant, the Academy Award Room, follows through on the 1950s movie theme.

Location: The Movie Manor is west of town, on U.S. 160.

Hours: The motel is open all year. Make sure you specify that you want a room facing the screen.

Telephone: (719) 852-5921

Edsel and Eleanor Ford House

Grosse Pointe Shores, Michigan

The lakefront palace, with its elegant avenue of trees leading from the entry gate to the main house, is the sort of baronial residence one associates with the automotive giants. Built in 1929 for Henry Ford's oldest son, Edsel (yes, the one for which the ill-fated car was named) and his wife, the former Eleanor Clay, it is a huge Cotswold cottage, designed by Albert Kahn, the architect who put up the GM and Fisher buildings. The home was deliberately built at the opposite end of the Detroit metropolitan area from Henry's estate in Dearborn.

Edsel, a quiet and thoughtful man, was a disappointment to his father. Henry wanted a hard driver, a forceful leader to head the company he founded. While he groomed Edsel for leadership, he handed over more actual power to Harry Bennett, Henry's onetime bodyguard and a former sailor with ties to the underworld. After Edsel's death in 1940 it appeared that Bennett would be able to edge out Henry's grandson, Henry Ford II, from taking over the company.

But in a domestic drama played out in this home, Eleanor Ford confronted the old man and threatened to sell her stock unless Bennett was dismissed and her son named to head the company. Faced with loss of control over every-

1937: Smokers rejoice as the ashtray becomes standard equipment on Hudson automobiles.

00183

thing he had built, Henry acquiesced, then bitterly retired to Fair Lane. Bennett was stunned. "You're taking over a billion dollar organization that you haven't contributed a thing to," he allegedly told Henry Ford II upon his departure. But under the young Ford's leadership, the company entered its greatest period of expansion and prosperity.

The echoes of that great battle still resound in this house. It was furnished with a connoisseur's eye by Edsel and Eleanor. The bedrooms of their children, Henry II and William Clay, are regarded as some of the finest surviving examples of original Art Deco interior decoration in the country. The home's great hall is also used for special exhibits by the Detroit Institute of Arts.

Location: The house is at 1100 Lake Shore Road, about 9 miles northeast of downtown Detroit. Take Interstate 94 (the Edsel Ford Freeway) east to Nine Mile Road, then right to Jefferson and right again. The home is on the left.

Hours: Wednesday through Sunday, 1–4. Tours given on the hour.

Admission: $5 for adults, $4 for senior citizens, and $3 for children. Grounds only, $3.

Telephone: (313) 884-3400 (tours); (313) 884-4222.

Fair Lane

Dearborn, Michigan

He may very well have been the man of the century. He transformed Ameri-

can industry, the way we travel, where we live and work, the very texture of our lives. For a time, Henry Ford was also probably the richest living American. But he was a complex man of simple tastes. A farmer's son who went out and licked the world. A backyard shed tinkerer who had a clearer economic vision than any Wall Street wizard. A man who preached world peace but hated any part of the world that wasn't just like him.

Ford was born in this western Detroit suburb. He moved his company here as soon as he could, assembled his enormous museums here, and died in the home he built here. Fair Lane is a surprisingly simple house for a man of such stature. Built in 1915, it was dwarfed by the mansions built by some of his contemporaries and his offspring. But surrounded by hundreds of acres of forests and gardens, it offered the seclusion Ford wanted. As he lay dying, in 1947, the Rouge River overflowed its banks in a spring storm and cut off all electrical power to the home. So the man who was the leading industrial innovator of his time drew his last breath in an upstairs bedroom here by flickering candlelight.

There were several other inventors who were tinkering with gas-powered vehicles around 1900. Ransom Olds already had a car in production by the time Ford came crashing through the garage of his own workshop in down-

1938: First automobile air conditioning system is offered by Nash. This system filters and heats air from the outside before it enters the car's interior.

Henry Ford's estate, Fair Lane Manor, is surprisingly simple for the man who transformed American industry.

AP/Wide World Photos

town Detroit (he forgot to make the door wide enough for the car) and made his first successful run down Detroit's Bagley Avenue. History and geography conspired to make Detroit the center of the new industry. Many local companies experienced in assembling carriage bodies were there and it was the center of Great Lakes transportation, with access to both the iron mines of the north and the energy fields of the east. There was also an excess of investment capital, as the lumber industry was exhausted in Michigan and former timber barons were seeking new outlets for their money. All of this combined to bring autos and the men who dreamed about them to Detroit.

But Ford's major importance was not as an inventor. It was his ability to expand production by using the assembly line, and then to expand his market by raising wages to the then incredible level of $5 a day, that earned him a place in history. He was the first industrialist to understand that unless his workers could afford the products they were making, the possibilities for expansion were limited. This was the miracle that shook the world, changed the lives of working people forever, and put America on wheels.

Much of the Fair Lane property that Ford owned has been developed in recent years. A regional shopping center, office towers, and a college campus now occupy land that once surrounded

his home. But Fair Lane preserves some of the seclusion Ford treasured and the house and grounds still let visitors capture some sense of the man who lived there.

Location: Fair Lane is at 4901 Evergreen Road, just north of Michigan Avenue (U.S. 12).

Hours: Tours are given on the hour, Monday through Saturday, 10–3, and Sunday, 1–4:30.

Admission: $7 for adults, $6 for senior citizens and students; children 5 and under are free.

Telephone: (313) 593-5590

First Turnpike Tourist Town

Breezewood, Pennsylvania

When the first section of the Pennsylvania Turnpike opened in 1939, most observers were sure that something wonderful was accomplished. Only they weren't sure exactly what.

The first limited access roads, which were called parkways, had been built around New York City in the 1920s. They were seen as a way of easing traffic congestion, which even then was strangling that area. The roads were limited to cars, however, and were not linked to any continuous long-distance routes.

The Pennsylvania Turnpike was different. The mountain ranges that run the breadth of Pennsylvania had made east-to-west travel extremely difficult since colonial times. The first western

1938: First steering column gear shift in the United States is introduced by Cadillac and becomes common on most manual shift cars.

highway, the National Road, ran to the south of the state, where natural gaps existed in the mountains. The westbound pioneer road developed along mountainous Indian trails. Eventually, it became U.S. 30, the Lincoln Highway. But the drive from Philadelphia to Pittsburgh was still arduous and dangerous, making links between the state's two largest cities difficult to maintain.

The turnpike changed all that. It bypassed towns and traffic lights and tunneled through the mountains on new routes chosen by engineers. It was the prototype of the interstate system that would develop after World War II and transform American auto travel.

The first section of the turnpike ran from Carlisle to Irwin, through the most mountainous part of the route. One unanticipated problem cropped up right away. While the old roads passed through a succession of small towns, the turnpike ran around them. Moreover, much of its route ran across lightly populated areas where sleeping, eating, and service facilities did not exist.

Out of that came Breezewood. Near the mid-point of the turnpike, it was barely a collection of shacks when the highway opened. But after the war, when family car travel resumed, it developed into something brand new—a turnpike service city. It was the model for all the communities that grew up thereafter along the interstates. Franchise motels, fast food restaurants, and

gas stations made up Breezewood, and it would become a big part of the entire American travel landscape after the 1950s.

Location: Breezewood is at Exit 28 of the Pennsylvania Turnpike, at the junction of Interstates 70 and 76.

General Motors Building
Detroit, Michigan

When plans for this massive structure were announced in 1919 it was called the Durant Building. The building was to be a tribute to the founder of General Motors, William Durant. He came from Flint, Michigan, and succeeded in unifying several Michigan-based auto producers to form GM. While the company could not compete with Ford when it came to supplying basic transportation, it discerned early that there was a growing market for the buyer who wanted to move up. Ford made only the Model T. There was no way for a Ford customer to show his neighbors that he was getting ahead and was able to afford a more expensive car. GM gave him a way.

Durant, however, would not be around to finish the work on the building. By the time construction actually began on his intended monument, he had been booted out of the chief executive's office by the GM board of directors. Although he developed Chevrolet as a low-end model to go head-to-

---

1938: First year of the longest-ever automobile production run, the Volkswagen "Beetle." Designed as "the people's car" by Ferdinand Porsche in the early 1930s, it was sponsored and financed by Adolf Hitler's government.

The GM Building opened in 1923.
AP/Wide World Photos

head with Ford, he was also over-extended in the stock market. The Du Pont family had quietly bought up a controlling interest in the corporation and decided Durant was not their man. It would be left for Alfred Sloan to lead GM to dominance in the industry. All that remained of Durant were the large letter Ds, already carved into the stone above the main entrance to the new building, and which were never removed.

But GM's location for its new company headquarters was even more significant than what the building was called. The company announced that it was creating a "New Center." For the first time, a major business development was to be built outside the historic downtown area of a city. It was the success of GM's New Center that encouraged the planning of Rockefeller Center in the next decade. The choice also was a tacit acknowledgement that the automobile had changed the shape of the American community. With the nation on wheels, it was now possible to decentralize the urban commercial pattern. People were no longer limited to a single downtown business district. The New Center was the first step on the road to the suburban office park.

The company chose Albert Kahn as its architect. His Detroit-based firm had risen to prominence as the designer of the modern auto factory. When he turned his attention to this office build-

ing, he made a statement of unforgettable power. His repeated pattern of windows and setbacks, extending an entire city block in length, was the architectural embodiment of the assembly line, the visual image of the work its tenants directed. The building opened in 1923 and drew as much attention for its spacious ground-floor showrooms as anything else. Detroiters still flock here to see the latest line of GM cars. But the curiosity can't compare to the levels of the 1940s and 1950s, when car models changed annually.

The New Center grouping was completed in 1928 with the opening of the Fisher Building, directly across the street. Built by the company that supplied GM's chassis (Fisher Body), this building was another Kahn project. While he went for power at GM, Kahn designed grace into the Fisher Building. Its slender central tower and, especially, the rich decor and mosaic panels in its lobby, made it the most beautiful office building of its time and the perfect complement to its massive partner across the way.

Location: The GM Building is located at 3044 West Grand Boulevard (at Second Avenue), about three miles north of downtown Detroit.

Hours: Monday through Friday, 9–5. The lobby of the Fisher Building, across the street at 3011 West Grand Boulevard, is also open on weekends.

Telephone: (313) 556-5000

1939: Flashing turn signals for automobiles, developed by the Guide Lamp Division of the General Motors Corporation, are introduced by Buick.

Giant Tire

Allen Park, Michigan

There are towns that have songs, a town whose name is spelled out high on a dreamy hillside, a town with an arch to symbolize it as the gateway to the west . . . and a town with an 80-foot high, 5-ton tire on its rim. It's the world's largest tire—looming up in a vacant field alongside I-94, reminding 120,000 people who drive by daily and those coming into town from the west that they are in the automobile capital of the world.

The giant tire, standing just west of Detroit, started out as an impressive advertisement, but it has become an appropriate symbol for the Motor City. If you're from southeastern Michigan, you never tire of seeing the familiar landmark, and if you're from out of town your first reaction is probably, "that's odd." It's crazy, but since you're most likely to see the big ol' tire through a car window, let's call it car crazy.

The giant Uniroyal tire wasn't always a big ol' tire. Once it was a huge ferris wheel with 24 dangling gondolas in which 2 million people got queasy going round and round and round during the 1964 World's Fair in New York, New York (one of those song towns). The ferris wheel was purchased by the Uniroyal Tire Company, which once had a huge plant in Detroit. They paid

$250,000 to have the wheel taken apart and converted into a tire—a steel hub covered with fiberglass and flame resistant polyester resin—and parked it in its present locale in 1966. For the tire's 30th anniversary, its present owners—Michelin—had it carefully retreaded, gave it a new hubcap and fancier white lettering, and helped make it look more like today's radial tires.

Location: The giant tire is located on the side of the eastern route of I-94, just east of the intersection with M-39, in Allen Park; this is between the western boundary of Detroit and Detroit Metropolitan Airport.

Golden Gate Bridge

San Francisco, California

It is much more than a bridge. If there was any doubt of that, it was erased entirely in 1987 when the Golden Gate turned 50 years old. A celebration was planned, but no one was prepared for the form it took. An estimated 350,000 people showed up on May 24 to walk across the span. Traffic was clogged in all directions, but it was a festive, almost jubilant gathering. Because on the West Coast, the Golden Gate Bridge had become the symbol of America. To arriving immigrants from Asia it meant hope. To servicemen returning from wars in Japan, Korea, and Vietnam it meant home. It had become the West's Statue of Liberty. So when the bridge turned 50 they came out to rejoice and

1939: First Pope to use an automobile regularly is Pope Pius XII. Pius X was presented with an Italian car as early as 1909, but refused to ride in it.

turned a modest event into an overwhelming celebration of America.

The bridge was talked about for years before being built. The treacherous waters and the changeable weather made the construction a dangerous project. It took four years and cost 11 lives to place the span across the mouth of San Francisco Bay. It is as high as a 40-story skyscraper and 4,200 feet across at the main span (60 feet shorter than the Verranzano Narrows Bridge in New York, which is the longest suspension bridge in the country). Its reddish orange color was chosen for visibility as well as for its resistance to wind and sea spray.

From the beginning, it has been an accessible bridge. At any given time its pedestrian lane is filled with joggers, walkers, bikers, and skaters. And, of course, the other lanes are packed with cars.

And sometimes there are jumpers. For some reason, the bridge has attracted an extraordinary number of suicides—an average of 16 a year. That is the confirmed number. An additional 350 are listed as possibles (although no bodies were found) and through the years, another 2,000 were stopped just in time. "The public myth is that it is a glamorous way to die," said a medical director at a nearby hospital. But that is the other side of the Golden Gate.

Location: The Golden Gate carries U.S. 101 from San Francisco to Marin County. The best view is from Fort Point, directly below the

support on the San Francisco side. Watch for the turnoff going down and to the right, about half a mile before the entrance to the bridge toll plaza.

Goodyear World of Rubber

Akron, Ohio

The strange bounces of the rubber industry have always been a bit confusing. For example, the similar names of tire giants Goodyear and Goodrich have puzzled so many people that the latter company based an ad campaign on it: "No, we're not the ones with the blimp." Not only that, the man who invented vulcanized rubber, Charles Goodyear, had no real connection with the company that bears his name, having died 38 years before it was formed.

Still, after a period in which most American tire-makers were acquired by foreign firms, Goodyear remains a strong presence in the industry's hometown. Goodyear was organized by local businessman Frank Seiberling in 1898. His family had been a major backer of B. F. Goodrich when he went into the rubber business in 1870. It may be that the canny Seiberling was deliberately trying to muddy the waters in going back to the long-deceased Goodyear for his company name; the turn of the century was an especially competitive time to enter the business. Pneumatic tires had enjoyed a steady, if unspectacular market in the bicycle and carriage

---

1939: Total U.S. car production to date reaches 75 million.

industries. But there were stories coming out of Detroit about an experimental gas-driven automobile that would send the market for tires off the charts. When the automobile entered mass production and required something to ride on, Akron and its rubber companies grew almost as quickly as Detroit.

During World War I, Goodyear also entered the aircraft industry. It built 1,150 balloons and blimps for the war effort and, as a public relations strategy, maintained its connection with these aircraft. Overhead shots from a Goodyear blimp are a familiar part of every major sporting event on television.

The World of Rubber exhibit, at the Goodyear plant site, presents a historical overview of tires and of the company. Goodyear's laboratory, in which he worked out the formula for vulcanization, the heating process that gives rubber its flexibility and strength, also has been recreated here.

Location: World of Rubber is on the plant site, at 1201 East Market Street (Ohio 18).

Hours: Monday through Friday, 8:30–4:30.

Admission: Free

Telephone: (216) 796-7117

Henry Ford Museum and Greenfield Village

Dearborn, Michigan

As Henry Ford began approaching old age, he made an unnerving discovery.

The rural America he had grown up in and loved was disappearing. The little farm towns, the pace of life measured by the seasons, the traditions, the simple virtues. Vanishing before his eyes. And in no small measure what had destroyed them was Ford's automobile.

It was because of the automobile that people had greater freedom of mobility than at any other time in the history of the world to date. They were using it to live, work, and shop in ever more widely dispersed patterns. Why patronize the little country store when you could get in the Model T and drive to the county seat? Why go to the husking bee when you could drive to the movies? So Ford resolved to preserve what he could, gather all the elements of the ideal small town of his memory in one setting. But Ford was also an admirer of great men. So the buildings he concentrated on acquiring were those associated with some of the great names of the American past. Noah Webster. Stephen Collins Foster. His friend and mentor, Thomas Edison. The Wright Brothers. He bought their homes and their workshops and transported them to his own town, Greenfield Village, named for the rural township in which he was born, a few miles away.

For all that, Ford was a believer in technology—the American know-how that was changing the world. So he also set about to create a vast museum of

1939: Hood lock releases move under the dash, sealed-beam headlamps become common, and push-button radios are introduced.

00192

The evolution of the automobile is on display at the Henry Ford Museum.

From the collections of the Henry Ford Museum and Greenfield Village

these machines. Washing machines. Vacuum cleaners. Phonographs. Bicycles. From the very earliest models to the most contemporary examples. The Henry Ford Museum is a huge repository of everything that helped relegate Greenfield Village next door to the history texts. Its most interesting section, perhaps, is the Automobile in American Life. It details the changes that the car worked on our culture, from where we eat, to what we buy, to where we sleep. Even Henry himself might be astonished at the scope.

There are traditional crafts displays in both facilities and special exhibits throughout the year.

Location: The village and museum are at 20900 Oakwood Boulevard, just south of Michigan Avenue (U.S. 12).

Hours: Daily, 9–5.

Admission: $12.50 for those 13 and older; $6.25 for children 5–12. (Separate admissions are required for the museum and the village.)

Telephone: (313) 271-1620

Indianapolis Motor Speedway

Indianapolis, Indiana

They ran it the first time in 1911 when Ray Harroun tore around the oval track at an average speed of 74.602 mph. The country was aghast. Since then, the Indianapolis 500 has become the ultimate test of man and machine, a Memorial Day racing ritual.

It is the richest auto race in the world. More than a quarter of a million spectators attend, many of them buying their tickets on the day after the previous year's race just to make sure they get in. The Speedway is nicknamed The Brickyard, and every last brick on its two-and-a-half mile track is regarded as holy ground. The race was located here as a measure of the auto industry's importance in Indiana during the industry's early years. The track's avowed purpose was as a testing ground for innovations. Engineers once claimed that 70 percent of the improvements put in family cars and tires originated in the machines that raced here. Among them are rearview mirrors and balloon tires.

The cars go ever faster. By the race's 80th anniversary, Arie Luyendyk's winning speed was almost exactly two and a half times as fast as Harroun's. But it has also become an American original, a carnival at which speed-loving auto fans lose their inhibitions and rock this sedate midwestern city to its roots. It has been suspended only six times, during the two world wars.

The greatest names in the sport's history—most of them recognized as great by their triumphs here—are memorialized in the Speedway Museum: Gaston Chevrolet, who won in 1920; A. J. Foyt and Al Unser, who won it four times apiece; Bill Vukovich, who won twice in a row and died trying to make it three. The museum shows off

1941: Indianapolis Speedway is closed for the duration of World War II.

several of the winning cars, as well as exhibits of made-in-Indiana automobiles. There are also bus tours of the track, when no events are scheduled.

Location: The track is 7 miles west of downtown, at 4790 West 16th Street, in the suburb of Speedway.

Hours: Daily, 9–5.

Admission: $2 for museum and bus ride (separate tickets may be purchased for $1).

Telephone: (317) 481-8500

National Automobile Museum

Reno, Nevada

William Harrah got into gambling by running a blackjack club for his father in Venice, California. It was profitable but there was one small problem: It wasn't legal. So in 1937 he moved to Reno and with a borrowed $500 opened a bingo parlor. He parlayed that small beginning into the largest gambling operation in northern Nevada. In 1955 he opened another casino on the south shore of Lake Tahoe. The lake had been a summer resort for generations. But Harrah figured—based on his position on the California border—if he could invest in a fleet of snowplows to keep the roads clear from San Francisco, he could run the resort year round. He was right, and between the Tahoe and Reno operations he became a very wealthy man.

Before all of this, Harrah had attended the University of California to study mechanical engineering and he became fascinated by cars. "I was always interested in anything that moved, and if it moved fast so much the better," he said in a 1963 interview. His first buy was a 1908 Maxwell. At least, the seller told him that's what it was. When he started restoration work on it, he found that it was actually a 1911 model, worth far less. But after that initial misstep, Harrah became known as one of the shrewdest buyers of historic cars in the world. His collection grew into the largest in America. Many of them were not even displayed "because they can still be seen too often on the street," he said. He admired Henry Ford and had a complete inventory of every model the company ever made. But he kept models in a garage until they were 20 years old.

Harrah began the car collection as a promotional tool for his casinos. But when the casino operation went public in 1971 and was run by full-time managers, Harrah turned full-time to collecting cars. This museum opened in 1989 and permanently displays more than 200 cars—a small portion of the 1,400 cars Harrah once owned, most of which were sold after his death in 1978. The Harrah collection is still the fullest expression of the country's infatuation with the automobile, and one man's passion for it. Its research library is regarded as the most complete resource of its kind in the world. Many of the cars are displayed in authentic historic street

1942: Car production is halted due to World War II. Automakers now switch to producing tanks, jeeps, aircraft, and other war-related materials.

Some Used Cars Just Can't Be Sold

Although William Harrah first opened his collection of cars to public view in 1962, the idea for the National Automobile Museum didn't develop until after Harrah's death. The Holiday Corporation purchased Harrah's car collection in 1980 and announced its plans to sell it. This resulted in tremendous public outcry from the citizens of Nevada, who wanted to save the collection. In response to this public outcry, Nevada Governor Robert List helped form the William F. Harrah Foundation—a private, nonprofit corporation—in 1981. The foundation was created to receive a gift of 175 cars and the extensive automotive research library from the Holiday Corporation. The National Automobile Museum held its grand opening on November 5, 1989. It covers 105,000 square feet and features one of the most unique and comprehensive public displays of automobiles anywhere.

scenes, with mannequins dressed in vintage clothing. Among the rare cars displayed is the 1907 Thomas Flyer that won the New York to Paris race in 1908.

Location: The National Automobile Museum overlooks the Truckee River, downtown, at Lake and Mill streets; 10 Lake Street, South.

Hours: Monday through Saturday, 9:30–5:30, Sunday, 10:00–4:00.

Admission: $7.50 for adults, $6.50 for senior citizens, $2.50 for children 6–18; children 5 and under are free.

Telephone: (702) 333-9300

Pikes Peak Highway
Manitou Springs, Colorado

Its first recorded sighting by a European was in 1806, when an American expedition led by Zebulon Pike caught a glimpse of it from far out on the Colorado plains. Standing apart from any other peak, it seemed to symbolize the mystery and power of the Rockies. Pike estimated its height at 18,000 feet, described it as the highest mountain he had seen, and wrote that it would never be conquered. Actually, he was off by almost 4,000 feet and Pike's Peak is only the 28th highest mountain in Colorado. Still, its lonely grandeur is a compelling sight and through the years of the western expansion, the motto "Pikes Peak or Bust" was a familiar sight on prairie wagons.

By the end of the century, the peak would be so tamed that a passenger train would run to its summit. Katherine Lee Bates stood there in 1893 and was moved to write a song that would become an alternate national anthem, "America, the Beautiful." Yet, the lonely peak remains a symbol of romance. It is the western frontier and the American Dream, attainable to those who dare to climb.

1942: National speed limit is reduced to 35 mph to help conserve fuel.

This 1911 Ford Model T—with a mother-in-law seat—is featured at the National Automobile Museum.

Courtesy of National Automobile Museum

Since 1915 the climb has been achievable in an automobile. The 18-mile toll-road ascends to the 14,110-foot peak and every July cars race to the summit in the annual Pikes Peak Hill Climb. The highway actually begins its ascent from an altitude of 7,773 feet above sea level but the drive still holds a grip on the American imagination. Climbing Pikes Peak is unlike any other mountain trip. Those who think they have driven to the roof of the Rockies have, like Pike, overestimated their peak. The road up Colorado's Mount Evans, in the Arapaho National Forest, actually ascends 150 feet higher. But no one ever said Mount Evans or Bust.

Location: The Pikes Peak Highway branches off U.S. 24, west of Manitou Springs, about 12 miles west of Colorado Springs. Summit House, at road's end, has lookout points and U.S. Forest Service displays.

Hours: The road is open daily, 7–6:30, June–August; 9–3, May, September, and October.

Admission: Toll is $5.

Telephone: (719) 684-9383

Richard Petty Museum

Randleman, North Carolina

There have been few athletes who have dominated their sport as thoroughly as Richard Petty ruled stock car racing in his prime. He won 200 races between 1958 and 1984, more than twice as many as anybody else. In his peak year, 1967, he won 27 out of 48 races, including an incredible 10 in a row. There is not an auto racing fan in America who doesn't think those marks will stand forever. Or, at least, hopes they do.

He was called King Richard, and in his trademark feathered hat and dark glasses and wide smile, Petty was every inch racing royalty. His last eight years on the NASCAR circuit, before his retirement in 1992, were winless, but still he was the one who drew the adulation of the fans. "He got three fans for every other driver's one," said one longtime rival.

In the Carolinas, where stock car racing is close to a religion, Petty occupied a place of special adulation. His race car number, 43, is as well known as Babe Ruth's number 3. Pro basketball star Brad Daugherty, who grew up in North Carolina, even insisted on wearing 43 as his uniform number as a tribute to Petty.

One writer once called him "Elvis behind the wheel of a race car," and that's a fair gauge of his position in this state. The museum, operated by the Petty family, contains memorabilia of his 34-year career, including three of his most famous cars.

Location: Randleman is located off U.S. 220, about 17 miles south of Greensboro. Turn left at the Level Cross exit onto Branson Mill Road and go about a mile; 311 Branson Mill Road.

Hours: Monday through Saturday, 9–5.

1943: Wartime conservation measures force the U.S. to order nationwide gas rationing, mainly to conserve dwindling rubber supplies. All motorists are assigned a gas ration sticker and pleasure driving is banned.

Admission: $3 for adults, $1.50 for students; children 6 and under are free.

Telephone: (910) 495-1143

Roadside America

Shartlesville, Pennsylvania

As long as people have been traveling by road, there have been roadside shrines offering balm for the weary. The American roadside culture developed its own kind of shrine, influenced by a strange passion for miniaturization. Throughout the country, as the highway system expanded, a cult of the cute grew along with it. Scaled down versions of religious scenes, local landscapes, famous parks, and gardens popped up along the new roads to amaze the traveler. Their creators seemed to feel that by compressing the familiar they made it more compelling.

By far the most ambitious of these projects is Roadside America, a representation of the growth of rural America. The late Laurence Gieringer spent about half a century assembling this tiny fanciful country. Mechanical figures wave and twirl, model trains race across the countryside, and in the evening the skies darken and the recorded voice of Kate Smith sings "God Bless America." The entire tableau covers 8,000 square feet and is housed in its own roadside structure.

It May Be a Miniature, but It Sure Is Big!

Roadside America began as creator Laurence Gieringer's boyhood dream. The idea was born in June of 1903 and has, from day to day and almost without interruption, grown—and grown and grown and grown—to be the largest miniature village of its type. Among the materials used to construct the display: 27,000 board feet of lumber; 175 gallons of paint; 5 special pumps to circulate 6,000 gallons of water per hour; 22 speaker systems for sound effects; 45,000 pounds of stone; 900 pounds of nails; 18,000 pounds of plaster; 8,000 pounds of sand; 184,000 feet of electrical wiring; 2,600 light bulbs; and 1,700 small surgical lamps (used for stars during the night scene). The weight of the entire display is estimated to be 45 tons.

Location: Roadside America is on U.S. 22, just off the Shartlesville exit of Interstate 78, about 35 miles west of Allentown.

Hours: Daily, 9–6:30, July to Labor Day; 10–5, rest of the year.

Admission: $3.75

Telephone: (610) 488-6241

Route 66 (The Last Segment)

Seligman, Arizona

John Steinbeck called it the "mother road," in his classic 1930s novel, *Grapes*

1943: Estimates indicate that production of 1 million Ford V8s required 69 million pounds of cotton, 3 million pounds of wool, 350,000 pounds of goat hair, and 2 million gallons of molasses.

More and More People Are Getting Their Kicks

Everybody loves a comeback, and the Route 66 story is a great one—from no more than 100 vehicles per year touring the highway in 1990 to over 15,000 annually today. More than 10 years after her obituaries were written, Route 66 draws eager travelers from across America and worldwide, thanks in part to the U.S. Route 66 Association. Formed in 1984 to help preserve the historic highway, this non-profit organization has assisted in creating local preservation groups and has supported successful Congressional legislation to restore the old road. The U.S. Route 66 Association remains dedicated to keeping travelers informed about Route 66, its rich history, and the two-lane adventure still to be found from Chicago to L.A.

Source: U.S. Route 66 Association

of Wrath. A 1940's hit song urged travelers to "get their kicks" by driving it from Chicago to Los Angeles. In the 1960s, a television series was built around the adventures of two guys cruising the road in their Corvette. This was U.S. Route 66, the most celebrated federal highway in America.

It started in Chicago and headed southwest, angling across Illinois and Missouri, then straightening out to

head due west across the southwestern states. For two generations, it symbolized the promise of California at the end of the road. One state away from that goal, in Arizona, it roared through the city of Flagstaff. Then, near the town of Seligman, it took a jog to the north, to avoid the rugged terrain around the Cottonwood Cliffs and Peacock Mountains. This is now the last remaining segment of the original Route 66. The rest of the route has been usurped by interstates.

Route 66, in the few areas where it survives, is a service drive. In an effort to drum up tourism, some local interests have put up markers identifying these disconnected segments as "Historic Route 66." But the route is not continuous and is no longer marked on most road maps. In Arizona, Interstate 40 runs where U.S. 66 used to, except for this one 119-mile strip, between Seligman and Kingman. Arizona has retained the old number for this last portion of Highway 66 even though it is maintained as a state road, not as a U.S. highway.

The route was originally surveyed by U.S. Army Lt. Edward Beale in 1857. He was charged with plotting a wagon road from Santa Fe to Los Angeles and was famous for importing camels from the Middle East to transport his equipment on this expedition. It was also the route followed by the Santa Fe Railroad when it came through in 1883.

1944: United States enacts Federal-Aid Highway Act calling for a National System of Interstate Highways connecting principle metropolitan areas, cities, and industrial centers. No funds are provided until 1952.

Highway 66 winds through the Hualapi Indian reservation to the town of Peach Springs, which is the departure point for nineteenth-century excursions to the most accessible part of the Grand Canyon. The highway bends back down through a few desert towns until it rejoins Interstate 40. That's all there is. But the drive is a part of history.

Location: Seligman, where the route begins, is about 75 miles west of Flagstaff.

Stock Car Hall of Fame and Museum
Darlington, South Carolina

At its opening in 1950, Darlington Raceway was regarded as the fastest and most complete auto racing facility in the South. But the experts doubted it would succeed. Its founder, H. W. Brasington, had chosen to build it 80 miles from the nearest city of any size, and this was in an age before interstate highways. The public was also taken aback when the first motorcycle event held here had to be canceled because two drivers in the first race were killed and the rest refused to participate because it was "too dangerous."

But Darlington survived its critics. It is now a revered venue of racing, the second oldest major track in the country behind Indianapolis. Its Southern 500, held on Labor Day weekend, is a major event on the stock car circuit and the races that have been run here wear

the patina of legend. This is an apt location for the Stock Car Hall of Fame, which is said to house the largest collection of race cars in the world. Exhibits, some of them underwritten by the auto companies, trace the evolution of stock cars from 1950 to the present, with special reference to those who were winners at Darlington.

Location: Darlington is about 80 miles northeast of Columbia, and is easily accessible from either Interstate 20 or 95. The Raceway is 2 miles west of town on South Carolina 34 (west of junction with U.S. 52 bypass).

Hours: Daily, 9–5.

Admission: $3

Telephone: (303) 395-8821

Studebaker Museum
South Bend, Indiana

Right after World War II, when Americans were ready to burst loose after years of pent-up demand for new cars, Studebaker came up with one of the most remarkable vehicles ever designed. The automaker had hired the famous packaging expert, Raymond Loewey, to rethink the appearance of the automobile. The result was the Hawk. Comics joked that you couldn't tell whether it was coming or going, since its front and rear ends were identically shaped. But consumers loved its low, sporty lines, different than any other car on the road, and its low price tag, too. By 1951, Studebaker was cm

1945: Mazda factories in Hiroshima are destroyed by the atomic bomb.

One of Bill Elliott's cars, on view at the Stock Car Hall of Fame and Museum.
Courtesy of Stock Car Hall of Fame and Museum

ploying 21,000 workers at its plant, the highest number in its history.

The Studebaker name goes all the way back to 1852 in South Bend. Two brothers, Henry and Clement Studebaker, arrived here from Ohio and went into business building wagons. Their products became known as the best in the country. Presidents Ulysses S. Grant and Benjamin Harrison used Studebaker carriages, as did many other famous and wealthy men of the day. In 1899, the company tentatively entered the new auto business, making bodies for electric cars. Three years later, it began manufacturing its own electric runabouts, and continued doing this for 10 years. By the 1920s, Studebakers were an established part of the industry and by the end of the Depression, South Bend was the last significant independent center of auto production outside of Detroit.

But even with the success of the Hawk, the company simply could not compete with the giant economies of the Big Three. In 1963, just 12 years after its peak, the Studebaker plant shut its doors for good. A consortium of local manufacturers continued to build the sporty Avanti at the old plant but even that limited production ceased in 1987.

Studebaker memories are preserved in a museum here, in the city's downtown Century Center. Displays go all the way back to wagon-making days

and run through a complete line of the company's best-known models. "More than we promised," was its slogan. And after seeing the still-striking lines of the Hawk, you may be inclined to agree.

Location: The museum and Century Center is located at 120 South Saint Joseph Street, downtown.

Hours: Monday through Saturday, 10–4; Sunday, 12–4.

Admission: $3

Telephone: (219) 284-9714

Wall Drug Store

Wall, South Dakota

The whole thing began with ice water. Dorothy Hustead and her husband Ted owned a gas station/drugstore in Wall, a town that got its name because it sits beside rock ramparts at the edge of the Badlands. Parched travelers would emerge from the Badlands, looking for the first place that served something cold. (This was in 1931, before cars were air conditioned.) Dorothy's gimmick was free ice water. Once their thirst was satisfied, they would probably step inside and buy a meal or a souvenir. Or a bottle of aspirin. Or, at least, a cup of coffee for a nickel.

Soon Wall became something of a landmark. After driving across miles and miles of miles and miles, here was this Dakota oasis, selling every conceivable sort of Western gear and postcard and corny souvenir. The Husteads

1945: Gasoline rationing ends the day after V-J (Victory in Japan) Day ends World War II.

The ice water is still free at Wall Drug.
Courtesy of Wall Drug Store

began putting up signs all along U.S. 16, the main highway from the east, and even more travelers showed up. It became kind of a national gag. "Only 500 more miles to Wall Drug." During World War II, Wall Drug milepost signs were spotted in North Africa, Guam, and Australia, all approximately correct in terms of distance. They covered almost as much territory in that era as the ubiquitous Kilroy.

Wall Drug is still a family enterprise, although it is now Interstate 90 that brings travelers to the store. It extends over the length of an entire block,

and it has room for 520 diners, who feast on buffalo burgers and homemade ice cream. There is animated entertainment, a clothing store stocking a complete line of Western togs, and—last but not least—the opportunity to view an authentic "jackalope." The ice water is still free and coffee still costs a nickel.

Location: Wall is due north of the western entrance to Badlands National Park, about 55 miles east of Rapid City.

Hours: Daily, 6 A.M.–10 P.M., Memorial Day to Labor Day. Hours vary rest of the year.

Admission: Free

Telephone: (605) 279-2175

1945: Car production resumes. Almost 50 percent of U.S. passenger cars on the road are at least seven years old.

00205

Stellar Sellers

Best-selling vehicles of 1995 (and number of units sold):

1. Ford F-Series pickups   691,452
2. Chevrolet C/K pickups   513,081
3. Ford Explorer sport/utility   395,227
4. Ford Taurus   366,266
5. Honda Accord   341,384
6. Toyota Camry   328,600
7. Ford Ranger pickup   309,085
8. Honda Civic   289,435
9. Saturn   285,674
10. Ford Escort   285,570

Source: *Detroit Free Press* and company reports

Popular Passenger Cars

Best-selling passenger cars of 1995 (and number of units sold):

1. Ford Taurus   366,266
2. Honda Accord   341,384
3. Toyota Camry   328,600
4. Honda Civic   289,435
5. Saturn   285,674
6. Ford Escort   285,570
7. Pontiac Grand Am   234,226

8. Chevrolet Lumina   214,595
9. Toyota Corolla   213,640
10. Chevrolet Cavalier 212,767

Source: *Detroit Free Press* and company reports

Keep on Truckin'

Best-selling Trucks of 1995 (and number of units sold):

1. Ford F-Series pickups   691,452
2. Chevrolet C/K pickups   513,081
3. Ford Explorer sport/utility   395,227
4. Ford Ranger pickup   309,085
5. Dodge Ram pickup   271,501
6. Dodge Caravan minivan   264,937
7. Jeep Grand Cherokee sport/utility   252,186
8. Ford Windstar minivan   222,147
9. Chevrolet Blazer sport/utility   214,661
10. Chevrolet S-series pickups   207,193

Source: *Detroit Free Press* and company reports

Some Nicknames for Cars

Banzai Bullet (a hot Japanese car)
Beemer (BMW)
Betsy or Bessie (any old car)
Bug (VW Beetle)

1945: Henry Ford steps down as head of Ford Motor Company, replaced by his grandson, Henry Ford II. "Hank the Deuce" hires a group of business school graduates—the "whiz kids"—who greatly improve the sluggish automaker.

Caddy (Cadillac)

Deuce Coupe (customized Ford 2-door)

Flathead (old Ford with the side-valve engine)

Land Yacht (any full-sized gas guzzling car)

Lead Sled (customized boulevard cruiser from
   the 40's or 50's)

Puddle Jumper (any small economy car)

Sleeper (innocent looking car with a large
   powerful engine)

'Stang (Mustang)

T-bucket (customized Model T)

'Vette (Corvette)

Woody (station wagon or other car with real
   wood sides)

Yuppie Wagon (Volvo or BMW station wagon)

Car-Related Seinfeld Episodes

Jerry's BMW with the non-removable B.O.

George's parking spot dispute.

Lost in the parking structure.

Kramer's cruise with the cigar store Indian.

Jerry surprises his parents with a new Cadillac.

Kramer and the ASSMAN license plate.

Cars From the Animal Kingdom

AMC Hornet

AMC Eagle

Audi Fox

Chevrolet Impala

Dodge Viper

Dodge Super Bee

Dodge Colt

Ford Falcon

Ford Mustang

Ford Maverick

Ford Pinto

Hudson Hornet

Jaguar

Mercury Lynx

Mercury Cougar

Mercury Bobcat

Plymouth Road Runner

Plymouth Barracuda

Plymouth Super Bird

Pontiac Firebird

Shelby Cobra

Studebaker Lark

Volkswagen Rabbit

Volkswagen Beetle

And Lumina spelled backwards is . . . Animul

Economy Cars

Cheapest 1995 model cars to repair (based on repair costs of 9 key items):

1.	Saturn SC	$1,483
2.	Saturn SL, SW	$1,547
3.	Hyundai Scoupe	$1,562
4.	Chevrolet Astro	$1,606
4.	GMC Safari	$1,606
6.	Eagle Vision	$1,617
7.	Dodge Intrepid	$1,631
8.	Hyundai Elantra	$1,639
9.	Hyundai Accent	$1,652
10.	Chevrolet/GMC Suburban	$1,655
11.	Hyundai Sonata	$1,667

Source: Your Money, April/May, 1995.

Money Machines

Most expensive 1995 model cars to repair (based on repair costs of 9 key items):

1.	Audi A6/S6	$3,822
2.	Ford Probe	$3,804
3.	Lexus SC 300/400	$3,694
4.	Mercedes-Benz E-Class	$3,680
5.	Mercedes-Benz C-Class	$3,549
6.	Mitsubishi Diamante	$3,496

1945: U.S. war effort: Automotive industry produced 92 percent of vehicles, 87 percent of aircraft bombs, 85 percent of helmets, 50 percent of engines, 56 percent of tanks, 47 percent of machine guns, and 10 percent of torpedoes.

7.	Mazda Millenia	$3,374
8.	Dodge Stealth	$3,343
8.	Mitsubishi 3000 GT	$3,343
10.	Acura Legend	$3,315
11.	Toyota Celica	$3,153

Source: Your Money, April/May, 1995.

Charge It!

Largest gasoline credit card programs in 1994 (and number of accounts):

1.	Amoco	8,700,000
2.	Texaco	8,497,167
3.	Chevron	7,230,000
4.	Mobil	7,000,000
5.	Shell	5,400,000
6.	Citgo	4,024,351
7.	Unocal	3,900,000
8.	BP	3,613,541
9.	Phillips 66	2,200,000
10.	Sunoco	1,872,000

Source: Card Industry Directory, Faulkner & Gray, 1995.

Twenty-Five Shades of Red

Arena Red
Aztec Red
Black Cherry
Candy Apple Red
Carmine
Chrysler Red
Coral Red
Coronado Red
Electric Red
Formula Red
Guards Red
Imperial Red
Matador Red
Monte Carlo Red
Monza Red
Pearl Red
Rallye Red
Renaissance Red
Roman Red
Signal Red
Sure-Fire Red
Torch Red
Toreador Red
Tudor Red
Vermillion Red

The Base Price of a Corvette

1953	$3,250
1957	$3,427
1960	$3,872
1963	$4,394
1965	$4,106
1969	$4,400
1975	$6,810
1978	$9,351
1980	$13,140
1984	$24,600
1996	$36,785 (LT1)

Source: Rasmussen, Henry, Four for the Road, Motorbooks International, 1989; and Motor Trend.

Rearview Mirror Attachments

Air fresheners
Baby shoes
Crystals
Fuzzy dice
Garters
Gold chains
Graduation tassles
Handcuffs
Mardi Gras beads
Parking passes

1946: France introduces a vehicle tax based on horsepower, a policy still in place in the 1990s and the reason why France does not produce cars with big engines, in case you were wondering.

Don's Drive-Thru Beer Store in Lancaster, Ohio.
Courtesy of Kathy Marcaccio

Rainbow suncatchers
Roach clips
Sunglasses

Things We Can Thank the Car For

Billboards
Car insurance
Car jackings
Car washes
Drive-by shootings
Drive-through businesses
Driveways
Freeways
Garages
Gas stations
Gridlock
Motels
O.J.'s Bronco chase
Parking lots
Potholes
Rest stops
Suburbs

Drive-Through Businesses

Funeral homes
Banks
Beer stores
Florists
Wedding chapels
Dry cleaners

Most Popular Car Colors of 1995

Luxury cars:

1. White
2. Light Brown
3. Dark Green
4. Black

Ford's Chameleon Color

Ford unveiled a new paint color—"Mystic"—for use on 2,000 of its 1996 Mustang Cobra coupes. Mystic looks black, purple, green, or gold, depending on which way the light hits it. The Mustang Cobras are the only cars that will get the special paint job. Ford plans to discontinue using the new color after finishing with the Mustangs to insure the collectibility of the cars. The chameleon color is quite costly to consumers: an $815 option, to be exact. But body shop owners will have it even rougher if they need to order some of the Mystic paint for a repair. It's expected to cost about $1,000 a gallon—10 times more than conventional automobile paint.

Source: USA TODAY

5. Medium Red

Full-size/intermediate cars:

1. White
2. Dark Green Metallic
3. Medium Red Metallic
4. Light Brown Metallic
5. Black

Sports/compact cars:

1. Dark Green
2. White
3. Medium Red
4. Black
5. Bright Red

1946: Network television advertising for automobiles is initiated by Chevrolet.

Trucks/vans

1. White
2. Dark Green Metallic
3. Black
4. Bright Red
5. Medium Red Metallic

Source: *USA TODAY and DuPont*

Steal Towns

Metropolitan areas with the highest vehicle theft rates in 1993 (and thefts per 100,000 residents):

1. Newark, NJ   4.073
2. Fresno, CA   3.443
3. Miami, FL   3.001
4. Tampa, FL   2.933
5. Detroit, MI   2.751
6. Bridgeport, CT   2.620
7. St. Louis, MO   2.600
8. Springfield, MA   2.449
9. Atlanta, GA   2.288
10. Gary, IN   2.209

Source: *Insurance Advocate, April 8, 1995.*

Better Lock Your Doors

Cities with the highest number of carjackings in 1992 (and number of incidents):

1. Los Angeles, CA   7,187
2. San Juan, PR   6,838
3. Dallas, TX   2,304
4. New York, NY   2,112
5. Detroit, MI   1,848
6. Chicago, IL   1,200
7. Baltimore, MD/Washington, DC 1,096
8. Cleveland, OH   672
9. Miami, FL   600
10. Newark, NJ   590

Source: *Sales & Marketing Management, November, 1994.*

Slow Down, You're Going Too Fast

Ten places with bad speed traps (in no particular order):

Wilmer, Alabama
Campbell, California
Firplay/Alma, Colorado
Waldo, Florida
Golf, Illinois
All of Louisiana
Washington County, Maryland
Taconic Parkway, New York
Decatur, Texas
Arlington County, Virginia

Source: *Andy Warner, WWW Speedtrap Registry (http://www.nashville.net/speedtrap)*

Some Bumper Stickers We Like

As long as there are tests there will be prayer in school.
Ask first if the animal wants to be killed.
Bad spellers of the world untie.
Hang up and drive!
Happiness is the ball in the fairway.
Honk once if you're Jesus, twice if you're Elvis.
Honk if you're Jesus, otherwise shut up!
I fear no weevil.
I like cats; they taste just like chicken.
I brake for hallucinations.
I'd rather be right than P.C.
If you do own the road, I'd like to talk to you about these potholes.
If you've got a problem ask a teenager while they're still young enough to know it all.
Life is like a box of chocolates: full of nuts.
Mean people suck.
My other car is a Zamboni.
My karma just ran over your dogma.
My other bumper sticker is funny.
My reality check bounced.

1947: Henry Ford dies. His funeral is attended by over 100,000 mourners.

To err is human; to really screw up you need a computer.

Visualize whirled peas.

Who needs Santa? I've got Grandma.

Wow! I could've had a V8!

You can't hug your kids with nuclear arms.

Cartoon Shows Built Around Cars

Hot Wheels

Penelope Pitstop

Speed Buggy

Speed Racer

Supercar

The Wacky Races

Wheelie and the Chopper Bunch

Wheeler-Dealers

Automobile dealers with the most retail sales in 1994 (and number of retail units sold):

1.	Longo Toyota (CA)	13,000 (estimate)
2.	Ricart Ford Inc. (OH)	11,320
3.	Galpin Ford (CA)	11,032
4.	Magic Ford (CA)	8,000 (estimate)
5.	Varsity Ford (MI)	7,500 (estimate)
6.	Mullinax Ford South (FL)	7,075
7.	Landmark Chevrolet Corp. (TX)	6,900 (estimate)
8.	Ed Mullinax Ford (OH)	6,836
9.	Brown & Brown Chevrolet (AZ)	6,817
10.	Earnhardt's Gilbert Dodge (AZ)	6,552

Source: Automotive News, Automotive News Market Data Book (annual), 1995.

An Insurance Company's Dream

1994 cars with the highest insurance premiums:

1. Porsche 911 Carrera
2. Chevrolet Corvette ZR-1
3. Mercedes-Benz SL600
4. Porsche 928 GTS
5. Mercedes-Benz S600
6. BMW 850CSI
7. Mercedes-Benz SL500
8. Mercedes-Benz SL320
9. Chevrolet Corvette
10. Porsche 968

Source: Medical Economics, April 10, 1995.

An Insurance Company's Nightmare

1994 cars with the lowest insurance premiums:

1. Ford Aspire
2. Chevrolet Cavalier (4-door)
3. Saturn wagon
4. Dodge/Plymouth minivan
5. Subaru Justy (4-door)
6. Ford F150 pickup
7. Saturn SL (4-door)
8. Ford Escort wagon
9. Ford Taurus wagon
10. Volkswagen Golf (4-door)

Source: Smart Money, February, 1995.

Excu-u-u-u-u-se Me!

Actual excuses for auto accidents, taken from insurance-company records:

"Coming home I drove into the wrong house and collided with a tree I don't have."

"The other car collided with mine without giving warning of its intentions."

"I thought the window was down, but I found out it was up, when I put my head through it."

"I collided with a stationary truck coming the other way."

1947: Driver's Education classes begin in many American high schools.

0 0 2 1 3

The AMC Pacer was ugly with a capital U.
Courtesy of American Automobile Manufacturers Association

"A truck backed through my windshield into my wife's face."

"A pedestrian hit me and went under my car."

"The guy was all over the road. I had to swerve several times before I hit him."

"I pulled away from the side of the road, glanced at my mother-in-law, and headed over the enbankment."

"In an attempt to kill a fly, I drove into a telephone pole."

"As I reached an intersection, a hedge sprang up, obscuring my vision, and I did not see the other car."

"I had been driving for 40 years when I fell asleep at the wheel and had an accident."

"I was on my way to the doctor with rear-end trouble when my universal joint gave way causing me to have an accident."

"As I approached the intersection, a sign suddenly appeared in a place where no stop sign had ever appeared before."

"To avoid hitting the bumper of the car in front, I struck the pedestrian."

"The indirect cause of the accident was a little guy in a small car with a big mouth."

"I was sure the old fellow would never make it to the other side of the road when I struck him."

"I was thrown from my car as it left the road. I was later found in a ditch by some stray cows."

"The telephone pole was approaching. I was attempting to swerve out of its way, when it struck the front end."

"I saw a slow-moving, sad-faced old gentleman as he bounced off the roof of my car."

Source: AIDE magazine

Ugly Cars

AMC Pacer
AMC Matador
AMC Gremlin
Buick Skylark (mid-1990s)
Chrysler K-Cars
Citroen 2CV
Edsel
Geo Metro convertible

Leaders in (Domestic) Luxury

Top U.S. luxury car models of 1994 (and number of units sold):

1.	Cadillac Deville	108,973
2.	Lincoln Town Car	107,074
3.	Chrysler New Yorker	64,090
4.	Chrysler Town & Country	31,875
5.	Lincoln Continental	30,583

Source: Brandweek, January 2, 1995.

Luxury from Afar

Best-selling imported luxury cars of 1994 (and number of units sold):

1.	Acura	105,952
2.	Lexus	78,608
3.	BMW	77,121
4.	Volvo	76,545
5.	Mercedes-Benz	65,648

Source: Brandweek, January 2, 1995.

Toll-Free Phone Numbers of Car Companies

Acura	(800) TO-ACURA
Alfa Romeo	(800) 245-ALFA
Audi	(800) FOR-AUDI
BMW	(800) 334-4BMW
Buick	(800) 4A-BUICK
Cadillac	(800) 333-4CAD
Chevrolet	(800) 950-2438

1947: World land speed record is set by John Cobb's Railton Racer with a speed of 394 mph on the Utah Salt Flats.

Road Test

MATCH THE CELEBRITY TO THE CAR THEY ENDORSED.

1. *Buzz Aldrin*   A. DeSoto
2. *Pat Boone*   B. Plymouth
3. *Sean Connery*   C. Oldsmobile
4. *Richard Dreyfuss*   D. Subaru
5. *Farrah Fawcett*   E. Volkswagen
6. *Ruth Gordon*   F. Buick
7. *Durwood Kirby*   G. AMC Gremlin
8. *Groucho Marx*   H. Aston Martin
9. *Bobby Riggs*   I. Lincoln-Mercury
10. *Tina Turner*   J. Chevy Impala

(Answers: 1.E 2.J 3.H 4.G 5.I 6.D 7.C 8.A 9.F 10.B)

Source: Advertising Age, January 8, 1996

Chevy Truck	(800) 962-2868	Lotus	(800) 24-LOTUS
Chrysler	(800) 4A-CHRYSLER	Mazda	(800) 639-1000
Dodge	(800) 4A-DODGE	Mercedes-Benz	(800) FOR-MERCEDES
Dodge Truck	(800) 4A-DODGE	Mitsubishi	(800) 447-4700
Geo	(800) GET-2-KNOW	Nissan	(800) NISSAN-3
GMC Truck	(800) GMC-TRUCK	Oldsmobile	(800) 242-OLDS
Honda	(800) 33-HONDA	Plymouth	(800) PLYMOUTH
Hyundai	(800) 826-CARS	Pontiac	(800) 762-4900
Infiniti	(800) 826-6500	Porsche	(800) PORSCHE
Isuzu	(800) 726-2700	Saab	(800) 582-SAAB
Jaguar	(800) 4JAGUAR	Saturn	(800) 522-5000
Jeep/Eagle	(800) JEEP-EAGLE	Subaru	(800) SUBARU-3
Kia	(800) 333-4KIA	Suzuki	(800) 447-4700
Land Rover	(800) FINE 4WD	Toyota	(800) GO-TOYOTA
Lexus	(800) 872-5398	Volkswagen	(800) 444-8987
Lincoln Mercury	(800) 446-8888	Volvo	(800) 458-1552

1947: The National Institute of Diaper Services threatens to picket Ford Motor Company over ads featuring a naked baby and the tagline "smooth as a '47 Ford." The NIDS claims that a naked, diaper-less baby is un-American.

Celebrities Who've Been in Car Commercials

Dustin Hoffman (Volkswagen)
Ricardo Montalban (Chrysler)
Lee Iacocca (Chrysler)
Frank Sinatra (Chrysler)
Barry Sanders (Cadillac)
Dinah Shore (Chevrolet)
Vivian Vance and William Frawley (Ford)
Christie Brinkley (Nissan)
Ringo Starr (Oldsmobile)
William Shatner (Oldsmobile)

Source: Advertising Age, January 8, 1996.

Car-Related Episodes of The Brady Bunch

Greg buys a lemon car from a wheeler-dealer friend.
Old man tries to take the Bradys for a ride after a fender bender with Carol.
Marcia bets Greg she can outscore him on a driving test.
Greg is grounded from driving the Brady cars.
Bobby accompanies Greg and his date to the drive-in.

Heavenly (Uni-) Bodies

Chevy Vega
Chevy Astro
Chevy Nova
Chrysler Cirrus
Dodge Stratus
Dodge Aries
Ford Galaxie
Ford Taurus
Mercury Comet
Merkur Scorpio

Mitsubishi Eclipse
Nissan Pulsar
Oldsmobile Rocket 88
Oldsmobile Starfire
Plymouth Satellite

Bumper to Bumper

U.S. Cities with the worst traffic in 1993 (based on Metro Traffic Control point system):

1. New York City
2. Chicago
2. Los Angeles
4. San Francisco
5. Seattle
6. Pittsburgh
7. Washington, D.C.
7. Atlanta
7. Houston
10. Kansas City, MO
10. Indianapolis

Source: Industry Week, March 21, 1994.

Famous People Killed in Car Crashes

Marc Bolan (British rock star)
Albert Camus (French writer)
Harry Chapin (singer-songwriter)
James Dean (actor)
Jack Johnson (heavyweight boxing champion)
Sam Kinison (comedian)
Ernie Kovacs (comedian)
Pelle Lindbergh (all-star NHL goaltender)
Jayne Mansfield (actress)
Billy Martin (baseball player/manager)
Margaret Mitchell (author)
Tom Mix (actor)
George S. Patton, Jr. (U.S. Army general)
Jackson Pollack (artist)
John D. Rockefeller III (philanthropist)
Bessie Smith (singer)

1948: Reliable tubeless tires are first made available in the United States by BFGoodrich.

Route 66 as it is today, just east of Williams, Arizona.
Courtesy of Tom Snyder/U.S. Route 66 Association

Ten Novels About Cars

Car (Harry Crews)
The Betsy (Harold Robbins)
The Car Thief (Theodore Weesner)
Christine (Stephen King)
David White and the Electric Wonder Car (W. E. Butterworth)
Grand National Racer (Margaret Ogan)
Hot Rod (Henry Grego Felsen)
The Last Convertible (Anton Myrer)
Tom Swift and His Electric Runabout or the Speediest Car on the Road (Victor Appleton, Jr.)
Wheels (Arthur Hailey)

Route 66 Road-Fan Info

Date Route 66 commissioned: November 11, 1926
Design standards set by: U.S. Department of Agriculture, Bureau of Public Roads
Highway officially decertified: June 28, 1985
Original mileage total from Chicago to Los Angeles: 2,448
Number of states crossed by Route 66: 8
Route 66 completely paved by: 1937
Percent of Route 66 roadway remaining: 117 (several alignments built through the years)
Percent of Route 66 still driveable: 90 (nearly all well-maintained by the various states)
Number of Interstate highways required to replace old Route 66: 9 (I-55, I-44, I-40, I-25, I-15, I-10, I-270, I-244, and I-215)
Miles of highway in the Interstate system: 42,545
Percent of traffic carried by the system: 20
Most popular songs written about the highway: "(Get Your Kicks on) Route 66," by Bobby Troup, and "Theme from Route 66," by Nelson Riddle.

Years when series *Route 66* appeared on TV: 1960–1964
Number of episodes actually filmed on Route 66: 3
Color of Corvettes used in the show: Beige
Source: U.S. Route 66 Association

Five Great Drives

Five roads that were featured on PBS's "Great Drives" series:

Highway 61
Route 66
Pacific Coast Highway
Highway 93
A1A

Scenic Highways and Byways

Scenic America's 10 most important scenic byways of 1996 (* = endangered):

San Mateo 1 (California)
Route 9* (Delaware)
Route A1A* (Florida)
Leon County Canopy Roads (Florida)
Route 2* (Illinois)
Route 40 (Indiana)
Route 41* (Michigan)
Cascade Lakes Highway (Oregon)
Delaware River Scenic Drive* (Pennsylvania)
Route 12* (Utah)

Source: Scenic America (a Washington, D.C.-based organization)

Twenty-Five Shades of White

Alabaster
Alpine White
Arctic White
Bright White

1948: Harley Earl's radical new design for the Cadillac initiates the tail-fin craze.

Cameo White
Champagne White
Classic White
Corinthian White
Cotillion White
Crystal White
Diamond White
Dover White
Ermine White
Frost White
Glacier White
Oxford White
Pastel White
Persian White
Polar White
Polo White
Porcelain White
Provincial White
Shetland White
Spinnaker White
Vail White

GLX	LX	SS	XT
GS	LXi	SSE	Z
GS-T	RL	SSEi	ZX

Biggest Pet Peeves of Drivers

1. Drivers who cut you off
2. Drivers who don't use turn signals
3. Drivers who tailgate
4. Drivers who drive too slow in the fast lane
5. Drivers who drive too fast
6. Drivers who use cellular phones while driving
6. Drivers who are rude
6. Drivers who run red lights
9. Drivers who change lanes too often

Source: Market Opinion Research

Early Names for the Automobile

The locomotive car
The autobat
The autovic
The self-propelled carriage
The locomotor
The self-motor

Source: Bryson, Bill, *Made in America,* William Morrow, 1994.

Suffixes, Suffixes, Suffixes

CL	GTI	RS	ST
CS	GTP	RT	STS
CRX	GXE	S	STX
CSE	HX	SC	SVX
CX	i	SD	SX
DL	iL	SE	TDI
DX	iS	SEI	ti
ES	JS	SEL	TL
Esi	JX	SHO	TSi
EX	JXi	Si	XE
G	L	SL	XJR
GL	LE	SLE	XJS
GLE	LS	SLS	XL
GLH	LSI	SLT	XLE
GLI	LSS	SLX	XLS
GLS	LT	SR	XLT
GLT	LTS	SRI	XS

The Auto Industry's 10 Greatest Achievements

1. The moving assembly line
2. The pneumatic tire
3. Seat belts/air bags
4. Electronic engine controls
5. The automatic transmission
6. Fuel injection
7. Hydraulic brakes
8. Air conditioning

1948: First torque converter-type automatic transmission offered on an American car is introduced by Buick. Buick calls the new system Dynaflow and puts it in its Roadmaster models.

The moving assembly line is the auto industry's greatest achievement.

Courtesy of American Automobile Manufacturers Association

9. The self-starter
10. The catalytic converter

Source: Society of Automotive Engineers

Popular Car Toys

Hot Wheels: One of the all-time great toys that actually worked as advertised. You could build long, intricate tracks, and the cars would usually stay on. The "superchargers" were really cool—kind of like a car wash, except the "brushes" were a battery-powered wheel that squeezed the car as it went through, and shot it out at high speed.

Matchbox Cars: A more serious version of the Hot Wheels. Matchboxes rolled but didn't "rocket" like Hot Wheels. Both of these little (1/43 scale) replicas are now highly collectible.

SST Racers: About six to eight inches in length, these speedy racers were powered by a flywheel and what the company called a "t-strip," both of which had teeth; you would insert the t-strip through a slot and yank it out real fast (the faster the better!), which would turn the flywheel and spin the back wheels. These things MOVED! One good pull would easily send the vehicle careening the length of an average suburban basement and into the opposite wall at high speed.

Slot cars: These ran on tracks made of plastic sections that snapped together, or on sheets of plywood into which grooves had been routed, and featured "slots" lined with metal from which the cars picked up their electrical power. The most fun was angling the roadway up and ending it, then seeing how far you could launch the car across the living room. (A few less imaginative types actually "raced" their slot cars.)

Plastic model kits: Every kid had to try a few of these. A few talented individuals actually succeeded in making highly accurate replicas of real production cars, race cars, or custom cars. But most of us ended up with a glue-fused chunk of shapeless plastic that vaguely resembled a canister vacuum.

Frequently Stolen Car Accessories

Cellular phones
T-Tops
Stereos
Radar detectors
Wheel covers
Gas caps
License plates/tabs

Some Vanity Plates We Like

4MYEGO
4U2NV
AHHSUMM
CELIB-8
CYBRPNK
EDITER
EYEMA10
FROMGOD
FUNVAN
GIRLIEQ
IM2BZ2P
IOU1DAD
JAZMAN
KIKINIT
NOTDADZ
NOTPOPS
OHTOBE18
PIGOUT
PPDOC
SOITNLY

1948: The Tucker 48 is introduced while Preston Tucker is on trial for fraud (he was acquitted in 1949). Though more conventional than planned, the rear-engined Tuckers feature several style and safety innovations.

URFAT
USOCRAZ
USONOZY

The Trends in Motors

Motor Trend magazine's "Car of the Year" award winners:

1949	Cadillac Motor Car Division
1950	no award
1951	Chrysler Corporation
1952	Cadillac Motor Car Division
1953	no award
1954	no award
1955	no award
1956	Ford Motor Company
1957	Chrysler Corporation
1958	Ford Thunderbird
1959	Pontiac Motor Division
1960	Chevrolet Motor Division
1961	Pontiac Tempest
1962	Buick Special
1963	AMC Rambler
1964	Ford Motor Company
1965	Pontiac Motor Division
1966	Oldsmobile Toronado
1967	Mercury Cougar
1968	Pontiac GTO
1969	Plymouth Road Runner
1970	Ford Torino
1971	Chevrolet Vega
1972	Citroen SM
1973	Chevrolet Monte Carlo
1974	Ford Mustang II
1975	Chevrolet Monza 2+2
1976	Chrysler: Dodge (Aspen), Plymouth (Volare)
1977	Chevrolet Caprice
1978	Chrysler: Dodge (Omni), Plymouth (Horizon)

To Steal this Stereo, You Have to Steal the Car

Think you're bad with that mega bass blasting, shaking and rattling the neighborhood? Try the sound system in Earl Zausmer's BMW 540i, which took about 1,800 hours to install and cost around $30,000. The system won the 1995 International Auto Sound Competition Association's national award. Some of the highlights:

—A laser beam locates car occupants and adjusts the system to ensure sound is being delivered directly to the listener.

—The bass notes come from two 13-inch woofer speakers, welded into the kick panels inside the front fenders.

—The fenders, doors, floor, and roof are filled with 370 pounds of insulation.

—Motorized lifts elevate $5,000 worth of high- and mid-range speakers from pockets on each side of the dashboard. The high range speakers are BMW Silver Signatures (with solid silver componentry).

—How many amplifiers? Three.

—Two 10-CD players; one in the trunk, the other under the front seat.

—A Sony ES control unit.

—Housings and connections are fashioned in aluminum and brass.

Source: Philadephia Inquirer

1949: Starting a car with a key—instead of the old method of pushing a button—is pioneered by Chrysler.

1979	Buick Riviera S
1980	Chevrolet Citation
1981	Chrysler K-Cars (Aries and Reliant)
1982	Chevrolet Camaro Z28
1983	Renault Alliance
1984	Chevrolet Corvette
1985	Volkswagen GTI
1986	Ford Taurus LX
1987	Ford Thunderbird
1988	Pontiac Grand Prix
1989	Ford Thunderbird SC
1990	Lincoln Town Car
1991	Chevrolet Caprice Classic LTZ
1992	Cadillac STS
1993	Ford Probe GT
1994	Ford Mustang
1995	Chrysler Cirrus
1996	Dodge Caravan

Source: Motor Trend

Branded a Winner (Part I)

Best automotive parts brands of 1994, according to discounters:

1. Pennzoil
2. Quaker State
3. Fram
4. Havoline
5. Valvoline
6. STP
7. Castrol
8. Prestone
9. Armor-All
10. AC/Delco

Source: Discount Store News, Top Brands Survey (annual), October 3, 1994.

Branded a Winner (Part II)

Best automotive parts brands of 1994, according to consumers:

1. Fram
1. Pennzoil
3. Quaker State
3. Valvoline
5. Turtle Wax
6. Castrol
6. Havoline
6. Armor-All
9. Michelin
9. Champion

Source: Discount Store News, Top Brands Consumer Survey—Pt. II (annual), October 17, 1994.

TV Shows with Cool Cars in the Cast

The Addams Family	The Druid Princess
The Banana Splits	Banana Buggies
Batman	The Batmobile
The Dukes of Hazard	The General Lee (Dodge Charger)
The Green Hornet	The Green Hornet limousine
The Monkees	The Monkeemobile
The Munsters	The Munstermobile and The Drag-u-la (Grandpa's car)

Mean Automobile Acronyms

Audi	Accelerates Under Demonic Influence
BMW	Big Money Waste; Bought My Wife; Bumbling Mechanical Wretch
Buick	Big Ugly Import Car Killer
Chevrolet	Can Hear Every Valve Rattle On Long Extended Trips; Cracked Heads, Every Valve's Rotten, Oil Leaks Every Time

1950: The Nash Rambler, a compact, is introduced. Nash president George Romney (later Governor of Michigan and a 1968 candidate for the Republican presidential nomination) views the compact as a serious challenge to the Big Three automakers.

Dodge	Dead On Day Guarantee Expires; Drips Oil, Drops Grease Everywhere
Edsel	Every Day Something Else Leaks
Fiat	Failure In Automotive Technology; Fix It Again, Tony
Ford	Fix Or Repair Daily; Found On Road, Dead; Fast Only Rolling Downhill
GM	General Maintenance
GMC	Generally Mediocre Cars
Honda	Had One Never Did Again
Hyundai	Hope You Understand Nothing's Drivable And Inexpensive
Jeep	Just Eats Every Part
MG	Money Guzzler
Pinto	Put In Nickel To Operate
Saab	Swedish Automobile—Always Broken
VW	Virtually Worthless

Things We Take for Granted on Cars of Today

5-mph bumpers
Brake lights
Bucket seats
Carpeting
Collapsible steering columns
Cup holders
Headrests
Heaters
Intermittent wipers
Radios
Rear-window defoggers
Safety glass
Seat belts
Side-impact protection
Tubeless tires
Turn signals
Windshield washers

Mobile Businesses

Pet grooming on wheels
Oil changes on wheels
Windshield repair on wheels
Bookmobiles
Meals on Wheels
Swimmobiles
Veterinarians

Don't Forget Your Wallet

Cities where it costs the most to own and operate an automobile (and the average annual expense):

1.	Los Angeles, CA	$8,375
2.	Boston, MA	$7,476
3.	Philadelphia, PA	$7,344
4.	Providence, RI	$7,277
5.	Hartford, CT	$7,195
6.	New York, NY	$7,162
7.	San Francisco, CA	$7,152
8.	Honolulu, HI	$6,832
9.	Phoenix, AZ	$6,772
10.	Detroit, MI	$6,731

Source: Ward's Auto World, June, 1995.

Wallet-Friendly Cities

Cities where it costs the least to own and operate an automobile (and the average annual expense):

1.	Sioux Falls, SD	$5,368
2.	Bismarck, ND	$5,445
3.	Burlington, VT	$5,459
4.	Boise, ID	$5,509
5.	Nashville, TN	$5,564
6.	Raleigh, NC	$5,566
7.	Des Moines, IA	$5,580
8.	Charlotte, NC	$5,617

1950: Tinted glass automobile windows first become available on Buick models. Designed initially to reduce glare and aid vision, they have evolved into today's sometimes totally darkened car windows.

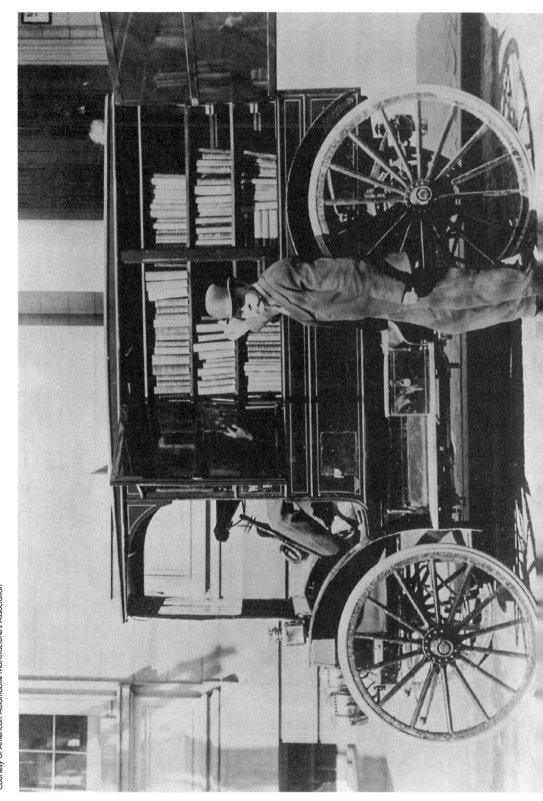

A bookmobile from around 1912.
Courtesy of American Automobile Manufacturers Association

9. Little Rock, AR $5,660
10. Birmingham, AL $5,668

Source: Ward's Auto World, June, 1995.

Teenage Dream States

States that allow driving at age 15:

Hawaii

Louisiana

Mississippi

New Mexico

Montana

(38 states allow driving at age 16; 5 allow driving at 17; 2 allow driving at 18)

Source: World Features Syndicate

0–60 Acceleration Times: Classic Cars

4.2 sec.	1965 AC Cobra 427
5.1 sec.	1985 Lamborghini Countach
5.4 sec.	1967 427 Corvette
5.4 sec.	1972 Aston Martin V8 Vantage
5.4 sec.	1968 Ferrari Daytona
5.9 sec.	1974 Plymouth Barracuda 440-6 pack
6.0 sec.	1967 Dodge Charger
6.1 sec.	1964 Mustang 289
7.3 sec.	1975 Ferrari 308 GTB
8.0 sec.	1969 Datsun 240Z
8.7 sec.	1983 Volkswagen GTI
9.3 sec.	1971 Mercedes 280SL
9.5 sec.	1955 Ford Thunderbird
9.6 sec.	1979 DeLorean DMC12
10.3 sec.	1959 Cadillac Convertible
10.5 sec.	1957 Buick Roadmaster
18.0 sec.	1980 Volkswagen Beetle
20.5 sec.	1963 Austin-Healey Sprite MK1 "Bug Eyed Sprite"

Source: Wilson, Quentin, The Ultimate Classic Car Book, Dorling Kindersley, 1995.

0-60 Acceleration Times: Recent Cars

3.7 sec.	1996 Porsche 911 Turbo
3.8 sec.	1994 Jaguar XJ 220
4.0 sec.	1994 McLaren F1
4.7 sec.	1995 Ferrari F355 Berlinetta
4.9 sec.	1995 Chevrolet Corvette ZR-1
5.2 sec.	1994 Ferrari 456 GT
5.2 sec.	1994 Dodge Viper GTS
5.2 sec.	1995 Ford Mustang Cobra R
5.3 sec.	1995 Pontiac SLP Firehawk
5.3 sec.	1996 Chevrolet Camaro Z28 SS
5.7 sec.	1995 Aston Martin DB7
5.8 sec.	1994 BMW 850CSi
6.4 sec.	1995 Cadillac STS
6.7 sec.	1995 Buick Roadmaster Limited
7.2 sec.	1996 Lincoln Mark VIII
8.0 sec.	1995 BMW 325i
8.0 sec.	1995 Dodge Neon Sport Coupe
8.0 sec.	1995 Toyota Camry LE V6
8.8 sec.	1995 Honda Accord EX V6
8.8 sec.	1996 Ford Explorer XLT V8
9.4 sec.	1995 Chevrolet Blazer LS
9.7 sec.	1994 Mazda Miata
11.6 sec.	1994 Ford Explorer XLT V6
13.9 sec.	1993 Suzuki Sidekick JX
16.2 sec.	1994 Volkswagen Eurovan Camper

Source: Road & Track Exotic Cars 1994 and Road & Track Road Test Review, March, 1996.

Some Memorable Car Slogans

Baseball, hot dogs, apple pie . . . and Chevrolet (Chevrolet)

Built for the human race (Nissan)

Fahrvergnugen (Volkswagen)

Have you driven a Ford . . . lately? (Ford)

I love what you do for me (Toyota)

It just feels right (Mazda)

Mark of excellence (General Motors)

Only in a Jeep (Jeep)

1951: Automobile power steering is first offered on the Chrysler Imperial models. Developed during World War II for use on military vehicles, it becomes very popular and is used on nearly all cars today.

Road Test

MATCH THE ADVERTISING SLOGAN WITH THE CAR OR CAR
COMPANY THAT USED IT.

1. *America's favorite fun car*
2. *Ask the man who owns one*
3. *First of the dream cars to come true*
4. *We make it simple*
5. *Live the dream*
6. *Smart to be seen in, smarter to buy*
7. *We build excitement*
8. *The rocket action car*

A. Studebaker
B. Oldsmobile
C. Packard
D. Ford Mustang
E. Pontiac
F. Chevrolet Corvette
G. DeLorean
H. Honda

(Answers: 1.D 2.C 3.F 4.H 5.G 6.A 7.E 8.B)

Ugly is only skin-deep (Volkswagen Beetle)
Wouldn't you really rather have a Buick? (Buick)

Some Great Races

Indy 500
Daytona
Pikes Peak
Sebring
Le Mans
Soapbox Derby

In the Winner's Circle

Top 20 NASCAR drivers in career wins
(through 1995):

1. Richard Petty..200
2. David Pearson..105
3. Darrell Waltrip..84
3. Bobby Allison...84
5. Cale Yarborough 83
6. Dale Earnhardt 68
7. Lee Petty 54
8. Ned Jarrett 50
8. Junior Johnson...50
10. Herb Thomas 48
11. Buck Baker 46
12. Rusty Wallace..41
13. Bill Elliott..40
13. Tim Flock 40
15. Bobby Isaac...37
16. Fireball Roberts 34
17. Rex White...28

1952: The first Holiday Inn opens for business in Memphis. This signals the dawning of a new era in
family motor travel.

Source: USA TODAY

Driving Essentials

Most important items for drivers to carry with them in their cars:

1. Car phone
2. Tire jack/tire tool
3. Flashlight
4. Jumper cables
5. Fire extinguisher

Source: Valvoline/Automotive Service Excellence poll

Winter Driving Essentials

A flashlight (Make sure the batteries work.)

A spare key (If you must have the car towed, you don't want to give away your only key.)

Warm blankets

A first-aid kit

Extra shoes (This is especially important for women, who often commute in pumps.)

Food (Like a candy bar or crackers, to munch on if help is slow in arriving.)

A "SEND HELP" sign to post in your window (So you don't have to leave your car.)

Flares (Hazard lights can freeze or burn out.)

A map of the areas you frequently drive as well as a list of local 24-hour towing services

Lock de-icer for your purse or briefcase (NOT in the car!)

Source: The Detroit News

Some Cars that Wouldn't Rust (Theoretically)

Hispano-Suiza custom (tulipwood body)

Mercedes-Benz 300SL Gullwing (aluminum)

Studebaker Avanti (fiberglass)

Vector (first 17 were Kevlar)

Saturn (plastic panels)

Chevrolet Corvette (fiberglass)

Chevrolet Lumina Minivan (plastic panels)

DeLorean (stainless steel)

Food, Next Exit

Most popular family dining restaurant chains (based on customer satisfaction surveys):

1. Cracker Barrel Old Country Store
2. Bob Evans Restaurants
3. Shoney's
4. Bakers Square
4. Perkins Family Restaurants
6. PoFolks
7. IHOP
8. Denny's
9. Friendly
10. Big Boy
11. Waffle House

Source: Restaurants & Institutions, Choice in Chains (annual), February 1, 1995.

Blowin' in the Wind

Chevrolet Typhoon (sport utility vehicle)

GMC Syclone (pickup)

Mercury Cyclone

Plymouth Breeze

Pontiac Tempest

Volkswagen Scirroco

Home, James

Top limousine companies of 1994 (and number of sedans):

1. Manhattan International Limousine   182

1952: Engineer John Hetrick develops the air bag and patents it in 1953. By the time the auto industry finally begins using them, Hetrick's patent has run out.

The DeLorean was made from stainless steel.
Courtesy of American Automobile Manufacturers Association

2.	A-1 Limousine Inc.	125
3.	Empire Transport Service	123
4.	London Towncars Inc.	108
5.	Carey New York	93
6.	Air Brook Limousine	90
7.	Dav-el New York	85
7.	Carey Michigan	85
9.	Rudy's Limousine Service	65
10.	Royal Coachman Ltd.	60

𝒮𝑜𝑢𝑟𝑐𝑒: *Limousine & Chauffeur*, January/February, 1995.

The Price of Getting in a Ferrari

1957	250 GT California	$12,000
1962	250 GT Lusso	$13,375
1964	275 GTS	$14,500
1966	330 GTC	$14,900
1967	275 GTB4	$14,680
1969	365 GTB4 Daytona	$19,500
1971	365 GTS 4 Spyder	$25,500
1971	365 GTC4	$27,500
1972	246 GTS Dino	$18,000
1977	BB 512 Boxer	$85,000
1978	308 GTS	$34,195
1995	F355 Berlinetta	$120,050

𝒮𝑜𝑢𝑟𝑐𝑒: *Rasmussen, Henry, Four for the Road, Motorbooks International, 1989; and Motor Trend.*

Your Mileage May Vary

Average number of miles driven annually per vehicle in the U.S.:

1980	9,500
1985	10,200
1990	11,250
1995	12,100 (estimate)

𝒮𝑜𝑢𝑟𝑐𝑒: *The New York Times,* Advocates for Highway and Auto Safety, Federal Highway Administration, Ford Motor Company, Bear Stearns, and American Petroleum Institute.

Easy Does It

Speed vs. fuel consumption (based on an average 1994 passenger car):

30 mph = 32 mpg
35 mph = 34 mpg
40 mph = 34 mpg
45 mph = 34 mpg
50 mph = 32 mpg
55 mph = 30 mpg
60 mph = 25 mpg
65 mph = 23 mpg
70 mph = 21 mpg
75 mph = 18 mpg

𝒮𝑜𝑢𝑟𝑐𝑒: *The New York Times,* Advocates for Highway and Auto Safety, Federal Highway Administration, Ford Motor Company, Bear Stearns, and American Petroleum Institute.

TV Shows Built Around Cars

Knight Rider
My Mother the Car
Viper
Taxi
Car 54, Where Are You?

TV Cops and Their Cars

The Saint	Volvo P1800
Columbo	Peugeot 403 Cabriolet
Magnum P.I.	Ferarri 308
Cannon	Lincoln Mark III
Sonny Crockett (*Miami Vice*)	Ferrari Testarossa, Ferrari Daytona
Knight Rider	Pontiac Firebird Trans Am
Starsky and Hutch	Ford Torino
#6 (Patrick McGoohan, Secret Agent)	Lotus Super 7
The Persuaders	Ferrari Dino 246
Jim Rockford	Pontiac Firebird

1953: First true American sports car is the Chevrolet Corvette. It is also the first series-production car with a reinforced fiberglass body fitted on a conventional steel frame.

Great Car Magazines

Motor Trend
Car and Driver
Automobile
duPont Registry
Road & Track
Hot Rod

Do-It-Yourselfers' Dream Stores

Top automotive aftermarket chains of 1993
(based on sales):

1. Western Auto Supply (MO)
2. Pep Boys (PA)
3. AutoZone (TN)
4. Northern Automotive (AZ)
5. Chief Auto Parts (TX)
6. WSR Group (NJ)
7. Trak Auto (MO)
8. Nationwise Automotive (OH)
9. Hi/Lo Automotives (TX)
10. Advance Auto Parts (VA)

Source: Discount Store News, Discount Industry
Annual Report, July 4, 1994.

Sales Up, Tops Down

Top convertibles of 1993 (and number of units
sold):

1.	Chrysler LeBaron	31,263
2.	Ford Mustang	23,405
3.	Mazda Miata	21,514
4.	Mercury Capri	9,853
5.	Chevrolet Cavalier	8,084
6.	Geo Metro	6,757
7.	Olds Cutlass Supreme	6,216
8.	Dodge Shadow	6,014
9.	Pontiac Sunbird	5,701
10.	Chevrolet Corvette	5,124

Source: Automotive News, September 19,
1994.

Famous Four-Wheeled Flops

Edsel
Vega
Pinto
Corvair
Yugo

Great Auto Shows

Detroit (of course)
Los Angeles
New York
Chicago
Miami
Tokyo

In the Black(walls)

Top tire manufacturers of 1993 (based on sales):

1. Michelin (France)
2. Bridgestone (Japan)
3. Goodyear (United States)
4. Continental (Germany)
5. Sumitomo Bank Ltd. (Japan)
6. Pirelli (Italy)
7. Yokohama (Japan)
8. Toyo (Japan)
9. Cooper (United States)
10. Kumho (South Korea)

Source: Financial Times, January 25, 1995.

European Sales Leaders

Automobile manufacturers selling the most cars
in Europe in1994 (and number of units sold):

1.	Volkswagen (including Audi and Seat)	148,500
2.	Peugeot SA (including Citroen)	125,850

1954: Cadillac becomes the first car manufacturer to adopt power steering as a standard feature on all its cars.

These plastic model Chevy Vegas wouldn't rust, unlike the real thing.
Courtesy of American Automobile Manufacturers Association

3. General Motors Corp.
(including Apel, Vauxhall, Isuzu) 116,000
4. Fiat Auto SpA 108,000
5. Renault 106,200
6. Ford Motor Co. (including Jaguar) 98,200
7. Mercedes-Benz 33,900
8. BMW 30,300
9. Nissan Motor Corp. 26,950
10. Toyota Motor Co. Ltd. 24,900

Source: Automotive News, November 21, 1994.

South of the Border

Best-selling cars in the Mexican domestic market in 1994 (and number of units sold):

1. Tsuru (Nissan) 9,444
2. Beetle (VW) 6,956
3. Jetta (VW) 5,382
4. Cavalier (GM) 4,150
5. Golf (VW) 3,250
6. Cutlass (GM) 1,285
7. Mystique (Ford) 1,169
8. Neon (Chrysler) 1,075
9. Spirit (Chrysler) 1,065
10. Tsubame (Nissan) 810

Source: Business Mexico, April, 1995.

Speaking of Sports

Top sporty cars of 1993 (and number of units sold):

1. Ford Mustang 98,648
2. Ford Probe 90,435
3. Chevrolet Camaro 68,773
4. Acura Integra 58,757
5. Mitsubishi Eclipse 57,083
6. Toyota Celica 29,237
7. Mazda MX-6 29,068
8. Eagle Talon 27,360

9. Pontiac Firebird 26,893
10. Toyota Paseo 24,466

Source: Advertising Age, February 7, 1994.

Faster than a Speeding Bullet?

Two street cars that went over 200 mph right from the factory:

1994 McLaren F1 220 mph
1994 Jaguar XJ220 212 mph

Body Language

Brougham
Cabriolet
Convertible
Coupe
Limousine
Roadster
Sedan
Station wagon
Touring car
Town car

Twenty-Five Shades of Blue

Aqua
Basin Street Blue
Blue Sky
Cambridge Blue
Carib Blue
Cayman Blue
Chesapeake Blue
Cobalt Blue
Diamond Blue
Dresden Blue
Glacier Blue
Gulf Blue
Jewel Blue

1954: Ford introduces the Thunderbird to compete with Chevrolet's popular Corvette.

The Levi's Gremlin featured a denim-like interior, complete with a Levi's "pocket tab."

Courtesy of American Automobile Manufacturers Association

Laguna Blue
Mariner Blue
Midnight Blue
Moonlight Blue
Nassau Blue
Regal Blue
Sapphire Blue
Starlight Blue
Tradewind Blue
Twilight Blue
Venetian Blue
Winter Blue

Cars with a Clothing Connection

Levi's AMC Gremlin
Eddie Bauer Ford Explorer
Orvis Jeep Grand Cherokee
Bill Blass Lincoln Continental
Nautica Mercury Villager

Rear Window Displays

Air freshener crowns
Baseball caps
Dogs with bobbing heads
Nativity scenes
Octopi
Stuffed animal collections
Toys

Cars and Their Famous Owners

Aston Martin: King Hussein of Jordan, Peter
    Sellers, Prince of Wales
Cadillac Eldorado: Dwight Eisenhower, Mari-
    lyn Monroe
Facel Vega: Ringo Starr, Ava Gardner, Danny
    Kaye, Tony Curtis, Francois Truffaut, Joan
    Fontaine, Albert Camus

Ferrari 400 GT: Sammy Davis, Jr.
Pantera: Elvis Presley
Porsche 930: Roy Orbison

For Rent

Top car rental companies by number of U.S.
locations in 1994:

1.	Enterprise	2,000
2.	Hertz	1,300
3.	Avis	1,200
4.	Budget	1,067
5.	National	950 (estimate)
6.	Thrifty	496
7.	U-Save	481
8.	Dollar	267
9.	Carey	212
10.	Payless	125
10.	Practical	125

Source: *Business Travel News*, Business Travel
    Survey (annual), May 29, 1995.

Things People (Shouldn't) Do While Driving

Brush their teeth
Change a diaper
Drink
Eat
Put on makeup
Read
Sleep
Switch seats
Talk on the phone
Use a computer

Old Songs About Cars

"In My Merry Oldsmobile" (1905)
"On an Automobile Honeymoon" (1905)

1955: The Dodge Custom Royal LaFemme is equipped with a matching rain cape, boots, umbrella, and purse.

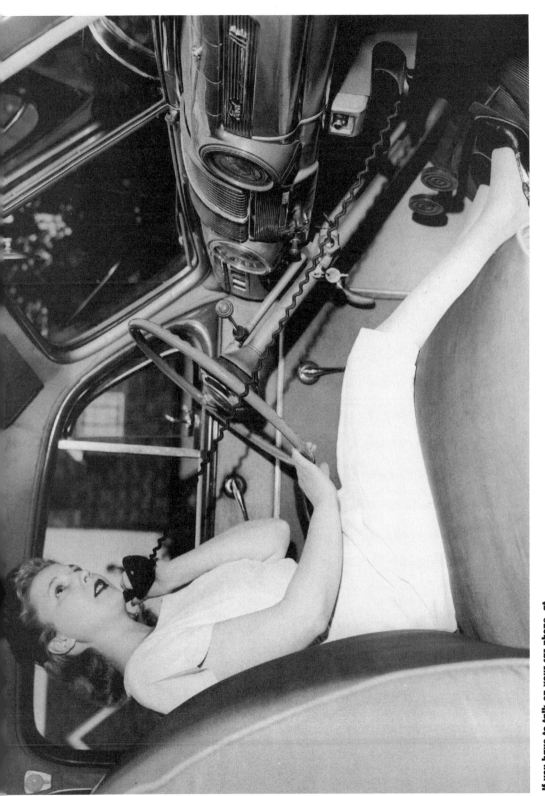

If you have to talk on your car phone, at least pull over to do it.

Courtesy of Ameritech

"Take Me 'Round in a Taxicab" (1908)

"Keep Away from the Fellow Who Owns an
Automobile" (1912)

"He'd Have to Get Under, Get Out and Get
Under, to Fix Up His Automobile" (1913)

"I'm Wild about Horns on Automobiles that
Go 'Ta-Ta-Ta-Ta' " (1928)

"The Low-Backed Car" (1934)

"Ridin' Around in the Rain" (1934)

"Traffic Jam" (1939)

"Headin' Down the Wrong Highway" (1945)

"There's Nothing Like a Model T" (1947)

"The Stanley Steamer" (1947)

More Recent Songs About Cars

"Car on a Hill" (*Joni Mitchell*)

"Car Wash" (*Rose Royce*)

"Cars" (*Gary Numan*)

"Devil in a Fast Car" (*Sheena Easton*)

"Fast Car" (*Tracy Chapman*)

"I'm In Love With My Car" (*Queen*)

"In My Car" (*The Beach Boys*)

"Let Me Be Your Car" (*Rod Stewart*)

"Our Car Club" (*The Beach Boys*)

"This Car of Mine" (*The Beach Boys*)

"Took the Car" (*John Mayall*)

"Used Cars" (*Bruce Springsteen*)

Songs About Cadillacs

"Big Black Cadillac Blues" (*Lightnin' Hopkins*)

"Brand New Cadillac" (*The Clash*)

"Cadillac Walk" (*Willie Deville*)

"Cadillac Brougham" (*The Beach Boys*)

"Cadillac Assembly Line" (*Albert King*)

"Cadillac Avenue" (*Don Henry*)

"Geronimo's Cadillac" (*Michael Martin Murphy*)

"Cadillac Ranch" (*Bruce Springsteen*)

"Guitars and Cadillacs" (*Dwight Yoakam*)

"Long White Cadillac" (*The Blasters*)

"Pink Cadillac" (*Bruce Springsteen/Natalie Cole*)

"Ray's Dad's Cadillac" (*Joni Mitchell*)

"Rusty Cadillac" (*Da Yoopers*)

"They've Downsized My Cadillac" (*Dick Siegel*)

Songs About Other Cars

"Chevy Van" (*Sammy Johns*)

"Corvair Baby" (*Paul Revere and the Raiders*)

"Ford Econoline" (*Nanci Griffith*)

"From a Buick 6" (*Bob Dylan*)

"Jaguar" (*The Tremolos*)

"Little GTO" (*Ronnie and the Daytonas*)

"Little Red Corvette" (*Prince*)

"Makin' Thunderbirds" (*Bob Seger and the Silver
Bullet Band*)

"Mercedes-Benz" (*Janis Joplin*)

"Mercury Blues" (*Steve Miller Band*)

"Pontiac" (*Lyle Lovett*)

Songs About Roads

"Autobahn" (*Kraftwerk*)

"Crossroads Blues" (*Robert Johnson*)

"Crosstown Traffic" (*Jimi Hendrix*)

"Expressway to Your Heart" (*Soul Survivors*)

"Farther Up the Road" (*Bobby Blue Bland*)

"Follow Your Road" (*Seawind*)

"Forty Miles of Bad Road" (*Duane Eddy*)

"Freeway of Love" (*Aretha Franklin*)

"Highway 51" (*Charlie Musselwhite*)

"L.A. Freeway" (*Jerry Jeff Walker*)

"Lookin' at the World Through a Windshield"
(*Del Reeves*)

"Mama Know the Highway by Heart" (*Hal
Ketchum*)

"Missouri Road Song" (*Bill Staines*)

"Ninety Miles an Hour Down a Dead-End
Road" (*Hank Snow*)

1956: United States begins a 41,000-mile network of modern freeways, spanning the country and
linking 90 percent of all the cities with populations of 50,000 or more.

"Racing in the Street" (*Bruce Springsteen*)

"Road Runner" (*The Gants*)

"Roll on Down the Highway" (*Bachman Turner Overdrive*)

"(Get Your Kicks on) Route 66" (*Nat King Cole*)

Songs About Accidents

"Crack-Up" (*The Routers*)

"Crawling from the Wreckage" (*Dave Edmunds*)

"D.O.A." (*Bloodrock*)

"Dead Man's Curve" (*Jan and Dean*)

"Hit and Run" (*The Bar Kays*)

"Last Kiss" (*J. Frank Wilson and the Cavaliers*)

"Teen Angel" (*Mark Denning*)

"Tell Laura I Love Her" (*Ray Peterson*)

"Wreck on the Highway" (*Roy Acuff*)

Songs About Driving

"Drive All Night" (*Dion*)

"Drive My Car" (*The Beatles*)

"Drive" (*The Cars*)

"Drive" (*R.E.M.*)

"Drivin' Home" (*Duane Eddy*)

"Drivin' Til the Break of Day" (*John Mayall*)

"Drivin' with Your Eyes Closed" (*Don Henley*)

"Driving My Life Away" (*Eddie Rabbitt*)

"Driving Wheel" (*Little Junior Parker*)

"Driving While Blind" (*ZZ Top*)

"Easy Driver" (*Kenny Loggins*)

"I Gotta Drive" (*Jan and Dean*)

"I Can't Drive 55" (*Sammy Hagar*)

"You Can Sleep While I Drive" (*Melissa Etheridge*)

Songs About Drivers

"Baby Driver" (*Simon and Garfunkel*)

"Back Seat Driver" (*The Bar Kays*)

"Cab Driver" (*The Mills Brothers*)

"Chauffeur Blues" (*The Jefferson Airplane*)

"Driver's Seat" (*Sniff and the Tears*)

"Lady Cab Driver" (*Prince*)

"Limousine Driver" (*James Taylor*)

Songs About Love in Cars

"Back Seat of My Car" (*Paul McCartney*)

"Cupid's Trash Truck" (*Lou and Peter Berryman*)

"Get Outta My Dreams (Get Into My Car)" (*Billy Ocean*)

"Heaven in the Back Seat" (*Eddie Money*)

"Paradise by the Dashboard Light" (*Meatloaf*)

"Radar Love" (*Golden Earring*)

"Rapture" (*Blondie*)

"Sitting in the Back Seat" (*Paul Evans*)

Hot Rod Songs by The Beach Boys

"409"

"Car Crazy Cutie"

"Cherry Cherry Coupe"

"Custom Machine"

"Don't Worry Baby"

"Fun Fun Fun"

"Little Deuce Coupe"

"No-Go Showboat"

"Our Car Club"

"Shut Down"

"This Car of Mine"

Hot Rod Songs by Jan and Dean

"'B' Gas Rickshaw"

"Bucket 'T'"

"Dead Man's Curve"

"Drag Strip Girl"

"Drag City"

"Hot Stocker"

1957: First cars fitted with twin double headlights (four headlights) are the Lincoln and Cadillac models.

The Man Behind the Hot Rod Songs

Gary Usher was the unknown name behind many hot rod songs and groups. He was the writer, producer, vocalist, and arranger for many hot rod songs of the 1960s. The groups he was involved with include The Captivations, The Competitors, The Customs, The Devons, The Four Speeds, The Hondells, The Revells, and The Super Stocks.

"I Gotta Drive"
"Little Old Lady from Pasadena"
"Move Out Little Mustang"
"My Mighty G.T.O."
"Rockin' Little Roadster"
"Schlock Rod"
"Surfin' Hearse"
"Three Window Coupe"

Hot Rod Songs by Other Groups

"Hot Rot Show" (*The Challengers*)
"Hot Rod Lincoln" (*Charlie Ryan*)
"Hot Rod Weekend" (*Donnie and Diane*)
"Hot Rod Ford" (*D.Y. and the Motivators*)
"Hot Rod High" (*The Hondells/The Surfaris*)
"Hot Rod City" (*The Hubcaps*)

"I'm a Hot Rodder" (*Jay Imus and Freddy Ford*)
"Hot Rod" (*The Lizards*)
"Hot Rod Volkswagen" (*Bill Parsons*)
"Hot Rod U.S.A." (*The Rip Chords*)
"Hot Rod Center" (*The Blasters*)
"Hot Rod Racer" (*Dick Dale and His Del-Tones*)
"Hot Rod Queen" (*The Dragsters*)
"Hot Rod Race" (*Charlie Ryan*)
"Hot Rod Car" (*Bobby Verne*)

Groups Named After Cars or Car Things

The Barracudas
The Bentleys
The Bonnevilles
The Cars
The Catalinas
The Chargers
The Chevelles
The Cords
The Corvettes
The Daytonas
The Deuce Coupes
The Fabulous Thunderbirds
Flash Cadillac and the Continental Kids
The Fleetwoods
The G.T.O.s
The Imperials
The Lincolns
REO Speedwagon
The Roadsters
The Sting Rays
The Thunderbirds
Traffic
The Triumphs
The Vettes

1957: A cruise control device is introduced on some cars by Chrysler.

ACTION JACKSON

Power-hungry auto tycoon Nelson tries to frame rebellious police sergeant Weathers for murder. Being a graduate of Harvard and a tough guy, the cop doesn't go for it. Nelson eats up the screen as the heavy with no redeeming qualities, while Weathers is tongue-in-cheek as the resourceful good guy who keeps running afoul of the law in spite of his best efforts. Lots of action, violence, and a few sexy women help cover the plot's lack of common sense. (1988; R)

Cast: Carl Weathers, Vanity, Craig T. Nelson, Sharon Stone.

Director: Craig R. Baxley. ●●

ACTION U.S.A.

A young woman witnesses the murder of her boyfriend by gangsters, who then pursue her to make sure she will never tell what she saw. Throughout Texas she rambles with the mob sniffing at her heels, grateful for the opportunity to participate in numerous stunts and car crashes. (1989)

Cast: Barri Murphy, Greg Cummins, William Knight, William Smith, Cameron Mitchell.

Director: John Stewart. ●(

AMERICAN FABULOUS

The posthumously released autobiography of an eccentric homosexual who lived life in the fast lane. Jeffrey Strouth performs his monologue from the back seat of a 1957 Cadillac, where the images of small-town America are seen to contrast sharply with his flamboyant style. His grotesque and candid recollections include his alcoholic Elvis-impersonator father, a stint as a teenage prostitute, drag queen friends, and drug addiction in New York. Strouth puts a comic twist on even the most brutal of his memories. He died of AIDS at the age of 33 in 1992. (1992)

Cast: Jeffrey Strouth.

Director: Reno Dakota. ●●(

AMERICAN GRAFFITI

Atmospheric, episodic look at growing up in the innocence of America before the Kennedy

●●●● *luxury ride*

●●●(*enjoyable ride*

●●● *handles well*

●●(*some bumps*

●● *time to rotate*

●(*slow leak*

● *needs some air*

◐ *totally flat*

1957: Ford Motor Company introduces a new car line, the Edsel. Swiftly rejected by the public, Edsel becomes synonymous with massive failure. Ford lost up to $350 million on this idea.

assassination and the Vietnam War. It all takes place on one hectic but typical night in the life of a group of recent California high school grads unsure of what the next big step in life is. So they spend their time cruising, listening to Wolfman Jack, and meeting at the drive-in. Slice of '60s life boasts a prudent script, great set design, authentic soundtrack, consistently fine performances by the young cast, and some of the coolest cars ever to show up on the silver screen. Worth the price of admission: the climactic race between Ford and LeMat. Catapulted Dreyfuss, Ford, and Somers to stardom, branded Lucas a hot directorial commodity with enough leverage to launch *Star Wars,* and steered Howard and Williams towards continued age-of-innocence nirvana on *Happy Days.* (1973; PG)

Cast: Richard Dreyfuss, Ron Howard, Cindy Williams, MacKenzie Phillips, Paul LeMat, Charles Martin Smith, Suzanne Somers, Candy Clark, Harrison Ford, Bo Hopkins, Joe Spano, Kathleen Quinlan, Wolfman Jack.

Director: George Lucas.

BABY ON BOARD

Kane plays the wife of a Mafia bookkeeper who is accidentally killed in a gangland murder. Out for revenge, she tracks her husband's killer to JFK airport with her four-year old daughter in tow. Just as she pulls the loaded gun from her purse and takes aim, a pickpocket snatches her purse, accidentally firing the gun. Now she's on the run and she jumps into the first cab she can find, driven by Reinhold. New York City is turned upside down as mother, daughter, and cabbie try to elude the mob in this funny but predictable comedy. (1992; PG)

Cast: Carol Kane, Judge Reinhold, Geza Kovacs, Errol Slue, Alex Stapley, Holly Stapley.

Director: Francis Schaeffer.

BACK TO THE FUTURE

When neighborhood mad scientist Doc Brown constructs a time machine from a De-Lorean, his youthful companion Marty accidentally transports himself to 1955. There, Marty must do everything he can to bring his parents together, elude the local bully, and get back . . . to the future. Solid fast-paced entertainment is even better due to Lloyd's inspired performance as the loony Doc while Fox is perfect as the boy completely out of his element. Soundtrack features Huey Lewis and the News. Followed by two sequels. (1985; PG)

Cast: Michael J. Fox, Christopher Lloyd, Lea Thompson, Crispin Glover, Wendie Jo Sperber, Marc McClure, Thomas F. Wilson, James Tolkan, Casey Siemaszko, Billy Zane, George DiCenzo, Courtney Gains, Claudia Wells, Jason Hervey, Harry Waters, Jr., Maia Brewton, J.J. Cohen. Cameos: Huey Lewis.

Director: George Zemeckis.

BAFFLED

Nimoy is a race car driver who has visions of people in danger. He must convince an ESP expert (Hampshire) of the credibility of his vision, and then try to save the lives of the people seen with his sixth sense. Made for television. (1972)

Cast: Leonard Nimoy, Susan Hampshire, Vera Miles, Rachel Roberts, Jewel Blanch, Christopher Benjamin.

Director: Philip Leacock.

1958: Aluminum automobile engines are developed in the United States. They are more resistant to wear and are 30 percent lighter than traditional cast-iron engines.

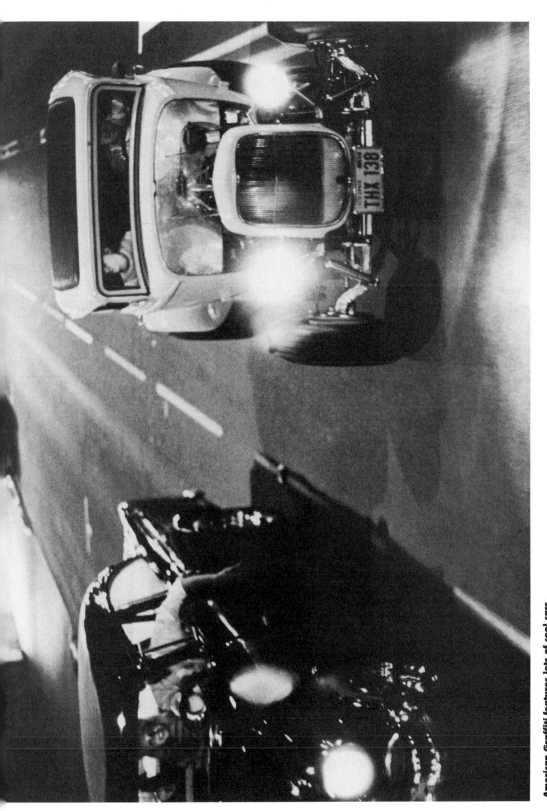

American Graffiti features lots of cool cars.
Lucas Films/Coppola Co./Universal/The Kobal Collection

BAIL OUT

Three bounty hunters, armed to the teeth, run a car-trashing police gauntlet so they may capture a valuable crook. (1990; R)

Cast: David Hasselhoff, Linda Blair, John Vernon, Tom Rosales, Charlie Brill.

Director: Max Kleven.

BANZAI RUNNER

A cop whose brother was killed in an exclusive desert-highway race decides to avenge by joining the race himself. (1986)

Cast: Dean Stockwell, John Shepherd, Charles Dierkop.

Director: John G. Thomas.

THE BETSY

A story of romance, money, power, and mystery centering around the wealthy Hardeman family and their automobile manufacturing business. Loosely patterned after the life of Henry Ford as portrayed in the Harold Robbins' pulp-tome. Olivier is the redeeming feature. (1978; R)

Cast: Laurence Olivier, Kathleen Beller, Robert Duvall, Lesley-Anne Down, Edward Herrmann, Tommy Lee Jones, Katharine Ross, Jane Alexander.

Director: Daniel Petrie.

THE BIG WHEEL

Old story retold fairly well. Rooney is young son determined to travel in his father's tracks as a race car driver, even when dad buys the farm on the oval. Good acting and direction keep this a cut above average. (1949)

Cast: Mickey Rooney, Thomas Mitchell, Spring Byington, Mary Hatcher, Allen Jenkins, Michael O'Shea.

Director: Edward Ludwig.

BLACK ICE

After an affair with a popular politician ends violently, Vanessa (Pacula) realizes her boss set up his death—and she's next in line. She finds the nearest taxi and offers the driver plenty of cash if he can quickly get her out of the country. It's going to be the ride of her life. (1992; R)

Cast: Michael Nouri, Michael Ironside, Joanna Pacula.

Director: Neill Fearnley.

BLACK MOON RISING

Based on an idea by John Carpenter (*Halloween*), this film deals with the theft of a new jet-powered car and its involvement in an FBI investigation. Solid performances and steady action enhance this routine effort. (1986; R)

Cast: Tommy Lee Jones, Linda Hamilton, Richard Jaeckel, Robert Vaughn.

Director: Harley Cokliss.

BLUE DE VILLE

Two young women buy a '59 Cadillac and journey from St. Louis to New Mexico, having adventures on the way. The rambling, free-spirited movie was a pilot for a prospective series that never set sail—but when *Thelma &*

1959: The Chevrolet Corvair—built to compete with small imports—is the first U.S. rear-engine, air-cooled car.

The Bluesmobile zooms over a police car in *The Blues Brothers*.
Universal/The Kobal Collection

Louise hit big this superficially similar item was hauled out on video. (1986; PG)

Cast: Jennifer Runyon, Kimberly Pistone, Mark Thomas Miller, Alan Autry, Robert Prescott.

Director: Jim Johnston.

BLUE JEANS AND DYNAMITE

A stuntman is hired to lift the "Golden Mask of the Duct Tomb" and is followed on land, water, and air. Great chase scenes and action-filled finale. (198?)

Cast: Robert Vaughn, Simon Andrew, Katia Kristine.

THE BLUES BROTHERS

As an excuse to run rampant on the city of Chicago, Jake and Elwood Blues attempt to raise $5,000 for their childhood orphanage by putting their old band back together. Good music, and lots of cameos. Loaded with car chases and crashes. (1980; R)

Cast: John Belushi, Dan Aykroyd, James Brown, Cab Calloway, Ray Charles, Henry Gibson, Aretha Franklin, Carrie Fisher, John Candy. Cameos: Frank Oz, Steven Spielberg, Twiggy, Paul (Pee Wee Herman) Reubens, Steve Lawrence, John Lee Hooker.

Director: John Landis.

BOBBY DEERFIELD

Cold-blooded Grand Prix driver comes face to face with death each time he races, but finally learns the meaning of life when he falls in love with a critically ill woman. Even with race cars, soap opera stalls. (1977; PG)

Cast: Al Pacino, Marthe Keller, Anny Duperey, Romolo Valli.

Director: Sydney Pollack.

BORDER RADIO

A rock singer decides to steal a car and try to outrun some tough thugs hot on his trail. (1988)

Cast: Chris D, Luana Anders.

Director: Allison Anders, Kurt Voss.

BORN TO RACE

In the world of competitive auto racing, a beautiful engineer is kidnapped for her new controversial engine design. (1988; R)

Cast: Joseph Bottoms, George Kennedy, Marc Singer, Marla Heasly.

Director: James Fargo.

BORN TO RUN

Nicky Donatello (Grieco) is a Brooklyn street drag racer who gets mixed up with the mob while trying to rescue his no-account brother. But he still finds time to fall for an uptown model who also happens to be the mobster's girlfriend. Made for television. (1993)

Cast: Richard Grieco, Jay Acovone, Shelli Lether, Christian Campbell, Brent Stait, Martin Cummins, Wren Roberts, Joe Cortese.

Director: Albert Magnoli.

1959: It's as big as a whale! Long-finned Cadillacs reach over 16 ½ feet.

BOYS ON THE SIDE

It's *Thelma & Louise* come to *Terms of Endearment* by way of *Philadelphia*. Goldberg is Jane, an unemployed lesbian singer, who connects with Ms. Priss real estate agent Robin (Parker) for a road trip to California. The two become a female version of the Odd Couple as Jane tags Robin as "the whitest woman in America." They stop off to pick up addle-brain friend Holly (Barrymore) who has just knocked her drug-crazed abusive beau in the head with a baseball bat. Holly's accident turns fatal and the threesome are on the run from cops. They bond like crazy glue and become a family as they face two huge setbacks—one's pregnant, another has AIDS. Strong performances by the lead actresses and a cool soundtrack may make up for this often trite movie of the week premise. (1994; R)

Cast: James Remar, Anita Gillette, Matthew McConaughey, Whoopi Goldberg, Mary-Louise Parker, Drew Barrymore.

Director: Herbert Ross.

BREAKING THE RULES

Predictable buddy-road movie with a tear-jerking premise and comedic overtones. Rob, Gene, and Phil were best buds growing up in Cleveland but young adulthood has separated them. They are reunited by Phil, who is dying of leukemia, and whose last wish is a cross-country road trip to California so he can appear as a contestant on *Jeopardy!* Along the way they meet brassy waitress Mary, who impulsively decides to join them and winds up bringing the trio's shaky friendship back together. Potts does well as the big-haired, big-hearted Mary but the actors must work hard to maintain any dignity given the story's melodrama. (1992; PG-13)

Cast: Jason Bateman, C. Thomas Howell, Jonathan Silverman, Annie Potts, Kent Bateman, Shawn Phelan.

Director: Neal Israel.

BREATHING LESSONS

Sweet look at a long-term marriage that renews itself on a road trip. Flighty Maggie and pragmatic Ira have been married for 28 squabbling but loving years. They're driving from their Baltimore home to a funeral in Pennsylvania and the road stops provide some small adventures and a great deal of conversation. Drama rests easily on the capable shoulders of the veteran performers. Based on the novel by Anne Tyler. Made for TV. (1994; PG)

Cast: James Garner, Joanne Woodward, Paul Winfield, Kathryn Erbe, Joyce Van Patten, Eileen Heckart, Tim Guinee, Henry Jones, Stephi Lineburg, Jean Louisa Kelly, John Considine.

Director: John Erman.

BULLITT

A detective assigned to protect a star witness for 48 hours senses danger; his worst fears are confirmed when his charge is murdered. Based on the novel, *Mute Witness* by Robert L. Pike, and featuring one of filmdom's most famous car chases. (1968; PG)

Cast: Steve McQueen, Robert Vaughn, Jacqueline Bisset, Don Gordon, Robert Duvall, Norman Fell, Simon Oakland.

Director: Peter Yates.

CADILLAC MAN

Williams is the quintessential low-life car salesman in this rather disjointed comedy. A

1960: DeSoto automobiles will no longer be manufactured as one of the cars offered by Chrysler Corporation. This announcement discontinues a line of cars Chrysler had made since 1928.

A Dodge Charger goes airborne in *Bullitt.*
Warner Brothers/The Kobal Collection

lesser comedic talent might have stalled and been abandoned, but Williams manages to drive away despite the flat script and direction. One storyline follows his attempt to sell 12 cars in 12 days or lose his job, while another follows his confrontation with a gun-toting, mad-as-hell cuckolded husband. Williams and Robbins are often close to being funny in a hyperkinetic way, but the situations are dumb enough to rob most of the scenes of their comedy. Watch for a movie-stealing bit by the spunky waitress at the local Chinese restaurant. (1990; R)

Cast: Robin Williams, Tim Robbins, Pamela Reed, Fran Drescher, Zack Norman, Annabella Sciorra, Lori Petty, Paul Guilfoyle.

Director: Roger Donaldson.

CALENDAR GIRL

In 1962 three high school best friends borrow a convertible and travel from their Nevada homes to Hollywood to meet their pinup idol, Marilyn Monroe. Roy's (Priestley) a rebel, Ned's (Olds, in his film debut) sensitive, and Scott's (O'Connell) just a nice guy. They stay with Roy's Uncle Harvey (Pantoliano), an aspiring actor, and work to meet their dream girl. Which they finally do, in a notably weak sequence which fits in with this notably uninspired film. The three actors at least have enough comradery to make realistic buddies—one of the few true touches in the film. (1993; PG-13)

Cast: Jason Priestley, Jerry O'Connell, Joe Pantoliano, Gabriel Olds, Stephen Tobolowsky, Kurt Fuller, Steve Railsback, Emily Warfield, Stephanie Anderson. Cameos: Chubby Checker.

Director: John Whitesell.

CANNONBALL

Assorted ruthless people leave patches of rubber across the country competing for grand prize in less than legal auto race. Not top drawer New World but nonetheless a cult fave. Inferior to Bartel's previous cult classic, *Death Race 2000.* Most interesting for plethora of cult cameos, including Scorsese, Dante, and grandmaster Corman. (1976; PG)

Cast: David Carradine, Bill McKinney, Veronica Hamel, Gerrit Graham, Robert Carradine, Sylvester Stallone, Jonathan Kaplan. Cameos: Martin Scorsese, Roger Corman, Joe Dante.

Director: Paul Bartel.

CANNONBALL RUN

So many stars, so little plot. Reynolds and sidekick DeLuise disguise themselves as paramedics to foil cops while they compete in cross-country Cannonball race. Shows no sign of having been directed by an ex-stuntman. One of 1981's top grossers—go figure. Followed by equally languid sequel *Cannonball Run II.* (1981; PG)

Cast: Burt Reynolds, Farrah Fawcett, Roger Moore, Dom DeLuise, Dean Martin, Sammy Davis, Jr., Jack Elam, Adrienne Barbeau, Peter Fonda, Molly Picon, Bert Convy, Jamie Farr.

Director: Hal Needham.

CANNONBALL RUN II

More mindless cross-country wheel spinning with gratuitous star cameos. Director Needham apparently subscribes to the two wrongs make a right school of sequels. (1984; PG)

Cast: Burt Reynolds, Dom DeLuise, Jamie Farr, Marilu Henner, Shirley MacLaine, Jim Nabors, Frank

1960: The first Daytona 500 car race is held at Daytona International Speedway and won by Lee Petty.

Sinatra, Sammy Davis, Jr., Dean Martin, Telly Savalas, Susan Anton, Catherine Bach, Jack Elam, Sid Caesar, Ricardo Montalban, Charles Nelson Reilly. Cameos: Henry Silva, Tim Conway, Don Knotts, Molly Picon.

Director: Hal Needham.

CAR CRASH

Organized crime hits stock car racing head on to produce crashing bore. (19??)

Cast: Joey Travolta, Anna Obregon, Vittorio Mezzogiorno.

CAR TROUBLE

Young English husband buys new Jaguar and wife's not so minor car trouble causes major marital trouble. Funnybone-tickling pairing of Walters and Charleson. (1986; R)

Cast: Julie Walters, Ian Charleson.

Director: David Green.

CAR WASH

An L.A. car wash provides a soap-opera setting for disjointed comic bits about owners of dirty cars and people who hose them down for a living. Econo budget and lite plot, but serious comic talent. A sort of disco car wash version of *Grand Hotel.* (1976; PG)

Cast: Franklin Ajaye, Sully Boyer, Richard Brestoff, George Carlin, Richard Pryor, Melanie Mayron, Ivan Dixon, Antonio Fargas.

Director: Michael A. Schultz.

THE CARS THAT ATE PARIS

Parasitic town in the Parisian (Australia) outback preys on car and body parts generated by deliberate accidents inflicted by wreck-driving wreckless youths. Weir's first film released internationally, about a small Australian town that survives economically via deliberately contriving car accidents and selling the wrecks' scrap parts. A broad, bitter black comedy with some horror touches. (1974; PG)

Cast: Terry Camillieri, Kevin Miles, John Meillon, Melissa Jaffe.

Director: Peter Weir.

CATCH ME . . . IF YOU CAN

High school class president Melissa doesn't want to see the school torn down. To raise fast cash, she teams up with a drag racer and the fun begins. (1989; PG)

Cast: Matt Lattanzi, Loryn Locklin, M. Emmet Walsh, Geoffrey Lewis.

Director: Stephen Sommers.

CHANGES

A young man leaves home and thumbs across the California coast in order to find himself. On the road again. (1969; PG)

Cast: Kent Lane, Michele Carey, Jack Albertson, Marcia Strassman.

Director: Hall Bartlett.

THE CHASE

Not realizing that his boss-to-be is a mobster, Cummings takes a job as a chauffeur. Natural-

1961: Jaguar introduces its legendary E-Type, a sleek sports car with aerodynamic lines, independent rear suspension, and front disc brakes. It is the first 150 mph production car.

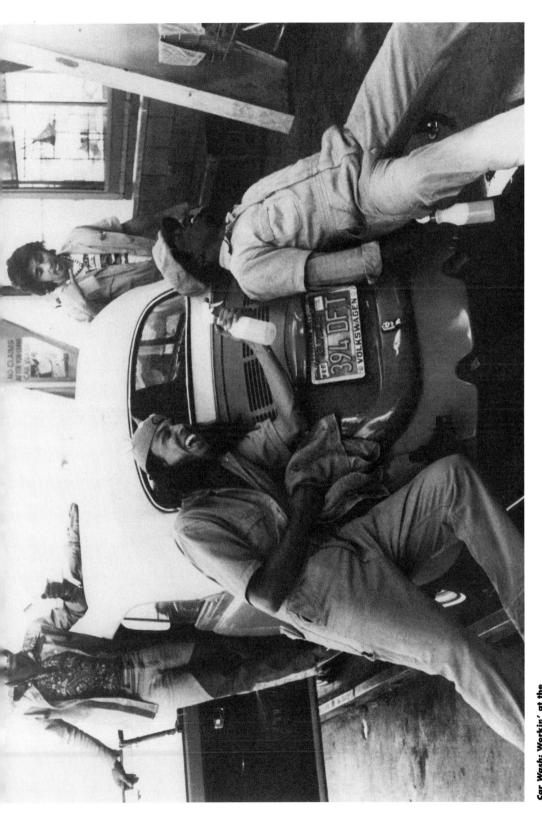

***Car Wash:* Workin' at the
car wash, yeah!**
Universal/The Kobal Collection

ly, he falls in love with the gangster's wife (Morgan), and the two plan to elope. Somewhat miffed, the cuckolded mafioso and his bodyguard (Lorre) pursue the elusive couple as they head for Havana. The performances are up to snuff, but the story's as unimaginative as the title, with intermittent bouts of suspense. (1946)

Cast: Robert Cummings, Michele Morgan, Peter Lorre, Steve Cochran, Lloyd Corrigan, Jack Holt, Don Wilson.

Director: Arthur Ripley.

THE CHASE

Heiress Natalie Voss (Swanson) is in the wrong place at the wrong time when she's carjacked by escaped con Jack Hammond (Sheen) who uses a Butterfinger for his weapon. Frantic chases ensues as it turns out that Daddy Voss is a media hungry millionaire and he's followed by not only the cops but the media as well. One-dimensional characters aren't helped by a one-dimensional script, but slick filmmaking and a little charm helps. Skewers the media hype that surrounds crime, taking on news programs that offer immediate coverage and reality based shows with glee. (1993; PG-13)

Cast: Kristy Swanson, Charlie Sheen, Josh Mostel, Ray Wise, Henry Rollins, Flea.

Director: Adam Rifkin.

THE CHECKERED FLAG

Lame auto-racing drama about an aging, millionaire race car driver with an alcoholic wife who would like nothing more than to see him dead. She talks a young rookie into helping her dispose of hubby. Plans go awry—with horrify-

ing results. Racing scenes overshadow incredibly weak script and performances. (1963)

Cast: Joe Morrison, Evelyn King, Charles G. Martin, Peggy Vendig.

Director: William Grefe.

CHEECH AND CHONG: THINGS ARE TOUGH ALL OVER

Stoner comedy team are hired by two rich Arab brothers (also played by Cheech and Chong in acting stretch) and unwittingly drive a car loaded with money from Chicago to Las Vegas. Tired fourth in the series. (1982; R)

Cast: Richard "Cheech" Marin, Thomas Chong, Shelby Fiddis, Rikki Marin, Evelyn Guerrero, Rip Taylor.

Director: Tom Avildsen.

CHITTY CHITTY BANG BANG

An eccentric inventor spruces up an old car and, in fantasy, takes his children to a land where the evil rulers have forbidden children. Poor special effects and forgettable score stall effort. Loosely adapted from an Ian Fleming story. (1968; G)

Cast: Dick Van Dyke, Sally Ann Howes, Lionel Jeffries, Gert Frobe, Anna Quayle, Benny Hill.

Director: Ken Hughes.

CHRISTINE

Unassuming teen gains posession of a classic auto equipped with a murderous will. The car more than returns the care and consideration its owner provides it. Based on a novel by Stephen King. (1984; R)

1962: First ever "million year" for a European car manufacturer is achieved by Volkswagen of Germany. Its popular Beetle is the largest selling import to the United States.

An evil car is the star of *Christine*.
Columbia/The Kobal Collection

Cast: Keith Gordon, John Stockwell, Alexandra Paul, Robert Prosky, Harry Dean Stanton, Kelly Preston.

Director: John Carpenter.

CLASS ACTION

Ethics from the 1960s and 1990s clash when a father and daughter, both lawyers, wind up on opposing sides of a litigation against an auto manufacturer. Hackman and Mastrantonio give intense, exciting performances, almost surmounting the melodramatic script. (1991; R)

Cast: Mary Elizabeth Mastrantonio, Gene Hackman, Joanna Merlin, Colin Friels, Laurence "Larry" Fishburne, Donald Moffat, Jan Rubes, Matt Clark, Fred Dalton Thompson, Jonathan Silverman, Dan Hicks.

Director: Michael Apted.

COMIC CABBY

A day in the life of an introvert cabby seems to last forever. From *New York City Cab Driver's Joke Book* by Jim Pietsch. (1987)

Cast: Bill McLaughlin, Al Lewis.

CORVETTE SUMMER

After spending a semester restoring a Corvette in his high school shop class, an L.A. student must journey to Las Vegas to recover the car when it is stolen. There he meets a prostitute, falls in love, and steps into the "real world" for the first time. Potts intriguing as the low-life love interest, but she can't save this one. (1978; PG)

Cast: Mark Hamill, Annie Potts, Eugene Roche, Kim Milford, Richard McKenzie, William Bryant.

Director: Matthew Robbins.

COUPE DE VILLE

Three brothers are forced by their father to drive mom's birthday present from Detroit to Florida in the summer of '63. Period concerns and music keep it interesting. (1990; PG-13)

Cast: Patrick Dempsey, Daniel Stern, Arye Gross, Joseph Bologna, Alan Arkin, Annabeth Gish, Rita Taggart, James Gammon.

Director: Joe Roth.

CRY PANIC

A man is thrown into a strange series of events after accidentally running down a man on a highway. Made for television. (1974)

Cast: John Forsythe, Anne Francis, Earl Holliman, Claudia McNeil, Ralph Meeker.

Director: James Goldstone.

CUJO

A rabid dog goes berserk and attacks a mother and her child who are trapped inside a broken-down (surprise, surprise) Pinto. Frighteningly realistic film is based on Stephen King's bestseller. (1983; R)

Cast: Dee Wallace Stone, Daniel Hugh-Kelly, Danny Pintauro, Ed Lauter, Christopher Stone.

Director: Lewis Teague.

1962: Debut of the Shelby AC Cobra, a high performance sports car designed by Carroll Shelby, combining an AC Bristol body with a Ford V8 engine.

DADDY-O

Drag racer Daddy-O traps the killers of his best friend and lands the blonde bombshell Jana. It might seem bad since it's dated, but, hey, it may have been bad in 1959, too! (1959)

Cast: Dick Contino, Sandra Giles.

Director: Lou Place.

DANGEROUS CURVES

Two friends are assigned to deliver a new Porsche to a billionaire's daughter—one of them talks the other into taking a little detour, and the trouble begins. This one went straight to video. (1988; PG)

Cast: Robert Stack, Tate Donovan, Danielle von Zernaeck, Robert Klein, Elizabeth Ashley, Leslie Nielsen.

Director: David Lewis.

DARK OF THE NIGHT

A young woman, new to the city, purchases a used Jaguar and finds she must share it with the car's former owner—a woman murdered inside the Jag. Decent psycho-thriller with some suspenseful and amusing moments. (1985)

Cast: Heather Bolton, David Letch, Gary Stalker, Michael Haigh, Danny Mulheron, Kate Harcourt.

Director: Gaylene Preston.

DAYS OF THUNDER

It's *Top Gun* in race cars! Cruise follows the same formula he has followed for several years now (with the notable exception of *Born on the Fourth of July*). Cruise co-wrote the screenplay concerning a young kid bursting with talent and raw energy who must learn to deal with his mentor, his girlfriend, and eventually the bad guy. First film that featured cameras that were actually on the race cars. If you like Cruise or race cars then this is the movie for you. (1990; PG-13)

Cast: Tom Cruise, Robert Duvall, Randy Quaid, Nicole Kidman, Cary Elwes, Michael Rooker, Fred Dalton Thompson, John C. Reilly.

Director: Tony Scott.

D.C. CAB

A rag-tag group of Washington, D.C. cabbies learn a lesson in self-respect in this endearing comedy. Though not without flaws, it's charming all the same. (1984; R)

Cast: Mr. T, Leif Erickson, Adam Baldwin, Charlie Barnett, Irene Cara, Anne DeSalvo, Max Gail, Gloria Gifford, Gary Busey, Jill Schoelen, Marsha Warfield.

Director: Joel Schumacher.

DEADLINE AUTO THEFT

A fun lovin' guy drives fast cars and meets beautiful women. Nudge, nudge, wink, wink. (1983)

Cast: H.B. Halicki, Hoyt Axton, Marion Busia, George Cole, Judi Gibbs, Lang Jeffries, Jr.

Director: H.B. Halicki.

DEATH DRIVER

In order to make a comeback, a stuntman attempts to do a stunt that was responsible for

---

1962: The first fuel-injected, turbocharged V8 engine is introduced in Oldsmobile's Jetfire car.

A rebel assassin is tossed from a car in *Death Race 2000*.
New World/The Kobal Collection

ending his career 10 years earlier. Obviously brave but none too smart. (1978)

Cast: Earl Owensby, Mike Allen, Patty Shaw, Mary Ann Hearn.

Director: Jimmy Huston.

DEATH RACE 2000

In the 21st century, five racing car contenders challenge the national champion of a cross country race in which drivers score points by killing pedestrians. Gory fun. Based on the 1956 story by Ib Melchior, and followed by *Death Sport.* Made for television. (1975; R)

Cast: David Carradine, Simone Griffeth, Sylvester Stallone, Mary Woronov.

Director: Paul Bartel.

DEATH SPORT

In this sequel to the cult hit *Death Race 2000,* a group of humans play a game of death in the year 3000. The object is to race cars and kill as many competitors as possible. Not as good as the original, but still watchable. (1978; R)

Cast: David Carradine, Claudia Jennings, Richard Lynch, William Smithers, Will Walker, David McLean, Jesse Vint.

Director: Henry Suso, Allan Arkush.

DESERT STEEL

Rival racers risk their lives in the big off-road race. (1994; PG)

Cast: David Naughton, Amanda Wyss, Russ Tamblyn, Brian Skinner.

Director: Glenn Gebhard.

DETOUR

Considered to be the creme de la creme of "B" movies, a largely unacknowledged but cult-followed noir downer. Well-designed, stylish, and compelling, if a bit contrived and sometimes annoyingly shrill. Shot in only six days with six indoor sets. Down-on-his-luck pianist Neal hitches cross-country to rejoin his fiancee. His first wrong turn involves the accidental death of the man who picked him up, then he's en route to Destiny with a capital "D" when he picks up fatal femme Savage, as vicious a vixen as ever ruined a good man. Told in flashback, it's also been called the most despairing of all "B"-pictures. As noir as they get. (1946)

Cast: Tom Neal, Ann Savage, Claudia Drake, Edmund MacDonald.

Director: Edgar G. Ulmer.

THE DEVIL ON WHEELS

Inspired by his dad's reckless driving, a teenager becomes a hot rodder and causes a family tragedy. A rusty melodrama that can't be described as high-performance. (1947)

Cast: James B. Cardwell, Noreen Nash, Darryl Hickman, Jan Ford, Damian O'Flynn, Lenita Love.

THE DEVIL THUMBS A RIDE

A naive traveller picks up a hitchhiker, not knowing he's wanted for murder. Will history repeat itself in this interesting noir? (1947)

Cast: Ted North, Lawrence Tierney, Nan Leslie.

Director: Felix Feist.

1963: Chrysler introduces the first 5 year/50,000 mile warranty (covering engine and powertrain parts).

DIAMONDS ARE FOREVER

Agent 007 once again battles his nemesis Blofeld, this time in Las Vegas. Bond must prevent the implementation of a plot to destroy Washington through the use of a space-orbiting laser. Fabulous stunts include Bond's wild drive through the streets of Vegas in a '71 Mach 1, escaping police by going down a narrow alley on two wheels. Connery returned to play Bond in this film after being offered the then record-setting salary of one million dollars. (1971; PG)

Cast: Sean Connery, Jill St. John, Charles Gray, Bruce Cabot, Jimmy Dean, Lana Wood, Bruce Glover, Putter Smith, Norman Burton, Joseph Furst, Bernard Lee, Desmond Llewelyn, Laurence Naismith, Leonard Barr, Lois Maxwell, Margaret Lacey, Joe Robinson, Donna Garrat, Trina Parks.

Director: Guy Hamilton.

DIRTY MARY CRAZY LARRY

A race car driver, his mechanic, and a sexy girl hightail it from the law after pulling off a heist. Great action, great fun, and an infamous surprise ending. (1974; PG)

Cast: Peter Fonda, Susan George, Adam Roarke, Vic Morrow, Roddy McDowall.

Director: John Hough.

DRAGSTRIP GIRL

An 18-year-old girl comes of age while burning rubber at the dragstrip—the world of boys, hot rods, and horsepower. A definite "B" movie that may seem dated. (1957)

Cast: Fay Spain, Steven Terrell, John Ashley, Frank Gorshin.

Director: Edward L. Cahn.

DREAM MACHINE

A childish teen comedy, based on that old urban legend of the lucky kid given a free Porsche by the vengeful wife of a wealthy philanderer. The gimmick is that the husband's body is in the trunk; the murderer is in pursuit. The tape includes an anti-drug commerical—but nothing against reckless driving, which the picture glorifies. (1991; PG)

Cast: Corey Haim, Evan Richards, Jeremy Slate, Randall England, Tracy Fraim, Brittney Lewis, Susan Seaforth Hayes.

Director: Lyman Dayton.

DRIVE-IN

A low-budget bomb showing a night in the life of teenage yahoos at a Texas drive-in. (1976; PG)

Cast: Lisa Lemole, Glen Morshower, Gary Cavagnaro.

Director: Rod Amateau.

DRIVE-IN MASSACRE

Two police detectives investigate a bizarre series of slasher murders at the local drive-in. Honk the horn at this one. (1974; R)

Cast: Jake Barnes, Adam Lawrence.

THE DRIVER

A police detective will stop at nothing to catch "The Driver," a man who has the reputation of

1963: President John F. Kennedy is assassinated in Dallas while riding in a specially-built Lincoln Continental. The car includes a power-operated backseat capable of lifting passengers up 10 inches for better crowd-viewing.

driving the fastest getaway car around. Chase scenes win out over plot. (1978; PG)

Cast: Ryan O'Neal, Bruce Dern, Isabelle Adjani, Ronee Blakley, Matt Clark.

Director: Walter Hill.

DRIVING FORCE

In an effort to capitalize on the popularity of the "Road Warrior" movies, features a lone trucker battling a gang of roadhogs in another post-holocaust desert. Ultimately, runs off the road. (1988; R)

Cast: Sam Jones, Catherine Bach, Don Swayze.

Director: A.J. Prowse.

DRIVING ME CRAZY

When an East German car inventor comes to America, it's laughs in the fast lane in this all-star comedy. (1991; PG-13)

Cast: Billy Dee Williams, Thomas Gottschalk, Dom DeLuise, Milton Berle, Steve Kanaly, Michelle Johnson, Richard Moll, Morton Downey, Jr., George Kennedy.

Director: Jon Turteltaub.

DUEL

Spielberg's first notable film, a made-for-television exercise in paranoia. A docile traveling salesman is repeatedly attacked and threatened by a huge, malevolent tractor-trailer on an open desert highway. (1971; PG)

Cast: Dennis Weaver, Lucille Benson, Eddie Firestone, Cary Loftin.

Director: Steven Spielberg.

DUMB & DUMBER

Dumb sells: $125 million at the box office and counting, plus a hit soundtrack. Not bad for moronic limo driver Lloyd Christmas (Carrey) and equally dense dog groomer Harry Dunne (Daniels), who travel (in the hilarious "sheep dog" van) from Rhode Island to Colorado—at one point going east!—to return a briefcase full of cash to a beautiful socialite (Holly). Engaging in all sorts of gross-out bathroom, bodily function, and slapstick humor, this one will definitely not appeal to the stuffy critic or art-house snob. It will provide plenty of laughs, however embarrassingly rendered, for everyone else. Daniels proves a convincing dimwit sidekick, while Carrey mugs shamelessly. Occasional *Seinfeld* writer Farrelly makes his directorial debut. (1994; PG-13)

Cast: Jim Carrey, Jeff Daniels, Lauren Holly, Teri Garr, Karen Duffy, Mike Starr, Charles Rocket, Victoria Rowell, Felton Perry.

Director: Peter Farrelly.

EAT MY DUST

Teenage son of a California sheriff steals the best stock cars from a race track to take the town's heartthrob for a joy ride. Subsequently he leads the town on a wild car chase. Brainless but fast-paced. (1976; PG)

Cast: Ron Howard, Christopher Norris, Warren Kemmerling, Rance Howard, Clint Howard, Corbin Bernsen.

Director: Charles B. Griffith.

FANDANGO

Five college friends take a wild weekend drive across the Texas Badlands for one last fling be-

1964: The first fully automatic automobile air conditioning system is Cadillac's "climate control" system.

00259

fore graduation and the prospect of military service. Expanded by Reynolds with assistance from Steven Spielberg, from his student film. Provides a look at college and life during the '60s Vietnam crisis. (1985; PG)

Cast: Judd Nelson, Kevin Costner, Sam Robards, Chuck Bush, Brian Cesak, Elizabeth Daily, Suzy Amis, Glenne Headly, Pepe Serna, Marvin J. McIntyre.

Director: Kevin Reynolds.

THE FAST AND THE FURIOUS

On the lam after being falsely charged with murder, Ireland picks up a fast car and a loose woman (or is it a loose car and a fast woman?) and makes a run for the border by entering the Pebble Beach race. (1954)

Cast: John Ireland, Dorothy Malone, Bruce Carlisle, Iris Adrian.

Director: John Ireland, Edwards Sampson.

FAST COMPANY

The life story of champion race car driver Lonnie Johnson including women, money, and the drag racing sponsors. (1978)

Cast: William Smith, John Saxon, Claudia Jennings, Nicholas Campbell, Don Francks.

Director: David Cronenberg.

FASTER PUSSYCAT! KILL! KILL!

It doesn't get any better than this! Three sexy go-go dancers get their after-work kicks by hot-rodding in the California desert. They soon find themselves enveloped in murder, kidnapping, lust and robbery after a particular race

gets out of hand. Easily the most watchable, fun and funny production to spring from the mind of Russ Meyer. Those who haven't seen this cannot truly be called "cool."(1966)

Cast: Tura Satana, Haji, Lori Williams, Susan Bernard, Stuart Lancaster, Paul Trinka, Dennis Busch, Ray Barlow, Mickey Foxx.

Director: Russ Meyer.

FERRIS BUELLER'S DAY OFF

It's almost graduation and if Ferris can get away with just one more sick day—it had better be a good one. He sweet talks his best friend into borrowing his dad's antique Ferrari and sneaks his girlfriend out of school to spend a day in Chicago. Their escapades lead to fun, adventure, and almost getting caught. Broderick is charismatic as the notorious Bueller with Grey amusing as his tattle-tale sister doing everything she can to see him get caught. Early Sheen appearance as a juvenile delinquent who pesters Grey. Led to TV series. One of Hughes' more solid efforts. (1986; PG-13)

Cast: Matthew Broderick, Mia Sara, Alan Ruck, Jeffrey Jones, Jennifer Grey, Cindy Pickett, Edie McClurg, Charlie Sheen, Del Close, Virginia Capers, Max Perlich, Louis Anderson.

Director: John Hughes.

FIREBIRD 2015 A.D.

Dreary action adventure set in a 21st century society where automobile use is banned because of an extreme oil shortage. Private cars are hunted down for destruction by the Department of Vehicular Control. One over-zealous enforcer decides to make it a package deal and throws in the owners as well. Everyone connected with effort should have been cited for running stop sign. (1981; PG)

1964: The Ford Mustang is introduced and becomes an instant best-seller. Much credit is given to the Lee Iacocca-designed sales package.

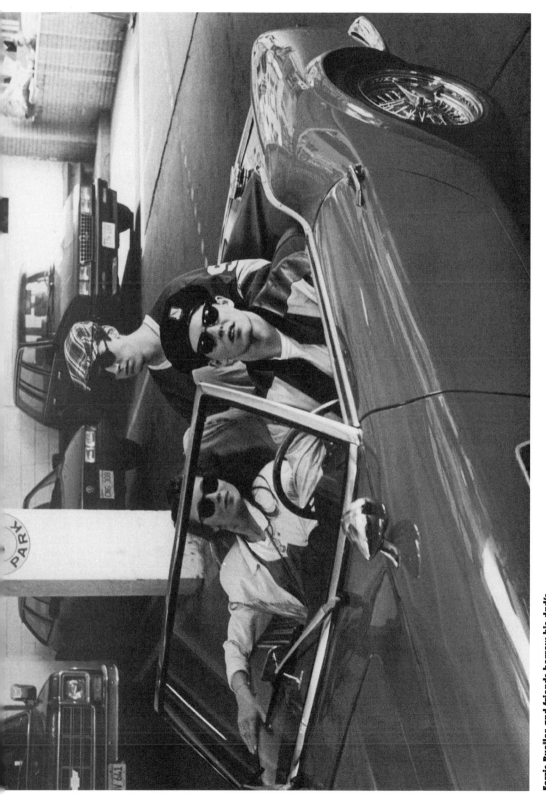

Ferris Bueller and friends borrow his dad's antique Ferrari in *Ferris Bueller's Day Off*.
Paramount/The Kobal Collection

Cast: Darren McGavin, George Touliatos, Doug McClure.

Director: David Robertson.

FLASH & FIRECAT

A beautiful blonde and a crazy thief steal and race their way across the country in a dune buggy with the police hot on their trail. (1975; PG)

Cast: Roger Davis, Tricia Sembera, Dub Taylor, Richard Kiel.

Director: Ferd Sebastian.

FOR THE LOVE OF IT

Television stars galore try to hold together this farce about car chases in California, stolen secret documents, and (of course) true love. Outstandingly mediocre. Made for television. (1980)

Cast: Deborah Raffin, Jeff Conaway, Tom Bosley, Norman Fell, Don Rickles, Henry Gibson, Noriyuki "Pat" Morita, William Christopher, Lawrence-Hilton Jacobs, Adrian Zmed, Barbi Benton, Adam West.

Director: Hal Kanter.

FOR YOUR EYES ONLY

In this James Bond adventure, 007 must keep the Soviets from getting hold of a valuable instrument aboard a sunken British spy ship. Sheds the gadgetry of its more recent predecessors in the series in favor of some spectacular stunt work and the usual beautiful girl and exotic locale—not to mention a gorgeous Lotus Espirit Turbo. Glen's first outing as director, though he handled second units on previous Bond films. Sheena Easton sang the hit title tune. (1981; PG)

Cast: Roger Moore, Carol Bouquet, Chaim Topol, Lynn-Holly Johnson, Julian Glover, Cassandra Harris, Jill Bennett, Michael Gothard, John Wyman, Jack Hedley, Lois Maxwell, Desmond Llewelyn, Geoffrey Keen, Walter Gotell, Charles Dance.

Director: John Glen.

FORD: THE MAN & THE MACHINE

Episodic biography of ruthless auto magnate Henry Ford I, from the building of his empire to his personal tragedies. The cast lacks spark and Robertson (Ford) is positively gloomy. The only one appearing to have any fun is Thomas (Ford's mistress). Based on the biography by Robert Lacey. (1987)

Cast: Cliff Robertson, Hope Lange, Heather Thomas, Michael Ironside, Chris Wiggins, R.H. Thomson.

Director: Allan Eastman.

48 HRS.

An experienced San Francisco cop (Nolte) springs a convict (Murphy) from jail for 48 hours to find a viscious murdering drug lord. Murphy's film debut is great and Nolte is perfect as his gruff foil. Some great chase scenes through the streets of Detroit. Also, Nolte's ragtop Cadillac and Murphy's classic Porsche provide more car-related interest. (1982; R)

Cast: Nick Nolte, Eddie Murphy, James Remar, Annette O'Toole, David Patrick Kelly, Sonny Landham, Brion James, Denise Crosby.

Director: Walter Hill.

1964: Plymouth releases the Barracuda to compete with the successful Ford Mustang.

Road Test

MATCH THE CAR WITH THE MOVIE.

1. Mustang GT	A. 48 Hrs.
2. Armored car	B. Goldfinger
3. Pontiac Trans Am	C. The Blues Brothers
4. Aston Martin DB5	D. Harold and Maude
5. Volkswagen Beetle	E. Bullitt
6. 1957 Chevy	F. Christine
7. Dodge police car	G. The Italian Job
8. 1957 Plymouth	H. Smokey and the Bandit
9. Cadillac convertible	I. American Graffiti
10. Jaguar E-Type	J. Herbie Goes Bananas

(Answers: 1.E 2.G 3.H 4.B 5.J 6.I 7.C 8.F 9.A 10.D)

FREE RIDE

A kooky kid steals a sports car to impress a girl, and gets involved with local hoods. They chase each other around. (1986; R)

Cast: Gary Hershberger, Reed Rudy, Dawn Schneider, Peter DeLuise, Brian MacGregor.

FREEBIE & THE BEAN

Two San Francisco cops nearly ruin the city in their pursuit of a numbers-running mobster. Top-flight car chases and low-level, bigoted humor combine. Watch for Valerie Harper's ap-pearance as Arkin's wife. Followed by a flash-in-the-pan television series. (1974; R)

Cast: Alan Arkin, James Caan, Loretta Swit, Valerie Harper, Jack Kruschen, Mike Kellin.

Director: Richard Rush.

FREEDOM

A young man finds the price of freedom to be very high when he tries to escape from Australian society in a silver Porsche. (1981)

Cast: Jon Blake, Candy Raymond, Jad Capelja, Reg Lye, John Clayton.

1965: Detroit industrialist Heinz C. Prechter begins what will become a $350 million business by introducing the sunroof to American automobiles.

cut to the Chase

Bullitt and *The French Connection* are considered my most to be the first two movies to incorporate big-time car chases.

FREEWAY

A nurse attempts to find the obsessive killer who shot her husband. The murderer phones a radio psychiatrist from his car, using Biblical quotes, while cruising for new victims. Okay thriller, based on the L.A. freeway shootings. (1988; R)

Cast: Darlanne Fluegel, James Russo, Billy Drago, Richard Belzer, Michael Callan, Steve Franken, Kenneth Tobey, Clint Howard.

Director: Francis Delia.

THE FRENCH CONNECTION

Two New York hard-nosed narcotics detectives stumble onto what turns out to be one of the biggest narcotics rings of all time. Cat-and-mouse thriller will keep you on the edge of your seat; contains one of the most exciting chase scenes ever filmed. Hackman's portrayal of Popeye Doyle is exact and the teamwork with Scheider special. Won multiple awards. Based on a true story from the book by Robin Moore. Followed in 1975 by *French Connection II.* (1971; R)

Cast: Gene Hackman, Roy Scheider, Fernando Rey, Tony LoBianco, Eddie Egan, Sonny Grosso, Marcel Bozzuffi.

Director: William Friedkin.

FURY ON WHEELS

Tale of men who race cars and wreak havoc and vice versa. (1971; PG)

Cast: Judd Hirsch, Tom Ligon, Paul Sorvino, Logan Ramsey, Collin Wilcox-Horne.

GATOR

Sequel to *White Lightning* (1973) follows the adventures of Gator (Reynolds), who is recruited to gather evidence to convict a corrupt political boss who also happens to be his friend. Reynolds in his good ol' boy role with lots of chase scenes. Talk show host Michael Douglas made his film debut in the role of the governor. First film Reynolds directed. (1976; PG)

Cast: Burt Reynolds, Jerry Reed, Lauren Hutton, Jack Weston, Alice Ghostley, Dub Taylor.

Director: Burt Reynolds.

GENEVIEVE

A 1904 Darracq roadster is the title star of this picture which spoofs "classic car" owners and their annual rally from London to Brighton. Two married couples challenge each other to a friendly race which becomes increasingly intense as they near the finish line. (1953)

Cast: John Gregson, Dinah Sheridan, Kenneth More, Kay Kendall.

Director: Henry Cornelius.

1965: World land speed record (600 mph) is achieved by Craig Breedlove in the Spirit of America Sonic 1 at the Bonneville Salt Flats.

THE GETAWAY

McQueen plays a thief released on a parole arranged by his wife (McGraw) only to find out a corrupt politician wants him to rob a bank. After the successful holdup, McQueen finds out his cohorts are in the politician's pocket and trying to doublecross him. McQueen and McGraw are forced into a feverish chase across Texas to the Mexican border, pursued by the politician's henchmen and the state police. Completely amoral depiction of crime and violence with McQueen taciturn as always and McGraw again showing a complete lack of acting skills. Based on a novel by Jim Thompson. McQueen and McGraw had a romance during filming and later married. Remade in 1993. (1972; PG)

Cast: Steve McQueen, Ali MacGraw, Ben Johnson, Sally Struthers, Al Lettieri, Slim Pickens, Jack Dodson, Dub Taylor, Bo Hopkins.

Director: Sam Peckinpah.

THE GETAWAY

It was a bad movie in 1972 and the remake hasn't improved the situation. Doc and Carol are husband and wife crooks (played by marrieds Basinger and Baldwin). Doc gets doublecrossed and winds up in a Mexican jail; Carol gets a well-connected crook (Woods) to spring her hubby—by sleeping with him and promising Doc will pull off another heist. The robbery's botched, there are double-crosses galore, and the couple go on the run. The stars are pretty but everything's predictable. (1993; R)

Cast: Alec Baldwin, Kim Basinger, James Woods, Michael Madsen, Jennifer Tilly, David Morse.

Director: Roger Donaldson.

GIRL IN A CADILLAC

Modern-day B-movie wannabe loosely adapted from the James M. Cain novella *The Enchanted Isle.* Seventeen-year-old freespirited Amanda (Eleniak) wants to get out of stifling small town Texas. She buys a bus ticket to find her long-gone daddy and winds up with not-too-smart cowpoke Rick (McNamara) instead. A bank robbery gone bad finds the twosome on the loose with $75,000, a cherry-red Eldorado convertible, and Rick's partners after them. Appealing lead performers can't overcome the cliches. (1994; R)

Cast: Erika Eleniak, William McNamara, Michael Lerner, Bud Cort, Valerie Perrine, Ed Lauter, William Shockley.

Director: Lucas Platt.

GOLDENEYE

Bond is back and Brosnan's got him—after an 8-year wait—in the 18th adventure of legendary Brit Agent 007. Since we're through the cold war, Bond has to make do with the villainy of the Russian Mafia, who are planning to sabotage global financial markets utilizing the "Goldeneye" satellite weapon. There's a spectacularly impossible stunt to start things out in familiar territory and lots more noisy (if prolonged) action pieces. Brosnan (who looks great in a tux) is slyly self-aware that his character is more myth than man and Janssen does a suitably over-the-top job as bad Bond girl Xenia Onatopp. The film debut for BMW's Z3 Roadster—looking equally great! (1995; PG-13)

Cast: Pierce Brosnan, Famke Janssen, Sean Bean, Joe Don Baker, Robbie Coltrane, Izabela Scorupco, Judi Dench, Tcheky Karyo, Gottfried John, Alan Cumming, Desmond Llewelyn, Michael Kitchen, Serena Gordon, Samantha Bond. Cameos: Minnie Driver.

1965: The Dodge Charger is introduced to compete with the Ford Mustang; the competition is made especially memorable in car chase scenes in the 1968 movie *Bullitt.*

The Best Advertising of All?

Movies can have a huge impact on car sales and prices. After its appearance in the 1995 James Bond thriller *Goldeneye*—along with a spot in the Neiman-Marcus Christmas catalog—the BMW Z3 roadster almost completely sold out of its first production run. And director Francis Ford Coppola's 1988 film *Tucker: The Man and His Dream* caused the value of the 49 remaining Tuckers in the world to sky-rocket.

Source: *Detroit Free Press*, November 15, 1995; and February 15, 1996.

Director: Martin Campbell.

GOLDFINGER

Ian Fleming's James Bond, Agent 007, attempts to prevent international gold smuggler Goldfinger and his pilot Pussy Galore from robbing Fort Knox. Features villianous assistant Oddjob and his deadly bowler hat. The third in the series is perhaps the most popular. Especially famous for the debut of Bond's gadget-laden Aston Martin DB5 (machine guns, oil slick, passenger ejection seat, etc.). Shirley Bassey sings the theme song. (1964; PG)

Cast: Sean Connery, Honor Blackman, Gert Frobe, Shirley Eaton, Tania Mallet, Harold Sakata, Cec Linder, Bernard Lee, Lois Maxwell, Desmond Llewelyn, Nadja Regin.

Director: Guy Hamilton.

GONE IN 60 SECONDS

Car thief working for an insurance adjustment firm gets double-crossed by his boss and chased by the police. Forty minutes are consumed by a chase scene which destroyed more than 90 vehicles. (1974)

Cast: H.B. Halicki, Marion Busia, George Cole, James McIntyre, Jerry Daugirda.

Director: H.B. Halicki.

GOODBYE PORK PIE

With the police on their trail, two young men speed on a 1,000-mile journey in a small, brand-new, yellow stolen car. Remember: journey of thousand miles always begin in stolen car. (1981; R)

Cast: Tony Barry, Kelly Johnson.

Director: Geoff Murphy.

GRAND PRIX

A big-budget look at the world of Grand Prix auto racing, as four top competitors circle the world's most famous racing circuits. Strictly for those who like cars racing round and round; nothing much happens off the track. (1966)

Cast: James Garner, Eva Marie Saint, Yves Montand, Toshiro Mifune, Brian Bedford.

Director: John Frankenheimer.

1965: Shirley "Cha Cha" Muldowney becomes the first woman licensed by the National Hot Rod Association to race dragsters. She goes on to become the second most successful drag racer, behind Don Garlits.

Two cars jockey for position in *The Great Race*.
Warner Brothers/The Kobal Collection

GRAND THEFT AUTO

In Howard's initial directorial effort, a young couple elopes to Las Vegas in a Rolls-Royce owned by the bride's father. The father, totally against the marriage and angered by the stolen Rolls, offers a reward for their safe return and a cross-country race ensues. (1977; PG)

Cast: Ron Howard, Nancy Morgan, Marion Ross, Barry Cahill, Clint Howard.

Director: Ron Howard.

GREASED LIGHTNING

The story of the first black auto racing champion, Wendell Scott, who had to overcome racial prejudice to achieve his success. Slightly-better-than-average Pryor comedy vehicle. (1977; PG)

Cast: Richard Pryor, Pam Grier, Beau Bridges, Cleavon Little, Vincent Gardenia.

Director: Michael A. Schultz.

GREAT AMERICAN TRAFFIC JAM

A made-for-television farce about the humorous variety of characters interacting on the interstate during a massive California traffic jam. (1980; PG)

Cast: Ed McMahon, Vic Tayback, Howard Hesseman, Abe Vigoda, Noah Beery, Jr., Desi Arnaz, Jr., John Beck, Shelley Fabares, James Gregory.

Director: James Frawley.

THE GREAT RACE

A dastardly villain, a noble hero and a spirited suffragette are among the competitors in an uproarious New York-to-Paris auto race circa 1908, complete with pie fights, saloon brawls, and a confrontation with a feisty polar bear. Overly long and only sporadically funny. (1965)

Cast: Jack Lemmon, Tony Curtis, Natalie Wood, Peter Falk, Keenan Wynn, George Macready.

Director: Blake Edwards.

THE GREAT TEXAS DYNAMITE CHASE

Two sexy young women drive across Texas with a carload of dynamite. They leave a trail of empty banks with the cops constantly on their trail. (1976; R)

Cast: Claudia Jennings, Jocelyn Jones, Johnny Crawford, Chris Pennock, Tara Strohmeier, Miles Watkins, Bart Braverman.

Director: Michael Pressman.

GUMBALL RALLY

An unusual assortment of people converge upon New York for a cross-country car race to Long Beach, California, where breaking the rules is part of the game. (1976; PG)

Cast: Michael Sarrazin, Gary Busey, Raul Julia, Nicholas Pryor, Tim McIntire, Susan Flannery.

Director: Chuck Bail.

GUNG HO

A Japanese firm takes over a small-town U.S. auto factory and causes major cultural collisions. Keaton plays the go-between for em-

1965: Pontiac introduces the GTO—the first "muscle car." The car and a song, "Little GTO," by Ronnie and the Daytonas, become instant hits.

ployees and management while trying to keep both groups from killing each other. From the director of *Splash* and *Night Shift.* Made into a short-lived television series. (1985; PG-13)

Cast: Michael Keaton, Gedde Watanabe, George Wendt, Mimi Rogers, John Turturro, Clint Howard, Michelle Johnson, So Yamamura, Sab Shimono.

Director: Ron Howard.

HARD DRIVIN'

Rowdy action featuring Southern stock car drivers with well shot race scenes from the Southern 500. (1960)

Cast: Rory Calhoun, John Gentry, Alan Hale, Jr.

Director: Paul Helmick.

HAROLD AND MAUDE

Cult classic pairs Cort as a dead-pan disillusioned 20-year-old obsessed with suicide (his staged attempts are a highlight) and a loveable Gordon as a fun-loving 80-year-old eccentric. They meet at a funeral (a mutual hobby), and develop a taboo romantic relationship, in which they explore the tired theme of the meaning of life with a fresh perspective. A few interesting tidbits for car crazies, including Corts's custom Jaguar E-Type hearse! (1971; PG)

Cast: Ruth Gordon, Bud Cort, Cyril Cusack, Vivian Pickles, Charles Tyner, Ellen Geer.

Director: Hal Ashby.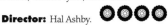

THE HEARSE

Incredibly boring horror film in which a young school teacher moves into a mansion left to her by her late aunt and finds her life threatened by a sinister black hearse. (1980; PG)

Cast: Trish Van Devere, Joseph Cotten.

Director: George Bowers.

HEART LIKE A WHEEL

The story of Shirley Muldowney, who rose from the daughter of a country-western singer to the leading lady in drag racing. The film follows her battles of sexism and choosing whether to have a career or a family. Bedelia's perfomance is outstanding. Fine showings from Bridges and Axton in supporting roles. (1983; PG)

Cast: Bonnie Bedelia, Beau Bridges, Bill McKinney, Leo Rossi, Hoyt Axton, Dick Miller, Anthony Edwards.

Director: Jonathan Kaplan.

HELL ON WHEELS

Two successful brothers in the racing industry are torn apart by the same girl. Brotherly love diminishes into a hatred so deep that murder becomes the sole purpose of both. (1967)

Cast: Marty Robbins, Jennifer Ashley, John Ashley, Gigi Perreau, Robert Dornan, Connie Smith, Frank Gerstle.

Director: Will Zens.

HERBIE GOES BANANAS

While Herbie the VW is racing in Rio de Janeiro, he is bothered by the syndicate, a pickpocket, and a raging bull. The fourth and final entry in the Disney "Love Bug" movies, but Herbie later made his way to a television series. (1980; G)

1966: *Unsafe at Any Speed,* written by American consumer activist Ralph Nader, exposes safety faults in U.S. automobiles and is partly responsible for the National Traffic and Motor Vehicle Safety Act.

Herbie Goes to Monte Carlo is one of several "Love Bug" movies.
Disney/The Kobal Collection

Cast: Cloris Leachman, Charles Martin Smith, Harvey Korman, John Vernon, Alex Rocco, Richard Jaeckel, Fritz Feld.

Director: Vincent McEveety.

HERBIE GOES TO MONTE CARLO

While participating in a Paris-to-Monte-Carlo race, Herbie the VW takes a detour and falls in love with a Lancia. Third in the Disney "Love Bug" series. (1977; G)

Cast: Dean Jones, Don Knotts, Julie Sommars, Roy Kinnear.

Director: Vincent McEveety.

HERBIE RIDES AGAIN

In this sequel to *The Love Bug*, Herbie comes to the aid of an elderly woman who is trying to stop a ruthless tycoon from raising a skyscraper on her property. Humorous Disney fare. Two other sequels followed. (1974; G)

Cast: Helen Hayes, Ken Berry, Stefanie Powers, John McIntire, Keenan Wynn.

Director: Robert Stevenson.

HIGH GEAR

Heartstring-tugger about a race car driver, his girlfriend and the orphan son of a driver killed in a crash. Try to guess the outcome. (1933)

Cast: James Murray, Joan Marsh, Jackie Searl, Theodore von Eltz, Lee Moran, Gordon DeMain.

Director: Leigh Jason.

HIGH ROLLING IN A HOT CORVETTE

Two carnival workers leave their jobs and hit the road in search of adventure and excitement, eventually turning to crime. (1977; PG)

Cast: Joseph Bottoms, Greg Taylor, Judy Davis, Wendy Hughes.

Director: Igor Auzins.

HIGHWAY 61

Shy barber Pokey Jones lives in the small Canadian town of Pickerel Falls and becomes a celebrity when he discovers the frozen corpse of an unknown young man in his backyard. Jackie Bangs, a rock roadie who's stolen her band's stash of drugs, finds herself stranded in the same small town. So begins a wild road trip. Lackluster direction undercuts much of the first-rate acting and amusing story quirks. (1991; R)

Cast: Valerie Buhagiar, Don McKellar, Earl Pastko, Peter Breck, Art Bergmann.

Director: Bruce McDonald.

THE HITCHER

A young man picks up a hitchhiker on a deserted stretch of California highway only to be tormented by the man's repeated appearances: is he real or a figment of his imagination? Ferociously funny, sadomasochistic comedy with graphic violence. (1986; R)

Cast: Rutger Hauer, C. Thomas Howell, Jennifer Jason Leigh, Jeffrey DeMunn, John M. Jackson.

Director: Robert Harmon.

1966: U.S. Department of Transportation is created at the cabinet level to provide leadership in the identification of transportation problems and solutions and to stimulate technological advances.

00271

HITCHHIKERS

Trash film about a bunch of scantily clad female hitchhikers who rob the motorists who stop to pick them up. Keep right on going when you spot this roadkill. (1972; R)

Cast: Misty Rowe, Norman Klar, Linda Avery.

Director: Ferd Sebastian.

HOMETOWN U.S.A.

Set in Los Angeles in the late '50s, this teenage cruising movie is the brainchild of director Baer who is better known as Jethro from that madcap television series *The Beverly Hillbillies*. (1979; R)

Cast: Brian Kerwin, Gary Springer, David Wilson, Cindy Fisher, Sally Kirkland.

Director: Max Baer, Jr.

HOOTCH COUNTRY BOYS

A film packed with moonshine, sheriffs, busty country girls, and chases. (1975; PG)

Cast: Alex Karras, Scott MacKenzsie, Dean Jagger, Willie Jones, Bob Ridgely, Susan Denbo, Bob Ginnaven, David Haney.

Director: Harry Z. Thomason.

HOT ROD

A young California hotrodder battles the evil sponsor of a drag race championship. (1979)

Cast: Greg Henry, Robert Culp, Pernell Roberts, Robin Mattson, Grant Goodeve.

Director: George Armitage.

HOT ROD GIRL

A concerned police officer (Conners) organizes supervised drag racing after illegal drag racing gets out of hand in his community. (1956)

Cast: Lori Nelson, Chuck Connors, John W. Smith.

Director: Leslie Martinson.

HOT WIRE

Tired comedy about the unscrupulous side of the car repossession racket. (197?)

Cast: George Kennedy, Strother Martin.

HOW I LEARNED TO LOVE WOMEN

A British comedy of errors involving a car-loving youth who learns about women and love. (196?)

Cast: Anita Ekberg.

IL SORPASSO

A braggart, who has failed at everything, spends all his time traveling around Italy in his sports car. He takes a repressed law student under his wing and decides to teach him how to have fun. In Italian with English subtitles. (1963)

Cast: Vittorio Gassman, Jean-Louis Trintignant.

Director: Dino Risi.

1966: The Ford Mustang reaches one million in sales faster than any automobile in history.

IT TAKES TWO

A young man spends his last 10 days of bachelorhood cruising down Texas highways with a beautiful car saleswoman. Meanwhile, back at the altar, his bride waits patiently. Upbeat with some genuinely funny moments. From the director of *Pass the Ammo*. (1988; PG-13)

Cast: George Newbern, Leslie Hope, Kimberly Foster, Barry Corbin.

Director: David Beaird.

THE ITALIAN JOB

Caine and Coward pair up to steal $4 million in gold by causing a major traffic jam in Turin, Italy. During the jam, the pair steals the gold from an armored car. Silliness and chases through the Swiss mountains ensue, culminating in a hilarious ending. (1969; G)

Cast: Michael Caine, Noel Coward, Benny Hill, Raf Vallone, Tony Beckley, Rossano Brazzi, Margaret Blye.

Director: Peter Collinson.

JON JOST'S FRAMEUP

Cocky ex-con Ricky Lee hooks up with dizzy waitress Beth Ann and they head out on a 3000-mile nightmare road trip to California. Free-form story shot in 10 days. (1993)

Cast: Howard Swain, Nancy Carlin.

Director: Jon Jost.

JOSH AND S.A.M.

Road movie for youngsters with a twist: the driver can barely see over the dashboard. Josh and Sam are brothers (and terrific kids!) whose parents are splitting. They cope by taking off on their own. Sam, meanwhile has been convinced by Josh that he's not a real boy at all, but rather a S.A.M.: Strategically Altered Mutant. Weber's directorial debut will appeal to young kids, but adults will see over the dashboard and through the transparent plot. Of special interest to car crazies whose sons are named Josh and Sam. (1993; PG-13)

Cast: Martha Plimpton, Christopher Penn, Stephen Tobolowsky, Joan Allen, Noah Fleiss, Jacob Tierney, Ronald Guttman.

Director: Billy Weber.

JOY RIDE TO NOWHERE

Two young women steal a Cadillac with $2 million in the trunk and ride away with the owner hot on their tail. (1978; PG)

Cast: Leslie Ackerman, Sandy Serrano, Len Lesser, Mel Welles, Ron Ross, Speed Stearns.

JOYRIDE

Mistreated by a union official, three friends steal a car for a joy ride and plummet into a life of crime. (1977; R)

Cast: Desi Arnaz, Jr., Robert Carradine, Melanie Griffith, Anne Lockhart.

Director: Joseph Ruben.

THE JUNKMAN

Movie maker whose new film is about to be premiered is being chased by a mysterious killer. Promoted as "the ultimate car chase film" since the production used and destroyed over

1967: A *Motor Trend* magazine survey of 1,100 married couples reveals that nearly 40 percent of the marriage proposals were made in automobiles.

150 automobiles. From the makers of *Gone in 60 Seconds.* (1982; R)

Cast: H.B. Halicki, Christopher Stone, Susan Shaw, Hoyt Axton, Lynda Day George.

Director: H.B. Halicki.

KALIFORNIA

It's *Badlands* meets the '90s in a road trip with the hitchhikers from hell. Early Grayce (Pitt) is your average slimeball who murders his landlord and hops a ride with his waifish girlfriend Adele (Lewis) from Kentucky to California with Brian (Duchovny), a yuppie writer interested in mass murderers, and his sultry photographer girlfriend Carrie (Forbes). Pitt and Lewis were still an item when they made this. Pitt reportedly wanted to play against type, and as pretty boy gone homicidal, he succeeds. Extremely violent and disturbing. (1993; R)

Cast: Brad Pitt, Juliette Lewis, David Duchovny, Michele Forbes, Sierra Pecheur, Lois Hall, Gregory Mars Martin.

Director: Dominic Sena.

KILLING CARS

A German car designer's pet project, a car that runs without gas, is halted by the influence of an Arab conglomerate. He nevertheless tries to complete it, and is hunted down. (1985; R)

Cast: Juergen Prochnow, Senta Berger, William Conrad, Agnes Soral.

Director: Michael Verhoeven.

KING OF THE MOUNTAIN

The "Old King" and the "New King" must square off in this tale of daredevil road racers who zoom through the streets of Hollywood. Interesting cast trapped by tired script. (1981; PG)

Cast: Richard Cox, Harry Hamlin, Dennis Hopper, Joseph Bottoms, Deborah Van Valkenburgh, Dan Haggerty.

Director: Noel Nosseck.

THE LAST AMERICAN HERO

The true story of how former moonshine runner Junior Johnson became one of the fastest race car drivers in the history of the sport. Entertaining slice of life chronicling whiskey running and stock car racing, with Bridges superb in the lead. Based on a series of articles written by Tom Wolfe. (1973; PG)

Cast: Jeff Bridges, Valerie Perrine, Gary Busey, Art Lund, Geraldine Fitzgerald, Ned Beatty.

Director: Lamont Johnson.

LAST CHASE

Famed race car driver becomes a vocal dissenter against the sterile society that has emerged, in this drama set in the near future. Made for television. (1981; PG)

Cast: Lee Majors, Burgess Meredith, Chris Makepeace, Alexandra Stewart.

Director: Martyn Burke.

1968: A Lincoln Continental is specially built as the U.S. president's limousine. It weighs 5.5 tons, including 2 tons of steel plate, and, at $500,000, is the most expensive car ever produced.

**Steve McQueen and the race car
he drove in** *Le Mans.*
Solar/Cinema Center/The Kobal Collection

LE MANS

The famous 24-hour Grand Prix race sets the stage for this tale of love and speed. McQueen (who did his own driving) is the leading race driver, a man who battles competition, fear of death by accident, and emotional involvement. Excellent documentary-style race footage almost makes up for weak plot and minimal acting. (1971; G)

Cast: Steve McQueen, Elga Andersen, Ronald Leigh-Hunt, Luc Merenda.

Director: Lee H. Katzin.

LICENSE TO DRIVE

When teen Haim fails the road test for his all-important driver's license, he steals the family car for a hot date with the girl of his dreams. The evening starts out quietly enough, but things soon go awry. If Haim survives the weekend, he'll definitely be able to pass his driving test on Monday morning. Semi-funny in a demolition derby sort of way. (1988; PG-13)

Cast: Corey Feldman, Corey Haim, Carol Kane, Richard Masur.

Director: Greg Beeman.

THE LIVING DAYLIGHTS

After being used as a pawn in a fake Russian defector plot, our intrepid spy—Bond . . . James Bond—tracks down an international arms and opium smuggling ring. Fine debut by Dalton as 007 in a rousing, refreshing, cosmopolitan shoot-em-up. Let's be frank: we were all getting a little fatigued of Roger Moore. Also noteworthy for an appearance of a new Aston Mar-

tin: a Volante, sporting wheel-axle lasers, missles, and a self-destruct button. (1987; PG)

Cast: Timothy Dalton, Maryam D'Abo, Jeroen Krabbe, John Rhys-Davies, Robert Brown, Joe Don Baker, Desmond Llewelyn, Art Malik, Geoffrey Keen, Walter Gotell, Andreas Wisniewski.

Director: John Glen.

LOST IN AMERICA

After deciding that he can't "find himself" at his current job, advertising executive David Howard and his wife sell everything they own and buy a Winnebago to travel across the country. This Albert Brooks comedy is a must-see for everyone who thinks that there is more in life than pushing papers at your desk and sitting on "Mercedes leather." (1985; R)

Cast: Albert Brooks, Julie Hagerty, Michael Greene, Tom Tarpey, Garry Marshall, Art Frankel.

Director: Albert Brooks.

LOVE AND A .45

Satirical and violent road movie finds petty career criminal Watty Watts (Bellows) living in a Texas trailer park with gal Starlene (Zellweger), for whom he's just purchased an expensive engagement ring. But he's borrowed the money from some crazed gangster types who want the loan repaid in a timely fashion. Soon, the dippy duo are on the run to Mexico with a trail of dead bodies behind them and the media just delighted to make them the next tabloid darlings. (1994; R)

Cast: Renee Zellweger, Rory Cochrane, Ann Wedgeworth, Peter Fonda, Gil Bellows, Jeffrey Combs, Jace Alexander.

Director: C.M. Talkington.

1968: The United States requires antipollution devices on all cars to control hydrocarbon emissions.

THE LOVE BUG

A race car driver (Jones) is followed home by Herbie, a white Volkswagen with a mind of its own. Eventually, Jones follows the "Love Bug" to a life of madcap fun. Followed by several sequels. (1968; G)

Cast: Dean Jones, Michele Lee, Hope Lange, Robert Reed, Bert Convy.

Director: Robert Stevenson.

MAD MAX

Set on the stark highways of the post-nuclear future, an ex-cop seeks personal revenge against a rovin' band of vicious outlaw bikers who killed his wife and child. Futuristic scenery and excellent stunt work make for an exceptionally entertaining action-packed adventure. Followed by *The Road Warrior* (also known as *Mad Max 2*) in 1981 and *Mad Max Beyond Thunderdome* in 1985. (1980; R)

Cast: Mel Gibson, Joanne Samuel, Hugh Keays-Byrne, Steve Bisley, Tim Burns, Roger Ward.

Director: George Miller.

THE MAN WITH THE GOLDEN GUN

Roger Moore is the debonair Agent 007 in this ninth James Bond flick. Assigned to recover a small piece of equipment which can be utilized to harness the sun's energy, Bond engages the usual bevy of villains and beauties and executes a 360-degree roll in an AMC Hornet while jumping a broken bridge in the Louisiana Bayou. (1974; PG)

Cast: Roger Moore, Christopher Lee, Britt Ekland, Maud Adams, Herve Villechaize, Clifton James, Sonn-

Teck Oh, Richard Loo, Marc Lawrence, Bernard Lee, Lois Maxwell, Desmond Llewelyn.

Director: Guy Hamilton.

MOTORAMA

A 10-year-old juvenile delinquent becomes obsessed with winning a gas station contest which involves collecting game cards. So he steals a car and hits the road where he gets his first tattoo and encounters a beautiful "older" woman (Barrymore) and lots of trouble. (1991; R)

Cast: Jordan Christopher Michael, Martha Quinn, Flea, Michael J. Pollard, Meat Loaf, Drew Barrymore, Garrett Morris, Robin Duke, Sandy Baron, Mary Woronov, Susan Tyrrell, John Laughlin, John Diehl, Robert Picardo, Jack Nance, Vince Edwards, Dick Miller, Allyce Beasley, Shelley Berman.

Director: Barry Shils.

MOVING VIOLATIONS

This could be entitled *Adventures in Traffic Violations School*. A wise-cracking tree planter is sent to traffic school after accumulating several moving violations issued to him by a morose traffic cop. Bill Murray's little brother in feature role. (1985; PG-13)

Cast: John Murray, Jennifer Tilly, James Keach, Brian Backer, Sally Kellerman, Fred Willard, Clara Peller, Wendie Jo Sperber.

Director: Neal Israel.

MY CHAUFFEUR

When a wise-cracking female is hired on as a chauffeur at an all-male chauffeur service, sparks fly. And when the owner takes a definite

1968: Chevrolet introduces the Camaro, a belated competitor to the Mustang. Although successful, the Camaro reflects Chevrolet's slow response to market trends that threatens its status as GM's top division until an early-1970s turnaround.

00277

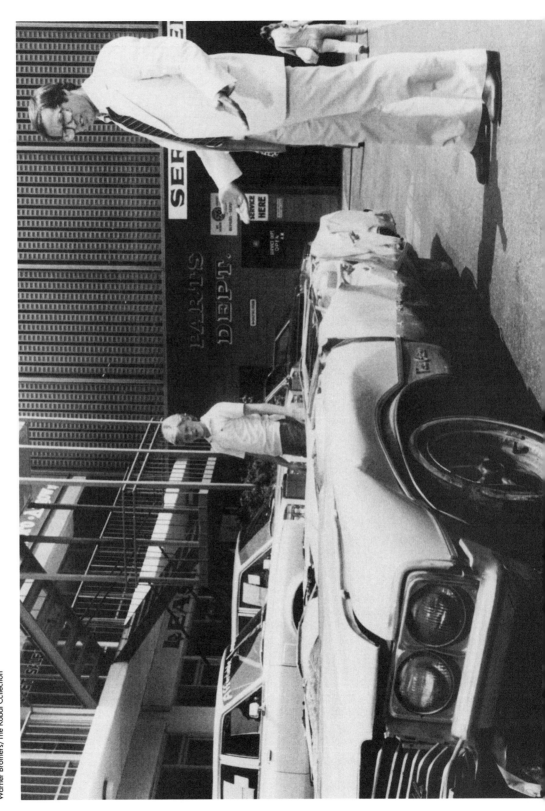

Chevy Chase surveys the damage to the family car in *National Lampoon's Vacation*.
Warner Brothers/The Kobal Collection

liking to her work, things take a turn for the worse. As these sort of sexploitation flicks go, this is one of the better ones. (1986; R)

Cast: Deborah Foreman, Sam Jones, Howard Hesseman, E.G. Marshall, Sean McClory.

Director: David Beaird.

NATIONAL LAMPOON'S VACATION

The Clark Griswold (Chase) family of suburban Chicago embarks on a westward cross-country vacation via car to the renowned "Wally World." Ridiculous and hysterical misadventures, including a falling asleep at the wheel sequence and the untimely death of Aunt Edna. (1983; R)

Cast: Chevy Chase, Beverly D'Angelo, Imogene Coca, Randy Quaid, Christie Brinkley, James Keach, Anthony Michael Hall, John Candy, Eddie Bracken, Brian Doyle-Murray, Eugene Levy.

Director: Harold Ramis.

NIGHT ON EARTH

Jarmusch's "road" movie comprises five different stories taking place on the same night in five different cities—Los Angeles, New York, Paris, Rome, and Helsinki—between cabbies and their passengers. As with any anthology some stories work better than others but all have their moments in this ambitious film with its outstanding international cast. Subtitled in English for the three foreign segments. (1991; R)

Cast: Winona Ryder, Gena Rowlands, Giancarlo Esposito, Armin Mueller-Stahl, Rosie Perez, Beatrice Dalle, Roberto Benigni, Paolo Bonacelli, Matti Pellonpaa, Kari Vaananen, Sakari Kuosmanen, Tomi Salmela.

Director: Jim Jarmusch.

NO WAY OUT

Career Navy man Costner is involved with a beautiful, sexy woman who is murdered. Turns out she was also the mistress of the Secretary of Defense, Costner's boss. Assigned to investigate the murder, he suddenly finds himself the chief suspect. A tight thriller based on 1948's *The Big Clock,* with a new surprise ending. Famous for it's backseat scene. (1987; R)

Cast: Kevin Costner, Sean Young, Gene Hackman, Will Patton, Howard Duff, George Dzundza, Iman, Chris D, Marshall Bell, Jason Bernard, Fred Dalton Thompson, David Paymer.

Director: Roger Donaldson.

ON HER MAJESTY'S SECRET SERVICE

In the sixth 007 adventure, Bond again confronts the infamous Blofeld, who is planning a germ-warfare assault on the entire world. Australian Lazenby took a crack at playing the super spy, with mixed results. Many feel this is the best-written of the Bond films and might have been the most famous, had Sean Connery continued with the series. Still, it's worth a look for a couple shots of a nice Aston Martin DBS. (1969; PG)

Cast: George Lazenby, Diana Rigg, Telly Savalas, Gabriele Ferzetti, Ilse Steppat, Bernard Lee, Lois Maxwell, Desmond Llewelyn, Catherine Schell, Julie Ege, Joanna Lumley, Mona Chong, Anouska Hempel, Jenny Hanley.

Director: Peter Hunt.

ONE DEADLY OWNER

A made-for-television film about a possessed Rolls-Royce torturing its new owner. Quite a

1968: Plymouth introduces the Road Runner, which becomes one of America's most popular street racers.

00279

vehicle for the usually respectable set of wheels. (1974)

Cast: Donna Mills, Jeremy Brett, Robert Morris, Laurence Payne.

PATHS TO PARADISE

Compson and Griffith share criminal past, re-unite at gala event to snatch priceless necklace, and head south of the border. World-class chase scene. (1925)

Cast: Raymond Griffith, Betty Compson, Thomas Santschi, Bert Woodruff, Fred Kelsey.

Director: Clarence Badger.

PEPPER AND HIS WACKY TAXI

Father of four buys a '59 Cadillac and starts a cab company. Time-capsule fun. (1972; G)

Cast: John Astin, Frank Sinatra, Jr., Jackie Gayle, Alan Sherman.

Director: Alex Grasshof.

PINK CADILLAC

A grizzled, middle-aged bondsman is on the road, tracking down bail-jumping crooks. He helps the wife and baby of his latest target escape from her husband's more evil associates. Eastwood's performance is good and fun to watch, in this otherwise lightweight film. (1989; PG-13)

Cast: Clint Eastwood, Bernadette Peters, Timothy Carhart, Michael Des Barres, William Hickey, John Dennis Johnston, Geoffrey Lewis, Jim Carrey, Tiffany Gail Robinson, Angela Louise Robinson.

Director: Buddy Van Horn.

PLANES, TRAINS & AUTOMOBILES

One-joke Hughes comedy saved by Martin and Candy. A straight-laced businessman (played straight by Martin) on the way home for Thanksgiving meets up with an oafish, bad-luck-ridden boor who turns his efforts to get home upside down. Martin and Candy both turn in fine performances, and effectively straddle a thin line between true pathos and hilarious buffoonery. Bacon and McClurg, both Hughes alumni, have small but funny roles. (1987; R)

Cast: Steve Martin, John Candy, Edie McClurg, Kevin Bacon, Michael McKean, William Windom, Laila Robins, Martin Ferrero, Charles Tyner, Dylan Baker.

Director: John Hughes.

POWWOW HIGHWAY

Remarkably fine performances in this unusu-al, thought-provoking, poorly-titled foray into the plight of Native Americans. Farmer shines as the unassuming, amiable Cheyenne travel-ing to New Mexico in a beat-up Chevy with his Indian activist buddy, passionately portrayed by Martinez. On the journey they are constant-ly confronted with the tragedy of life on a reservation. A sobering look at government in-justice and the lingering spirit of a people lost inside their homeland. (1989; R)

Cast: Gary Farmer, A. Martinez, Amanda Wyss, Rene Handren-Seals, Graham Greene.

Director: Joanelle Romero, Jonathan Wacks.

PRIVATE ROAD: NO TRESPASSING

A stock-car racer and a top engineer compete

1969: This is the worst year for road fatalities in United States history, as 54,895 people are killed. In this century, more than 25 million people have been killed on the world's roads.

over a military project, cars, and a rich heiress. (1987; R)

Cast: George Kennedy, Greg Evigan, Mitzi Kapture.

Director: Raphael Nussbaum.

RACE FOR LIFE

A race car driver attempts to make a comeback despite objections from his wife. He races around Europe (great scenery); she leaves him; he tries to win her back and salvage his career. Standard, un-gripping story. Car scenes are great. (1955)

Cast: Richard Conte, Mari Aldon, George Coulouris.

Director: Terence Fisher.

RACE WITH THE DEVIL

Vacationers are terrorized by devil worshipers after they witness a sacrificial killing. Heavy on car chases; light on plot and redeeming qualities. Don't waste your time. (1975; PG)

Cast: Peter Fonda, Warren Oates, Loretta Swit, Lara Parker.

Director: Jack Starrett.

THE RACERS

Douglas brings power to the role of a man determined to advance to the winners' circle. Exciting European location photography, but not much plot. (1955)

Cast: Gilbert Roland, Kirk Douglas, Lee J. Cobb, Cesar Romero, Bella Darvi.

Director: Henry Hathaway.

RAIN MAN

When his father dies, ambitious and self-centered Charlie Babbit finds he has an older, autistic brother who's been institutionalized for years. Needing him to claim an inheritance, he liberates him from the institution and the two take to the road in their father's 1949 Buick Roadmaster (definitely a '49). On the road, both brothers undergo subtle changes. The Vegas montage is wonderful. Critically acclaimed drama and a labor of love for the entire cast. Cruise's best performance to date as he goes from cad to recognizing something wonderfully human in his brother and himself. Hoffman is exceptional. (1988; R)

Cast: Dustin Hoffman, Tom Cruise, Valeria Golino, Jerry Molen, Jack Murdock, Michael D. Roberts, Ralph Seymour, Lucinda Jenney, Bonnie Hunt, Kim Robillard, Beth Grant.

Director: Barry Levinson.

REBEL WITHOUT A CAUSE

James Dean's most memorable screen appearance. In the second of his three films, he plays a troubled teenager from the right side of the tracks. Dean's portrayal of Jim Stark, a teen alienated from both his parents and peers, is excellent. He befriends outcasts Wood and Mineo in a police station and together they find a common ground. The climactic game of chicken is a real "cliff-hanger." Superb young stars carry this in-the-gut story of adolescence. All three leads met with real-life tragic ends. (1955)

Cast: James Dean, Natalie Wood, Sal Mineo, Jim Backus, Nick Adams, Dennis Hopper, Ann Doran, William Hopper, Rochelle Hudson, Corey Allen, Edward Platt.

Director: Nicholas Ray.

1970: Head restraints fitted to the back of front car seats become compulsory in the United States. These reduce the extent of neck injuries when a car is hit from behind.

RED LINE 7000

High stakes auto racers drive fast cars and date women. Excellent racing footage in otherwise routine four-wheel fest. (1965)

Cast: James Caan, Laura Devon, Gail Hire, Charlene Holt, John Crawford, Marianna Hill, George Takei.

Director: Howard Hawks.

THE REIVERS

Young boy and two adult pals journey from small town Mississippi (circa 1905) to the big city of Memphis in a stolen car. Picaresque tale is delightful on-screen, as in William Faulkner's enjoyable last novel. (1969; PG)

Cast: Steve McQueen, Sharon Farrell, Will Geer, Michael Constantine, Rupert Crosse.

Director: Mark Rydell.

REPO JAKE

Jake Baxter learns the myth of the carefree life of a repossession man in this action thriller. His illusion is destroyed by angry clients, pornography, a deadly underworld racetrack, and a sinister crime boss. (1990)

Cast: Dan Haggerty, Robert Axelrod.

REPO MAN

An inventive, perversely witty portrait of sick modern urbanity, following the adventures of a punk rocker taking a job as a car repossessor in a barren city. The landscape is filled with pointless violence, no-frills packaging, media hypnosis, and aliens. Executive producer: none other than ex-Monkee Michael Nesmith. (1983; R)

Cast: Emilio Estevez, Harry Dean Stanton, Sy Richardson, Tracey Walter, Olivia Barash, Fox Harris, Jennifer Balgobin, Vonetta McGee, Angelique Pettyjohn.

Director: Alex Cox.

RETURN TO MACON COUNTY

Tale of three young, reckless youths who become involved with drag racing and a sadistic law enforcement officer. Nolte turns in a good performance in his first film, as does Johnson, despite a mediocre script and dialogue. Sequel to 1974's *Macon County Line*. (1975)

Cast: Nick Nolte, Don Johnson, Robin Mattson.

Director: Richard Compton.

THE RICHARD PETTY STORY

The biography of race car driver Richard Petty, played by himself, and his various achievements on the track. (1972; G)

Cast: Richard Petty, Darren McGavin, Kathie Browne, Lynn Marta, Noah Beery, Jr., L.Q. Jones.

RISKY BUSINESS

With his parents out of town, a teenager becomes involved in unexpected ways with a quick-thinking prostitute, her pimp, and assorted others. Cruise is likeable, especially when dancing in his underwear (to a tune by the Motor City's own Bob Seger). Funny, well-paced, stylish prototypical '80s teen flick reintroduced Ray-Bans as the sunglasses for the wannabe hip. Features a memorable car chase,

1970: Sixty-two-year-old Miriam Hargrave of England finally passes her driving test on the 40th try, following 212 lessons and 39 previous attempts in eight years.

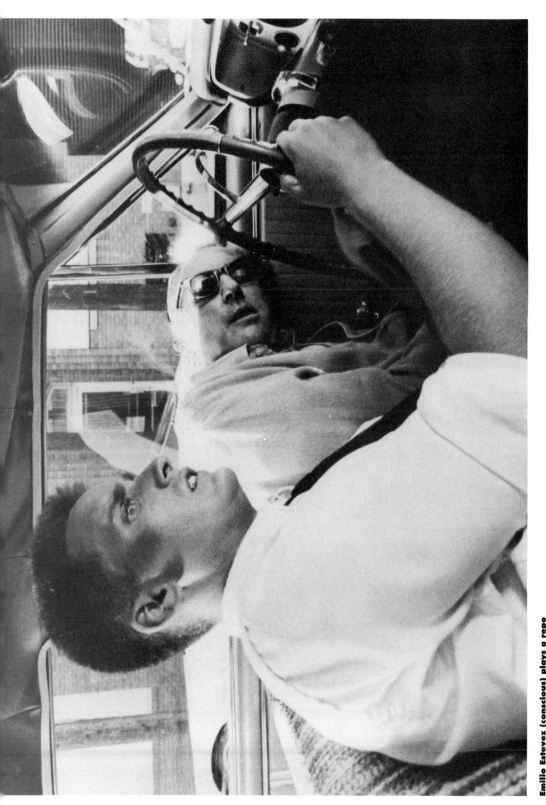

Emilio Estevez (conscious) plays a repo man in the cleverly titled *Repo Man*.
Edge City/Universal/The Kobal Collection

but the car-craziest scene is the one where Cruise allows his dad's Porsche 928 to fall into Lake Michigan. (Later, an unsympathetic service manager asks, "Who's the U-boat commander?") (1983; R)

Cast: Tom Cruise, Rebecca DeMornay, Curtis Armstrong, Bronson Pinchot, Joe Pantoliano, Kevin Anderson, Richard Masur, Raphael Sbarge, Nicholas Pryor, Janet Carroll.

Director: Paul Brickman.

ROAD KILL USA

Two sleazy drifters on a cross-country murder spree pick up a hitchhiking college student and expect him to join in the fun. When he refuses, he has two choices: kill or be killed. (1993)

Cast: Andrew Porter, Sean Bridges, Deanna Perry.

Director: Tony Elwood.

THE ROAD KILLERS

Sickening psycho Cliff (well-played by Sheffer) is head of a brutal quartet that terrorizes a family driving along a remote desert highway. Cliff kidnaps the family daughter and her mild-mannered dad (Lambert) must rescue her. (1995; R)

Cast: Christopher Lambert, Craig Sheffer, Adrienne Shelly.

Director: Deran Sarafian.

ROAD RACERS

The roar of the engine, fast cars, and family ties combine in this movie about the thrill of speed. (1959)

Cast: Joel Lawrence, Marian Collier, Skip Ward.

Director: Arthur Swerdloff.

THE ROAD WARRIOR

The first sequel to *Mad Max* takes place after nuclear war has destroyed Australia. Max helps a colony of oil-drilling survivors defend themselves from the roving murderous outback gangs and escape to the coast. The climactic chase scene is among the most exciting ever filmed. This film virtually created the "action-adventure" picture of the 1980s. (1982; R)

Cast: Mel Gibson, Bruce Spence, Emil Minty, Vernon Wells.

Director: George Miller.

THE ROARING ROAD

Romantic comedy about a car salesman named Toodles, who drives for his company in a big race. Vintage racing footage. Silent with original organ music. (1919)

Cast: Wallace Reid, Ann Little, Theodore Roberts.

Director: James Cruze.

ROARING ROADS

An heir to a fortune acquires a lust for race car driving and, his family thinks, a reckless death wish. (1935)

Cast: Gertrude Messinger, David Sharpe.

ROCKIN' ROAD TRIP

A guy meets a girl in a Boston bar, and finds himself on a drunken, slapstick road trip down

---

1971: The first manned-vehicle on the moon is a General Motors Lunar Roving Vehicle. The moon-buggy is powered by batteries and cruises at 10 mph—and it's still there.

the eastern seaboard with a rock band. (1985; PG-13)

Cast: Garth McLean, Katherine Harrison, Margeret Currie, Steve Boles.

ROGER & ME

Hilarious, controversial, and atypical semi-documentary details Moore's protracted efforts to meet General Motors president Roger Smith and confront him with the poverty and despair afflicting Flint, Michigan, after GM closed its plants there. Includes some emotionally grabbing scenes: a Flint family is evicted just before Christmas; a woman makes a living by selling rabbits for food or pets; and a then soon-to-be Miss America addresses the socioeconomic impact of GM's decision. One of the highest-grossing non-fiction films ever released, and Moore's first. (1989; R)

Cast: Michael Moore, Bob Eubanks, Pat Boone, Anita Bryant.

Director: Michael Moore.

ROUND TRIP TO HEAVEN

Party guy Larry (Feldman) and his innocent cousin (Galligan) take off in a borrowed Rolls-Royce to go meet Larry's dream centerfold in a supermodel contest. Unfortunately, the Rolls' trunk is loaded with stolen money and Stoneface (Sharkey), the felon who stashed the cash, wants the money back. With Stoneface in pursuit these guys are in for the ride of their lives. For the teen set only. (1992; R)

Cast: Corey Feldman, Zach Galligan, Julie McCullough, Rowanne Brewer, Ray Sharkey.

Director: Alan Roberts.

RUN

A high-energy action cartoon, with little plot but lots of stunts. Dempsey is a super-smart law student hired to drive a car to Atlantic City. A stop on the way starts trouble. Instant romance with a local girl balances mayhem from crime boss. Expect no more than physical feats and you'll be happy with this lightweight fare. (1991; R)

Cast: Patrick Dempsey, Kelly Preston, Ken Pogue, Alan C. Peterson, Sean McCann.

Director: Geoff Burrowes.

RUNNING SCARED

Hip, unorthodox Chicago cops Hines and Crystal have to handle an important drug arrest before taking an extended vacation in Key West. Not as relentless as *48 Hrs.,* but more enjoyable in some ways. Ever wonder what it's like to ride in a car at high speed on the tracks? Find out here. (1986; R)

Cast: Gregory Hines, Billy Crystal, Dan Hedaya, Jimmy Smits, Darlanne Fluegel, Joe Pantoliano, Steven Bauer.

Director: Peter Hyams.

SAFARI 3000

A *Playboy* writer is assigned to do a story on a 3-day, 3,000 kilometer car race in Africa. Doesn't take itself too seriously, and neither should we. Dumb, dull, and disjointed. (1982; PG)

Cast: Stockard Channing, David Carradine, Christopher Lee.

Director: Harry Hurwitz.

1973: First automobile air bag is offered by General Motors. The auto industry resists adopting this safety system and it takes another 20 years before the air bag is standard equipment on most cars.

Burt Reynolds: Actor and Car Salesman

Burt Reynolds appeared in Pontiac sales literature in 1981. He was promoting the limited edition "Bandit" replicas, Firebird Trans Ams made to look like the star of the "Smokey and the Bandit" movies.

Source: Smith, Mark, and Naomi Black, *America on Wheels*, William Morrow, 1985.

SHAKER RUN

A stunt-car driver and his mechanic transport a mysterious package. They don't know what to do—they're carrying a deadly virus that every terrorist wants! Car chases galore, and not much else. However, if you like chase scenes . . . (1985)

Cast: Leif Garrett, Cliff Robertson, Lisa Harrow.

Director: Bruce Morrison.

SIX PACK

The Gambler goes auto racing. Rogers, in his theatrical debut, stars as Brewster Baker, a former stock-car driver. He returns to the racing circuit with the help of six larcenous orphans (the six-pack, get it?) adept at stripping cars. Kinda cute if you're in the mood for sugar-powered race car story. (1982; PG)

Cast: Kenny Rogers, Diane Lane, Erin Gray, Barry Corbin, Anthony Michael Hall.

Director: Daniel Petrie.

SLITHER

Caan and Boyle become wrapped up in a scheme to recover $300,000 in cash, stolen seven years previously. Along the way they pick up speed freak Kellerman, who assists them in a variety of loony ways. Frantic chase scenes are the highlight. (1973; PG)

Cast: James Caan, Peter Boyle, Sally Kellerman, Louise Lasser, Allen (Goorwitz) Garfield, Richard B. Shull, Alex Rocco.

Director: Howard Zieff.

SMASH PALACE

A compelling drama of a marriage jeopardized by his obsession with building a race car and her need for love and affection. Melodramatic, but worth watching. Robson as their young daughter is wonderful. (1982)

Cast: Bruno Lawrence, Anna Jemison, Greer Robson, Keith Aberdein.

Director: Roger Donaldson.

SMOKEY AND THE BANDIT

If you don't know how to end a movie, you call for a car chase. The first and best of the horrible series about bootlegger Reynolds is one long car chase. Reynolds makes a wager that he can have a truck load of Coors beer—once unavailable east of Texas—delivered to Atlanta from Texas in 28 hours. Gleason is the "smokey" who tries to stop him. Field is the hitchhiker

1973: Oil shortages begin as the Organization of Petroleum Exporting Countries (OPEC) embargoes shipments to the United States. Gas shortages and subsequent steep price increases soon become a major factor in all transportation planning.

Reynolds picks up along the way. Great stunts; director Needham was a top stunt man. (1977; PG)

Cast: Burt Reynolds, Sally Field, Jackie Gleason, Jerry Reed, Mike Henry, Paul Williams, Pat McCormick.

Director: Hal Needham.

SMOKEY AND THE BANDIT II

Pathetic sequel to *Smokey and the Bandit* proved a box-office winner, grossing $40 million. The Bandit is hired to transport a pregnant elephant from Miami to the Republican convention in Dallas. Sheriff Buford T. Justice and family are in hot pursuit. (1980; PG)

Cast: Burt Reynolds, Sally Field, Jackie Gleason, Jerry Reed, Mike Henry, Dom DeLuise, Pat McCormick, Paul Williams.

Director: Hal Needham.

SMOKEY AND THE BANDIT 3

You thought the second one was bad? Another mega car chase, this time sans director Needham. (1983; PG)

Cast: Burt Reynolds, Jackie Gleason, Jerry Reed, Paul Williams, Pat McCormick, Mike Henry, Colleen Camp.

Director: Dick Lowry.

SMOKEY & THE HOTWIRE GANG

A convoy of truckers try to track down a beautiful woman driving a stolen car. (1979)

Cast: James Keach, Stanley Livingston, Tony Lorea, Alvy Moore, George Barris.

SMOKEY BITES THE DUST

Car-smashing gag-fest about a sheriff's daughter kidnapped by her smitten beau. Near-plotless and literally unoriginal: lifted footage from several other Roger Corman-produced flicks, a technique that can aptly be called garbage picking. (1981; PG)

Cast: Janet Julian, Jimmy McNichol, Patrick Campbell, Kari Lizer, John Blythe Barrymore, Jr.

Director: Charles B. Griffith.

SPEED CRAZY

A psychotic madman with a fast car fetish risks it all to find a place to go crazy. (1959)

Cast: Brett Halsey, Yvonne Lime, Charles Wilcox, Jackie Joseph.

Director: William Hole, Jr.

THE SPEED LOVERS

Stock-car driver Lorenzen plays himself as an inspiration to a young man to join the auto-racing circuit. More of a pat on the industry's back than a serious drama. Features footage from a number of race tracks around the country although shot principally in Atlanta. (1968)

Cast: Fred Lorenzen, William F. McGaha, Peggy O'Hara, David Marcus, Carol Street, Glenda Brunson.

Director: Willima F. McGaha.

THE SPEED SPOOK

Silent ghost races car and steals documents. (1924)

Cast: Johnny Hines, Warner Richmond.

1974: American Motors Company is the only American automaker with increased sales. Ninety percent of AMC cars are compacts.

Road Test

MATCH THE CAR MOVIE WITH ITS STAR.

1. *Bobby Deerfield*
2. *Corvette Summer*
3. *Days of Thunder*
4. *Grand Prix*
5. *Le Mans*
6. *Speedway*
7. *Thunder Road*
8. *Tucker: The Man and His Dream*
9. *Used Cars*
10. *Winning*

A. Tom Cruise
B. Steve McQueen
C. Elvis Presley
D. Jeff Bridges
E. Kurt Russell
F. Al Pacino
G. Paul Newman
H. James Garner
I. Mark Hamill
J. Robert Mitchum

(Answers: 1.F 2.I 3.A 4.H 5.B 6.C 7.J 8.D 9.E 10.G)

Director: Charles Hines.

SPEED ZONE

Comic celebrities take over a high speed auto race when a redneck cop locks up the real drivers. Unfunny sequel to *Cannonball Run.* (1988; PG)

Cast: Melody Anderson, Peter Boyle, Tim Matheson, Donna Dixon, John Candy, Eugene Levy, Joe Flaherty, Matt Frewer, Shari Belafonte, Tom Smothers, Dick Smothers, Brooke Shields, Lee Van Cleef, Jamie Farr, John Schneider, Michael Spinks.

Director: Jim Drake.

SPEEDTRAP

Typical chase scenes and cross-gender sparring characterize this tale of a private detective and a police officer pursuing car thieves. Good cast and fun chemistry between the leads; weak, typical script. (1978; PG)

Cast: Joe Don Baker, Tyne Daly, Richard Jaeckel, Robert Loggia, Morgan Woodward, Timothy Carey.

Director: Earl Bellamy.

SPEEDWAY

Elvis the stock car driver finds himself being chased by Nancy the IRS agent during an im-

1974: The Emergency Highway Energy Conservation Act goes into effect in the United States. This law establishes a national speed limit of 55 mph in order to reduce gasoline consumption.

**James Bond's Lotus turns into a
submarine in *The Spy Who Loved Me*.**
United Artists/The Kobal Collection

portant race. Will Sinatra keep to the business at hand? Or will the King melt her heart? Some cameos by real-life auto racers. Watch for a young Garr. Movie number 27 for Elvis. (1968; G)

Cast: Elvis Presley, Nancy Sinatra, Bill Bixby, Gale Gordon, William Schallert, Carl Ballantine, Ross Hagen. Cameos: Richard Petty, Cale Yarborough, Terri Garr.

Director: Norman Taurog.

SPINOUT

A pouty traveling singer decides to drive an experimental race car in a rally. Usual Elvis fare with the King being pursued by an assortment of beauties. (1966)

Cast: Elvis Presley, Shelley Fabares, Carl Betz, Diane McBain, Cecil Kellaway, Jack Mullaney, Deborah Walley, Una Merkel, Warren Berlinger, Will Hutchins, Dodie Marshall.

Director: Norman Taurog.

THE SPY WHO LOVED ME

James Bond teams up with female Russian Agent XXX to squash a villain's plan to use captured American and Russian atomic submarines in a plot to destroy the world. The villain's henchman, 7'-2"Kiel, is the steel-toothed Jaws. Carly Simon sings the memorable, Marvin Hamlisch theme song, "Nobody Does It Better." The Bondmobile for this film: a Lotus Espirit that does double-duty as a submarine, complete with torpedoes and surface-to-air missles! (1977; PG)

Cast: Roger Moore, Barbara Bach, Curt Jurgens, Richard Kiel, Caroline Munro, Walter Gotell, Geoffrey Keen, Valerie Leon, Bernard Lee, Lois Maxwell, Desmond Llewelyn.

Director: Lewis Gilbert.

STARMAN

An alien from an advanced civilization lands in Wisconsin. He hides beneath the guise of a grieving young widow's recently deceased husband. He then makes her drive him across country to rendezvous with his spacecraft so he can return home. Well-acted, interesting twist on the "Stranger in a Strange Land" theme. Bridges is fun as the likeable starman; Allen is lovely and earthy in her worthy follow-up to *Raiders of the Lost Ark.* (1984; PG)

Cast: Jeff Bridges, Karen Allen, Charles Martin Smith, Richard Jaeckel.

Director: John Carpenter.

STEEL ARENA

Several real life stunt-car drivers appear in this action-packed film, crammed with spins, jumps, explosions, and world-record-breaking, life-risking stunts. (1972; PG)

Cast: Dusty Russell, Gene Drew, Buddy Love.

Director: Mark L. Lester.

STINGRAY

Two guys buy a Corvette, not knowing it's loaded with stolen heroin. Gangsters with an interest in the dope come after them, and the chase is on. Very violent and not all that funny. (1978; PG)

Cast: Chris Mitchum, Sherry Jackson, Les Lannom.

Director: Richard Taylor.

1975: American Motors introduces the Pacer, a small, wide car which is among the first American automobiles to offer rack-and-pinion steering. Despite its quality, the Pacer suffers in a languishing market.

STROKER ACE

Flamboyant stock car driver tries to break an iron-clad promotional contract signed with a greedy fried-chicken magnate. Off duty, he ogles blondes as dopey as he is. One of the worst from Reynolds—and that's saying something. (1983; PG)

Cast: Burt Reynolds, Ned Beatty, Jim Nabors, Parker Stevenson, Loni Anderson, Bubba Smith.

Director: Hal Needham.

SUNSET LIMOUSINE

An out-of-work stand-up comic gets thrown out by his girlfriend, then takes a job as a chauffeur. Standard vehicle with occasional bursts of speed. (1983)

Cast: John Ritter, Martin Short, Susan Dey, Paul Reiser, Audrie Neehan, Lainie Kazan.

Director: Terry Hughes.

SUPERBUG SUPER AGENT

Dodo the wonder car puts the brakes on crime in this silly action-adventure tale. A lemon in a lot full of Herbies. (1976)

Cast: Robert Mark, Heidi Hansen, George Goodman.

TEENAGE CRIME WAVE

Route 66 provides thrills for a couple of teen punks, but things get out of hand when they blow a sheriff's head off. They scoop up a couple of babes and hightail it with the police

close behind, ultimately confronting their destiny at a mountain top observatory. (1955)

Cast: Tommy Cook, Mollie McCart, Sue England, Frank Griffin, James Bell, Kay Riehl.

Director: Fred F. Sears.

THELMA & LOUISE

Hailed as the first "feminist-buddy" movie, Sarandon and Davis bust out as best friends who head directly into one of the better movies of the year. Davis is the ditzy Thelma, a housewife rebelling against her dominating, unfaithful, abusive husband (who, rather than being disturbing, provides some of the best comic relief in the film). Sarandon is Louise, a hardened and world-weary waitress in the midst of an unsatisfactory relationship. They hit the road for a respite from their mundane lives, only to find violence and a part of themselves they never knew existed. Outstanding performances from Davis and especially Sarandon, with Pitt notable as the stud who gets Davis' motor revved. (1991; R)

Cast: Susan Sarandon, Geena Davis, Harvey Keitel, Christopher McDonald, Michael Madsen, Brad Pitt, Timothy Carhart, Stephen Tobolowsky, Lucinda Jenney.

Director: Ridley Scott.

THIS MAN MUST DIE

A man searches relentlessly for the driver who killed his young son in a hit-and-run. When found, the driver engages him in a complex cat-and-mouse chase. Another stunning crime and punishment tale from Chabrol. (1970; PG)

Cast: Michael Duchaussoy, Caroline Cellier, Jean Yanne.

Director: Claude Chabrol.

1975: American car registrations pass the 100 million mark for the first time.

THOSE DARING YOUNG MEN IN THEIR JAUNTY JALOPIES

Daring young men in noisy slow cars trek 1,500 miles across country in the 1920s and call it a race. (1969; G)

Cast: Tony Curtis, Susan Hampshire, Terry-Thomas, Eric Sykes, Gert Frobe, Peter Cook, Dudley Moore, Jack Hawkins.

Director: Ken Annakin.

THUMB TRIPPING

A dated '60s/hippie film. Two flower children hitchhike and encounter all kinds of other strange people in their travels on the far-out roads. (1972; R)

Cast: Meg Foster, Michael Burns, Bruce Dern, Marianna Hill, Michael Conrad, Joyce Van Patten.

Director: Quentin Masters.

THUNDER AND LIGHTNING

A mismatched young couple chases a truckload of poisoned moonshine. Action-packed chases ensue. Nice chemistry between Carradine and Jackson. (1977; PG)

Cast: David Carradine, Kate Jackson, Roger C. Carmel, Sterling Holloway, Eddie Barth.

Director: Corey Allen.

THUNDER ROAD

Mitchum comes home to Tennessee from Korea and takes over the family moonshine business, fighting both mobsters and federal agents. An exciting chase between Mitchum and the feds ends the movie with the appropriate bang. Mitchum not only produced, wrote, and starred in this best of the moonshine-running films, but also wrote the theme song, "Whippoorwill" (which later became a radio hit). A cult favorite, still shown in many drive-ins around the country. Features the film debut of Mitchum's son, James. (1958; PG)

Cast: Robert Mitchum, Jacques Aubuchon, Gene Barry, Keely Smith, Trevor Bardette, Sandra Knight, Jim Mitchum, Betsy Holt, Frances Koon.

Director: Arthur Ripley.

THUNDERBALL

The fourth installment in Ian Fleming's James Bond series finds 007 on a mission to thwart SPECTRE, which has threatened to blow up Miami by atomic bomb if 100 million pounds in ransom is not paid. One of the more tedious Bond entries but a big box-office success. Includes a repeat performance by the tricked-out Aston Martin DB5. Tom Jones sang the title song. Remade as *Never Say Never Again* in 1983, with Connery reprising his role as Bond after a 12-year absence. (1965; PG)

Cast: Sean Connery, Claudine Auger, Adolfo Celi, Luciana Paluzzi, Rik von Nutter, Martine Beswick, Molly Peters, Guy Doleman, Bernard Lee, Lois Maxwell, Desmond Llewelyn.

Director: Terence Young.

TO LIVE & DIE IN L.A.

Fast-paced, morally ambivalent tale of cops and counterfeiters in L.A. After his partner is killed shortly before his retirement, a secret service agent sets out to track down his ruthless killer. Lots of violence; some nudity. No-

1976: The Volkswagen Golf breaks the Ford Mustang's record for quickest one million sales (31 months for the Golf compared to the Mustang's 36).

table both for a riveting car chase and its dearth of sympathetic characters. (1985; R)

Cast: William L. Petersen, Willem Dafoe, John Pankow, Dean Stockwell, Debra Feuer, John Turturro, Darlanne Fluegel, Robert Downey, Jr.

Director: William Friedkin.

TO PLEASE A LADY

Romantic comedy-drama about race car driver Gable and reporter Stanwyck. Although leads do their best with the script, they're unable to generate any sparks. However, race scenes are excellent. Filmed at the Indianapolis Speedway, the spectacular racing footage makes up for overall average film. (1950)

Cast: Clark Gable, Barbara Stanwyck, Adolphe Menjou, Will Geer, Roland Winters.

Director: Clarence Brown.

TOMBOY

A pretty auto mechanic is determined to win not only the race but the love and respect of a superstar auto racer. (1985; R)

Cast: Betsy Russell, Eric Douglas, Jerry Dinome, Kristi Somers, Richard Erdman, Toby Iland.

Director: Herb Freed.

TRAFFIC

Eccentric auto designer Monsieur Hulot tries to transport his latest contraption from Paris to Amsterdam for an international auto show. As usual, everything goes wrong. Tati's last feature film and his fifth to feature Hulot. French with subtitles. (1971)

Cast: Jacques Tati, Maria Kimberly, Marcel Fraval.

Director: Jacques Tati.

TRAFFIC JAM

A light comedy about a Japanese family's attempt to travel on a holiday weekend. Tokyo couple and their two young children decide to visit the husband's family who happen to live on a distant island. Naturally, the traffic's horrendous, they have very little time, and things continuously go wrong. Japanese with English subtitles. (1991)

Cast: Kenichi Hagiwara, Hitomi Kuroki, Ayako Takarada, Shingo Yazawa, Eiji Okada.

Director: Mitsuo Kurotsuchi.

TROUBLE BOUND

Madsen is Harry, a guy just out of prison, on his way to Nevada with trouble dogging him every step. He's got a dead body in the car trunk, drug dealers after him, and when he offers a lift to a pretty cocktail waitress (Arquette) his luck only gets worse. She plans to kill a Mob boss and it's no secret. Chases and violence. (1992; R)

Cast: Michael Madsen, Patricia Arquette, Florence Stanley, Seymour Cassel, Sal Jenco.

Director: Jeff Reiner.

TUCKER: THE MAN AND HIS DREAM

Portrait of Preston Tucker, entrepreneur and industrial idealist, who tried to build the car of the future in the 1940s and was effectively run out of business by the powers-that-were. Ravishing, ultra-nostalgic lullaby to the American Dream. Watch for Jeff's dad, Lloyd, in a bit role.

1977: A.J. Foyt becomes the first four-time winner of the Indianapolis 500, and Janet Guthrie becomes the first woman to compete at Indy.

00293

Jeff Bridges plays Preston Tucker in *Tucker: The Man and His Dream.*
Lucas Films/The Kobal Collection

One of the best car movies ever made. (1988; PG)

Cast: Jeff Bridges, Martin Landau, Dean Stockwell, Frederic Forrest, Mako, Joan Allen, Christian Slater, Lloyd Bridges, Elias Koteas, Nina Siemaszko, Corin "Corky" Nemec, Marshall Bell, Don Novello, Peter Donat, Dean Goodman, Patti Austin.

Director: Francis Ford Coppola.

USED CARS

A car dealer is desperate to put his jalopy shop competitors out of business. The owners go to great lengths to stay afloat. Sometimes too obnoxious, but often funny. (1980; R)

Cast: Kurt Russell, Jack Warden, Deborah Harmon, Gerrit Graham, Joe Flaherty, Michael McKean.

Director: Robert Zemeckis.

VALET GIRLS

Two Hollywood parking services engage in comedic competitive warfare by offering "special service" to their customers. (1986)

Cast: Meri D. Marshall, April Stewart, Mary Kohnert, Christopher Weeks.

THE VAN

A recent high school graduate passes on the college scene so he can spend more time picking up girls in his van. A lame sex (and sexist) comedy. (1977; R)

Cast: Stuart Getz, Deborah White, Danny DeVito, Harry Moses, Maurice Barkin.

Director: Sam Grossman.

VAN NUYS BLVD.

The popular boulevard is the scene where the cool southern California guys converge for cruising and girl watching, so naturally it's where a country hick comes to test his drag racing skills and check out the action. (1979; R)

Cast: Bill Adler, Cynthia Wood, Dennis Bowen, Melissa Prophet.

Director: William Sachs.

VANISHING POINT

An ex-racer bets that he can deliver a souped-up car from Denver to San Francisco in 15 hours. Taking pep pills along the way, he eludes police, meets up with a number of characters, and finally crashes into a roadblock. Rock score helps attract this film's cult following. (1971; PG)

Cast: Barry Newman, Cleavon Little, Gilda Texler, Dean Jagger, Paul Koslo, Robert Donner, Severn Darden, Victoria Medlin.

Director: Richard Sarafian.

VIVA LAS VEGAS

Race car driver Elvis needs money to compete against rival Danova in the upcoming Las Vegas Grand Prix. He takes a job in a casino and romances fellow employee Ann-Margret, who turns out to be his rival for the grand prize in the local talent competition. Good pairing between the two leads, and the King does particularly well with the title song. (1963)

Cast: Elvis Presley, Ann-Margret, William Demarest, Jack Carter, Cesare Danova, Nicky Blair, Larry Kent.

Director: George Sidney.

1978: Seventy-seven-year-old American Fannie Turner finally passes her written driving examination on the 104th try.

**Paul Newman tries to win
the Indy 500 in *Winning*.**
Universal/The Kobal Collection

WEEKEND

A Parisian couple embark on a drive to the country. On the way they witness and are involved in horrifying highway wrecks. Leaving the road they find a different, equally grotesque kind of carnage. Godard's brilliant, surreal, hyper-paranoiac view of modern life was greatly influenced by the fact that his mother was killed in an auto accident in 1954 (he himself suffered a serious motorcycle mishap in 1975). In French with English subtitles. (1967)

Cast: Mireille Darc, Jean Yanne, Jean-Pierre Kalfon, Valerie Lagrange, Jean-Pierre Leaud, Yves Beneyton.

Director: Jean-Luc Godard.

WHEELS OF TERROR

Possessed black car stalks children in isolated village. Bus driver Cassidy gets behind the wheel of V8 super-charged school bus to initiate most interminable chase scene in screen history. (1990; R)

Cast: Joanna Cassidy, Marcie Leeds, Carlos Cervantes, Arlen Dean Snyder.

Director: Christopher Cain.

WHITE LIGHTNING

Good ol' boy Reynolds plays a moonshiner going after the crooked sheriff who murdered his brother. Good stunt-driving chases enliven the formula. The inferior sequel is *Gator.* (1973; PG)

Cast: Burt Reynolds, Ned Beatty, Bo Hopkins, Jennifer Billingsley, Louise Latham.

Director: Joseph Sargent.

WINNING

A race car driver (Newman) will let nothing, including his new wife (Woodward), keep him from winning the Indianapolis 500. Newman does his own driving. Thomas' film debut. (1969; PG)

Cast: Paul Newman, Joanne Woodward, Robert Wagner, Richard Thomas, Clu Gulager.

Director: James Goldstone.

THE WRAITH

Drag-racing Arizona teens find themselves challenged by a mysterious, otherworldly stranger. Hot cars; cool music; little else to recommend it. Lousy script; ludicrous excuse for a premise. Most of the stars herein are related to somebody famous. (1987; PG-13)

Cast: Charlie Sheen, Nick Cassavetes, Sherilyn Fenn, Randy Quaid, Matthew Barry, Clint Howard, Griffin O'Neal.

Director: Mike Marvin.

YOU ONLY LIVE TWICE

Agent 007 travels to Japan to take on archnemesis Blofeld, who has been capturing Russian and American spacecraft in an attempt to start WWIII. Great location photography; theme sung by Nancy Sinatra. Though implausible plot is a handicap, there's a nice car chase involving a rare Toyota 2000 GT convertible. (1967; PG)

Cast: Sean Connery, Mie Hama, Akiko Wakabayashi, Tetsuro Tamba, Karin Dor, Charles Gray, Donald Pleasence, Tsai Chin, Bernard Lee, Lois Maxwell, Desmond Llewelyn.

Director: Lewis Gilbert.

1978: Ford's F-Series pickup is the best-selling vehicle in the United States, beginning a trend in which cars will eventually be outsold by trucks and wagons—pickups, minivans, and sport utility vehicles.

ZERO TO SIXTY

Newly divorced man finds his car has been re-possessed for nonpayment. Seeking out the manager of the finance company, he gets a job as a repo man with a sassy 16-year-old girl as his assistant. Repartee develops, stuff happens, and the movie ends. (1978; PG)

Cast: Darren McGavin , Sylvia Miles, Denise Nickerson, Joan Collins.

Director: Don Weis.

1978: Henry Ford II fires Lee Iacocca as President of Ford. Iacocca moves to Chrysler and leads it out of bankruptcy with the help of a federal loan.

Car Repairs 101

Here's an old standard that I used a few times: When you blow out an exhaust pipe, you cut both ends out of a beer can, smear the inside of it with muffler-repair goop, wrap it around the hole in the pipe, then secure it with a hose clamp at each end. At one time I had a '66 Datsun Roadster with three of these set-ups."

Peter Gareffa

We were out cruising in a friend's black GTO. It started to rain and his windshield wipers broke. We took the coat hanger out of the antenna, wrapped one end around the windshield wiper on the passenger side, and then the passenger had to pull it back and forth to operate the wipers. It worked OK, but you got soaked."

Don Boyden

That happened to me, too, only I didn't even have a hanger. In 1982, I was still driving my 1970 Malibu that I had 'inherited' after my grandpa had died. I was living in Ann Arbor (Michigan), driving east on Huron, between Seventh and Main, during one of those awful combination rain/sleet/snow/ice storms. Those of you familiar with Ann Arbor may know that that particular part of Huron is a giant hill. The windshield wiper (on the driver's side, of course) must have overheated because it just went limp. The only way I could see, as the rain/sleet/snow/ice built up on the windshield, was by rolling down the window and using my hand and coat sleeve to continually wipe off the windshield. And, oh yeah, it was terribly icy and I had to keep the other hand on the wheel. Cars sliding all over the place and I

1978: A 1957 Mercedes-Benz 180D owned by Robert O'Reilly of Olympia, Washington, gets into the *Guiness Book of World Records* for highest authenticated mileage accumulated. The odometer on O'Reilly's Mercedes reads 1,184,880.

come to that awful part of Huron. Slip-slidin' I go. Miraculously I was able to maintain some sort of control and eventually made my way home. The most harrowing driving experience I can remember."

Larry Baker

My dad regularly used coat hangers to hold up mufflers and exhaust systems. I think of this one as one of THE classic fix-its, though I have yet to do it myself. Dad would also try to patch mufflers with tin cans and whatever he could find to hold them on (more coat hangers?). But that never worked so well. Of course, our clothes were always all over the floor . . . but the car was quiet at least."

Charlie Montney

And of course there's the bent-up coat hanger you could use to unlock your car door after locking your keys inside. That was before cars were made with hermetically-sealed doors and theft-deterrent locks. Boy, I challenge anyone to use a coat hanger to unlock a car door these days. Come to think of it, I seem to recall hearing about someone

who unlocked their car door with a golf ball retriever after locking their keys inside. That must've been something to see."

Dean Dauphinais

In early 1972, my brother and I were cruising in his blue Ford Econoline van (V8 302, headers, big carb, black racing stripe, carpeted back, a true high school boy's dream) when he decided he needed to do an engine repair that could only be done while moving. We found a large parking lot and switched places, with me driving—for the first time ever. On early Ford Econolines the engine sat squarely between the driver and passenger inside the vehicle, and was covered by a big plastic or fiberglass cowling. Dave pulled the engine cowling off and proceeded to tinker with the engine as I drove the van around in slow circles. He fixed the problem, and told me to stop. Not having any real driving experience and being anxious to please my motor head brother, I put it in park from about 15 mph. Well, Dave bounced off the engine, I bounced off the dash, and the van bounced merrily to a stop. It's a good thing I'm a lot bigger than my brother, or he

1979: A nationwide gasoline shortage leads to long lines—and sometimes fisticuffs—at fuel stations.

would have hurt me a lot more than he did."

Don Boyden

Six years ago I was working in Nebraska. The wind chill was about 40 below but I wanted to get home to Omaha, three hours away. I went to start my '81 Mazda 626 and it was just barely turning over. I knew if I kept cranking it I would just drain the charge from the battery. AAA couldn't get anyone there for hours. I knew the car was a quart low on oil, so before adding it I decided to heat it up. I put the oil in a pan, and put in a candy thermometer since I guessed it might boil around 285 degrees, which is the temperature I use for cracking toffee. It started scorching around 260 so I put it in and the car turned right over.

"I tried this again on one other occasion, but the car didn't need any more oil and I wasn't going to crawl under the car in that cold to drain out oil. So, after adding the boiling oil I later found that I had oil leaking out around the valve cover gasket."

Anonymous

From my years on the Range (that's the Iron Range of Min-

nesota, boyhood home of Bob Dylan and assorted Lake Wobegon types) and in The Cities (what Rangers call Minneapolis/St. Paul), here are two tales of life in an intemperate zone:

"During the winter in rural northern Minnesota it can be very difficult to start a car that has been parked even for a few hours. This is assuming one would want to try. Sometimes we would get warnings over the radio that the temperatures were so low that tires were apt to shatter. A common practice for keeping cars startable was to dig a shallow pit, fill it with heated stones, wood, or charcoal embers, and a layer of soil, and then park the car over it. Enough heat would rise to keep the engine warm and the battery alive. Hot stones covered with light soil or gravel can stay warm quite a while—sort of the luau concept adapted to northern culture. And where would one get heated stones? In Minnesota they come from saunas.

"In The Cities the temperatures weren't much higher and one faced the same car-starting problems but without ready access to a pit most of the time. The solution was plug-ins. These are electrical leads that

---

1980: Six years after the U.S. speed limit is set at 55 mph, 470,000 radar detectors are sold in one year. In 1985, some 1.7 million are sold, indicating widespread belief that this speed is unrealistically slow for highways.

0 0 3 0 1

attach to a car battery overnight and keep it warmed up. Plug-ins were a routine part of life. Often ads for apartments would say things such as '3 bdrms; gd view; new kitch; plug-ins.' Plug-ins were the most important part, out-ranking fireplaces, pools, and second bathrooms as desirable real-estate features."

Barb Beach

While visiting my parents in Texas, I took a friend to Houston Intercontinental Air-port on the other side of Houston. Just after dropping her off I noticed steam. I stopped at the gas station and found a hole in a radiator hose about six inches from the end. The station did not have the hose I needed and there wasn't another for miles. I got a knife and cut off the hose to the edge of the hole. I loosened the other end, and moved it so it was just barely on and clamped it down. I then pulled the loose end as hard as I could to get it on and clamped it on. I filled the radiator and it held fine for the drive to my parents house. Within two weeks I had to re-peat this maneuver on the other hose to the radiator. So I should have replaced it at the same time as the first

since they wear out at the same rate."

Anonymous

I had a Mercury Lynx with a trailer hitch installed. They offered to sell me a rust pre-vention cap for the ball. In-stead I used a rubber baby doll head with grease in it. It looked rather punk."

Kelly Stevens

Car Trouble

One July my parents' 1973 Ford LTD (green, of course) was not starting in their driveway. After several at-tempts to jump it, etc., they and their houseguests went back inside the house to call for a tow truck, have another cup of coffee, and generally cool their heels. It being summer, the windows and doors were all open to let breeze in through the screens. So they had no trouble hearing when the LTD suddenly fired itself up and began to run, with no one in sight, no key in the ignition, nothing but hot July air anywhere near it."

Diane Dupuis

1980: Facing bankruptcy, Chrysler receives a large loan from the U.S. government. Chrysler quickly rebounds and pays off the loan by 1983, seven years early.

Modern car trouble pales in comparison to that of the early days of driving.

Courtesy of American Automobile Manufacturers Association

My first car trouble came when I was four. I was waiting in the car—which was parked in our driveway—for my mom, who ran back into the house to get something she forgot and evidently needed badly for our shopping trip to the mall. So I thought I'd be really cool and play with the shifter on the family station wagon. Well, I got it into neutral and the car started rolling down our sloping driveway. I didn't know what to do so I just enjoyed the ride. The car came to a stop in the middle of the street. Next thing I know, here comes a car down the street. Uh-oh. I thought I was history. Well, the car stopped just in time (or so it seemed) and started honking its horn. Out came mom, and her face had a look of horror on it that I'll never forget. Boy, did I get in trouble. Never made it to the mall, either."

Dean Dauphinais

When I was three, the folks used to let me sit in the car in the driveway (probably to shut me up) and play. I had pretty much the same experience as Dean: slipped the transmission into neutral and rolled the old man's '53 Buick out into the street. I don't

remember what happened after that."

Peter Gareffa

My mother had an orange Volvo 240 station wagon, a car which is in the book *Worst Cars Ever Made,* and it deserves the distinction. Not only was it a lemon, it was jinxed . . .

"We were driving the car back from Maine and the engine started to sound real funny, then there was a horrible grinding noise. The air conditioning compressor had fallen off and was rattling around.

"I downshifted in it once, and blew the muffler off.

"A tree fell on it in our driveway, crushing the hood and roof.

"I put it through a fence and into a tree, smashing in the front and putting teeth marks on the leather wrap on the steering wheel.

"It was hit in a parking lot (so we believe, we never saw the accident and we suspect the car may have done it to itself).

"We were towing snowmobiles behind it and one of them fell off the trailer, rolling across several lanes of Rte. 128.

1981: Germany's BMW introduces a new on-board computer that tells the driver when the car needs to be serviced. In 10 years, nearly every non-economy car will have computer chips to control and monitor its systems.

"It was the first car we ever had with the new 5 mph bumpers. We tested them one night in the high school parking lot by repeatedly driving it at 5 mph into an abandoned car. They really worked, although the black rubber bushings got a little scarred.

"We finally sold it to a used car dealer in Florida when we moved down there. He deserved it."

Don Boyden

My dad had a Dodge Dart that would start itself, but then he had to go and get it fixed and ruin all of the fun."

Terri Schell

I was driving in my rusty old VW Bug one winter. A car with two guys inside pulled up alongside me and tried several times to get my attention by shouting something that started with an 'F.' I could tell they weren't swearing at me even though I'm not real good at lip reading. Since my fenders were then wired onto the car by means of bent coathangers, I thought they were telling me my fenders were falling off, which of course I already knew, hence the creative repair job. It turns out my engine (as in all Beetles,

in the rear of the car) was on fire, which must be why they sped away after my cavalier dismissal of their concerns. I only learned this after I called my ex to have him pick up the @#$%# car from an I-75 entrance ramp, where it had died. He said later that the gas line had a hole and I was lucky to be alive. I never saw that car again."

Debra Kirby

Two vehicles is not a safety net. It's tempting fate.

"The Toyota has a broken headlight (not burned out, broken, like from a flying rock) that'll cost $250+ at a dealership or garage to replace, or $100+ if we can find a junkyard with the right headlight. My temporary solution has been to drive the truck so I don't have to drive half-blind coming home in the evenings.

"But the heater in the truck stopped working this weekend, just when the cold spell hit. So maybe it's finally time to investigate that bus schedule.

"Also: Last winter the car wouldn't start one morning. For the first time since I was 17, I'd left the lights on. *#!@. So I got in the truck.

1981: The much-anticipated and delayed release of the stainless steel DeLorean sports car leaves the buying public unimpressed; quality, finance, and legal problems quickly overcome the car and its designer, John DeLorean.

Dead battery, wouldn't even hold a charge. Synchronicity again."

Christa Brelin

This is not my direct story, but my husband's. He used to own what he calls "The #%*!# Horizon from Hell," that, along with all kinds of unending mechanical problems, once backfired so loudly it blew out its hatchback window."

Debbie Burek

I had a Horizon in college and it was the worst car I ever owned. Wheel bearings went out on three tires in the span of three months, I had the carburetor rebuilt twice, and the car still had awful run-on. (In fact, it was part of the club of cars that would run without the key in. When it first happened, my mechanic was in awe—'I've never seen a car do that before!' Needless to say, I just reached for the wallet when I heard that.) In addition, whenever it was rainy or damp, the car would stall at every intersection; and in the winter, if we got even a hard frost, the locks would freeze solid and I would have to crawl in through the back hatch to get in. Now that was a sight.

These cars were clearly the work of the devil."

Brad Morgan

Those Omnis and Horizons were the scourge of the road. I once traveled 28 round-trip hours in the backseat of one as an adult (next to my adult sister) on a family Thanksgiving trip to my aunt and uncle's house. The misery of being crammed into that non-ride-engineered space was prolonged by the fact that the thing couldn't really muster highway speed. My parents had all kinds of mechanical trouble with it before it finally died. Once in a while I see one that's still chugging along on the freeway at 50 mph and I wonder why someone hasn't performed a mercy killing by now."

Diane Dupuis

My friend in college had one, and we called it the 'Rolls Canardly.' Because every time we tried to go up a certain hill on campus (wasn't even a big hill!), it would sputter and smoke. Therefore, it *rolls* down hills and *can hardly* make it back up. I know, I know, a very poor play on words. But that car ranked

---

1982: The first Japanese-owned automobile plant in the United States begins producing the 1983 model Honda Accord in Marysville, Ohio.

even higher on the lemon scale than my '87 Tempo."

Erin Holmberg

Don't veer, smear the deer!! At least, that's what my cousin had to do on a trip up to Michigan a couple of years ago in her Horizon. Coming up US-23, she had a choice of hitting a deer that was already downed in her lane, or veering into the next lane, which was filled by a nice big semi. Needless to say, she chose the deer, which acted as a ramp for her poor little Horizon. She bottomed out, and had to make the rest of the trip with just third gear and reverse (and the pleasant smell of roast venison). Strangely enough, the only repair needed (besides a strong bath) was to flip a little lever near the gearbox that had gotten out of alignment. The dealer didn't charge her. This episode was the last in a series of car-related troubles my cousin had every Thanksgiving for about four years, as her trips all seemed to be cursed."

Diane Telgen

My husband's car that I inherited was a 1984 Renault Encore that I learned how to drive (my first stick) in Chicago when I took a job that required traveling. It died exactly five years to the month after he wasted his money on it. Anyway, it started overheating in February, but I kept driving it (I stopped occasionally when the smoke got too bad) because I had to get to work and school. Turns out I warped the engine or something by driving it—we finally took it in and payed $600 we didn't have to get the stupid thing fixed. By March, the transmission was gone, the speedometer was broken, the heat didn't work, and you couldn't use the driver's side door (I don't remember why). The radio was already long gone (stolen). I don't even remember how we got it to the dealership, who let us trade it in for $500. My husband swears I killed it, but everybody knows that the Encore was a piece of crap. That's why they stopped making them soon after"

Lisa DeShantz-Cook

Two experiences:

"One, as a newly licensed 16-year-old in Chicago, I was dropping my mom off at the Belmont Harbor off of Lake Shore Drive. I parked in the last space in a row of one of

---

1982: After being the first of the Big Three to stop producing convertibles (in 1970), Chrysler is the first to reintroduce the ragtop option (on the LeBaron).

the big lots they have there, walked her to where her boyfriend's boat was, and left. As I was getting ready to pull out (hadn't actually begun moving yet) a car sped around the curve and slammed directly into my passenger door. I about died. I jumped out, they jumped out (girl driver switched seats with boy passenger), and people started gathering. I am naive. I know this now. I asked them to stay right there while I called the police, and as I ran to a pay phone, off they sped. Totally kicking myself for forgetting to get the license plate number (GOD, what heat of the moment) I had to run and get my mom, who (for once) wasn't too mad, and drove me to the police station where they laughed at my inquiry as to how long it would take to find the perpetrators.

"Second, having moved to Detroit on a whim (with all my worldly belongings—including two cats—stuffed into a car with 220,000 miles on it that I bought for $250 the day I left), and in need of a job, I drove in this dear Toyota to Royal Oak (Michigan) from the east side to take some sort of government test (I can't remember the name now). It lasted till almost 11 P.M., and off I drove for home. On I-696—

I'll never forget the spot—I started hearing this very strange grinding noise. I began to pray, hoping to just get home, when BLAM! Luckily I was in the far right lane and pulled over, shaken but alive. Luckily (again!) a very nice woman and her friend saw my car blow, and pulled over to help. (Side note: I'd lived here a couple of months, it's 11:30 P.M., and all my old friends had said 'DETROIT?!? What are you NUTS?!?' I was very grateful for the rescue.) Not only did they drive me the rest of the way home, but the woman worked as a recruiter for an ad agency and got me a job interview. Car report? My baby had blown pistons right through the engine. Trash it, the repair guy said. So I did. I've never felt truly problem-free in a car since—always worried something beyond my control is gonna blow."

Jane Hoehner

The first vehicle I ever owned had a standard transmission, which I probably damaged trying to learn to drive it after I bought it and nearly killed myself on the way home, stalling at every intersection. It took me two days to get up the nerve to go buy some gas for it and

1983: A new world land speed record (633 mph) is set by Richard Noble in the Thrust 2 jet car at Black Rock, Nevada.

try again. And maybe I was waiting for a paycheck."

Diane Dupuis

I'm from Illinois and when I was barely 15, I took my Mom's Ford Something-or-other out for a drive in the country. It was summertime and the corn was high. And, nobody had taught me how to drive yet. I stopped at a stop sign to make a left turn. First, I cranked the wheel all the way around till it could turn no more. Then, I slammed down the accelerator and proceeded to make a VERY sharp left turn. I flew down a huge ditch and literally PLOWED through a cornfield. All I could see around me were corn stalks flying everywhere. Somehow, I miraculously ended up back on the road.

"I tried to sneak the car back into the garage, but I forgot to pull the stalks of corn out. Plus, the alignment was a little off and it rattled a bit. Of course, I was busted . . . got grounded . . . sad story being 15 and all. Anyhow, Mom made me go APOLO-GIZE to the farmer for driving through his cornfield. I found out that the farmer sold his corn crop to Orville Reden-bacher Popcorn. So, if you see

tire tracks on your popcorn kernels, you'll know where they came from."

Sarah Mallory-Lucas

When my husband and I were about to start our first teaching jobs, we had to drive from Kalamazoo (Michigan) to Saginaw (Michigan) on December 31 to look for an apartment. We were driving Brunhilde, the mighty warrior Ford (when my dad first saw it, he asked Mike where the hell the cement came out, and Mike—unwilling to offend his new father-in-law who wasn't very fond of him—looked for an opening) and, mid-afternoon, we went over a bump and seemed to lose a muffler.

"We drove into a gas station near where we were going to be teaching, and asked for a quick muffler repair/re-moval/gum-and-glue job to get the car back to its final resting place in Brighton (Michigan). The owner set a 17- or 18-year-old young man on the task, and he was furi-ous! He obviously had a hot date, thrashed the muffler right off, and closed the gas station all around us.

"We had one more stop, found an apartment, and decid-ed we needed gas to get to

1984: New York becomes the first U.S. state to require drivers, front seat passengers, and children under 10 to wear seat belts.

00309

Brighton. So we pulled into another gas station, and—much to our chagrin—discovered the muffler thrashing had put a hole in the brake lining. We circled the pumps several times, bounced off a back wall, and eventually came to a stop. The attendant stood there watching us and said, 'Sorry, I'm closing,' and got into his car.

"So here we were, two destitute new teachers, 6:00 on New Year's Eve, one more trip to take in the clunker, no brakes and no gas. God was smiling on us (so was the rest of the known universe!), and several blocks down the road, a dear little man in a World War I flying ace aviator cap with an almost unintelligible foreign accent listened to our plea. He said, 'Omma feexa you opp!' He pulled us into his gas station, tied off the holey brake, refilled the other three with fluid, and, several hours later, let us go after we wrote him a check he couldn't cash until January 2nd. He gave us instructions that all we had to do was turn right every time we wanted to stop. Then, as we pulled out, he waved us off with a hearty 'Omma hope-a you make it!'

"We did, and you can believe we drove to the other side of town to frequent his establishment all the time we lived in Saginaw. And my first day of class as a twelfth grade English teacher, first hour of the day, who should seat himself right in front of me but the surly young man who poked the hole in the brake! Oh, the look on his face when he figured out where he'd seen me! Oh, the sweet revenge for the rest of the year!

"Turns out that hot date was with the boss' daughter, and was probably the occasion of them getting her pregnant. He shoulda fixed the Ford."
Pamela Dundas

After my Godfather passed away, we drove his red, '65 Mustang. Old Red was probably nine years old by then, but still a very sharp car.

"Now, my husband is a real car buff—he loves cars the way I love computers! (Scary thought, to say the least!) John can make any car purr. But Old Red liked me better than John. Winter mornings, he would be out there, trying to get the Mustang started. The harder he tried, the more he fiddled and analyzed, the more obstinate the Mustang got, simply refusing to turn over.

"Finally, John would storm into the house and tell me to

1984: About 18 million used cars are purchased in the U.S., twice as many as are purchased new.

start MY car. I would get in the front seat, sweet talk Old Red for a minute, then turn the key. He started for me every time. If I wasn't around, the Mustang would start without a problem for John.

"This love/hate relationship between the Mustang and my husband continued until Old Red died of old age."

Carol Wojtowicz Bimberg

Driver's Ed

I took Driver's Ed in 1980, at the peak of the ugly Chrysler K-car/Ford Fairmont time period. You know—back when the U.S. automakers didn't have to worry about the Japanese and thus built some of the ugliest and mechanically inept cars in history. Well, we had about six Fairmonts that we used for Driver's Ed, and one had this little quirk that it idled at 35 miles per hour. You would start the car, and it would just roar. Drop it into gear, and you'd get a little squawk from the tires without even trying. The worst was on the narrow streets that we did our road training on—you had to ride the brakes the entire way

just to keep the car at or near 25 mph. What a trip."

Brad Morgan

In Driver's Ed we were required to put in some hours on a standard-transmission model training car. I was unsure of that whole procedure, so I just snuck by using a car that had automatic transmission in a stick format on the floor to the right of the driver's seat. I don't know if the instructor was fooled or not, but he never made me learn to drive a real standard-transmission car."

Diane Dupuis

During the actual driving part of Driver's Ed, we were assigned three to a car with one instructor. Luckily, I got assigned to the same car as my best friend at the time, so that took some of the pressure off. Our instructor, however, added mucho pressure—it was 6'-5", 300 lb., gruff-but-lovable, voice like a foghorn, math teacher/city mayor (gulp!) Mr. Smith. Definitely not cool to screw up with the mayor in the car.

"The first day we were out, the third driver in our car took the wheel first. It was his first time driving ever,

1985: General Motors announces the formation of Saturn Corporation, a new division that will focus exclusively on import-fighting compact cars.

and it showed. Every time a large truck came towards us, he veered off the road, clearly terrified. Smith finally blew up at him and told him to stop the car and let one of us take over. We didn't think we were going to make it home on that one.

"Later on, I was driving and decided I could squeak by a bus that was pulled over to let off passengers. I thought I had plenty of room, but my friend later told me I missed the bus by no more than two inches, and that Mr. Smith had turned a little pale when I pulled off that stunt. During that same day, with my friend at the wheel, I could see a large rock in the road ahead of us, smack in the center of our lane. 'No problem,' I thought, 'Gary (my friend) will just change lanes.' Wrong. We hit that thing at about 40 mph, and it just ripped at the undercarriage, somehow not causing any parts to fall off. Well, that was it. Mr. Smith blew, wondering if we were both blind, and why didn't we react to what we saw, and what the hell was wrong with us, and we were never going to pass Driver's Ed. Bad day at Black Rock all the way around. All three of us *did* pass, however."

Brad Morgan

The high school I went to provided Driver's Ed to students based on their age; the oldest students went first. I happened to be the youngest student signed up, so I went dead last.

"A local Chevrolet dealer had provided a fleet of brand new Citations for us to use, but by the time it was my turn, they had all been returned to the dealer. After much scrounging around, my instructor (who was also my social studies teacher) located a beat up Plymouth Fury for us to use. The car belonged to the son of the school superintendent, and had seen better days. Besides the tendency for the engine to stall if you let it idle, it had a steering wheel that was about 45 degrees off center and a healthy pull to the right, thanks to hitting a curb.

"We headed off one afternoon after school, and I was instructed to make a left turn onto Grand River (in Brighton, Michigan). Lucky me, the car stalled right in the middle of the busiest intersection in that small town, and I couldn't get it to start. After what seemed like ages, my instructor managed to get it started, and we wobbled off down the road.

1985: Ford introduces the Taurus, which competes against similarly sized, high quality imports. The Taurus and the Honda Accord are the best-selling cars for the next decade.

"The other students may have had brand new cars, but three of them had to share one on each lesson. As I was last, it was just me and the instructor. He wound up having me drive him around to run his errands for him, since I guess he hadn't planned on having this one last student cutting into his after work time. After we had stopped at the post office so he could mail some letters, he opened the window, leaned back, lit up a cigarette, cranked up the radio and told me that we had 'a half hour to kill. Drive wherever you want to go.' We just wandered around aimlessly for half an hour, and then called it a day.

"After repeating this twice more (stumbling around Ann Arbor in a downpour on the last lesson) I was deemed fit to receive the treasured learners permit."

Todd Nessel

It's not good to have (cause) accidents. It's even WORSE to have accidents when your parent—specifically your father—is in the car.

"(Really bad Rod Serling impression going on here.) Picture if you will a young man, 15 to be exact, motoring home from a great day at Driver's Ed, on a perfectly wonderful summer day, in the 'sacred' family car, he in the driver's seat, Dad in the passenger seat, discussing the wonders of driving and the awesome responsibility of unleashing a 15-year-old on the road, behind the wheel of a 5,000-pound mechanized behemoth (this was circa 1975, when men were men, and cars were still BIG . . . the family car was a '73 Caddy Deville . . . a big motor scooter!). They approach a red light, stopping next to, of all things, an auto tow truck. The light changes to green . . . the cars proceed . . . Dad says, 'Get in the right lane.' 'Sure thing, dear old Dad of mine,' the lad says. Then, suddenly, a bump . . . then a scraping sound . . . finally the crunch . . . aaaaaggggh!!! The father spews the requisite expletives such an event would precipitate . . . the son sits motionless . . . uninjured, in shock (and in fear of his life at the moment!).

"Thinking to himself, he pondered, 'I'm dead, I'm dead, but how will he do it? The Family Car . . . The SACRED FAMILY CAR! DESTROYED!!! I'm dead!!!' The Dad and the truck driver exchange a few words . . . and a laugh??? HUH? WAIT A

MINUTE?? WHAT UP? I'm (I mean, the lad is) pondering the manner in which I—uh, I mean HE—is to die and they're laughing. The truck drives off into the distance . . . 'Drive home, boy.' Uh-oh . . . the tone of the voice!!! (Can't you *hear* it?) The lad arrives at the family home, pulls into the family driveway, disembarks from the Sacred Family Car and sees . . . (dramatic, climactic music here)

"A lil' scratch, a broken taillight, and a slightly dented taillamp bezel. No death, no punishment (except the agony of driving with the father to get estimates, and make arrangements for repair, and obtaining rental cars, a $500 repair bill, and washing the car 'EACH AND EVERY SATURDAY MORNING TILL SCHOOL STARTED AGAIN!' BUT DO I SOUND BITTER? NOOOOOO, I'M NOT BITTER!) As it turns out, Dad told the truck driver that his kid was taking Driver's Ed, and the truck driver said he had a similar situation—his daughter was taking DE (taking DE . . . sounds like some kind of illegal substance, huh?), which was pretty funny. Dad had one more page for the 'Son, haven't I always told you' files, but he did allow me to drive the Sacred Family Car when I passed DE."

Reggie Carlton

This insult wasn't perpetrated on me by a Driver's Ed instructor but by my own dear mother. Learner's permit in hand, I was performing my requisite training session on a beat-up old Datsun pickup—a stick. My mother, being possessed by the Devil, decided it would be fun to take me driving in Ann Arbor. On a football Saturday. Down Hoover Street. (For those of you unfamiliar with the area, this is about two blocks north of Michigan Stadium, and prior to games is filled with people walking to the stadium.)

"You can imagine the fun I was having, creeping along the road trying to avoid hitting a pedestrian, especially as this was one of my first sessions with a stick shift. Putter putter JERK! Stall. Putter putter JERK! Putter putter. Some long-haired student (probably drunk) yelled at me to watch where the hell I was going. But at least my mom stuck up for me (never mind that she put me there in the first place): she bellowed out the window, 'Hey! Leave her alone! She's only 15!' My mom bellowing being a fearsome event even for someone who's sober, the student quickly apologized with a sheepish grin and got out of my way. I

1987: Automotive statistics reveal that 10,000 teenagers die each year in automobile accidents, more than from any other single cause. About $1 billion is spent annually to treat and rehabilitate another 130,000 injured teens.

made it through without knocking anyone over, and learned a valuable lesson about how to intimidate pedestrians in Ann Arbor."

Diane Telgen

I remember going 'on the road' with my mother when I was 15. (On the road meant in the subdivision not going more than 20 mph.) Anyway my mom gripped the handle on the door the entire time I was driving. I think my mom really wished that our Citation had both a steering wheel on the passenger side and another set of brakes there, too. She made constant motions with her hands as if she wished she could steer, and constant motions with her foot as though she were stepping on a brake pedal. Needless to say after about five minutes of this I was a nervous wreck; I turned around and came home. My mom swore that she would never get in the car with an unlicensed driver again. Funny thing though, even now, 14 years later, if I'm driving and my mom is in the passenger seat, she still looks apprehensive, and still makes motions with her foot as though that imaginary brake pedal will actually stop the car."

Holly Selden

When we saw the Driver's Ed movie *Mechanized Death,* we were told we could leave the room if we couldn't take the blood and stuff."

Andy Malonis

I don't remember any feature films. But we practiced driving in devices called simulators while watching a film that was supposed to make you feel as if you were in traffic, kinda like flight simulators. Being 15-going-on-16-year-olds, we of course called them 'stimulators.'"

Peg Bessette

We saw *Death on the Highway,* a colorized black and white film where only the blood was a garish red."

Don Boyden

There was also a film on the IPDE System: Identify Predict Decide Execute. In this film an older gentleman in a convertible told you how to use the IPDE System. The beauty of this film was that the guy spent the entire movie talking to the camera as he drove, he never looked at the road, and he was constantly taking his

1988: According to a Motor Vehicle Manufacturers Association report, 386 million automobiles are in use; 135 million registered automobiles are in the U.S.; and Americans devote 20 percent of annual household expenses to owning and operating a car.

Driver's Ed teachers of the 1960s try to master the driving simulator.

hands off the wheel to make lots of gestures."

Brad Morgan

I remember IPDE also. One annoying thing the narrator advised was honking the horn every single time you: a) pass someone on a multi-lane highway; b) approach a driveway that someone's backing out of; c) cross an intersection where a car is waiting at the stop sign. He called it a 'friendly honk.'"

Christa Brelin.

I think there was a Disney cartoon where Goofy played the bad driver who slammed on his brakes in traffic, thus causing 'the box-car effect' accident."

Sarah Mallory-Lucas

Our Driver's Ed focused on defensive driving techniques and looking out for 'accident situations.' For the rest of our high school cruising careers we'd get that stentorian voice and say 'accident situation' like the robot from *Lost in Space* whenever we were knocking over mailboxes with our cars or practicing bat turns or doing lawn jobs."

Don Boyden

Driveway Dangers

I quoted to my mother on the phone the other day the entry I made to this database about the bumper sticker 'Answer My Prayers, Steal This Car' that was on my parents' 1970-something station wagon. She told me that her favorite story involving this car was when my two oldest sisters were of driving age, my sister Sandi (the second oldest) was driving the wagon, and my sister Lori (the oldest) was driving another car (I think it was an MG). My one sister was backing out of the driveway (in the wagon), while my other sister was pulling in the driveway. I guess neither one of them was paying attention, and CRASH, they collided in our driveway. (Not going very fast, but colliding nonetheless.) But this isn't the only accident that has happened in that driveway.

"We have a large family and a lot of drivers. At one point we had two cars parked in the garage (mom and dad's of course), and three cars parked in the driveway. It always took a lot of planning on where each of us parked on the driveway, so that we all could get out/in without a hitch. Well, we worked it out so that my car would always be parked in the position nearest the

---

1989: The Honda Accord becomes the largest selling automobile in the United States.

street, because I usually worked late and left early. Anyway, I got used to always being the 'last' car in the driveway. So I got used to not checking behind me when backing out of the driveway.

"One Saturday evening, I was on my way to a dinner party. Good friends of my parents were over playing cards. They had parked behind me (last in the driveway). My arms were loaded down with stuff for the party. I put some of the stuff on top of my car, loaded up the car, and totally forgot that my parents' friends car was right behind me. I got in, turned the key, and put that baby in reverse. CRASH. I had hit their car, and caused more damage than I thought possible, because they were parked on an incline and I was parked on a flat surface.

"I thought I would die of humiliation. They all came running out of the house to see what had happened. I was upset and embarrassed. My parents' friends were so incredibly good-natured about it. We had a good laugh about it a few months later and we still laugh about it today."

Holly Selden

Something very similar happened to me. The house I grew up in was at the end of a cul-de-sac. One day I was in a hurry to get somewhere. Since no traffic ever came down to the end of our street, the usual routine was to get in the car, start it up, and back out. So, that's what I did. Only this time my '85 VW Jetta backed right into an '82 Horizon—driven by my sister! I broke one of her headlights, but my car was okay. Talk about embarassing."

Dean Dauphinais

My grandparents used to have a two-car garage with a garage door for each car. You guessed it. One day Gram, bless her heart, lifted the door behind the Chevy, then backed the Ford out—right through the closed door.

"Another day—this time in the Chevy—Gram couldn't figure out why the turn signal wasn't turning on, and why the engine was suddenly making all those horrible noises. Gently as possible, eight-year-old me said, 'Um, isn't the turn signal on the other side of the steering wheel?' She'd been shifting gears while driving on down the highway."

Christa Brelin

1990: For the first time in U.S. automotive history, air bags are installed in a sizeable (approximately 3 million) number of automobiles.

Back in '73 (a follow-up to an old Bob Seger tune?), the family took a month-long trip out West—in the family station wagon, of course. Dad had everything planned to a tee, complete with AAA maps and Tour Guides, estimated drive times, mileage estimates, and I'll bet he even had a stop-watch.

"Much of this trip included getting up at ungodly hours of the morning so that we could 'make our time.' Yuck. Getting up at 5:00 to be on the road at 5:30 was pure torture, even if, as Dad always said, 'You can sleep in the car.' Yup. Scrunchin' up in the back seat of a car, with a seat belt on, going 65 mph certainly compares favorably to a comfy pillow and bed.

"Anyhoo, at 5:30 on the very first day of the trip, all the packing had been completed, the family was in the car, doors slammed, car started, gear put in reverse, and we were ready to leave lovely Livonia (Michigan) for points west. As Dad accelerated, we heard this sad, crunching groaning sound of metal. Turns out Dad had opened the garage door only part way (that was before automatic garage door openers). So we hadn't even left the ding dang garage when we had a delay. Dad spent the next half hour banging and pushing the metal garage door (but trying to do it in an inconspicuous way, since it was the crack of dawn) just so he could get it flat enough to get it closed and locked for a month. He did it, though we had the funniest looking garage door for months.

"Oh, and an hour or so later we had a flat tire in Coldwater (Michigan)—ironically, my dad's home town. But even with all these interruptions, we still wound up in Columbia, Missouri that night. And even managed to stop in St. Louis to go up the Gateway Arch."

Larry Baker

My sister Chris backed our '72 Ventura into the garage door, too. I can't believe how common this seems to be. My dad banged it into shape so the door would open and close, and for years the paint kind of peeled and generally looked tacky. Finally my dad broke down and replaced the garage door, ending my mother's complaints."

Julie Winklepleck

I was 15, just days away from turning in my learner's permit

1991: The first Saturns—GM's answer to compact imports—arrive and feature front-wheel drive and a lightweight steel and plastic body.

for a real driver's license. It was Sunday, and we were getting ready to go to my older sister's bridal shower. I didn't have any shoes to go with my dress, and needed to go to my friend's house to borrow a pair of hers.

"She lived one street over. Since I wasn't going to be driving on any major surface streets, my father agreed to let me drive by myself. My older sister let me take her car, and my younger sister Rosey asked to go along for the ride.

"When we got back, I had to turn the car around to park it in the street. Our situation was much like Holly's, where everyone had a set place to park. My sister's car was always parked on the street in front of our house. I pulled into the driveway of our neighbor across the street, looked both ways, and let off of the brakes, chatting to Rosey the whole time. We were two feet (if not fewer) away from my neighbor's garage door when Rosey and I paused our conversation long enough to realize that I *was not* in reverse, and had in fact never shifted gears!

"Panicked, I stomped on the brakes. Alas, I was wearing the high-heeled shoes that I

had borrowed from my friend and, not being used to them (they throw my foot-eye coordination off) I only partially placed my foot on the right side of the brake pedal. My slippery-soled shoe, of course, slid right off of the brake pedal and onto the accelerator. We lurched right through their garage door. Luckily, no one was home, meaning that there was no car in the garage for me to smash into.

"Rosey and I paused for a minute. I asked her what I should do (as if my 13-year-old sister would know any better than I would), and she suggested that I just park the car. 'No one will know,' she said, 'because there's no damage to *our* car, and no one saw us, anyway.' This made sense to me, in the just-go-about-your-business-and-no-one-will-notice kind of way, so Rosey got out of the car, and I parked it as if nothing happened.

"Of course, while no one may have seen my damage, people certainly *heard* it. When we got into the house, my sisters asked us what that horrible sound was. Rosey said, 'Oh, nothing. It was probably a garbage truck or something like that.' Little did we know, my father, who had been

---

1992: An estimated 350,000 deer are killed this year in collisions with cars. Auto accidents with deer also injure as many as 7,000 people, 100 of them fatally.

reading the paper in the front room, saw the whole thing through the window. He yelled at us, then called the police, who came and took a report. The policeman then had to find our neighbors, who were still out, to let them know what happened. They came back from wherever they were, and the looks on their faces were enough to make me burst into tears. They were very nice to me, even though they had every right to hate my guts.

"We ended up being late to my sister's shower. Rosey told everyone there what I did—I cried again (humiliation twice!). On Monday, Rosey then made sure everyone in our neighborhood knew that I was the one who destroyed the neighbor's house (humiliation three times!). People I didn't even know were coming up to me at school and asking if I was the one who went through someone's garage.

"My father still brings up the fact that he had to lie and tell the policeman that he was with me so the insurance company would cough up the $1,000 it cost to replace the neighbor's garage door ('So, sir, were you in the car?' 'No, I wasn't.' 'The insurance company won't pay if you weren't in the car. So, were you in the car?' 'Yes, yes I was.').

"I got my license, but I was grounded for a month—a really big deal, because I had never been grounded before (I was the Golden Child up until this point). But, the really horrible part for me was having to look out of my bedroom window every day for a week and reliving the destruction that I had created. The day they replaced that door was a great-big-sigh-of-relief day for me. The neighbors still live there, and for about three years after 'the garage incident,' I was still too ashamed to meet their gazes.
Eva Felts

Favorite Cars

A 1969 Jaguar E-Type roadster. It was beautiful. It was fast. It handled better than anything I've ever driven, including a couple all-out racing cars. And it attracted attention like crazy.

"I still love it. I'm an idiot for selling it. I'll never be able to afford another one. For penance, the automotive gods have decreed that I drive Honda Accords for the rest of my mortal existence."
Peter Gareffa

1992: Race car driver Lyn St. James is named Indy Rookie of the Year, the first woman to be honored with that title.

Peter Gareffa's 1969 Jaguar E-Type roadster.
Courtesy of Peter Gareffa

I stumbled upon a gem: a 1989 Chevy Camaro Z28 Monster Machine! (Similar to the kind of thing they do with the Pontiac Firebird 'Firehawk' performance package.) It was special ordered by some GM Chevrolet exec who wanted a hot rod in plain clothes. After the car was delivered, apparently he decided he didn't want it and the dealer handling the order put it on the sales lot. Guess who bought it? You guessed it! Used the folk's option plan, got it at a great price. It wasn't fast . . . it was INCREDIBLY FAST!! I used to blow away Mustang GT's (and an occasional Vette) like blowing away leaves. Funny too (though not funny at the time), the day I picked the car up from the dealership, as I was driving it home, my appendix ruptured and I had to drive myself to the hospital.

"I just barely was able to park the thing, then went into the emergency room and proceeded to get REALLY sick. While they were prepping me for surgery, the attending ER physician, who felt really bad for poking me in my side (over and over again . . . 'Does this hurt still?') and making me scream in blood-curdling agony, tried to take my mind off my misery by making small talk:

'So, Reg, what's new?' (He actually said that, no lie!)

'Well, doc,' I said, 'I just bought a new car.'

'Oh yeah, when?'

'About 20 minutes ago (moan).'

'Do you like it?'

'Gee, doc, I don't know . . . I haven't had a chance to really drive it, you know? Would YOU like to drive it (ha-ha, groan)?'

"Before I could get into the 'options list' (narf!), I passed out, they eventually did the surgery, and my kid brother drove the car home and parked it in the garage . . . where it sat . . . for three-and-a-half weeks!!!! A brand new Chevy Camaro, stickers still on the windows, new-car smell and everything, and all I could do was look at it. Didn't actually get in it again till I went to visit my office at the end of the three-and-a-half weeks—and SOMEBODY ELSE had to drive then 'cause I couldn't control the blasted thing. But I eventually did and it was a dream car until the winter of '91 when (sob), during a rainstorm, I was broadsided by a drunk driver! I survived, but, alas, my car did not. They even tried to fix it ($7,800 was the final repair bill tally!) but it was never the same (in and out of

1992: Vangie Jones, a forklift driver at the Dodge City Truck Plant in Warren, Michigan, is presented with a new truck in honor of never having missed a day of work (never late, never took a vacation) in 50 years.

service constantly). Got rid of it and got a Pontiac. Definitely a way-cool car though!!!"

Reggie Carlton

I never owned anything fun, but my brother had a hot rod Vega he would let me drive. It was a green Vega GT hatchback. My brother used a Don Hardy conversion kit to shoe horn a 350 V8 out of a crashed Camaro. It had a B & M trick shifter, headers exiting before the rear wheels, and a monster four-barrel. It was the ultimate sleeper. No posi, so great burnouts. Handled like a bathtub. I would pick up hitchhikers just to scare them."

Don Boyden

First Cars

My brother actually owned it. I learned how to drive in it, stole it from him when I could, and I loved it dearly. It was a black, '67 Pontiac Bonneville (renamed 'Bon evil' after we pried some letters off) and it was BEAUTIFUL. My brother bought it for $200 and we terrorized downriver Detroit in it for about a year before it met with a tragic end. A head-on collision on a

rainy late night tilted the engine and screwed up some other stuff. It was carted away, along with my heart, to the junk yard. I've never been the same."

Lisa DeShantz-Cook

A 1963 Volkswagen Beetle. White, or so said the factory; actually, it was cream. Sporting Pirelli red-striped tires, with tubes, no less. Red, German pseudo-leather interior. And, best of all, one of those really cool canvas full-length sunroofs. Paid $300 for it, and got it a couple weeks before I actually turned 16.

"I immediately added a few 'tasteful' custom touches of my own: really large back tires; hot-rod engine components; woodgrain dashboard; school decal in the back window; various dangly things on the rearview mirror (at different times, a garter, saxophone neck straps, fuzzy dice, girlfriend's graduation tassel, my tassel, etc.).

"This thing was perfect for pulling 'donuts' in the winter. (Well, probably could've done it in the summer, too, although I never tried it.) Also good for beating Corvettes off the line. For

1993: A new power plant—owned by Texaco—in Montebello, California, uses old automobile tires as fuel. The plant uses a form of energy production called gasification, which turns solid fuel (tires) into a gas.

about the first 30 yards, anyway. But the best thing about it was driving down the street with various inebriated individuals hanging out the sunroof. Sigh, those were the good old days."

Peter Gareffa

It was big as a whale but it could never, ever set sail, except down the highway. A '72 Pontiac Catalina, large enough to house a family of four comfortably. Bought it with $500 of my high school graduation open-house money with the explicit parental understanding that it was for the summer only—come the University of Michigan in the fall, that sucker was gone. Which was fine with me anyway—I just needed summertime transportation.

"It was a really faded tan (with rust of course) color, with a white landau top that was peeling in several spots and a white faux leather interior. Power locks, power windows, and of course really BIG rear speakers that I added. It ran beautifully, but it honestly got less than 10 miles to the gallon. A trip to the mall that was 20 miles away meant a stop at the Shell station and contributions from my friends for gas money.

"It got me through the summer, and I sold it for $500 at the end of August, so things worked out perfect."

Brad Morgan

When my mom was a senior at Eastern Michigan University, her dad, an engineer at Ford, asked her, if she could have *any* car she wanted, what kind of car would that be? My mom, being of a very practical nature, replied that she would like a black sedan with four doors. What she ended up with was a '63 Mercury Comet convertible. It was red, with a white and black vinyl interior, and a black top. There are pictures of my mom and my uncle Paul in cute red sweaters sitting in the car, standing next to the car, and sitting on the back with the top down, smiling, but looking as though they are humoring my grandfather. ('Please, not one more picture!')"

Leslie Norback

The first car that was specifically 'mine' was a little Datsun B-210 my dad picked up for $500 when I was in college and needed it to get to work. It had 85,000 miles on it, and he bought it sight unseen from a buddy at a car dealership.

1993: Lincoln introduces a system that offers—at the touch of a button—automatic memory settings for 12 different auto systems (for two different drivers).

A 1963 Mercury Comet convertible.
Courtesy of American Automobile Manufacturers Association

Of course, my first question was, 'What color it is?' He said, 'I don't know, I didn't ask.' I said, 'Oh, well, as long as it's not green.' (This being the 1980s and the era of olive-green, lime-green, and otherwise-putrid-green cars).

"Of course, we picked up the car and it was not only green, but two tones of green where primer had been put over areas where the rust had been sanded away. But my little B-210 was a faithful car, only giving out after 105,000 miles when the engine mounts rusted out and collapsed after I crossed a set of railroad tracks two miles from home. (It made a very cool sound, the engine fan hitting the front grille.)"

Diane Telgen

I bought a 1980 burgundy Chevette with 100,000 miles on it for $1,000 when I was 17 (man, what was I thinking!). I earned the money by working after school and in the summer. It ran pretty well and the body had very little rust. After a year of driving it all over the place, all sorts of things went wrong—the starter went bad (twice), the shock tower had to be welded, the catalytic converter was wasted, and the floorboard on the

driver's side rusted through (imagine Fred Flintstone). It managed to last one more year. When I traded it in, the dealership only gave me $25 for it (and the exhaust was barely hanging on)."

Dawn DesJardins

I was born in 1964, and by age five, I started noticing cars. The first car to be implanted in my impressionable mind was the Ford Mustang. The coolest adults I can remember drove Mustangs or Cougars. I grew up, joined the Navy, and was sent to schools in Mare Island, California. This was an isolated base, and without a car you were going to be stuck on base. I went on a Mustang hunt. I wanted a 1966 red fastback.

"I could have had a perfect primer gray, ready to finish, 1967 fastback for $1,400. I am a motor head, but the cost of a paint job frightened me. Cheap looks won out, and I bought a 1969 coupe for $1,100. I slowly replaced anything that was worn. The carpet, headliner, trunkliner, wheel covers, and dashboard were all redone. I drove it for two or three years and it started having various problems so I sold it for $650 in San Diego. The sailor that

1993: Libby-Owens-Ford develops an infrared transmitter and sensor that detects rain on a car's windshield and automatically turns on its wipers.

bought the car test drove it on I-5 at 110 mph and looked at me and said, 'I'll take it.'

"I miss that car. My mid-life crisis (in about 15 years) will include buying an old Mustang."

Kelly Stevens

I got my first car, a 1977 Thunderbird, the summer after I turned 16. It was gold and bigger than a cabin cruiser, but FREE. More importantly, it had a 350 horsepower V8 engine that beat almost anything that challenged it (usually silly high school boys driving 323s, Cavaliers, and Chevettes that thought they could beat a girl in anything)! I drove it until 1989 when someone bought it for the engine, which had well over 100,000 miles on it and was still better than most new ones.

"As much as people made fun of that car, it was still my favorite until last week when I got my Explorer. The T-Bird was ridiculed and abused by those same car-less friends who had no other method of transportation, but I loved it, even as it sucked up all my money with its 25-gallon gas tank. In fact, instead of collecting gas money I let my friends support my drinking habits (soft drinks, of course). Come to think of it, I miss that car more than those friends."

Wendy Mason

My first car was given to me as a hand-me-down from my brother-in-law. It was an Olds Cutlass, rechristened 'Gutless' due to a continuing problem with starting from a stop—which later developed into a stalling-out problem that made every left turn a challenge. It was brown. I hated that car . . . it was too big and had a problem with the catalytic converter that made it smell like rotten eggs. At least that's what the repair guy told me. What did I know?

"The first car I ever bought with my own money (and a cosigner) was a 1988 Ford Escort. It was sky blue. It was cute. I liked it, but it was a real lemon. I owned it for five years, and there was no end to the problems I had with it. The last straw was when it completely died a mile from home . . . I left it at the side of the road. It only had 33,000 miles on it (after five years!) and the repair guy thought the counter had already rolled over. He said every moving piece of metal on

1993: First production delivery is made of a vehicle-mounted head-up display (HUD). Called DataVision, it creates a "virtual image" of vital driving information that appears to hover beyond the windshield.

the car was worn out. I later learned that Escorts of that year were made with some kind of experimental metal that was too soft and wore out too quickly. (Thanks, Ford!) At least that's what they told me. What do I know? I sold it to a motorhead friend of my husband's for $200. A week later, the transmission blew. Since then, he's completely rebuilt the car and it runs great. I guess it just needed to be owned by somebody who could fix cars."
Peggy Kneffel Daniels

My first (and favorite) car was a '76 Buick Regal (A.K.A. Annabelle). It was an awful brown, with an AM radio. But it had a dent-free body and the whitest leather seats imaginable. She was huge, and in 1989 it took $30 worth of gas to fill her up.

"I too was ridiculed for driving such a big car. But of course everybody traveling by foot was quick to beg for a ride. I was also the one volunteered by parents on the block to chaperone their teenage children to parties (the car could hold six passengers comfortably). Annabelle also remained undamaged in a few fender benders; however, the opposing vehicles were not so lucky.

"I suppose Annabelle found another love, because she left the front of my house one day never to return. Annabelle, I love you man! (SOB)"
Kristine Burns

The first car that was technically mine was a present from my parents. A '66 Dodge Coronet. They bought it from a neighbor for $100. It took me about two months to blow up the transmission doing neutral-to-drive drop burnouts. It was painted at Earl Scheib for $59, taxi cab yellow.

"The first car I bought (cosigner, of course) was a used mid-70's Grand Prix, sun roof, leather power seats, console shift, and two-tone brown and cream. I actually took real good care of her, which made it all the worse the first dent she got (courtesy of an evil hitchhiker I didn't pick up who beaned my car with a brick). A few months later I blew up the transmission and sold her (I had to sell my coin collection to pay for the new transmission). After that it was a motorcycle until I met my wife, who convinced me that it is not a smart thing to do burnouts in cars that we own."
Don Boyden

1994: A record is set at Atlanta Motor Speedway for miles traveled in 24 hours by an electric vehicle. A battery-powered pickup truck built by Electric Power Technology, Inc., travels 831.8 miles at an average speed of 35 mph.

My first car was a hand-me-down from my grandpa, who was going blind and had been deaf for years and finally had to give up his beloved 1948 Buick Special. It wasn't so hard because he told himself his granddaughter had to have it for college; otherwise he could still drive.

"The starter was underneath the accelerator. Better make sure that sucker wasn't in gear! It must have weighed 85 tons. It was a stick shift (of course) and I couldn't drive it faster than five mph for the first week, because I didn't know how to get out of first gear.

"I called it the Purple Princess, but purple was one of the very few colors that wasn't 'bondoed' on the side. The hood opened up from the side, and I used to love to pull into gas stations and freak out the hotshot pumpboys by asking them to check the oil. I couldn't even get it serviced at a Buick dealership.

"I drove it up hills and down valleys in Kalamazoo in the winter. During snowstorms there would be nobody on the road but me and the Bronco Transit bus system. I hit a Volkswagen at dusk at the bottom of a hill once, and the VW owner thought my car was so cool. He asked how I kept it running, and I told him I fed it a Beetle once a week. He ceased being amused and called the police, who cited me.

"I still miss her."
Pamela Dundas

The first car that I was officially responsible for (insurance, gas, oil changes, general maintenance, etc.) was a Plymouth Horizon that I inherited from my mom after college. Starting this car in the winter was a cold, long, torturous process. As I recall, this car also needed its carburetor replaced twice. This car was put out of its misery when I hit a car that had stopped on the expressway for a man laying in the road trying to commit suicide."

Leslie Norback

After high school graduation, I spent the summer working in the housekeeping department of a local hospital to earn enough money to cover books and transportation for my first year at Wayne State University in Detroit. In search of my first car, I consulted the classified ads in the *Grosse Pointe* (Michigan)

1994: At the Tokyo Motor Show, Toyota exhibits the EV-50, an experimental electric car that uses rechargeable lead-acid batteries, has a top speed of 72 mph, and a range of 150 miles.

News. I don't remember how many cars I looked at (with my father, of course), before I came across the 1966 Dodge Coronet I purchased for $300. It was already nine years old, but the body was rust-free, the interior was clean, and it had relatively low mileage, so I bought it. It was a nifty ride—working radio and all. And gas was cheap that summer—only a couple bucks to fill the tank!!

"A couple weeks after buying it, in anticipation of its first road trip (up to Michigan State University to visit friends), I bought a set of four retread tires for $2 each—and they installed and balanced them, too! Lansing, here we come!

"About five weeks after classes began, I came down with a monster case of mononucleosis, and was housebound for about six weeks. During that time, my father allowed my younger sister and brother to use my car to drive to school. After all, why let it sit in the backyard unused? Well, one day after school, my brother (a junior in high school) thought that he would do a bit of showing off by driving my car from its spot on the street a block away through the school parking lot. Only he didn't get that far. He pulled into a driveway to turn around and neglected to check both ways before backing out. Yes, my perfect used car got mangled. The rear passenger door got crunched pretty bad. I don't remember it ever opening again. (Unfortunately, this wasn't the last time he ever got to wreck one of my cars.)

"I drove that car pretty hard for the next year and a half (lots of trips out to Metro Beach during the summer and up to Michigan State during the school year!). Then I had an accident on the Wayne State campus, leaving the left front end so badly crunched that I was unable to make a left turn. (Have you ever tried getting where you are going using right turns only?) Thus it was shipped off to the junkyard. I got $35 for its undriveable hulk."

Kathy Marcaccio

The prefix to the number on my winning 50-cent ticket was PP, so of course I had to name her Penelope, and called her Penny for short. Penny was a two-toned robin's egg blue 1947 four-door, 60-horsepower Nash, and I won her at the Detroit Fireman's Field Day drawing. This annual event was held each August at Briggs Stadium (now Tiger Stadium) as a benefit for the Detroit Fireman's Fund Association. Twenty-five people became the lucky owners of new cars. My number was drawn 14th and I had the choice of 12 cars. I had no trouble picking Penny.

"After the drawing Penny was sent to the dealer for final preparation. Though I was 19 or 20 at the time, I couldn't drive yet, so I had to ask a friend to take me and my father to pick up the car. My family's big concern was how to pay for the income tax on my winnings. In fact, Mom and Dad cashed in an insurance policy held on my younger sister in order to pay for this unexpected expense.

"Then somebody had to learn to drive Penny! As a junior at Detroit's Wayne University, I was very busy with classes and student teaching, so I deferred driving lessons. My sister, a high school junior, soon learned to drive and began chauffeuring her friends to and from Grosse Pointe (Michigan) High School.

"The battle of the gas tank began in this way: My fiancé, who also attended Wayne University, would take the bus or streetcar to my house and take possession of Penny either on Friday or Saturday night, whenever we had a date. He would drive the Nash home after our date, drive it to Wayne on Monday, and take me home after Monday classes. Money was tight with students, so my fiancé would usually run the gas tank pretty close to empty before parking Penny in our garage on Monday. When my sister went to get the car for her school run, she would have to collect change from her friends to buy some gas before school. On good days they might be able to afford 50 cents' worth. On Friday afternoons, my sister would ease the car into the garage with little more than vapors in the tank. And so it went, week after week!

"I loved that cute little car with the burgundy steering wheel and the stick shift on the tree. I smiled constantly for two years over my good luck at winning her. I finally learned to drive and Penny carried us through our courtship, on our honeymoon, and through the first year of our marriage. Then we traded her in for a 1950 four-door Pontiac. But it didn't have the soul or romance of Penny."

Jean Dupuis

1994: Traffic fatalities decrease from 5.5 per 1 million miles driven in 1966 to 1.7 per 1 million miles driven in 1994. More than twice as many miles are driven in 1994 than in 1966.

The 1966 Dodge Coronet was the first car of more than one car crazy.
Courtesy of American Automobile Manufacturers Association

Games People Play

Perdunkles: When you were on a date and saw a car with one headlight out, you'd yell 'perdunkle' and could get a kiss—first date, or whatever. A perdiddle was a car with both headlights out and you'd get two kisses."

Lauri Taylor

For us, perdiddles worked this way. When you saw a perdiddle you got to punch the person next to you, or kiss them. This covered you if you were sitting next to someone you didn't like. Real depressing, though, if you liked the girl sitting next to you and she punched you!"

Don Boyden

We would give a punch in the arm and yell 'Slug Bug' in the ear when spotting a VW Beetle."

Anonymous

We played Sting 'Stang, which involved pinching your opponent when you saw a Mustang. Having three older siblings, I lost at these games quite a bit (ouch)."

Dean Dauphinais

When my sister and brother and I were little we used to say, 'Piggy Punch, Slug Bug' whenever we saw a VW go by. As we said this we would curl our hands in a hitchhiker's shape and clap them together."

Larry Baker

When my sister Slug Bugs me she calls out the color of the Beetle (Slug Bug yellow!—smack!). This is especially useful when you are passing an Auto Haus or other shop where little sick Slug Bugs go to get better. It also gives you credit for each identification."

Terri Schell

When we played Slug Bug we called out the color, also. It was like the license plate game where you called out the state to keep someone else from using it."

Julie Winklepleck

Slide over baby!' was when the driver swerved hard to do a favor for the guy in the back seat. (Guess he and his date weren't wearing their seat belts!)"

Carol Wojtowicz Bimberg

1994: BMW introduces HID (High-Intensity Discharge) lighting technology on some of its models. An HID headlamp is twice as bright as a low-beam halogen lamp, burns 10 times longer, and uses less electricity.

Road Test

WHICH OF THE FOLLOWING ARE WITHIN THE ACTUAL CITY LIMITS OF DETROIT?

1. Ford world headquarters
2. GM world headquarters
3. Chrysler world headquarters
4. The Dodge Viper assembly plant
5. Detroit Metropolitan Airport
6. The Motown Historical Museum
7. Joe Louis Arena (home of the Detroit Red Wings)
8. The Silverdome (home of the Detroit Lions)
9. Tiger Stadium (home of the Detroit Tigers)
10. The Palace (home of the Detroit Pistons)

(Answers: 2, 4, 6, 7, 9)

Was it called 'fire stop' when you got out of the car at a red light and everyone ran around the car and tried to get back in before the light changed?"

Lauri Taylor

In my part of town, switching seats in the car while at a light was known as a 'Chinese fire drill.'"

Dave Schulte

Story Time

My most amazing car story is about a near-miss accident I once had driving from Chicago to Detroit. There was a lot of construction, it was night, and I was in a particularly convoluted stretch of highway. I'd just come out of a confusing section of detours when I noticed headlights directly ahead of me. I chalked it up to the construction and assumed there would be another turn before our two cars met. Imagine my

---

1995: Siemens Corporation develops the SideMinder, an inexpensive infrared transmitter-detector and microprocessor that monitors a car's blind spot.

surprise when, from about 50 feet away, the other car HONKED at me! Yes, there was some fool playing Chicken on I-94 at 70 mph! Luckily, there was no one on my right, so I swerved, missed the car, exited at the (conveniently located) exit ramp, stopped at the first gas station and reported the incident to the (also conveniently) stopped police. I never found out if they caught the fool, but the police tore out of the gas station like a bat out of hell!"

Linda M. Bohanon

When I was 28, I DEFIED (yes at 28, the Catholic guilt still existed) my father, a retired steelworker, and bought my first foreign car, a Honda Accord with a manual transmission. Why a manual transmission? I don't know what got into me. I had NEVER driven a car with a manual transmission in my life but I thought it would be cool.

"I was living in Charlottesville, Virginia, at the time but I purchased the car in Harrisonburg, Virginia, about an hour away across the Shenandoah Mountains in the 'Valley' as that neck of the woods is called. The salesman gave me a 15-minute lesson on the stick. 'Cool', I thought, 'this is easy!' I took off from Harrisonburg for Charlottesville and the drive back was without incident. 'Wow, I can drive a manual transmission! Hot damn!' ran through my head.

"Spending large sums of money is stressful for me and having forked out $12,000, I needed a nap. That nap lasted for 13 hours! I woke up the next day an hour earlier than usual. A little nervous, I left for work 40 minutes early. I started the car very carefully, tried to back out of the space but succeeded only in grinding the gears each time I tried reverse. I finally just gave up and drifted out of the space in neutral. I was so happy I pulled into a parking space the night before facing up the inclined parking lot AND had the presence of mind to use neutral to drift backward when I couldn't get reverse to work! I finally did manage to get the car into first gear and I was all set for the ride to work.

"Between my apartment and the entrance to my small apartment complex, I stalled the car three times. After the third stall, I decided to make a game out of it, knowing I'd probably stall at each of the

1995: Chrysler shareholder Kirk Kerkorian is unsuccessful in his bid to buy the company—through stock purchases—for $21 billion.

traffic lights between my apartment and my office. After a total of four traffic lights on three miles of rural winding roads, I arrived at my office in need of a shirt change, perspiring from nervousness, and ever so glad I made it to work. Total number of stalls: 19.

"I'm still driving a Honda Accord with a manual transmission, not the same car, but I still manage to stall it every now and then. And I always smile when it happens . . . Always."
Joe Connolly

I was 17 years old and used to work down at a local restaurant and go with the owner at 5:00 A.M. (ugh!!) down to Eastern Market [a large farmer's market in Detroit] for produce runs. (I'd work till 10:00 A.M. and then go to school; couldn't miss Brother Steven's English class.) We had a former Sears appliance service van (I think it was a Chevy) that had a manual COLUMN transmission on the steering wheel. I was always amazed that HE could drive it.

"Well, while at the market one day near Christmas, we were a bit overloaded and he needed to 'negotiate in the

back room' (i.e., Christmas cheer). My boss told me to drive back to the restaurant and unload and then come back and get him.

"Eastern Market is very busy with people at 5:00 A.M. Well, after stalling about 20 or more times trying to back up and turn around, about 10 people just grabbed the van and pushed me out onto Gratiot Avenue, where I could finally get going for a long and torturous ride.

"I love manual transmissions on the floor though. Had 'em for six cars and 20 years before opting for the four-door sedan and minivan household."
Dave Schulte

One of the last great muscle cars, a 1970 Dodge Challenger T/A, 340 Six-Pak, stock fiberglass hood with high-rise intake. Canary yellow with black racing stripes and black interior. He was a good-looking guy . . . and what a ride! He rumbled into my parent's driveway to pick me up. My kid sister looked at me with astonished awe. Our first-date destination was the local drive-in (of course), now the site of a Ford auto plant. I banged the passenger door against a pole . . . I

1995: For the first time in its history, Ford's trucks (pickups, sport utility vehicles, and minivans) outsell its cars.

 00337

The 1970 Dodge Challenger T/A packed a lot of muscle.
Courtesy of American Automobile Manufacturers Association

cringed. He winced. We married."

Karen Hill

When my daughter, Jennifer Ann Gareffa (yes, we really did), was little, we owned a yellow 1969 Jaguar E-Type roadster, a 1964 Plymouth station wagon, and a relatively new Honda. Although the latter two cars had all the room in the world for diapers, toys, and all the other accessories needed to travel with a kid, she would often get in these moods where she would tolerate nothing but the Jag. She'd shriek, 'Wanna go in the yellow car,' in that high-pitched, grating voice common to all ankle-biters, which causes electrical impulses to start at the base of a parent's spine and travel directly to the annoyance center of the brain.

"So rather than travel in relative comfort, we'd cram whatever we could into the two-seater and head off down the road. (Not that ol' dad really minded all that much.) Of course, Jen always insisted that we put the top down, too: 'Open top. Open top.'

"Chapter 2: The kid, now 21, went to the auto show Sunday. When she got back she asked, 'Did you see those Jaguars? There was one convertible that was the perfect color for me, sapphire blue. It's my birthstone; it's my favorite color; and it matches my eyes.' So now the cry has become, 'I want the blue one.'"

Peter Gareffa

Back in 1987 I had only two children, and drove an '81 Dodge Colt (stick). My son Johnny was four (he went to preschool) and Kristofer was one (he stayed with a sitter). Every morning I religiously dropped the youngest son off to the sitter, while the four-year-old waited in the car. One morning as the sitter closed her door. I spotted my Dodge rolling out of her driveway and down the street. Johnny was laughing and hanging his head out of the back window like a happy puppy going for a Sunday drive. I remember running frantically after the car and trying to grab it before it ran into a vehicle parked on the other side of the street. Fortunately the street was clear and the vehicle that it hit was a 'Deuce and a Quarter' (225) and therefore unharmed. Needless to say that at this point of the morning I'm ruined mon-

---

1995: Volvo of Sweden becomes the first car company to offer side-impact airbags on some of its models.

tally, but to top that off, I drove to work with Johnny still in the back seat! I aged that day."

Kristine Burns

Just recently, my dad was traveling to pick up his brand new Ford Contour. The dealer didn't have the exact one he wanted on the lot, so they were trading with another dealership. The dealer's dad drove the truck to be traded out to the other dealer, and my dad rode along. On the way back, my dad drove the new Contour (loves that V6 engine).

"They weren't even two miles from reaching the home dealership when the driver of a van in the oncoming lane either fell asleep or had a seizure. The car in front of my dad swerved and avoided the van as it crossed into the lane, but by the time my dad put the Contour on the shoulder, the van was there too, hitting the Contour just behind the passenger seat and spinning it into a ditch 12 inches deep in mud and water. No one was injured, thank goodness.

"They managed to drive the Contour back to the dealership, where there was much exclaiming over the condition of the new vehicle. Luckily for my dad, the papers had not yet been signed; needless to say, when the dealer asked if he still wanted that car, he declined."

Diane Telgen

When my dad was in college he was parking with a date on a deserted back country road. When it came time to drive home he discovered his lights didn't work. He was trying to figure out what to do when he saw the headlights of a car coming along heading back to town. When the car passed him on the side of the road he zoomed up behind him and followed him back to town. The other driver thought he was some kid playing a stunt and kept driving faster. Don't know if he got a second date."

Don Boyden

My mother had to get rid of her '87 Celebrity shortly after my parents moved to Boca Raton, Florida, and replace it with a more 'upscale' car. On several occasions, despite being dressed up, the security guards (at two different complexes!) told her that cleaning people were not supposed to use the main gate!"

Anonymous

1996: Chrysler announces that its new Sebring convertible has new integrated seat belts that are built into the seat. These eliminate dangling belts and bulky floor and side-panel mountings.

When my youngest daughter, Rebecca, was about two years old, she threw three one-hundred dollar bills out of the car window. My oldest, Samantha, said to me—after I discovered what the child from h - - l had done, 'Mommy, I told you Becky was in your purse, but you didn't listen to me.' What can I say, I was doing about 70 mph down I-94. But things work out in the end. The same day, I played the number '300' in the lottery, and guess what? I WON $500!!! And for those of you who are wondering, Rebecca is still among the living."

Robin Sabbath

We had a car when I was a kid, a Pinto I believe. It had a very leaky back window. With just me and my Mom, no one ever had call to get in the back seat. One day we had to put some boxes back there or something and discovered that, along with the moisture, some grass seed had made its way in. It looked better than what was in front of the house. Kind of a greenhouse effect, I guess."

Kristin Kahrs

Very fitting. As cars, Pintos always did make good planters."

Peter Gareffa

Very Superstitious

It was bad luck if, when you were driving in a car and got stopped by a train or a funeral procession, you counted the number of train cars/funeral cars that passed by."

Terri Schell

In our family, we'd get fair warning of an upcoming RR crossing and my brothers and I would yell out: 'Dat datta dat dat'—and then let the tracks make the final 'dat dat.' We were so musical."

Monica Hubbard

I remember something about lifting your feet off the floor when you went over railroad tracks. If you didn't, something bad was supposed to happened (although I don't remember what it was.)"

Lauri Taylor

1996: Toyota moves a new vehicle, the RAV4, into some showrooms. Priced at about $15,000, this "recreational activity vehicle" is a miniature four-wheel-drive, sport utility vehicle with a small, four-cylinder engine.

My friends told me that if I didn't lift my feet going over RR tracks I would die."

Carol Wojtowicz Bimberg

We lifted our feet off the ground and put our hands on the ceilings to avoid night-mares (of course this could have been my mother's twisted way of keeping us occupied on road trips).

"We also held our breath when driving past cemeteries in order to avoid becoming the dreaded old maid."

Linda Irvin

We held our breath while passing cemeteries, but it was because whoever didn't would be the next to die."

Julia Furtaw

When I was in the Girl Scouts, we had this thing about driving past cemeteries: you had to give the 'thumbs-up' to show the dead spirits the way to heaven."

Anonymous

You must touch the dome light when you go through a yellow light."

Todd Flanders

It's bad luck, and in terribly bad taste, to speak kindly of one's automobile in its presence.

"Also, your car runs better immediately after filling up the gas tank and is fastest when coming out of the drive-through car wash"

Jeff Lehman

1996: GM announces plans to introduce its electric EV1 sports coupe through Saturn dealers in southern California and Arizona. The front-wheel-drive, two-seat car is powered by lead-acid batteries, can go 60 miles between charges, and can reach a top speed of 80 mph.

MAKE/MODEL-SPECIFIC WEB SITES

AC Cobra
http://www.xs4all.nl/~luukb

Acura Integra
http://integra.ico.net

Acura NSX
http://ganglion.anes.med.umich.edu/NSX
http://www.scp.caltech.edu/~bryan/autos

American Motors AMX
http://home.worldweb.net/~stoneji/amx.html

Audi
http://www.audi.com
http://coimbra.ans.net/quattro.html

BMW
http://www.bmwusa.com
http://cbsgi1.bu.edu/bmw/bmw.html
http://www.trader.com/bmwcca

Bugatti
http://dutoc74.io.tudelft.nl/bugatti.htm

Buick
http://www.buick.com

Buick Turbo Regal
http://ni.umd.edu/gnttype/www/buick.html

Cadillac
http://www.cadillac.com

Chevrolet
The Chevy Spot
http://www.chevrolet.com

> *View the entire Chevy/Geo product line and get just about any related information you could possibly need: Prices, options, reviews; you name it, it's here. You can even buy Chevy souvenirs, collectibles, and wearables (sorry, no bowties) or e-mail Chevrolet. Look in the "Cool" section for free netsurfing software.*

> *EXCERPT: Welcome to the Chevy Spot. Here you'll find alost everything you want to know about Chevy Cars, Chevy Trucks, and Geos. You'll find plenty of surprises, too.*

Chevrolet Camaro
http://www.z28.com

Chevrolet Chevelle
http://www.awinc.com/users/amckenzi/club.html

Chevrolet Corvair
http://haycorn.psy.cmu.edu/virtualVairs

Chevrolet Corvette
http://www.dcc.edu/vettenet
http://www.geopages.com/colosseum/1299
http://www.vannevar.com/votn/index.html

Chrysler
http://www.chryslercars.com
Chrysler Technology Center
http://www.chryslercorp.com

> *Take a virtual tour of the Chrysler Technology Center in Auburn Hills, Michigan. Watch video clips of concept cars, go to the Chrysler library, tour the executive offices, and more. Just be sure to wipe your feet.*

> *EXCERPT: Get prepared to experience what many consider to be the most technologically advanced vehicle development operation in the world. Of course, due to the highly classified information we're about to show you, the first thing you'll need is a Chrysler Corporation Identification Badge.*

Citroen
http://huizen.dds.nl/~toi/ds.htm

DeLorean
http://www.delorean-owners.org
http://www.peak.org/~takeuchi/delorean.html

DeSoto
http://w3.one.net/~desoto/index.html

Dodge
http://www.4adodge.com

Dodge Dart
http://www.wam.umd.edu/~sragow/dart/
dart.html

Dodge Stealth/Mitsubishi 3000GT
http://users.aimnet.com/%7Edragnet/stealth

Eagle
http://www.eaglecars.com

Ferrari
http://pscinfo.psc.edu/%7Ersnodgra/Ferrari
http://www.physics.monash.edu.au/~davidz/
ferrari.html
Ferrari: The Official Web Site
http://www.ferrari.it/ferrari

> *Can't afford to buy a Ferrari? Then go window shopping at the company's impressive web site. Check out photos and specs of Ferraris past and present, catch up on the latest Ferrari racing news, or take a look at the company test track. You can even practice reading Italian by clicking on the Italian menu option.*

> *EXCERPT: There are many people in the world who love Ferrari and want to know about its history and everyday life. We have opened this web site in order to satisfy their curiosity and passion.*

Fiat
http://www.mirafiori.com

Ford
http://www.ford.com
http://www.mame.mu.oz.au/salman/Ford/
fpage.html
http://www.me.mtu.edu/~prater/ford.html

Ford Falcon
http://judith.www.media.mit.edu/Falcon/home/
html

Ford Mustang
http://www.dwx.com/~bob/topics/mustang/mustang.html
http://www.best.com:80/~mustang
http://www.corral.net

Ford Probe
http://www.wpi.edu/~ss/PGT/probe.html
http://www.bh.org/ford-probe.html

Ford SVT Cobra Mustang
http://crunch.Colorado.EDU/~cobra

Ford Thunderbird
http://www.autopro.com/tbird

General Motors
General Motors Homepage
http://www.gm.com

> *About what you'd expect from the web site of the world's biggest corporation. Video. Audio. Graphics. Free cars. (Just kidding about the free cars.) View the entire GM product line, "Take a Spin" using Quicktime VR technology (it's downloadable here), or take the GM trivia quiz.*

> *EXCERPT: This site is designed to give you the fullest, most interesting, and up-to-date web experience possible today. Enjoy.*

Gillet Vertigo
http://www.skynet.be/gillet.html

Honda
http://www.honda.com

Honda Prelude
http://rookery.acns.nwu.edu/~harrier/prelude/hmpg.html

Hyundai
http://www.hmc.co.kr

Jaguar
http://www.jaguarvehicles.com
http://www.oslonett.no/home/nick/jaguar.html

Jeep
http://www.indirect.com/www/a4x4/jeep.html
Jeep Unpaved
http://www.jeepunpaved.com

> *In addition to the obligatory product line rundown, this site offers an interesting "Create Your Own Destination" section. You state your preferences and a destination is suggested to allow you to experience nature on your own terms. And with your own money.*

> *EXCERPT: Welcome to Jeep Unpaved, where current information on Jeep vehicles and Jeep technology is at your fingertips. And since this is the Jeep site, you can count on us to continually conquer new ground by adding to, expanding, or revising this site.*

Jensen
http://hugh.pharmacol.su.oz.au/jensen.html

Lamborghini
http://www.csv.warwick.ac.uk/~bsuqg/lambo/
lambo.html

Lancia
http://www.c2.org/~mark/lancia/lancia.html

Land Rover
http://www.cs.monash.edu.au/~lloyd/tildeLand-Rover
http://www.ridgecrest.ca.us/RoverWeb

Lexus
http://www.lexuscar.com

Lincoln
http://www.lincolnvehicles.com

Lotus
http://lotuscars.com

Maserati
http://stone.america.com/maserati

Mazda Miata
http://www.csv.warwick.ac.uk/~esuqg
Miata.net
http://www.miata.net

> *A plethora of information about one of the world's most popular roadsters. Miata photos, Miata brochures, Miata clubs, Miata classifieds, Miata stories. This is Miata mania! The "Tips from the Garage" section will help keep your MX-5 running (and looking) like new.*
>
> *EXCERPT: Welcome! You've found the web home for Mazda MX-5 Miata enthusiasts around the world. Miata.net contains more information specifically relating to the Miata than almost any other resource.*

Mercedes-Benz
http://www.daimler-benz.com/mb/mb_e.html

Mercury
http://www.mercuryvehicles.com

MG
http://www.mgcars.org.uk

Mitsubishi
http://www.Mitsubishi-Motors.co.jp

Morgan
http://www.tay.ac.uk/mcsweb/staff/amm/morgan.html

Nissan
http://www.nissanmotors.com

Nissan/Datsun (Z-Cars)
http://www.cs.princeton.edu/~snd/z-car

Plymouth
http://www.plymouthcars.com

Plymouth Valiant
http://www.mordor.com/valiant/valiant.html

Peugeot
http://www.peugeot.com

Pontiac
http://www.pontiac.com

Pontiac Fiero
http://www.cen.uiuc.edu/~pz3900/fiero.html

Pontiac Firebird/Chevrolet Camaro (F-Bodies)
http://wj.net/f-body

Porsche
http://tta.com/Porschephiles/home.html
http://www.cs.cmu.edu/afs/andrew.cmu.edu/usr18/mset/www/porsche.html
http://192.253.114.31/Stuttgart/Porsche/Porsche_contents.html

Saab
http://www.saabusa.com

Saturn
http://www.physics.sunysb.edu/Saturn
The Saturn Site
http://www.saturncars.com

> *Saturn customers are extremely loyal and here they get a great big cyberhug from Saturn Corporation. Search the "Extended Family Database" (translation: Saturn owners), peruse photos from the 1994 Homecoming, or check up on the Saturn Cycling Team. Coolest thing here? Info on GM's new EV1 electric car, to be sold exclusively through Saturn dealers.*
>
> *EXCERPT: The Saturn Site is one more way that we can keep in touch with everyone and anyone who's interested in Saturn. We've designed the site to be as straightforward and easy to navigate as possible (heck, we're not cyberpunks, we're a car company).*

Studebaker
http://www.cris.com/~kjohnson/syudebaker.shtml

Subaru
http://www.subaru.com

Toyota
@Toyota
http://www.toyota.com

> *Yes, this is Toyota's web site, but it's easy to forget that once you click on "The Hub." There you'll find "magazines" dealing with men's and women's issues, the arts, sports, and more. (Image is everything.) Oh, I almost forgot. There's stuff about Toyotas here, too.*
>
> *EXCERPT: Where else in the world wide web can you get fit fast, plan a perfect garden, rate your mate, chart a financial future, swap hoop rookies, learn to talk hardware, and find a path through the woods. Welcome to the Hub @ Toyota. If it isn't here, humans don't do it.*

Toyota Land Cruiser
http://www.indirect.com/www/a4x4/tlc/tlc.html

Toyota MR-2
http://www.mr2.com

Triumph
http://www.mit.edu:8001/afs/athena.mit.edu/user/z/i/zimerman/www/tr6.html
http://www.sanders.com/vtr/vtr.html
http://www.team.net:80/TR8

Tucker
http://www.grfn.org/~cmille1/tucker.html

Volkswagen
http://www.volkswagen.com
http://www.oroad.com/volkswebbin
http://www.metrics.com/VW/vw.html

Volvo
http://www.volvocars.com
http://www.cs.earlham.edu/~davel/swedishbricks.
html

OTHER CAR-RELATED SITES

Art Cars
http://www2.nse.com/artcars
http://www.panix.com/~oval/artcar

Audio
http://www.ksu.ksu.edu/~spdtrap/caraudio/
CarAudio.html
http://bingen.cs.csbsju.edu/~mrgoff

Automobilia
http://www.ewacars.com

Automotive Engineering
http://www.sae.org

Bad Drivers
Highway 17 Page of Shame
http://www.got.net/~egallant/the_road.html
*Two guys and a camera look for bad drivers
during their daily commute on the busy California highways. If you cut 'em off, chances
are your car's picture will show up on this
web site. Features the "Jerque du Jour."
(Parental guidance suggested)*

*EXCERPT: This page was born out of my
frustration of seeing the world's worst drivers
and not being able to actually reach out and
"educate" them. Hopefully, one of those bad
drivers will surf on over to this page, see a picture of their car and a description of their
awful driving, then change their wicked ways.*

Books
http://www.primenet.com/~komet/speed/
speedway.html

Classic Cars
http://www.primenet.com/~komet/classic/clascars
.html
http://www.mines.edu:8080/students/g/gbragalo/
bump/bumpstop.html
Classic Car Source
http://www.classicar.com
*Everything for and about classic cars—and
then some. Find that hard-to-find part, check
out classic car shows and museums worldwide, or place a classified ad. A neat link puts*

you in touch with people and companies that
offer restoration services. This site is destined
to become a classic!

*EXCERPT: Here's where you'll find the most
detailed road map on the web to help you find
your way to whatever it is that interests you
about classic vehicles. Looking for that special
part? Try a search on our blazingly fast, cus-
tom-made database.*

Collectible/Exotic Cars for Sale
http://www.collectorcar.com
http://www.clark.net/pub/networx/autopage/auto
page.html
http://www.kars.com
http://www.seanet.com/Vendors/kongkars/
kongkars.html
http://vmarketing.com/auto.html

Electric Cars
http://northshore.shore.net/~kester

Exotic Cars
http://www.abc.se/~m8938/cars/index.html

4 x 4s
The 4 x 4 Web Page
http://www.indirect.com/www/a4x4/4x4.html
*Nirvana for 4 x 4 owners. Photos of 4 x 4s in
hard-to-believe places (how did they get
there?), trip reports from 4 x 4 owners, information on off-road racing, 4 x 4 clubs and
associations to join, etc. A section on land
issues helps promote responsible use of off-
road vehicles.*

*EXCERPT: This site is dedicated to the 4 x 4
and off-road enthusiast who likes to get their
rig OFF-HIGHWAY!*

History
http://hfm.umd.umich.edu/SHOW/show.intro.html
http://www.ford.com/archive/FordHistory.html
http://www.st.rim.or.jp/~iwat

Hot Rods
http://www.america.net/com/hotrods/hrhome.
html
http://www.Nashville.Net:80/~hotrod

Humor
http://pubweb.acns.nwu.edu/~bil874/comedy/
trans.htm
http://genie.resnet.upenn.edu:8080/~humorarchive
/drivingfun

Lemon Law/Automobile Fraud
http://www.directnet.com/~rbrennan

License Plates
http://licplate.andhra.com
http://www-chaos.umd.edu/misc/plates.html

Lowriders
http://expert.cc.purdue.edu/~jschaefe

Magazines

http://www.autoweek.com

http://popularmechanics.com/popmech/auto/
1HOMEAUTO.html

http://www.magicnet.net/~joeg/turbo_mag

http://www.mobilia.com

http://www.sover.net/~hemmings/hmn.html

http://www.carcollector.com

http://www.cs.umanitoba.ca/~gdueck/aao.html

http://www.MotorCity.com/site/MC/Autonaut/
autonaut.html

Car and Driver

http://www.caranddriver.com

> *The electronic version of one of the best car magazines around. A fabulous "Buyer's Guide" gives you crucial data for all the latest cars and "Car Chat" is there for on-line automobile discussion. And, of course, there are articles from the current edition of the paper product. All in all, a great "magazine" that you don't have to recycle at the end of the month.*
>
> *EXCERPT: Welcome to Car and Driver on the web! Search or browse our complete guide of . . . new cars and trucks. New vehicles continually updated.*

Microcars (cars made to carry just one person)

http://www.homeless.com/homepages/jhock
@pullman.com.html#home

Miscellany

http://www.webcom.com/~autodir

http://www.mindspring.com/~labrams/a2cartop.
htm

http://www.sover.net/~autojum

http://www.route66.com

http://www.car-trek.com

http://www.cftnet.com/members/rcbowden/home
car.htm

Motorist Associations

http://www.motorists.com

Museums

http://www.product.com/AutoZonLine/
carbarn.html

http://www.tgimaps.com/MPLS/ELLINGSON/|
ellingson.html

http://www.fastnet.ch/LSNE/ARTCUL/MUSEE/
musauto_e.html

http://www.classicar.com/museums.htm

New and Used Cars (Dealers/Classifieds)

http://www.dealernet.com

http://www.autoweb.com

http://www.autorow.com

http://www.motorcity.com

http://www.webfoot.com/lots/international.car.lot.
html

Oscar Mayer Wienermobile

http://www.oscar-mayer.com/wienermobile/
history.html

Pickup Trucks

http://www.rtd.com/~mlevine/pickup.html

Posters

http://www.westworld.com/~rasachs/carart.html

Racing

http://www.starnews.com/speednet

http://www.racecar.com

http://www.primenet.com/~thomasj/index.html

http://www.inetdirect.net/home/racing.html

http://www.motorsport.com

http://www.io.org/~raceweb

http://chiller.compaq.com/dragnet

Route 66

http://route66.netvision.be

http://www.marketplaza.com/route66/route66.
html

Specialty Cars

http://www.SpecialCar.com

Speedtraps

The WWW Speedtrap Registry

http://www.nashville.net/speedtrap

> *Divided into sections for all 50 states—with separate sections for Canada, the United Kingdom, Australia, and Sweden—the Speedtrap Registry lists speed traps that ensnare unwary drivers. Also includes a "Cop Car Registry" so you know what kinds of police cars—marked and unmarked—to keep your eyes peeled for while traveling.*
>
> *EXCERPT: This registry was started . . . to cut down the number of speeding tickets resulting from speed traps. The Registry is not meant to be a tool to undercut the efforts of law enforcement to keep our roads safe.*

Sports Cars

http://www.highway-one.com

Swap Meets

http://www.mm.com/swapmeet

http://www.carsnet.com

Tires

http://www.goodyear.com

Toy Cars

http://www.interaccess.com/diecast

Abarth Register, U.S.A.
c/o Gerald Rothman
1298 Birch St.
Uniondale, NY 11553-2008
(516) 481-2092
Fax: (516) 583-7118

> Owners of Abarth automobiles, vintage Italian race cars manufactured from 1951 to 1971. Established to restore, preserve, and enjoy the Abarth marque. Members gather three to four times a year in the U.S. and Europe to participate in races with their Abarths. Maintains hall of fame.

Airflow Club of America
c/o William H. Gordon
796 Santree
Las Vegas, NV 89110
(702) 438-4362

> Owners and fanciers of Chrysler and DeSoto airflow automobiles (1934–37). Dedicated to the restoration and preservation of these automobiles and their related history and lore.

Alfa Romeo Owners Club
2468 Gum Tree Ln.
Fallbrook, CA 92028
(619) 728-4875

> Owners and enthusiasts of Alfa Romeo automobiles. Promotes knowledge of the history and tradition of the Alfa Romeo marque; provides technical information for efficient and safe operation of Alfas. Chapters organize socials and amateur driving events and conduct technical seminars and driver's schools to teach safe and skillful driving on the highway and in competitions.

Allard Owners Club U.S.A.
33 Underwood Rd.
Montville, NJ 07045
(201) 471-5000

> Individuals united to restore, race, and exhibit Allard automobiles.

AMC Pacer Club
c/o Frank Wrenick
2628 Queenston Rd.
Cleveland Heights, OH 44118
(216) 371-0226

> Persons interested in the Pacer automobiles manufactured by American Motors Corporation from 1975–1980. Promotes and encourages the preservation, restoration, and collection of Pacers as well as the collection and preservation of all forms of information and printed material relating to them.

AMC Rambler Club
2645 Ashton Rd.
Cleveland Heights, OH 44118
(216) 371-5946

> Individuals interested in 1958–1969 American Motors Corporation automobiles. Encourages and promotes the preservation, restoration, and collection of these automobiles, as well as the collection and preservation of all forms of information and printed material relating to them. Provides a parts locator service and technical and mechanical assistance services. Plans to establish a museum.

AMC World Clubs
7963 Depew St.
Arvada, CO 80003-2527
(303) 428-8760
Fax: (303) 428-1070

> Individuals dedicated to the preservation and restoration of American Motors cars from 1950 to 1988. Assists members and others in the restoration of their vehicles. Conducts research for magazine articles. Operates museum.

American Austin/Bantam Club
c/o Helen Jean White
351 Wilson Rd.
Willshire, OH 45898-9551
(419) 495-2569

> *Owners and enthusiasts of American Austin and American Bantam cars, trucks, jeeps, and trailers built in Butler, PA from 1930 to 1941. Aims to promote preservation and restoration of American Austin (1930–35) and American Bantam (1938–41) vehicles. Offers free classified advertisement service to members; conducts car show competitions.*

American Automobile Association (AAA)
1000 AAA Dr.
Heathrow, FL 32746
(407) 444-7000
Fax: (407) 444-7380

> *Federation of automobile clubs (1,000 offices) providing domestic and foreign travel services, emergency road services, and insurance. Sponsors public services for traffic safety, better highways, more efficient and safer cars, energy conservation, and improvement of motoring and travel conditions.*

American Automobile Manufacturers Association
1401 H St. NW, Ste. 900
Washington, DC 20005
(202) 326-5500
Fax: (202) 326-5567

> *Trade association whose members are Chrysler Corporation, Ford Motor Company and General Motors. Reviews economic, social and public policies for their impact on the motor vehicle industry and its customers. Monitors, analyzes, and responds to Federal and state legislative and regulatory initiatives affecting motor vehicles and their use. Sponsors basic research projects in such areas as emissions, energy use, safety, recycling , and noise. Maintains analytical and statistical information about the U.S. motor vehicle industry. Distributes publications on motor vehicle related issues and statistics to news media, educators, community leaders and the public through a variety of public information programs.*

American Bugatti Club
4484 Howe Hill Rd.
Camden, ME 04843
(207) 236-8288
Fax: (207) 236-0869

> *Promotes the preservation and appreciation of the work of Ettore Bugatti (1881–1947), provides network for owners of Bugatti motor cars and other enthusiasts. Maintains a Registar of Bugattis in North America.*

American Hot Rod Association
N. 111 Hayford Rd.
Spokane, WA 99204
(509) 244-2372
Fax: (509) 244-2472

> *Professional and amateur drag racers from the U.S. and Canada. Goal is to sponsor a series of national drag racing championships. Conducts track operators meeting for racetrack owners. Sponsors competitions. Maintains hall of fame.*

American Lancia Club
Turkhill Rd.
Brewster, NY 10509
(914) 279-9463
Fax: (914) 941-1729

> *Owners and enthusiasts of Lancia automobiles. Disseminates information on the Lancia automobile including technical tips and advertisements. Maintains library and biographical archives.*

American MGB Association
PO Box 11401
Chicago, IL 60611
(312) 878-5055, (800) 723-MGMG
Fax: (312) 769-6262

> *MGB car owners and enthusiasts. Purpose is to assist owners in the upkeep and maintenance of their cars. Local groups sponsor technical sessions, rallies, and picnics. Provides information on MG Marque history. Compiles statistics on chassis numbers, engine numbers, and other information on cars.*

American MGC Register
34 Park Ave.
Asheville, NC 28803
(704) 274-2269
Fax: (704) 274-2269

> *Owners and enthusiasts of the MGC automobile. Dedicated to the preservation and use of the car. Assists members in restoring and locating parts. Makes available regalia, including patches, pins, and buckles. Sponsors competitions; compiles statistics.*

American Motors Owners Association
c/o Darryl A. Salisbury
6756 Cornell St.
Portage, MI 49002-3412
(616) 323-0369
Fax: (616) 387-4806

> *Owners and enthusiasts of AMC vehicles built from 1958–1988. To aid and encourage ownership, use, and enjoyment of AMC vehicles; to encourage preservation and restoration of these vehicles; and to increase communications and fellowship among owners.*

American Motorsport International

7963 Depew St.
Arvada, CO 80003
(303) 428-8760
Fax: (303) 428-1070

Collectors and admirers of AMC cars and Jeeps. (American Motors Corporation was formed in 1954 by the merger of the Hudson and Nash companies. AMC operated as an independent automobile manufacturer from 1954 to 1987, when it was absorbed by the Chrysler Corporation.) Functions as a clearinghouse of information on all AMC products. Provides technical assistance to members involved in restoring or preserving AMC automobiles. Maintains library and archive of sales and engineering literature and artifacts pertaining to AMC products. Sponsors national concours for AMC cars and Jeeps. Makes available novelty items and memorabilia.

American Supercharger Club and Owner's Association

9302 Livernois
Houston, TX 77080
(713) 461-BLWN

Owners, manufacturers, and users of supercharging and nitrous oxide injection engines used in automobiles, boats, and in racing. Promotes new developments and improvements in these systems and encourages information exchange among enthusiasts. Offers technical assistance and guidance to individuals using supercharged engines. Conducts educational and research programs. Offers discounted pricing on performance parts and blowers. Offers referral service.

Amphicar Owners Club

382 Vassar Rd.
Poughkeepsie, NY 12603
(914) 297-2510
Fax: (914) 297-6523

Owners, former owners, dealers, and distributors of Amphicars and parts; others interested in Amphicars. (Amphicars, manufactured 1960–67 by the Industrie Werke Karlesruhe in Germany, are vehicles which can be driven on land or in water.) Aids owners in restoring their Amphicars and in locating other owners to exchange ideas and parts; disseminates information concerning the substitution of American car parts for hard-to-locate Amphicar parts. Compiles statistics.

Antique Auto Racing Association

PO Box 486
Fairview, NC 28730
(704) 628-3428

Persons interested in the history of auto racing and in preserving, restoring, and driving antique race cars as well as collecting memorabilia related to antique race cars.

Antique Automobile Club of America

501 W. Governor Rd.
Hershey, PA 17033
(717) 534-1910
Fax: (717) 534-9101

Collectors, hobbyists, and others interested in the preservation, maintenance, and restoration of automobiles and in automotive history. Encourages historical research.

Antique Studebaker Club

PO Box 28845
Dallas, TX 75228
(214) 709-6185, (800) 527-3452
Fax: (214) 296-7920

Private collectors and restorers. United to promote the collection, restoration, and preservation of antique Studebaker vehicles produced before World War II.

Arnolt-Bristol Registry

PO Box 60
Brooklandville, MD 21022
(410) 484-1834

Owners and enthusiasts of Arnolt-Bristol automobiles English-Italian-American two-seater roadsters manufactured between 1954 and 1959; only 142 were made). Maintains registry that lists owners of the marque. Provides updated information on the automobile and activities such as vintage auto racing and concours d'elegance car shows.

Auburn-Cord-Duesenberg Club

9NO89 Corron Rd.
Elgin, IL 60123
(708) 464-5767

Persons interested in preserving Auburn, Cord, and Duesenberg automobiles. Collects historical material pertaining to ACD automobiles and associated companies; maintains library of books, pamphlets, articles, and photographs. Sponsors competitions.

Austin-Healey Sports and Touring Club

PO Box 3539
York, PA 17402
(215) 536-6912

Austin-Healey automobile owners and enthusiasts. Provides social activities, technical information, and vehicle maintenance assistance. Maintains library of repair and technical manuals, historical information, data on cars, and serial numbers.

Automobile Competition Committee for the United States FIA
1500 Skokie Blvd., Ste. 101
Northbrook, IL 60062
(708) 272-0090
Fax: (708) 272-0101

United States representative on the International Sporting Commission of the International Automobile Federation. National racing organizations (6) and individuals who direct the committee (22); organization members are Sports Car Club of America, United States Auto Club, National Hot Rod Association, National Association for Stock Car Auto Racing, Championship Auto Racing Teams, and International Motor Sports Association (see separate entries). Coordinates activities between the member organizations and the FIA on such matters as: rules and regulations; automobile specifications; international calendar listing of major motor sports events; interchange of drivers, cars, and participants among members and between the U.S. and Europe. Works with manufacturers for international recognition of American-built automobiles. Issues international racing driver and entrant licenses.

Automobile License Plate Collectors Association
PO Box 77
Horner, WV 26372
(304) 842-3773

Persons interested in collecting license plates or related data. Compiles statistics and disseminates information about current and expired license plates, systems of registration, and laws.

Automobile Objects d'Art Club
252 N. 7th St.
Allentown, PA 18102
(610) 432-3355
Fax: (610) 820-9368

Individuals interested in objects d'art of early automobiles, such as prints, paintings, and bronzes. Seeks to preserve the history of early motoring. Conducts expositions at art museums; gives lectures and slide presentations. Maintains speakers' bureau and museum; conducts research, educational, and charitable programs.

Automotive Hall of Fame
PO Box 1727
Midland, MI 48641
(517) 631-5760
Fax: (517) 631-0524

Individuals who have been or are now engaged in the automotive industry or related industries. Dedicated in 1976, the Hall of Fame contains exhibits and histories of the people of the industry. Purpose is to perpetuate the memory of pioneers in the automotive industry among present and future generations. Cooperates with business schools and colleges that have automotive-related courses. Elects up to five automotive pioneers to Hall of Fame annually.

Automotive Service Association
1901 Airport Fwy., Ste. 100
PO Box 929
Bedford, TX 76095-0929
(817) 283-6205, (800) 272-7467
Fax: (817) 685-0225

Automotive service businesses including body, paint, and trim shops, engine rebuilders, radiator shops, brake and wheel alignment services, transmission shops, tune-up services, and air conditioning services; associate members are manufacturers and wholesalers of automotive parts, and the trade press. Represents independent business owners and managers before private agencies and national and state legislative bodies. Promotes confidence between consumer and automotive technician, safety inspection of motor vehicles, and better highways.

Avanti Owners Association International
PO Box 322
Uxbridge, MA 01569
(508) 278-3242

Owners of Avanti and Avanti II automobiles. (Fewer than 5,000 Avantis were built by Studebaker; the last came off the production line December 30, 1963. Another company, the Avanti Motor Corporation of South Bend, Indiana, started producing an Avanti II in 1965.) Provides members with historical and technical data about the Avanti.

Berkeley Exchange
46 Elm St.
North Andover, MA 01845
(508) 687-3421

Owners and enthusiasts of the Berkeley, a British sports car manufactured in Great Britain from 1956 to 1961. The exchange is dedicated to the preservation and restoration of the Berkeley automobile and serves as a network for the exchange of information. Participates in car meets.

Berkeley Newsletter
PO Box 162282
Austin, TX 78716
(512) 327-6231

Owners of Berkeley automobiles; interested others. Promotes the preservation, restoration, *and enjoyment of Berkeley automobiles, which were manufactured from 1956 to 1961.*

BMW Automobile Club of America
PO Box 3828
City of Industry, CA 91744-0828
(909) 595-2439
Fax: (909) 594-5178
Individuals who own a BMW automobile. Purposes are to further the BMW marque, to provide more enjoyment from the car, and to meet other owners of BMW automobiles. Sponsors two annual driving schools. Maintains charitable program.

BMW Car Club of America
2130 Massachuetts Ave., No. IA
Cambridge, MA 02140
(617) 492-2500, (800) 878-9292
Fax: (617) 876-3424
Owners of BMW automobiles and other interested persons. Promotes interest in BMW automobiles through technical, social, and driving events; encourages the exchange of information among members. Club is independent of any commercial interests. Conducts charitable programs.

BMW Vintage Club of America
PO Box S
San Rafael, CA 94913
(415) 897-0220
Fax: (415) 898-0831
Owners and admirers of pre-war, Veritas, 501, and V-8 models of BMW automobiles. Promotes the restoration and preservation of these cars. Facilitates information exchange among members; helps members locate parts.

Borgward Owners' Club
77 New Hampshire
Bay Shore, NY 11706
(516) 273-0458
Owners and enthusiasts of Borgward, Goliath, and Lloyd vehicles. Provides members with information about repairs and availability of parts at discount prices.

Boss 429 Owners Directory
4228 S. Conklin
Spokane, WA 99203
(509) 455-9369
Owners of 1969–1970 Ford Boss 429 Mustangs; other interested individuals. Facilitates exchange of information among members; operates restoration and parts services. Maintains Boss 429 Registry to preserve and record vehicle information.

Boss 302 Registry
1817 Janet Ave.

Lebanon, PA 17046-1845
(717) 274-5280
Works to locate all factory Ford Mustang Boss 302s. Compiles statistics; conducts research programs.

Bricklin International Owners Club
213 Southwoods
Fredericksburg, TX 78624
(210) 997-6134
Fax: (805) 269-2729
Local car clubs and individuals united for meets, rallies, and technical assistance in the preservation of the out-of-production Bricklin automobile. Compiles statistics.

Bristol Owners Club, U.S. Branch
PO Box 60
Brooklandville, MD 21022
(410) 484-1834
Owners of cars manufactured from 1946 to present by the Bristol Aeroplane Company in England. Seeks to further interest in Bristol cars and promote the preservation and restoration of Bristol vehicles and development of a spare parts register. Sponsors events such as a driving competition, tours, concours, and social gatherings.

Buick Club of America
PO Box 401927
Hesperia, CA 92340-1927
(619) 947-2485
Fax: (619) 947-2485
Promotes the development, publication, and interchange of technical, historical, and other information among members who are interested in Buick automobiles; also promotes fellowship among members. Encourages the maintenance, restoration, and preservation of all models produced by the Buick Motor Division of General Motors.

Buick GS Club of America
1213 Gornto Rd.
Valdosta, GA 31602
(912) 244-0577
Owners and enthusiasts of the Buick Gran Sport automobile, manufactured from 1965 to 1973, and the Buick Grand National, manufactured in 1986 and 1987. Promotes the collectibility of the high-performance Buick muscle cars. Assists in the upkeep and maintenance of GS and GN automobiles. Provides parts sources and technical information.

Butterfield Trail Antique Auto Club
c/o Roger Lohrmeyer
2509 Henry Dr.
Hays, KS 67601
(913) 628-8712

Car owners and enthusiasts. Promotes interest in automobiles as a hobby. Members do not have to own a special interest vehicle.

Cadillac Convertible Owners of America
PO Box 269
Ossining, NY 10562
Cadillac convertible owners who wish to preserve and enhance the value of their automobiles.

Cadillac-LaSalle Club
c/o Jay Ann Edmunds
PO Box 359
Devon, PA 19333
(610) 688-7747
Persons interested in Cadillac or LaSalle automobiles. Seeks to preserve, restore, and enjoy Cadillac and LaSalle cars of all models.

California Association of Tiger-Owners
18321 Vista Del Lago
Yorba Linda, CA 92686
(714) 777-3744, (310) 404-7755
Fax: (818)541-1784
National organization of owners of Sunbeam Tiger and Alpine automobiles. Objectives are to provide information about the Sunbeam marque and to manufacture and supply parts for members. Conducts social functions. Sponsors research programs and specialized education. Compiles statistics.

Car Care Council
1 Grande Lake Dr.
Port Clinton, OH 43452
(419) 734-5343
Fax: (419) 732-3780
Educates the public about the importance of preventive vehicle maintenance. Provides public service messages on auto maintenance to radio, TV newspapers and magazines. Coordinates National Car Care Month each October.

Cartercar Registry
2060 Bethel Rd.
Lansdale, PA 19446
(610) 584-4294
Owners of Cartercars. Purpose is to promote the care and pleasure driving of Cartercars (The Cartercar was invented in 1904 by Byron Carter who was then the superintendent of Michigan State Prison where the first car was assembled. William Durant, at that time president of General Motors, secured the Cartercar rights from Carter in 1906 and produced the car until 1914. The Cartercar, of which only 50 are believed to be in existence, has a friction drive transmission.)

Championship Auto Racing Teams (IndyCar)
390 Enterprise Ct.
Bloomfield Hills, MI 48302
(810) 334-8500
Fax: (313) 334-8560
Race car owners who compete for series championships. Serves as the scheduling and rule-making body for Indianapolis 500 car type motor racing events. Seeks to enhance the sport of automobile racing. Organizes and sanctions annual PPG Indy Car World Series throughout North America.

Checker Car Club of America
c/o Steven D. Wilson
15536 Sky Hawk Dr.
Sun City West, AZ 85375-6512
(602) 546-9052
Individuals interested in Checker automobiles. Promotes the preservation, enjoyment, and exchange of information on Checker automobiles, produced by the Checker Motors Corporation from 1922 to 1982 and traditionally used as taxicabs. Plans to hold national meets.

Chevrolet Nomad Association
8653 W. Hwy. 2
Cairo, NE 68824
(308) 384-2622
Individuals interested in Chevrolet Nomad automobiles manufactured from 1955–57. Works to preserve and show Nomads.

Chrysler Performance Parts Association
Box 1210
Azusa, CA 91702
(818) 303-6220
Fax: (818) 303-2481
Clearinghouse for information on from whom, where, and how to obtain vintage, muscle, and high-tech Chrysler performance parts.

Chrysler Products Owners Club
8919 Moreland Ln.
Annandale, VA 22003
Collectors and restorers of Chrysler-product automobiles. Promotes the collection, preservation, restoration, maintenance, exhibition, and enjoyment of all Chrysler product cars, trucks, and other vehicles, including Chrysler, DeSoto, Dodge, Imperial, and Plymouth. Offers technical advice; provides list of cars, parts, and services. Though the group maintains national interest, membership is concentrated in the Washington, D.C. metropolitan area.

Chrysler 300 Club International
4900 Jonesville Rd.
Jonesville, MI 49250
(517) 849-2783
Fax: (517) 849-7445

Individuals interested in the preservation of 1955–1965 and 1970 Hurst letter-series 300 automobiles built by Chrysler Corporation. Conducts national and local meets; compiles statistics. Maintains complete up-to-date list of letter Series 300s and owners; also maintains authentication service. Projects include: reproduction parts, N.O.S. parts locating, and copies of factory specifications.

Chrysler Town and Country Owners Registry

c/o Bob Porter
12540 Edgewater Dr., No. 1707
Lakewood, OH 44107
(216) 228-1169
Fax: (216) 228-0465

Objectives are the restoration and promotion of the Chrysler Town and Country automobile of 1941–1950, the Chrysler Royal Station Wagon of 1949–1950, and the Chrysler Le Baron Town and Country Convertible of 1983–1986.

Citroen Car Club

PO Box 743
Hollywood, CA 90078

Individuals who are interested in the promotion, preservation, or restoration of Citroen and Panhard automobiles. Provides information exchange; assists in locating hard-to-find parts and in selling of vehicles. Conducts social activities, automotive clinics, caravans, and group tours.

Citroen Quarterly Car Club

PO Box 30
Boston, MA 02113
(617) 742-6604

Promotes the preservation of Citroen automobiles.

Classic AMX Club International

7963 Depew St.
Arvada, CO 80003
(303) 428-8760
Fax: (303) 428-1070

Automobile buffs interested in preserving and restoring the 1968, 1969, and 1970 American Motors AMX auto and promoting national recognition of the AMX as a valuable collector's car.

Classic Chevy Club International

PO Box 607188
Orlando, FL 32860-7188
(407) 299 1957, (800) 456 1957
Fax: (407) 299-3341

Promotes the preservation and restoration of 1955, 1956, and 1957 Chevrolets. Compiles statistics. Supplies variety of reproduction parts for restoration.

Classic Comet Club of America

100 Sandhill Rd.
Fleetwood, PA 19522-9363

Owners of Comet automobiles manufactured by Mercury in the 1960s and 1970s. Promotes the history, restoration, and preservation of Comet automobiles. Facilitates purchase, sale, and trade of auto parts among members. Works to establish a Comet registry and to develop a rare auto parts hot line. Sponsors car shows; attends other sanctioned events; compiles statistics.

Classic Jaguar Association

c/o Dr. Robert Sutter
1444 Key View
Corona del Mar, CA 92625
(310) 434-4712
Fax: (408) 625-1529

International organization of owners or enthusiasts of pre-war SS cars and post-war models of Jaguar; also accepts membership of later model Jaguar owners. Has members and officers in 16 countries. Promotes ownership and operation of these automobiles. Conducts technical and historical research. Maintains spare parts coordination worldwide. Gives technical assistance to members and will provide consultation or proofreading service to persons writing about the vehicles. Holds regional concours d'elegance shows, social events, and driving activities.

Classic Thunderbird Club International

PO Box 4148
Santa Fe Springs, CA 90670
(310) 945-6836

Owners of 1955, 1956, and 1957 Ford Thunderbird cars. Encourages the upkeep and preservation of "classic" Thunderbird automobiles. Maintains library consisting mainly of Ford Motor Co. sales literature, repair manuals, and parts books related to the 1955–1957 Fords and Thunderbirds. Sponsors competitions at local, regional, and national levels.

Club Elite of North America

6238 Ralston Ave.
Richmond, CA 94805-1519
(510) 232-7764
Fax: (510) 232-7764

Owners of the 1959–63 Lotus Elite automobile or early Lotus sports racing models. Aids owners in the maintenance of their cars.

Cobra Owners Club of America

c/o Tom McIntyre
313 N. Lake St.
Burbank, CA 91502
(818) 953-2240
Fax: (818) 845-0896

Individuals owning automobiles manufactured by Shelby-American, Inc. (Mustang GT 350 or GT 500, Cobra 289, Cobra 427, and Ford GT 40 MK 1, MK 2, or MK 4). Organized for the appreciation, preservation, and restoration of the marque. Conducts social activities and technical and racing programs.

Continental Mark II Owner's Association

Holiday Ranch Airport
26676 Holiday Ranch Rd.
Apple Valley, CA 92307
(619) 247-4758
Fax: (619) 247-7679

Owners and enthusiasts of the Continental Mark II automobile, built from 1956 to 1957. Provides assistance, advice, parts, and information for the purpose of restoring and preserving the Mark II. Compiles statistics.

Cooper Car Club

14 Biscayne Dr.
Ramsey, NJ 07446
(201) 825-4548
Fax: (201)825-8285

Owners and enthusiasts of Cooper race cars. Promotes presentation of Cooper automobiles.

Corvair Society of America

PO Box 607
Lemont, IL 60439
(708) 257-6530
Fax: (708) 257-5540

Enthusiasts of the Corvair automobile united for technical assistance and parts availability. Holds national and local meets.

Corvette Club of America

PO Box 9288
Glenwood, FL 32722
(904) 736-6467
Fax: (904) 734-3330

Promotes the restoration, reconstruction, and customizing of Chevrolet Corvette automobiles. Sponsors racing events. Bestows awards. Conducts educational and charitable programs and children's services. Maintains speakers' bureau.

Cougar Club of America

c/o John W. Baumann
0-4211 N. 120th Ave.
Holland, MI 49424
(616) 396-0390
Fax: (616) 396-0366

Owners and enthusiasts dedicated to the preservation of Mercury Cougar automobiles manufactured from 1967 to 1973. Compiles statistics.

Crosley Automobile Club

217 N. Gilbert
Iowa City, IA 52245
(319) 338-9132

Individuals interested in the Crosley automobile. Conducts national yearly meets. Assists members in locating and selling parts and cars and in restoration.

Crown Victoria Association

PO Box 6
Bryan, OH 43506
(419) 636-2475
Fax: (419) 636-8449

Individuals with an interest in Ford automobiles manufactured during the 1954–1956 era. Purposes are to disseminate general information on these cars and to inform members of available automobiles and parts.

Curved Dash Olds Owners Club

7 Kiltie Dr.
New Hope, PA 18938
(215) 862-2353

Persons who own and are interested in preserving and restoring Curved Dash Oldsmobile automobiles.

Daimler and Lanchester Owners Club of North America

c/o David Ford
316 Prospect St.
Ridgewood, NJ 07450
(201) 445-0853
Fax: (212) 552-7467

Owners and enthusiasts of Daimler, B.S.A., and Lanchester automobiles. Acts as forum for discussion on matters of common interest to owners; explores and develops sources of spare parts; organizes displays.

D.A.R.T.S.

PO Box 9
Wethersfield, CT 06129-0009
(203) 257-8434, (860) 257-8434

Promotes the preservation, restoration, and enjoyment of Dodge Dart automobiles.

Datsun Fairlady Registry

c/o Frank Beer
13701-416 Riverside Dr.
Sherman Oaks, CA 91423-2483
(619) 940-6365
Fax: (818) 982-1042

Enthusiasts and owners of the Datsun Fairlady. Promotes exchange of history and information on Datsun automobiles. Provides opportunities for Datsun owners to gather and display their automobiles. Sponsors competitions.

Delahaye Club of America
1015 Stewart
Seattle, WA 98101
(206) 292-9906
Fax: (206) 292-9908
> *Drivers and collectors of Delahaye automobiles; interested others. Promotes and preserves the Delahaye automobile and its history. Conducts research.*

DeLorean Club International
PO Box 23040
Seattle, WA 98102
> *Owners, dealers, and enthusiasts of DeLorean automobiles, produced by the DeLorean Motor Company from 1981 through January of 1983. Promotes fellowship among members; provides for the exchange of technical and maintenance information.*

DeLorean Owners Association
879 Randolph Rd.
Santa Barbara, CA 93111
(805) 964-5296
> *Owners and enthusiasts of the DeLorean automobile. Single largest group devoted exclusively to the DeLorean.*

DeSoto Club of America
403 S. Thornton
Richmond, MO 64085
(816) 776-3048
> *Individuals interested in DeSoto automobiles. Seeks to preserve and advance future restoration of the DeSoto; promote the participation in events of DeSotos for public appreciation and gratification, with special emphasis on models from 1928 to 1961. Sponsors meets and flea markets.*

Dodge Brothers Club
c/o Mike Wenis
PO Box 151
N. Salem, NY 10560
(914) 669-5509
> *Owners and others interested in the preservation and enjoyment of Dodge Brothers motor vehicles of model year 1938 and earlier. Serves as an information exchange.*

Durant Family Registry
2700 Timber Ln.
Green Bay, WI 54313-5899
(414) 499 8797
> *Owners and others interested in automobiles produced by William C. Durant during the years 1921–1932. Cars include Durant, Star, Flint, Rugby (commercial and export), DeVaux, and Canadian Frontenac. Purpose is to gather and distribute information on main-*

> *tenance and restoration of these automobiles. Compiles statistics.*

Early Ford V-8 Club of America
Box 2122
San Leandro, CA 94577
(510) 606-1925
> *Persons interested in restoration of the early Ford V8 automobile.*

Eastern Museum of Motor Racing
1 Speedway Dr.
Mechanicsburg, PA 17055
(717) 528-8279, (717) 236-9577
Fax: (717) 236-0843
> *Individuals interested in the history of American auto racing and the preservation of auto racing artifacts. Operates museum that features restored vintage cars and other memorabilia. Restored race track for exhibition racing of vintage cars. Sponsors research projects; conducts educational programs. Maintains hall of fame.*

Eastern Packard Club
PO Box 5112
Hamden, CT 06518
(718) 324-8093
> *Enthusiasts and owners of Packard automobiles. Promotes the preservation and restoration of the Packard. Provides activities for the exchange of information on the history of the Packard automobile. Encourages participation in automobile shows and parades.*

Edsel Owner's Club
PO Box 6784
Fullerton, CA 92634
(714) 738-1958
> *Owners and others interested in the preservation and restoration of the Edsel automobile. The Edsel, produced by the Ford Motor Company in the late 1950s, was phased out of production in 1959. Local groups hold individual meets.*

Electric Auto Association
2710 SE Giles Ln.
Mountain View, CA 94040
(415) 591-6698, (800) 537-2882
> *Engineers, technicians, and hobbyists. Encourages development of electric vehicles for street use and sponsors public exhibitions of vehicles built by members. Conducts research on electric vehicles.*

Elva Owners of America
318 Adrian
Berea, OH 44017
(216) 243-2894

Individuals interested in Elva cars. Promotes the preservation and history of Elva cars. Sponsors competitions.

Erskine Register
441 E. St. Clair
Almont, MI 48003
(810) 798-8600
    Owners of Erskine cars, built by Studebaker from 1927 to 1930. Exchanges ideas and parts. Compiles statistics.

Fabulous Fifties Ford Club of America
PO Box 286
Riverside, CA 92502
(909) 591-2168
    Dedicated to the restoration, preservation, and enjoyment of passenger cars and commercial vehicles built by the Ford Motor Company in the years 1949–1960, including Lincolns, Edsels, and Mercuries.

Falcon Club of America
PO Box 113
Jacksonville, AR 72076
(501) 982-9721
    Owners of the Ford Falcon automobile devoted to its preservation and restoration. Provides a medium of exchange for ideas, technical information, and parts availability.

Ferrari Club of America
PO Box 720597
Atlanta, GA 30358
(800) 328-0444
Fax: (404) 936-9392
    Individuals and firms having an interest in Ferrari automobiles. Purposes are: to inspire ownership, operation, restoration, and preservation of Ferrari automobiles; to serve members as a source of information regarding Ferrari history and technical data; to organize meets and exhibits; to assist members in locating Ferrari automobiles and parts.

Ferrari Data Bank
Rte. 3, Box 425
Jasper, FL 32052
(904) 792-2480
Fax: (904) 792-3230
    Owners, clubs, dealers, and enthusiasts of Ferrari automobiles manufactured from 1948 to the present. Collects and publishes data on individual Ferrari cars. Acts as an information resource; compiles statistics; maintains museum.

Ferrari Owners Club
8642 Cleta St.
Downey, CA 90241-5201
(619) 462-1254

Fax: (619) 462-1217
    Ferrari owners and enthusiasts. Promotes and seeks to further the enjoyment of the Ferrari automobile. Sponsors special events.

Fiat Club of America
PO Box 192
Somerville, MA 02143-0004
(617) 776-8576
    Persons who own or who are interested in Fiat cars. Activities include information exchange and social and educational meetings. Maintains a list of dealers giving discounts to members.

Fiero Owners Club of America
2165 S. Dupont Dr., No. I
Anaheim, CA 92806-6103
(714) 978-3132
Fax: (714) 978-3059
    Pontiac Fiero automobile owners interested in learning more about the Fiero, produced by Pontiac between 1984 and 1988. Provides a network for the sharing of knowledge and information through publications, rallies, conventions, and local chapters. Maintains museum-archive and hall of fame. Compiles statistics; conducts research programs.

Fifty 567 Club Inc.
2021 Wiggins Ave.
Saskatoon, SK S7J 1W2
Canada
(306) 343-0567
Fax: (306) 343-5670
    Owners and enthusiasts of 1955, 1956, and 1957 Chevrolets, including Chevy and GMC trucks, Corvettes, and Pontiacs. Provides advice and technical information on how to locate parts and build vehicles; locate and build vehicles and parts. Coordinates events enabling interested individuals to convene and exchange information. Compiles statistics.

FOMOCO Owners Club
3633 Akron Ct.
Loveland, CO 80538
(303) 669-8767
    Individuals dedicated to the exhibition, preservation, and restoration of Edsel, Ford, Lincoln, and Mercury automobiles. Conducts charitable activities; sponsors educational programs. Bestows awards.

Ford Galaxie Club of America
PO Box 360
Salkum, WA 98582-0360
(206) 985-7675
    Owners and admirers of the Galaxie automobile, built by the Ford Motor Company between the years 1959 and 1974. Promotes

the restoration, preservation, and enjoyment of Galaxies; seeks to unite Galaxie owners.

Formula One Spectators Association
8033 Sunset Blvd., No. 60
Los Angeles, CA 90046
(818) 982-9529
Fax: (818) 982-9529

Individuals interested in Formula One (Grand Prix) auto racing. Works to secure more thorough press coverage of the sport of Formula One racing. Compiles information files on Formula One circuits for use by members. Maintains seat reservation service and information centers at Formula One events; offers special tours and travel packages.

Gardner Registry
228 Revell Rd.
Grenada, MS 38901
(601) 226-9060

Individuals interested in the Gardner automobile, produced in St. Louis, Missouri, between 1920–1931. Promotes the study and preservation of the Gardner automobile. Maintains registry of the vehicles; offers clearinghouse of information on cars and parts available. Compiles statistics.

Graham Owners Club International
c/o Roberta Heath
5262 NW Westgate Rd.
Silverdale, WA 98383
(360) 692-2149

Owners of Graham, Graham Paige, Graham Brothers antique automobiles and trucks, and others interested in the Graham-Paige marque. Compiles statistics.

GTO Association of America
5829 Stroebel Rd.
Saginaw, MI 48609
(800) GTO-1964

Persons owning or interested in Pontiac GTO and GT-37 automobiles produced between 1964 and 1974. Promotes the preservation and restoration of GTO automobiles. Appoints technical advisors to assist members with repair and restoration of their cars. Sponsors swap meet and competitions at which members' cars are judged. Maintains library of service manuals, books, sales literature, advertisements, and press releases for member use. Compiles statistics on GTO production.

Gullwing Group International
PO Box 1569
Morgan Hills, CA 95038-1569
(408) 776-1788
Fax: (408) 776-1788

Owners of either a Mercedes-Benz 300SL Gullwing Coupe or Mercedes-Benz 300SL Roadster; associate members need not own a car. Seeks to maintain and preserve, to the highest standards, the type 300SL Mercedes-Benz automobile, manufactured from 1954 through 1963. Holds technical instruction sessions.

H. H. Franklin Club
Cazenovia College
Cazenovia, NY 13035
(703) 768-8437

Works to collect and publish the history of the Franklin and other air-cooled automobiles of the period. Encourages preservation of such cars and related material. Maintains library of Franklin Car Company.

Haynes-Apperson Owners Club
3256 S. 400 W
Kokomo, IN 46902
(317) 883-5939

Owners of Haynes-Apperson, Haynes, and Apperson automobiles. Objectives are to provide information to owners and to keep a record of all Haynes and Apperson cars still in existence. Gives lectures; compiles statistics. Maintains museum and 100-volume library including catalogs, papers, and biographical archives.

Henry Nyberg Society
17822 Chicago Ave.
Lansing, IL 60438
(708) 474-3416
Fax: (708) 474-3416

Individuals interested in auto manufacturer Henry Nyberg and the vehicles he designed and produced between 1903 and 1913. Promotes research, education, and scientific activities associated with the design, production, preservation, and acquisition of the Nyberg automobile, truck, fire apparatus, race car, and motorcycle. Collects information, photographs, artifacts, advertisements, and items related to Nyberg vehicles for public display in museums; disseminates information to the public.

Historic Motor Sports Association
PO Box 30628
Santa Barbara, CA 93130
(805) 966-9151
Fax: (805) 966-5028

Individuals interested in auto racing history. Conducts races each June and August in Monterey, California.

Horseless Carriage Club of America
128 S. Cypress St.
Orange, CA 92666-1314

(714) 538-HCCA
Fax: (714) 538-5764

> *Hobbyists who are interested in the preservation, accessories, archives, and romantic lore of old cars. Sponsors four annual tours and three swap meets for larger cars and for one- and two-cylinder cars. Maintains museum.*

Hubcappers

Box 54
Buckley, MI 49620
(616) 269-3555

> *Persons interested in preserving a piece of automotive history through the collecting of threaded hubcaps manufactured prior to 1930. Objective is to try to locate as many of these hubcaps as possible.*

Hudson-Essex-Terraplane Club

100 E. Cross St.
Ypsilanti, MI 48198
(313) 482-5200

> *Persons from 21 countries interested in preserving and restoring automobiles built by the Hudson Motor Car Company from 1909 to 1957, including the Hudson, Essex, Terraplane, Dover, Jet, Railton, Brough Superior, and any of the custom body styles built during the classic era from 1925 to 1936.*

Hurst/Olds Club of America

c/o Steve LaCoe
1600 Knight Rd.
Ann Arbor, MI 48103-9371
(517) 337-0444, (313) 994-8778

> *Hurst/Olds enthusiasts. Seeks to perpetuate interest in and promote preservation of Hurst/Olds automobiles, which have been produced since 1968 by the Oldsmobile Division of the General Motors Corporation. Maintains Hurst/Olds registry. Holds car shows in conjunction with the Oldsmobile Club of America.*

Inliners International

c/o Walter Skoczylas
20045 SW Jaylee St.
Aloha, OR 97007-2864
(503) 642-9513
Fax: (503) 642-9513

> *Admirers, collectors, racers and mechanics of inline engines. Acts as a forum for the exchange of information on inline engines.*

International Camaro Club

2001 Pittston Ave.
Scranton, PA 18505
(717) 585-4082

> *Chevrolet Camaro enthusiasts and local Camaro clubs. Provides a forum for the exchange of information and parts. Sponsors shows and rallies. Operates Trim Tag ID Project, which compiles codes for trim tags that appear on the Camaro; these codes are used to aid in restorations and purchasing of cars. Maintains a pace car registry.*

International Edsel Club

c/o Murray and Judy Zegers
PO Box 371
Sully, IA 50251
(515) 594-4284

> *Individuals in 11 countries interested in the preservation, restoration, and collection of Edsels. Distributes information.*

International Ford Retractable Club

PO Box 389
Marlborough, MA 01752
(508) 460-5101

> *Individuals interested in the Ford retractable hardtop automobile (ownership not necessary). Purposes are: to increase interest in and encourage restoration and preservation of 1957–59 Ford Skyliner retractable hardtops; to exchange historical and technical information, buying tips, and parts location. Holds competitions. Conducts research and educational programs. Compiles statistics.*

International Hot Rod Association (IHRA)

PO Box 3029
Bristol, TN 37625
(423) 764-1164
Fax: (423) 764-4460

> *Promotes safety and encourages sportsman participation in drag racing. Through the sanctioning of numerous drag strips throughout the country, strives to be the most responsive organization of its kind for both promoters and competitors. Conducts IHRA World Championship Series for professional and sportsman drag racers. Sponsors competitions and compiles statistics.*

International Mercury Owners Association

6445 W. Grand Ave.
Chicago, IL 60635-3410
(312) 622-6445
Fax: (312) 622-3602

> *Owners of, and individuals interested in, Mercury automobiles. Offers owners and collectors assistance in locating parts, sharing information, and buying/selling cars. Sponsors national car shows.*

International Motor Sports Association

PO Box 10709
Tampa, FL 33679
(813) 877-4672
Fax: (813) 876-4604

Governing body for four separate and distinctly different series of auto races: EXXON World Sports Car Championship with exotic and domestic sports car; EXXON Supreme GT Championship comprised of production-based cars; Supercar Championship comprised of purebred luxury sports cars; and Street Stock Endurance Championship, which features the best American, Japanese, and European sports coupes and sedans. Sponsors competitions and compiles statistics.

International Society of Corvette Owners

PO Box 740614
Orange City, FL 32774
(904) 775-1203
Fax: (904) 775-3042

Devoted Corvette and Chevy owners. Offers advice on Corvette restoration. Sponsors car meets and seminars. Certification of Corvettes and Chevys.

International Society for Vehicle Preservation

PO Box 50046
Tucson, AZ 85703
(602) 622-2201

Car clubs; automobile restorers and preservationists; automotive engineers and historians; interested others. Seeks to collect and preserve information related to the origin and development of self-propelled vehicles. Promotes preservation of self-propelled vehicles, literature, artifacts, and related products. Sanctions and conducts world class concours d'elegances and educational seminars. Is developing the International Museum of Self-Propelled Vehicles; plans to offer research services through an online database.

International Specialty Car Association

Rte. 3
Star Kustom Ave., No. 2
Afton, OK 74331
(918) 257-4233
Fax: (918) 257-8224

Owners of customized vehicles who exhibit these autos in sanctioned events; car enthusiasts. Provides show-related information and standard judging and classification rules; works with show producers on behalf of membership and acts as a service organization to producing companies. Sanctions Auto Shows. Organizes and oversees competitions; seeks sponsorships for competition winners; maintains competition point standings based on members' individual show statistics.

International Thunderbird Club

8 Stag Train
Fairfield, NJ 07004
(201) 227-1770

Seeks to encourage the use and preservation of classic and antique Thunderbirds. Researches and disseminates information; conducts educational programs; holds competitions.

Iso and Bizzarrini Owners Club

c/o Don Goldman
7853 Starling Dr.
San Diego, CA 92123
(619) 560-4370

Owners and enthusiasts of the high-speed automobiles Iso (manufactured from 1963 to 1974) and Bizzarrini (manufactured from 1966 to 1971) automobiles, including the Bizzarrini GT America, Bizzarrini GT 1900, Iso Fidia, Iso Grifo, Iso Lele, and Iso Rivolta. Encourages the preservation and restoration of the automobiles; promotes appreciation of the marques. Bestows awards; maintains biographical archives; compiles statistics.

Italian Car Registry

3305 Valley Vista Rd.
Walnut Creek, CA 94598-3943
(510) 458-1163

Individuals, museums, and organizations owning or interested in preserving unusual Italian automobiles. Records histories of Italian cars; brings together owners of similar types of low-production Italian cars. Conducts research; collects and distributes information.

Jaguar Clubs of North America

Jaguar Cars Inc.
555 MacArthur Blvd.
Mahwah, NJ 07430
(201) 818-8144
Fax: (201) 818-0281

Jaguar clubs in U.S. and Canada representing a combined membership of 5200. Works to: foster and encourage a spirit of mutual interest and assistance for Jaguar automobile enthusiasts; promote public interest in motoring and motor sports; develop road safety; encourage an improved understanding of traffic laws; promote social and motoring events. Conducts individual vehicle history search services.

Jensen Interceptor Owners Club

8007 Aramara
Austin, TX 78750
(512) 338-1144, (800) 553-6736
Fax: (512) 338-1174

Owners and enthusiasts of the Jensen Interceptor automobile. Promotes public interest in the Jensen Interceptor; provides forum for information exchange. Makes spare parts available. Holds rallies and other social events; conducts workshops and seminars.

Jewett Owners Club
24005 Clawiter Rd.
Hayward, CA 94545
(510) 785-8433
Fax: (510) 783-3690
Owners of Jewett automobiles manufactured by the Paige Company from 1922 to 1927. Assists members in locating Jewett automobiles and parts. Maintains registry; distributes technical information.

Jordan Register
58 Bradford Blvd., Colonial Heights
Yonkers, NY 10710
(914) 337-5624
Owners and enthusiasts of Jordan automobiles, manufactured in Cleveland, Ohio, from 1916 to 1931. Seeks to expand information about the Jordan automobile and the life of Edward S. "Ned" Jordan (1882–1958), the company founder. (Jordan is recognized as having revolutionized auto advertising by shifting emphasis away from mechanical performance toward image and appeal to young professionals and women, focusing on "the sizzle instead of the steak." According to the group, information on Jordan is limited because he destroyed much of it in the wake of federal investigations into his commingling of company and personal funds.) Holds informal gatherings at flea markets and local and national auto shows. Compiles statistics.

The Judge GTO International
114 Prince George Dr.
Hampton, VA 23669
(804) 838-2059
Owners and admirers of 1969–71 Pontiac GTO Judge automobiles. Seeks to preserve the GTO Judge. Offers parts service; aids in restoration; provides advice; encourages collection of memorabilia; compiles statistics.

Kaiser-Darrin Owners Roster
RD 3, Box 36
Antram Rd.
Somerset, PA 15501-8814
(814) 445-6135
Fax: (814) 443-6468
Persons who own or are interested in preserving and restoring the Kaiser-Darrin, a limited production, two-seater, fiberglass bodied sportscar built by the Kaiser-Willys Corporation; only 435 Kaiser-Darrins were produced during its brief 1954 model year production run. Seeks to promote communication between owners for restoration help, maintenance advice, sources for parts, and support of parts remanufacturing projects. Conducts educational programs.

Kaiser-Frazer Owners Club International
2375 Leisure Lake Dr.
Atlanta, GA 30338
Persons who own or are interested in preserving and restoring Kaiser, Frazer, Henry-J, Allstate, and postwar Willys automobiles. Aids in problems of car maintenance, locating parts, and acquiring or trading cars. Maintains library of literature on Kaiser-Frazer automobiles.

Karmann-Ghia Registry
5705 Gordon Dr.
Harrisburg, PA 17112
Fax: (717) 540-9972
Karmann-Ghia automobile owners.

Kissel Kar Klub
147 N. Rural St.
Hartford, WI 53027
(414) 673-7999
Owners of automobiles manufactured by the Kissel Motor Car Co. of Hartford, Wisconsin (1906–1931); former Kissel officers and employees. Works to: protect the Kissel name; maintain a list of surviving Kissel-built motor cars; authenticate the model years of members' cars; assemble pertinent history and assist historians, librarians, and authors with accurate information; aid owners in restoring cars and obtaining parts; help prospective owners locate Kissel cars. Maintains library of magazine articles, copies of company records, and correspondence with company officers.

Kustom Kemps of America
RR 1, Box 1521A
Bill Hailey Dr.
Cassville, MO 65625-9724
(417) 847-2940, (417) 847-4998
Fax: (417) 847-3647
Enthusiasts of custom cars and trucks from 1935 to 1964. (Kemp is slang from the late 1950s indicating a customized car or truck.) Seeks to restore and manufacture custom cars of the hot-rodding industry. Operates Late Model Smoothie Division for nonstock cars and trucks produced from 1965 to the present. Maintains hall of fame.

Lagonda Club, U.S. Section
3237 Harvey Pky.
Oklahoma City, OK 73118-8652
(405) 232-3100
Fax: (405) 272-9381
Individuals who own or are interested in Lagonda cars. Purpose is to promote and preserve these cars. Maintains spare parts program. Sponsors rallies, races, and concours. Compiles statistics.

Lamborghini Club America
1 Northwood Dr.
Orinda, CA 94563-1613
(510) 254-2107
Fax: (510) 254-9397
> *Lamborghini automobile owners and enthusiasts. Provides assistance in locating parts and reputable service facilities. Disseminates information; sponsors social gatherings.*

Land Rover Owners Association, U.S.A.
PO Box 1144
Paradise, CA 95967-1144
(510) 569-8879
> *Owners and enthusiasts of Land Rover and Range Rover vehicles. Seeks to bring Land Rover owners together for outdoor activities and information sharing. Provides parts and technical information. Exchanges newsletters with Land Rover organizations worldwide. Conducts technical sessions; coordinates social gatherings.*

Late Great Chevrolet Association
PO Box 607824
Orlando, FL 32860
(800) 683-1961, (407) 886-1963
Fax: (407) 886-7571
> *Seeks to preserve and restore 1958–1964 Chevrolets. Sponsors competitions; supplies a variety of reproduction parts for restoration.*

Les Amis de Panhard and Deutsch Bonnet
c/o Andre L. Garnier
PO Box 1172
Minneola, FL 34755
(904) 394-7797
> *Owners and fans of DB and Panhard automobiles, which are of French manufacture. (The DB is named after Charles Deutsch and Rene Bonnet, who built fiberglass coupes and roadsters, using Panhard running gear and power train, from about 1957 to 1963.)*

Lincoln and Continental Owners Club
PO Box 157
Boring, OR 97009
(503) 658-3119, (800) 281-6606
> *Persons interested in preserving and restoring Lincolns and Continentals. Provides information on location and exchange of replacement parts and restoration service.*

Lincoln Owners Club
c/o Tom Powels
6933 Yolanda
Reseda, CA 91335
(818) 343-7332
> *Persons interested in preserving and restoring Lincoln cars produced from 1920–1940, ending with the K Series cars and not including the Zephyr or Continental.*

Lincoln Zephyr Owner's Club
PO Box 16-5835
Miami, FL 33116
> *Persons who own, or are interested in, the Lincoln-Zephyr automobile circa 1936–48. Promotes the preservation, restoration, and exhibition of this automobile class, including all cars that were based on the Zephyr mechanical elements.*

London Vintage Taxi Association—American Section
PO Box 1213
Hartwell, GA 30643-6213
(706) 376-3414
> *Owners and enthusiasts of retired taxicabs of London. Seeks to promote the restoration and preservation of vintage London taxis. Facilitates the exchange of technical information. Maintains historical records and restoration parts and data.*

Lotus
PO Box L
College Park, MD 20741
(301) 982-4054
Fax: (301) 982-4054
> *Owners and enthusiasts of Lotus automobiles (ownership not required for membership). Objective is to provide and exchange information on Lotus cars.*

Marlin Owners' Club
Rte. 5, Box 187
Coatesville, PA 19320
(215) 383-4664
> *Owners and enthusiasts of American Motors Corporation Rambler Marlin automobiles. Is concerned with the preservation and restoration of vehicles made by AMC or predecessors. Compiles and disseminates literature; collects items related to Marlin cars.*

Marmon Club
3044 Gainsborough Dr.
Pasadena, CA 91107
(818) 449-2325
> *Persons interested in the history, preservation, driving, and restoration of Marmon and Roosevelt automobiles built in the years 1902–1933.*

Maserati Information Exchange
Box 1015
Mercer Island, WA 98040
(206) 455-4449
> *Owners and enthusiasts of Maserati sports automobiles, manufactured in Italy from 1926*

to the present. Provides members with information and technical assistance and conducts meets. Maintains $10 million inventory of new and used parts. Publishes quarterly magazine (80 pages) for membership.

Maserati Owners Club of North America
Box 6554
Orange, CA 92667
Owners and enthusiasts of Maseratis. Provides forum for social contact between members. Disseminates technical information.

Mercedes-Benz Club of America
1907 Lelaray St.
Colorado Springs, CO 80909
(719) 633-6427, (800) 637-2360
Fax: (719) 633-9283
Owners and others interested in Mercedes-Benz cars. Sponsors national events and local section rallies, concours d'elegance, and gymkhanas. Provides technical information on maintenance and parts. Conducts educational and research programs; sponsors charitable activities.

Mercury Enthusiast Restorer Custom Performance Auto Club
Rte. 4, PO Box 116
Alexandria, IN 46001
(317) 724-7601
Owners of Mercury Comet, Meteor, and Montego automobiles manufactured between 1960–78; owners of larger class Mercury vehicles produced between 1939–78. Provides technical assistance to members wishing to restore Mercury automobiles; conducts research. Maintains library, museum, and hall of fame; sponsors charitable programs. Compiles statistics; sponsors competitions.

Metropolitan Owners Club of North America
5009 Barton Rd.
Madison, WI 53711
(608) 271-0457
Fax: (608) 833-2058
Seeks to preserve the Metropolitan automobile produced by Austin Motor Co., Ltd. of Birmingham, England for American Motors, Inc. between 1954 and 1961. Disseminates information concerning restoration and maintenance of the Metropolitan.

Metz Owners Club Library
2055 7 Lakes S.
Seven Lakes, NC 27376
Assists persons restoring or seeking information on Metz vehicles. Maintains extensive library. The Metz Co. manufactured automobiles from 1909 to 1921 and also produced motorcycles, light trucks, and an airplane.

Mid-Century Mercury Car Club
4411 Harrison Rd.
Kenosha, WI 53142
(414) 652-5621
Individuals united to promote the appreciation and preservation of the 1949–51 Mercury car, stock or custom.

Midstates Jeepster Association
12700 W. Cortez Dr.
New Berlin, WI 53151
(219) 326-5589
Seeks to promote the restoration of the Willys-Overland Jeepster. Supplies information and parts to be shared by all club members.

Midwest Sunbeam Registry
20700 Huntington Way
Prior Lake, MN 55372-9725
(612) 440-6300
Fax: (612) 440-5700
Collectors and enthusiasts of Sunbeam Alpine and Tiger sports cars throughout the U.S. who preserve and restore Sunbeam Alpine and Tiger sports cars manufactured in England. Promotes good fellowship among members through car-related activities. Conducts technical training sessions. Compiles statistics.

Milestone Car Society
PO Box 24612
Speedway, IN 46224
(314) 344-8520
Multi-marque automobile society established for the enjoyment of selected, nominated milestone era (1945–72) foreign and domestic cars.

Mini Registry
395 Summit Point Dr.
Henrietta, NY 14467-9606
(716) 359-1400
Fax: (716) 359-1428
Owners of Austin or Morris Mini automobiles or Mini variants. Maintains historical records and biographical archives.

Model A Drivers
c/o Paul Mastalir
PO Box 83
Shawano, WI 54166
(715) 524-3180
Individuals interested in purchasing and restoring the Model A Ford automobile, which was built from 1928 to 1931, with the intent to operate the vehicle.

Model A Ford Cabriolet Club
PO Box 515
Porter, TX 77365
(713) 429-2505

A special interest group of the Model A Ford Club of America and a Special Body Style Interest Region of the Model "A" Restorers Club. Owners and enthusiasts of the Cabriolet dedicated to its restoration and preservation. (Cabriolets are a rare body style of the Model A Ford manufactured from 1928 through 1931.) Provides for the collection and dissemination of information and parts. Compiles statistics; encourages gatherings at antique car shows. Ownership of a Cabriolet is not required.

Model A Ford Club of America

250 S. Cypress
La Habra, CA 90631
(213) 697-2712
Fax: (213) 690-7452
> Persons interested in restoring and preserving Model A Ford cars (1928–31).

Model A Ford Foundation

184 Steeple Chase Cir.
Sanford, FL 32771
(407) 322-2435
> Promotes the preservation of the Model A Ford and its era (1928–1931). Conducts charitable, educational, and research programs; maintains speakers' bureau and museum.

Model "A" Restorers Club

24800 Michigan Ave.
Dearborn, MI 48124
(313) 278-1455
> Automotive enthusiasts interested in preserving Model A Ford cars and trucks and related literature and accessories. (The Model A was produced between 1928 and 1931). Compiles statistics.

Model "T" Ford Club of America

PO Box 743936
Dallas, TX 75374-3936
(214) 783-7531
Fax: (214) 783-7531
> Individuals interested in the restoration and operation of the Model T Ford. Maintains collection of catalogs, photos, and pamphlets. Compiles statistics.

Model T Ford Club International

PO Box 438315
Chicago, IL 60643
> Hobbyists interested in the preservation and restoration of antique Model T Ford automobiles. Sponsors restoration, photography, and safety slogan contests. Local groups conduct activities including tours, restoration contest, parades, and parts exchanges.

Mopar Muscle Club International

879 Summerlea Ave.
Washington, PA 15301
(412) 225-5790
> Persons with an interest in Chrysler Corporation automobiles. Dedicated to the restoration and preservation of Chrysler's high-performance and regular production vehicles. Compiles statistics.

Mopar Scat Pack Club

PO Box 2303
Dearborn, MI 48123
(313) 563-5974
Fax: (313) 493-4700
> Individuals dedicated to the preservation and restoration of Chrysler high-performance cars. Collects and shares information and statistics on parts, technical matters, and car history. Sponsors shows, swap meets, and races. Offers members discounts on parts and services, restoration tips, and technical seminars at sponsored events. Compiles lists of Chrysler high-performance car production figures and parts needed for sale nationwide. Maintains historical collection of parts books, dealer brochures, and pictures.

Mopar Trans-Am Association

313 N. Stewart Rd.
Liberty, MO 64068
(816) 781-0095
> Individuals who own Chrysler automobiles. Makes available spare parts.

Morgan Car Club

616 Gist Ave.
Silver Spring, MD 20910
(301) 585-0121
> Morgan car owners, past owners, parts suppliers, and other interested parties. Promotes interest in the Morgan automobile; encourages fellowship among Morgan owners, drivers, and enthusiasts. Compiles statistics; maintains placement service.

Morgan Owners Register

c/o Richard D. Larrick
442 Haverhill Rd.
Lancaster, PA 17601
(717) 569-4448
> Owners of Morgan automobiles. Registers and sponsors research on Morgan automobiles. Maintains speakers' bureau; compiles statistics. Maintains a parts exchange program.

Morgan Plus Four Club

5073 Melbourne Dr.
Cypress, CA 90630
(714) 828-3127

Owners of Morgan cars. Enjoys and promotes the Morgan car.

Morgan Three-Wheeler Club—U.S.A Group
3708 California Ave.
Long Beach, CA 90807
(213) 595-6179
Owners and enthusiasts of Morgan three-wheeled automobiles, made in England from 1910 to 1952. Promotes the preservation of Morgan three-wheelers. Offers technical advice.

Morris Minor Registry
318 Hampton Park
Westerville, OH 43081-5723
(614) 899-2394
Fax: (614) 899-2394
Owners of Morris Minor automobiles and interested individuals united for mutual assistance in finding parts for and repairing the cars. Compiles statistics on the Morris Minor automobiles still on the road in the U.S. and Canada.

Muntz Registry
21303 NE 151st St.
Woodinville, WA 98072-7612
(206) 788-6587
Conducts research and disseminates information concerning the history, current ownership, restoration, and needed and available parts for Muntz jet automobiles, which were produced from 1951–53. Compiles statistics.

Mustang Club of America
PO Box 447
Lithonia, GA 30058
(404) 482-4822
Fax: (770) 682-9955
Owners and enthusiasts of Ford Mustang and Shelby automobiles produced since 1964. Purpose is to preserve and maintain Ford Mustang and Shelby cars and to serve as an accurate technical source of information concerning these automobiles. Offers restoration and maintenance advice. Sponsors camp-outs and other group events; holds a buy-sell-swap forum. Operates charitable program.

Mustang Owners Club International
2720 Tennessee NE
Albuquerque, NM 87110
(505) 296-2554
Owners and enthusiasts with an interest in the preservation and promotion of Ford Mustangs produced since 1965.

Nash Car Club of America
4151 220th St.
Clinton, IA 52732-8943
(319) 242-5490

Persons interested in Nash cars and their history. Purpose is to aid and promote the preservation and restoration of Nash and related vehicles. Maintains listing of reproduced parts and library research service. Provides advisors for nearly all models and years. Conducts restoration workshops. Holds regional and national meets, tours, and picnics.

National American Motors Drivers and Racers Association
PO Box 987
Twin Lakes, WI 53181-0987
(414) 396-9552
AMC automobile owners. Promotes use of AMC and Jeep vehicles in drag race competitions; sponsors car shows, swap meets, and races. Serves as information clearinghouse and parts exchange for members. Maintains library of owners' parts, shop manuals, and magazine articles on AMC vehicles. Bestows awards.

National Antique Oldsmobile Club
11730 Moffitt Ln.
Manassas, VA 22111-3122
Persons interested in Oldsmobile cars produced prior to 1964. Seeks to preserve Oldsmobile autos and encourage restoration of the cars. Promotes participation in events concerning Oldsmobiles.

National Association of Auto Racing Memorabilia Collectors
PO Box 12226
St. Petersburg, FL 33733
(813) 895-3482
Fax: (813) 895-3389
Collectors, hobbyists, and historians interested in auto racing memorabilia who participate in the annual Day Before the 500 Meet in Indianapolis, Indiana. Encourages and facilitates trading, buying, and selling among members. Maintains speakers' bureau.

National Association for Stock Car Auto Racing (NASCAR)
PO Box 2875
1801 Volusia Ave.
Daytona Beach, FL 32120-2875
(904) 253-0611
Fax: (904) 258-7646
To sanction and supervise stock car races. Compiles statistics.

National Auto Racing Historical Society
121 Mount Vernon
Boston, MA 02108
(617) 723-2661
Fax: (617) 227-5366
Auto racing historians. Assists advertising, public relations, and other media personnel in

using antique autos or automotive historical themes.

National Chevelle Owners Association

7343-J W. Friendly Ave.
Greensboro, NC 27410
(910) 854-8935

Individuals dedicated to the preservation of stock, modified, and custom 1964–1987 Chevelles and El Caminos. Offers technical and factory information and listings of parts available to members.

National Chrysler Products Club

c/o Patricia Murray
790 Marigold Ave.
Southampton, PA 18966

Collectors and fanciers of Chrysler Corporation product antique autos and trucks (Chrysler, Imperial, DeSoto, Dodge, Plymouth, Maxwell, and Chalmers). Objectives are: the preservation, restoration, exhibition, and use of Chrysler product cars and trucks; the collection, recording, and preservation of Chrysler product historical data; the dissemination to the public of the story of Chrysler Corporation contributions to the automotive industry. Sponsors competitions; compiles statistics.

National Corvette Owners Association

PO Box 777-A
Falls Church, VA 22046
(703) 533-7222
Fax: (703) 533-1153

Corvette owners and enthusiasts united to encourage and increase the enjoyment and popularity of Corvette automobiles. Provides members with benefits such as insurance, interior discounts, and auto supply discounts. Maintains reference book collection.

National Corvette Restorers Society

6291 Day Rd.
Cincinnati, OH 45252
(513) 385-8526
Fax: (513) 385-8554

Purposes are the preservation, restoration, and enjoyment of Corvettes produced from 1953 thru 1982 and of all related material. Encourages and publishes studies and research pertaining to their development and history. Conducts research projects and technical sessions. Compiles statistics.

National Council of Corvette Clubs

PO Box 813
Adams Basin, NY 14410
(800) 245-VETT

Federation of clubs of owners of Corvette automobiles. Raffles a new Corvette each year

with proceeds benefitting the Spina Bifida Association of America . Compiles statistics. Sanctions a full calendar of events.

National Demolition Derby Association

Tower Hill, IL 62571
(217) 567-3632

Seeks to develop standards of conduct and rules for the sport of demolition derbies. Trains officials; awards victory points for the top drivers.

National DeSoto Club

1521 Van Cleave NW
Albuquerque, NM 87107
(505) 344-6932, (404) 394-9578
Fax: (505) 344-6932

Owners and enthusiasts of the DeSoto car, manufactured 1928–61 by the Chrysler Corporation; companies selling or servicing antique automobiles. Encourages the preservation and restoration of the DeSoto. Assists members in locating complete vehicles and automobile parts. Maintains collection of sales literature and technical information on the DeSoto.

National Firebird Club

PO Box 11238
Chicago, IL 60611
(312) 769-6262
Fax: (312) 769-6262

Owners of Firebird automobiles, produced since 1967 by the Pontiac division of the General Motors Corporation. Promotes the magic of Firebird. Disseminates technical and historical information on the Firebird; acts as a Firebird registry. Conducts technical sessions; sponsors competitions.

National Hemi Owners Association

c/o Pete Haldiman
3732 Elm Ave.
Long Beach, CA 90807

Individuals interested in the preservation of Chrysler hemispherical head engines produced from 1951 to 1958 and from 1966 to 1971. Provides assistance in finding car and engine parts and technical and general information.

National Hot Rod Association (NHRA)

2035 Financial Way
Glendora, CA 91740
(818) 914-4761
Fax: (818) 963-5360

Persons interested in automobiles modified and designed for performance and acceleration. Sets competition rules and construction guidelines; sponsors regional and national drag races; conducts world championship points tournament and certifies official records. Conducts design and safety research; provides automotive data. Emphasizes safety, ingenuity, and sportsmanship in races and on the road; encourages civic activities by local groups. Sanctions racing events at 150 tracks in the U.S. and Canada. Maintains photographic file. Produces 15 television shows based on national racing events.

National Impala Association

830 3rd St.
PO Box 968
Spearfish, SD 57783
(605) 642-5864
Fax: (605) 642-5868

Owners of full-size automobiles manufactured by Chevrolet from 1958–69. Provides technical advisory staff and parts inventory for individuals wishing to restore full-size Chevys.

National Indy 500 Collectors Club

10505 N. Delaware St.
Indianapolis, IN 46280
(317) 848-4750

Individuals interested in auto racing and history of the Indianapolis motor speedway. Promotes and operates programs to preserve the history of the Indianapolis speedway. Conducts research programs.

National Institute for Automotive Service Excellence (ASE)

13505 Dulles Technology Dr.
Herndon, VA 22071-3415
(703) 713-3800
Fax: (703) 713-0727

Governed by a 40-member board of directors selected from all sectors of the automotive service industry and from education, government, and consumer groups. Encourages and promotes the highest standards of automotive service in the public interest. Conducts continuing research to determine the best methods for training automotive technicians; encourages the development of effective training programs. Tests and certifies the competence of automobile, medium/heavy truck, collision repair, and engine machinist technicians as well as parts specialists.

National Monte Carlo Owners Association

c/o Larry Ashcraft
PO Box 187
Independence, KY 41051
(606) 491-2378

Owners of all types of Monte Carlo automobiles, produced by the Chevrolet division of General Motors Corporation. Compiles statistics.

National Muscle Car Association

3404 Democrat Rd.
Memphis, TN 38118
(901) 365-3779
Fax: (901) 366-1807

Owners of and individuals interested in muscle cars. Offers an equitable set of standards by which all types of muscle cars can compete. Sponsors drag races and car shows. Compiles statistics on performance and participants. Sponsors Save the Muscle awareness coalition for anti-old car legislation.

National Nostalgic Nova

PO Box 2344
York, PA 17405
(717) 252-4192

Individuals interested in the Chevrolet Nova and Chevy II. Promotes interest in the preservation, restoration, and history of the 1962–79 Chevy Nova. Provides for fellowship, distributes information, and makes parts available.

National Old Timers Auto Racing Club

PO Box 991
Flemington, NJ 08822
(908) 832-7885

Former race car drivers, owners, builders, members of the race media, and interested others. Promotes the preservation of auto racing history. Maintains National Auto Racing Hall of Fame and Museum.

National Sport Custom Registry

1306 Brick St.
Burlington, IA 52601
(319) 752-0420

Persons interested in the research, restoration, and preservation of 1950s-style sport custom cars. Provides technical, historical, and restoration assistance; compiles statistics.

National Street Rod Association

4030 Park Ave.
Memphis, TN 38111
(901) 452-4030

Street rod builders and enthusiasts. Conducts automotive events; attempts to influence state and federal legislation that is auto-oriented. (Street rods are modified antique cars using new automotive parts. They are designed for street use as family cars, however, and not for drag racing.) Annual events include: Street Rod Nationals; Street Rod Nationals North; Street Rod Nationals West; Street Rod Nationals East; Street Rod Nationals South; Mid-American Street Rod Nationals; Northwest Street Rod Nationals; Rocky Mountain Street Rod Nationals; Southeast Street Rod Nationals; Southwest Street Rod Nationals.

National Vehicle Conversion Association
1003 Maple Dr.
Greenfield, IN 46140-1224
(317) 462-5033
Fax: (317) 462-7525

Van conversion manufacturers and suppliers; auto dealers; consumers. Promotes education, standardization, and safety in the industry. Has written and implemented certification program for van conversion manufacturers. Encourages certification and plans to develop certification programs for suppliers and manufacturers that serve the transportation needs of the disabled and elderly.

National Woodie Club
PO Box 6134
Lincoln, NE 68506
(402) 488-0990

Owners, restorers, and aficionados of wood-bodied cars. Seeks to: promote interest in the beauty, usefulness, and uniqueness of wood-bodied cars; unite owners of these cars to exchange information and compare building techniques.

New England MG "T" Register Limited
Drawer 220
Oneonta, NY 13820
(607) 432-6835, (800) 252-7764
Fax: (607) 432-3342

People who own vintage MG automobiles. United to maintain, preserve, and enjoy their cars.

Nifty Fifties Ford Club
PO Box 142
Macedonia, OH 44056

Collectors and admirers of 1950's-era Ford vehicles. Membership limited to northeast Ohio.

1948–50 Packard Convertible Roster
84 Hoy Ave.
Fords, NJ 08863
(908) 738-7859
Fax: (908) 738-7625

Owners of 1948–50 Packard convertible automobiles; interested others. Promotes preservation and enjoyment of the automobiles.

1949–1959 Ford Products Club
6355 Johnanne St.
Columbus, OH 43229
(614) 891-5004

Individuals interested in products manufactured by the Ford Motor Company from 1949–59.

1970 Dart Swinger 340s Registry
PO Box 9

Wethersfield, CT 06129-0009
(203) 257-8434, (860) 257-8434,

Owners of 1970 Dodge Dart "Swinger 340" automobiles. Works to locate and authenticate all 13,785 1970 Dodge Dart Swinger 340s known to have been produced.

1971 GTO and Judge Convertible Registry
14906 Ferness Ln.
Channelview, TX 77530
(713) 452-0855

Owners of 1971 GTO or Judge Convertibles. Collects vehicle registry information to locate, verify, and record data on the number of these vehicles still existing.

1965–66 Full Size Chevrolet Club
15615 St. Rd. 23
Granger, IN 46530
(219) 272-6964

Owners and enthusiasts interested in the preservation and restoration of Chevrolet 1965–66 Caprice, Impala SS, Impala, Bel Air, and Biscayne automobiles. Holds local and regional swap meets.

Nineteen Thirty-Two Buick Registry
3000 Warren Rd.
Indiana, PA 15701
(412) 463-3372
Fax: (412) 463-8604

Owners of 1932 Buick automobiles. Collects and disseminates information; reproduces needed parts by sharing tooling expenses. Sponsors lectures; compiles statistics.

North American Auto Union Register
260 Santa Margarita Ave.
Menlo Park, CA 94025
(415) 323-3913

Provides history, parts, sources, and information on Auto Union and DKW automobiles. (DKW cars were manufactured in Germany from 1930 to 1965; the car is the forerunner of the present day Audi.)

North American English Ford Registry
513 Deubler Rd.
Camp Hill, PA 17011
(717) 737-1119

Owners and enthusiasts of English Ford automobiles. (English Fords are automobiles manufactured or sold in the U.K.; models include the Anglia, Prefect, Consul, Cortina, Thames, Escort, Popular, Corsair, Capri, Zephyr, and Zodiac.) Promotes enjoyment of English Ford automobiles through cooperation, information sharing, and mutual encouragement. Provides parts exchange and source information.

North American Mini Moke Registry
1779 Kickapoo St.
PO Box 9110
South Lake Tahoe, CA 96158
(916) 577-7895

Individuals who own or are interested in the Austin Mini Moke, an English automobile designed by Sir Alec Issigonis and first produced in 1964. Works to facilitate communication among members.

North American Opel GT Club
29W 682 Vale Rd.
West Chicago, IL 60185
(708) 231-4938

Individuals who own or are interested in Opel GT sports cars. Promotes preservation of all Opel model sports cars, especially the GT, which were last produced in 1973. Facilitates communication among members. Gathers and disseminates technical and parts location information.

Nostalgia Drag Racing Association
PO Box 9438
Anaheim, CA 92812
(714) 539-6372
Fax: (714) 539-8524

Promotes nostalgia drag races at locations around the U.S. which feature street rods, muscle cars, and antique racers manufactured prior to 1974. All vehicles welcome for Saturday time trials regardless of car year.

NSU Club of America
717 N. 68th St.
Seattle, WA 98103
(206) 784-5084

Owners and enthusiasts of NSU automobiles. (NSU is an acronym for Neckarsulm, the German city where the cars were manufactured.) Conducts educational programs; maintains museum.

NSU Enthusiasts U.S.A.
11192 Prouty Rd.
Concord, OH 44077

Owners and enthusiasts of NSU automobiles. NSU is an acronym for Neckarsulm, the German city where the automobiles were manufactured. Promotes the preservation of NSU cars; provides information on such cars including the availability of parts and other reference materials; promotes social activities among members. Conducts interchange of technical material. Maintains library of repair manuals.

Oakland-Pontiac Enthusiast Organization
3520 Warringham Dr.
Waterford, MI 48329-1380

(810) 623-7573
Fax: (810) 623-6180

Owners and enthusiasts dedicated to the preservation and restoration of Oakland and Pontiac automobiles over ten years old.

Opel Motorsport Club
c/o Richard Graham
5161 Gelding Cir.
Huntington Beach, CA 92649-3601
(714) 846-3793
Fax: (714) 846-3793

Owners and enthusiasts of Opel automobiles. (Opel automobiles have been manufactured in Russelsheim, Federal Republic of Germany since 1899.) Promotes the Opel automobile, friendships among members, sportsmanship, and competence in vehicle maintenance and operation. Facilitates information exchange, especially technical information regarding service and parts. Sponsors auto-crosses.

Organization of Bricklin Owners
PO Box 24775
Rochester, NY 14624
(716) 247-1575

Owners of Bricklin SV-1 motorcars united for assistance in the maintenance and preservation of their cars. Provides members with technical, accessory, and service and parts information available upon request.

Pacific Bantam Austin Club
1589 N. Grand Oaks Ave.
Pasadena, CA 91104
(818) 791-2617

Individuals interested in the preservation and restoration of the American Austin and Bantam automobiles. Also interested in pre-World War II British Austin "7s" and cars using genuine Austin and Bantam parts.

Packard Automobile Classics
84 Hoy Ave.
Fords, NJ 08863
(908) 738-7859
Fax: (908) 738-7625

Individuals interested in preserving and restoring Packard automobiles, which were produced between 1899 and 1958. Sponsors annual summer national tour.

Packard Data Bank
Rte. 3, PO Box 425
Jasper, FL 32052
(904) 792-2480
Fax: (904) 792-3230

Packard automobile owners, clubs, dealers, and enthusiasts. (Packard automobiles were manufactured from 1899 to 1958 by the Packard Motor Car Co.) Collects information on Packards and compiles a history of the Packard Motor Car Co. and its employees. Compiles statistics; operates museum.

Packard V-8 Roster,'55-'56
84 Hoy Ave.
Fords, NJ 08863
(908) 738-7859
Fax: (908) 738-7625
Serves as clearinghouse of information on 1955–56 Packard and Clipper automobiles. Compiles statistics.

Packards International Motor Car Club
302 French St.
Santa Ana, CA 92701
(714) 541-8431
Packard owners and enthusiasts dedicated to the driving enjoyment and preservation of Packard automobiles. Sponsors driving tours.

Pantera International
18586 Main St., Ste. 100
Huntington Beach, CA 92648
(714) 848-6674
Fax: (714) 843-5851
Owners of the de Tomaso Pantera automobile and interested individuals united to share technical information on the car.

Peerless Motor Car Club
1749 Baldwin Dr.
Millersville, MD 21108
(410)923-2606
Individuals interested in the preservation of antique luxury cars produced between 1903 and 1932 by the Peerless Motor Car Company in Cleveland, Ohio. (Referred to as one of the "three P's" along with Pierce Arrow and Packard, the Peerless was considered a luxury car of the highest quality from 1907 through 1920.) Fosters communication between members including the sharing of resources and voicing of individual restoration needs.

Performance Ford Club of America, Inc.
13155 U.S. Rte. 23
Ashville, OH 43103
(614) 983-2273
Fax: (614) 983-9691
Car collectors and restorers, race car enthusiasts, and truck and tractor pullers. Provides restoration, promotion, and maintenance of Ford-powered products. Conducts research on past and present products. Sponsors specialized education; holds competitions.

Peugeot Owners' Club
6649 E. 65th St.
Indianapolis, IN 46220-4301
(317) 845-5050

Owners or enthusiasts of French-built Peugeot automobiles united for sharing of technical information and experiences.

Pierce-Arrow Society
135 Edgerton St.
Rochester, NY 14607
(716) 244-1664
Owners and enthusiasts interested in Pierce-Arrow automobiles. Provides technical answering service and restoration assistance.

Pioneer Automobile Touring Club
374 Harvard Ave.
Palmerton, PA 18071
(610) 826-2622
Owners of automobiles manufactured in or before 1915. Promotes touring of vintage automobiles.

Plymouth Barracuda/Cuda Owners Club
c/o Connie Sager
64898 Lutz Rd.
Constantine, MI 49042
(908) 388-6442
Owners and others interested in the preservation and restoration of 1964–74 Plymouth Barracuda automobiles.

Plymouth Owners Club
c/o Jim Benjaminson
PO Box 416
Cavalier, ND 58220
(701) 549-3746
Fax: (701) 549-3744
Persons interested in the collection, preservation, and use of 1928–1970 Plymouth cars, 1937–1941 trucks, and Fargo commercial vehicles; Plymouth Division of Chrysler Corporation is an honorary member. Promotes authentic restoration and exhibition of early models; provides technical assistance and exchange of information. Sponsors competitions with judging in 12 classes. Provides technical advice and copy service of out-of-print Plymouth materials. Maintains roster of all 1928–1970 Plymouth cars and trucks and Fargo commercial vehicles.

Pontiac Drag Sports
22456 Van Buren St.
Grand Terrace, CA 92324
(909) 783-0866
Individuals interested in Pontiac drag racing vehicles. Promotes the sport of drag racing. Sponsors racing events; conducts fundraising activities.

Pontiac-Oakland Club International
PO Box 9569
Bradenton, FL 34206

(813) 750-9234

Fax: (813) 747-1341

Persons interested in the history, restoration, and preservation of Pontiac and Oakland automobiles. Assists owners of Pontiac and Oakland automobiles with the restoration of their vehicles. Maintains staff of volunteer technical advisers. Conducts research pertaining to original specifications and production history. Provides computerized services.

Porsche Club of America

PO Box 30100

Alexandria, VA 22310

(703) 922-9300

Fax: (703) 922-9617

Persons owning Porsche automobiles.

Powell Sport Wagon Registry

c/o Jeff Peterson

PO Box 27871

Tempe, AZ 85285

(602) 834-4643

Owners and enthusiasts of Powell Sport Wagon automobiles made by the Powell Brothers between 1955 and 1957. Promotes preservation and restoration of Powell Sport Wagons; maintains registry. Provides for parts and information exchange among members.

Pro Stock Owners Association

c/o Kirk Racing Cars, Inc.

155 E. Braod St., 19th Fl.

Columbus, OH 43215

Owners and drivers of Pro Stock racing cars. Promotes the Pro Stock as the "most technologically advanced of all the eliminators." Seeks to: improve the overall image of Pro Stock automobiles; increase professionalism in Pro Stock racing; modify Pro Stock racing in order to meet the standards of sanctioning bodies and to accommodate crews televising Pro Stock events.

Professional Car Society

PO Box 09636

Columbus, OH 43209

(614) 237-2350

Automobile collectors interested in vintage funeral, rescue, livery, and related professional vehicles. Seeks to preserve and enhance appreciation of vintage professional vehicles.

Profile Automobile League

15 Anita St.

Rochester, NH 03867-3304

(603) 332-5518

Collectors and restorers of antique automobiles. Conducts tours, meets, and flea markets. Maintains historical records.

ProJet Association

PO Box 72

Enfield, CT 06082-0072

(203) 280-8285, (203) 745-1870,

Fax: (203) 253-9830

Jet race car owners, drivers, and associates. Works to increase the public's awareness of jet race cars; promotes the sport of drag racing. Acts as liaison between jet car racers and sanctioning bodies. Oversees racing safety by monitoring including performance levels, licensing, maintainence, and operating procedures. Sponsors research programs. Maintains hall of fame and speaker's bureau.

The Ranchero Club

1339 Beverly Rd.

Port Vue, PA 15133

Owners and collectors of Rancheros, Falcon Sedan Deliverys, Courier Sedan Deliveries, and other car-based commercial vehicles produced by the Ford Motor Company from 1952 to the present. Promotes the restoration and preservation of these vehicles; provides limited assistance in restoration research. Offers advertising space to members for listing vehicles and other related items; maintains collection of original printed material on club vehicles; compiles statistics.

Ranchero-Torino Club

8307 E. Calexico St.

Tucson, AZ 85730

(520) 886-3511, (520) 886-6420,

Owners and enthusiasts of Ford motor vehicles. Promotes the restoration and preservation of Ford motor vehicles of all years and models. Disseminates information on Rancheros-Torinos and other Ford vehicles.

REO Club of America

115 Cherry Rd.

Chesnee, SC 29323

(803) 461-2894

Persons interested in REO automobiles and trucks. (REO cars were manufactured by the Ramson E. Olds Factory in Lansing, MI from 1905 to 1936; trucks were manufactured at the same plant until 1976.) Serves as a forum for exchange of ideas, information, and parts for owners and admirers of early REO trucks and cars; to help members restore and preserve their vehicles. Maintains staff of technical advisers.

Riley Motor Club U.S.A.

c/o Varlie Gordon

13511 Broadway

Whittier, CA 90601-3718

(310) 693-2867

Owners of Riley automobiles and motorcycles. Purposes are to: promote restoration and enjoyment of all vintages of Riley products surviving in the U.S. and Canada; establish sources of information and services and parts; pass on technical data, techniques, and experiences in restoration and maintenance; hold or participate in concours d'elegances, rallies, tours, and automobile display events.

Road Race Lincoln Register
c/o Burr Oxley
461 Woodland Dr.
Wisconsin Rapids, WI 54494
(715) 423-9579

Persons interested in Lincoln automobiles built from 1949 to 1957. Promotes restoration and preservation of these vehicles and provides members with information on restoration and parts availability. Maintains historical files of production information; disseminates historical information on the production and performance application of these vehicles.

Rolls-Royce Owners' Club
191 Hempt Rd.
Mechanicsburg, PA 17055
(717) 697-4671

Persons interested in preserving and restoring automobiles produced by Rolls-Royce Ltd., Rolls-Royce Motors, Ltd., Rolls-Royce of America, and Bentley Motors (1931) Ltd. To exchange technical, historical, and general information. Reprints owners' manuals and technical materials.

Rometsch Registry
2510 N. Larchmont, Dept. VWT
Santa Ana, CA 92706
(714) 542-5217

Owners of Rometsch automobiles. Works to account for all remaining automobiles built by Rometsch of Berlin, Germany.

Saab Club of North America
2416 London Rd., No. 900
Duluth, MN 55812
(218) 724-1336
Fax: (218) 728-6307

Owners and enthusiasts of Swedish-manufactured Saab automobiles. Helps members exchange information on the care and maintenance of all Saab models.

Sabra Connection
7040 N. Navajo Ave.
Milwaukee, WI 53217
(414) 352-8408

Promotes the interest and history of rare Sabra automobiles which were manufactured in 1962 and 1963 by Reliant Corp. in Eng-

land and by Autocars Ltd. in Israel. Compiles serial numbers of existing Sabra vehicles; disseminates information. Maintains ownership lists.

Saxon Owners Registry
c/o Walter H. Prichard
5250 NW Highland Way
Corvallis, OR 97330
(503) 752-6231

Persons interested in acquiring, restoring, and preserving Saxon automobiles. Attempts to determine how many of the 90,000 Saxons that were manufactured are still in existence. Helps those restoring Saxons to locate parts and information.

Scripps-Booth Register
10 Bacon's Wood Dr.
Macomb, IL 61455
(309) 837-2593

Owners of Scripps-Booth automobiles and interested others. Promotes communication among members.

Sebring/Cimbria Kit Car Club
6 Dixie Dr.
Bel Air, MD 21014
(410) 836-5618
Fax: (410) 671-4941

Owners of Cimbria or Sebring kit cars. Acts as forum for the exchange of information on the construction of kit cars. Maintains library of technical and how-to books. Sponsors displays at car shows.

74-75-76 Cadillac Talisman Registry
404 La Vista Blvd.
Dodge City, KS 67801

Owners and enthusiasts of 1974–76 Cadillac Talisman automobiles. Collects information on this vehicle and maintains records on Cadillac Talisman owners.

'71 429 Mustang Registry
6250 Germantown Pike
Dayton, OH 45418
(513) 866-0690
Fax: (513) 438-2337

Owners and admirers of 1971 Ford Mustang automobiles. Promotes restoration and preservation of these cars.

Shelby American Automobile Club
PO Box 480
Chilmark, MA 02535
(508) 645-3471
Fax: (508) 645-2475

Owners and enthusiasts of Shelby GT 350 and GT 500, Cobra, Tiger, and Ford GT automobiles. Dedicated to the history, preservation, care, and enjoyment of the sports cars manufactured between 1962 and 1970 by Shelby American, Inc. Services include parts and technical assistance information and insurance assistance at reasonable prices.

Shelby Owners of America
577 14th St. SE
Le Mars, IA 51031
(712) 546-4045
Owners and enthusiasts of cars made by Shelby American 1962–73, and high performance Ford Motor Company cars, including Shelby GT 350, GT 500, GT 500 KR, Cobra, GT, Mustang, Boss, and Mach automobiles. Purpose is to collect and preserve high-performance Shelby and Ford cars. Sponsors drag races, autocross programs, car shows, and swap meets. Acts as technical information clearinghouse.

Siata/Fiat 8V Register
PO Box 1022
Cambria, CA 93428
(805) 927-5802
Fax: (805) 927-5802
Owners and enthusiasts of Siata and Fiat 8V automobiles. Maintains a register of known Siatas and Fiat 8Vs and a library of historical documents regarding these automobiles. Operates museum and archives. Compiles statistics.

66,67,68 High Country Special Mustang Registry
6874 Benton Ct.
Arvada, CO 80003
(303) 424-3866
Owners and enthusiasts of High Country Special Mustang automobiles, model years 1966, '67, and '68. Collects and decodes descriptive information contained in vehicle information numbers. Compiles statistics. Assists enthusiasts, owners and potential owners.

Slant 6 Club of America
Box 4414
Salem, OR 97302
(503) 581-2230
Collectors and restorers of Slant 6 vehicles, most notably mid-1960s Darts and Valiants, but includes all Slant 6 powered cars and trucks (Slant 6 vehicles are cars manufactured from 1960 to 1983 and trucks manufactured from 1961 to 1987 by the Chrysler Corporation. Slant 6 is a six cylinder engine that is slanted at a 30 degree angle). Promotes the maintenance, restoration, and preservation of Slant 6 powered vehicles.

Society of Automotive Historians
6760 E. County Rd., 800 North
Brownsburg, IN 46112
(317) 852-0431
Writers, researchers, librarians, students, educators, hobbyists, publishers, industry figures, museums, and other individuals. Purpose is the preservation and recording of the history of the automobile, the industry, its people, its attendant industries, and supporting structures. Conducts research. Activities include rescuing and placing historical material in publicly accessible libraries and archives.

Sports Car Club of America
9033 E. Easter Pl.
Englewood, CO 80112
(303) 694-7222
Fax: (303) 694-7391
Competition sports car owners and enthusiasts. Sanctions professional FIA international events and amateur national and regional races. Sanctions World Challenge and Trans-Am Tour series; also conducts race driver schools, rallies (professional European-style and precision driving tests over a given route at an exact speed), gymkhanas (intricate driving maneuvers in a cleared area), and concours d'elegance (rating cars by a correlation of age, condition, and equipment of the vehicle). Issues competition driver licenses. Establishes safety regulations for competitions. Conducts educational and charitable programs.

Sportscar Vintage Racing Association
PO Box 489
Charleston, SC 29402
(803) 723-7872
Fax: (803) 723-7372
Sanctioning body for vintage sports car races.

Squire SS-100 Registry
c/o Arthur R. Stahl
11826 S. 51st St.
Phoenix, AZ 85044-2313
(602) 893-9451
Owners and enthusiasts of Squire SS-100 automobiles. Traces ownership and maintains records of ownership of the Squire SS-100.

Stealth Club of America
1718A Northfield Sq.
Northfield, IL 60093
Owners and enthusiasts of Dodge Stealths. Promotes the enjoyment and preservation of the Dodge Stealth automobile. Works to exchange ideas, technical information, and reminiscences about Stealths among members.

Steam Automobile Club of America
PO Box 285
Niles, MI 49120
(616) 683-4269

Persons interested in restoration of antique steam cars, preservation of steam car history, and the design, development, and production of a modern steam car.

Stevens-Duryea Associates
3565 Newhaven Rd.
Pasadena, CA 91107
(818) 351-8237

Owners of Stevens-Duryea antique automobiles. Provides exchange of information, and assistance in the restoration and maintenance of the automobiles. Participates in meetings with Antique Automobile Club of America, Horseless Carriage Club of America, and Veteran Motor Car Club of America.

Studebaker Driver's Club
PO Box 1040
Oswego, IL 60543
(800) 527-3452

Owners of Studebaker automobiles and trucks. Attempts to aid in the restoration of, procure parts for, and reproduce old instruction manuals of the Studebaker car. Supports Studebaker Vehicle Museum in South Bend, IN. Compiles statistics.

Stutz Club
7400 Lantern Rd.
Indianapolis, IN 46256
(317) 849-3443

Stutz automobile owners and enthusiasts. Promotes fellowship and the maintenance and preservation of Stutz automobiles. Works to preserve Stutz literature, memorabilia, and technical information. Conducts exhibitions of Stutz automobiles for charitable organizations. Conducts research programs. Compiles statistics.

Subaru 360 Drivers' Club
1421 N. Grady Ave.
Tucson, AZ 85715
(520) 290-6492

Past, present, or potential owners and drivers of 1968 to 1970 two-cylinder Subaru 360 automobiles. Objective is to keep these vehicles functional. Provides information on parts availability and maintenance procedures. Forms united effort to keep parts available and licensing rights unrestricted for vehicles. Offers help in documenting value of Subaru 360s for insurance purposes.

Sunbeam Alpine Club
1752 Oswald Pl.
Santa Clara, CA 95050
(408) 984-1474

Owners of automobiles manufactured by Rootes Motors, primarily Sunbeam Alpine

owners. Seeks to preserve Sunbeam automobiles through events such as clinics, meetings, and track meets. Fosters competition through sponsorship of rallies and autocross races. Provides research information service; compiles statistics. Maintains record of all Rootes vehicles and small library; operates speakers' bureau.

Tigers East/Alpines East
PO Box 1260
Kulpsville, PA 19443
(717) 566-6813
Fax: (717) 566-6813

Promotes the restoration and preservation of the Sunbeam sports car.

Topolino Register of North America
3301 Shetland Rd.
Beavercreek, OH 45434
(513) 426-0098

Owners and others interested in Fiat Topolino automobiles and their derivatives. Serves as a central exchange for information, technical advice, and parts sources for owners of Fiat Topolino automobiles, and related vehicles including the Simca Cinq, Siata Amica, and Nardi-Crosley. Attempts to locate all remaining Topolinos in North America by serial numbers.

TR8 Car Club of America
266 Linden St.
Rochester, NY 14620
(716) 244-9693

Individuals who enjoy the TR8 automobile, which was manufactured from 1978 to 1982, and was the last model produced by British Leyland's Triumph division. Provides technical and parts location information to members.

Triumph Register of America
5650 Brook Rd. NW
Lancaster, OH 43130
(410) 974-6707

Owners and enthusiasts of Triumph sports cars of the TR-2/3 series, manufactured between 1953 and 1962. Aids owners in the preservation, maintenance, and enjoyment of their classic sports cars. Conducts technical workshops and rallies through local centers. Provides advertisement and information on new and secondhand spare parts.

Tucker Automobile Club of America
c/o Richard Jones
315 Arora Blvd.
Orange Park, FL 32073-3213
(904) 272-5982

Persons interested in the Tucker automobile, which was manufactured in 1948 by the Tucker Corporation of Chicago, Illinois. Plans to open museum.

TVR Car Club North America

4450 S. Park Ave., Apt. 1609
Chevy Chase, MD 20815
(301) 986-8679
Fax: (301) 986-9611

Owners and enthusiasts of TVR automobiles. (The TVR sports car is totally handcrafted by TVR Engineering, Ltd., of England.) Purpose is to preserve and maintain the TVR marque. Offers spare parts service for members.

United Drag Racers Association

7601 Hamilton Ave.
Burr Ridge, IL 60521
(708) 887-0442
Fax: (708) 887-0443

Drag racing teams; retail distributors of products related to drag racing; owners of drag racing cars; persons with an interest in the sport. Sponsors drag racing events; provides cars to other associations for races.

United Ford Owners

Box 32419
Columbus, OH 43232
(614) 265-8095

Owners of vehicles manufactured by the Ford Motor Company and interested individuals. Promotes interests of members. Maintains library of books, periodicals, and videos on automotive-related subjects.

United Four-Wheel Drive Associations

4505 W. 700 S
Shelbyville, IN 46176
(317) 729-5862, (800)44-UFWDA
Fax: (317) 729-5930

Advisory and individual members' clubs. Purpose is to work with land problems and establish better communication between four-wheelers and the government. Operates charitable program benefitting the March of Dimes Birth Defects Foundation. Compiles statistics.

United States Auto Club (USAC)

4910 W. 16th St.
Indianapolis, IN 46224
(317) 247-5151
Fax: (317) 247-0123

Officials, manufacturers' representatives, mechanics, drivers, and car owners. Purposes are to: provide qualified leadership and officiating at major automotive competitions; license personnel; sanction competitions; maintain permanent records of accomplishments; schedule events; execute other func-

tions necessary for the proper control of motorsports in the U.S.

United States Camaro Club

PO Box 608167
Orlando, FL 32860
(407) 880-1967, (800) CAMAROS
Fax: (407) 880-1972

Owners and enthusiasts interested in Camaro automobiles built between 1967 and 1994. Works with technicians and car dealers on writing educational and technical information concerning the Camaro. Holds swap meets, car shows, and other programs including trim tag code research and cruise-ins. Provides discount cards on parts and services from advertisers. Compiles statistics. Plans to create museum.

United Street Machine Association

430 N. Batchawana
Clawson, MI 48017
(810) 280-0342

Individuals interested in owning and showing muscle cars, street rods, customs, 4 x 4s, and trucks. Conducts charitable programs.

U.S. Route 66 Association

PO Drawer 5323
Oxnard, CA 93031
(805) 488-8613

Led successful movement to preserve and revitalize old Route 66, which had been officially decommissioned, helping to increase touring from 100 vehicles per year in 1983 to 10,000 annually today. Main focus had shifted from preservation and promotion to serving the Route 66 traveler. Works with affiliated Route 66 organizations overseas, together with tour sponsors to provide a memorable touring experience. Provides design services, cultural guidance and opportunities for socially responsible marketing.

Veteran Motor Car Club of America

c/o William E. Donze, M.D.
PO Box 360788
Strongsville, OH 44136

Collectors and others interested in antique automobiles and related items.

Vintage Chevrolet Club of America

PO Box 5387
Orange, CA 92667
(714) 633-1310

Persons interested in restoration and preservation of vintage Chevrolet automobiles. Currently recognizes all Chevrolet-built vehicles at least 15 years old. Sponsors meets and car shows. Provides insurance and technical sponsorship for all approved functions.

Vintage Sports Car Club of America
170 Wetherill Rd.
Garden City, NY 11530
> Vintage sports car owners and enthusiasts. Encourages acquisition, preservation, restoration, and operation of sports and racing cars built before World War II, and rare and unusual sports cars built between 1944 and 1959. Sponsors competitive events and exhibitions; serves as a source of technical information.

Vintage Thunderbird Club International
PO Box 2250
Dearborn, MI 48123-2250
(716) 674-7251
> Owners of 1958 to 1966 Ford Thunderbird automobiles. Encourages restoration and maintenance of the cars, exchanges pertinent information, and participates in group events of a car oriented nature. Provides technical assistance; maintains parts locator service.

Vintage Triumph Register
15218 W. Warren Ave.
Dearborn, MI 48126
(770) 932-8153
> Persons interested in preserving and enjoying Triumph automobiles. Purposes are to: provide advice and assistance for the maintenance, restoration, and preservation of the marque; investigate parts and literature sources and make them available to members; conduct research into the history of the marque.

Vintage Volkswagen Club of America
5705 Gordon Dr.
Harrisburg, PA 17112
(717) 540-9972
> Owners and enthusiasts of Volkswagen-based automobiles which are air-cooled. Promotes the acquisition, preservation, and restoration of the vintage cars. Facilitates exchange of technical and mechanical information and information concerning the location of original parts and old literature. Works to establish beneficial relationships with Volkswagen factories and dealers.

Volkswagen Club of America
PO Box 154
Department EA
North Aurora, IL 60542-0154
(708) 896-2803
> Owners and enthusiasts of Volkswagen and Audi automobiles. Disseminates information on maintenance and restoration of Volkswagen vehicles. Local clubs hold rallies, parties, and other automotive and social events.

Volvo Club of America
PO Box 16
Afton, NY 13730
(607) 639-2279
Fax: (607) 639-2279
> Owners and enthusiasts of Volvo automobiles produced from the 1930s to the present. Promotes ownership of Volvos and communication among Volvo owners. Provides technical information and assistance. Encourages safe driving and the use of safety devices such as seat belts. Sponsors regional and national activities.

Volvo Sports America 1800 Registry
1203 W. Cheltenham Ave.
Melrose Park, PA 19027
(215) 635-0117
Fax: (215) 635-4070
> Owners of 1800 Volvo sports cars, which are qualified by the Milestone Car Society as milestone cars. To encourage proper operation and maintenance, recognition, and the preservation and restoration of all 1800 Volvo sports models.

Wills Sainte Claire Owners Club
c/o William L. McKeand
721 Jenkinson
Port Huron, MI 48060
(810) 987-2425
> Owners of Wills Sainte Claire automobiles (about 82 cars accounted for), former owners, and interested individuals. Supplies members with information and parts needed in restoring cars. Maintains hall of fame honoring C. Harold Wills. Maintains library of original bulletins, factory letters, dealer and distributor letters, factory parts and prices, showroom bulletins and catalogs, and original photos of cars when new.

Willys Club
c/o Gordon Lindahl
795 N. Evans St.
Pottstown, PA 19464
> Individuals interested in Willys vehicles manufactured from 1933 to 1963. Purpose is the preservation and restoration of these vehicles.

Willys Overland Jeepster Club
PO Box 12042
El Paso, TX 79913-0042
(915) 581-2671
> Promotes interest in and respect for the Willys Overland Jeepster Phaeton, "the last touring car phaeton body style built in the U.S." According to club statistics, only 19,131 such convertibles were made between 1948 and 1951.

Willys-Overland-Knight Registry

1440 Woodacre Dr.

McLean, VA 22101-2535

(703) 533-0396

> *Persons interested in the restoration and maintenance of the Knight sleeve-valve engine and pre-World War II Willys-Overland automobiles. Provides historical and technical information and reproduces some hard-to-find parts.*

Winged Warriors/National B-Body Owners Association

216 12th St.

Boone, IA 50036

(515) 432-3001

> *Auto enthusiasts. Seeks to account for each produced 1962 to 1974 Bigblock Plymouth and Dodge B-Body, 1969 Charger Daytona, and 1970 Superbird automobiles. Assembles historical information on the vehicles; promotes local and regional meets; aids members in restoring their cars.*

Woodill Wildfire Registry

c/o Frank Cornell

52 Briggs Rd.

Lebanon, CT 06249

(860) 642-6144

> *Owners of Woodill Wildfire automobiles. (The Woodill Wildfire was produced from 1952 to 1958 by the Woodill Motor Company in Downey, California, and was one of the first fiberglass sports cars.) Serves as forum for exchange of information among members. Compiles statistics.*

WPC Club

PO Box 3504

Kalamazoo, MI 49003-3504

(616) 375-5535

Fax: (616) 375-5535

> *Individuals dedicated to the preservation, restoration, and enjoyment of Chrysler product cars. Conducts social activities; houses library.*

Zimmerman Registry

2081 Madelaine Ct.

Los Altos, CA 94024

(415) 967-2908

Fax: (415) 967-2908

> *Promotes the preservation of Zimmerman automobiles, which were produced in Auburn, Indiana, from 1907–1915. Conducts research and location programs. Provides restoration information. Compiles statistics.*

Alabama

International Motorsports Hall of Fame Museum
Speedway Blvd.
Talladega, AL 35160

Arizona

Hall of Flame Firefighting Museum
6101 E. Van Buren St.
Phoenix, AZ 85008

H.H. Franklin Museum
1405 E. Kleindale Road
Tucson, AZ 85719

Arkansas

The Castle-Museum at Inspiration Point
Rt. 2
Eureka Springs, AK 72362

Museum of Automobiles
Petit Jean Mountain
Rt. 3
Morrilton, AR 72110

Reed's Museum of Automobiles
714 Central Ave.
Hot Springs, AR 71901

California

Antique Automotive Museum
4124 Poplar St.
San Diego, CA 92105

Arciero Race Car Exhibit
2625 Hwy. 46E
Paso Robles, CA 93446

Behring Auto Museum
3750 Balckhawk Plaza Circle
Danville, CA 94506

Boses Collection/Hollywood Picture Vehicles
1028 N. Labrea Ave.
West Hollywood, CA 90038

Deer Park Car Museum
29013 Champagne Blvd.
Escondido, CA 92026

Dennis Mitosinka's Classic Cars
619 E. 4th St.
Santa Ana, CA 92701

Firehouse Museum
1572 Columbia St.
San Diego, CA 92101

Hays Antique Truck Museum
2000 E. Main St.
Woodland, CA 95695

Jim Lattin Racing Museum
1275 W. Second St.
Pomon, CA 91768

Merle Norman Classic Collection
15180 Bledso St.
Sylmar, CA 91342

Metropolitan Historical Collection
5330 Low Canyon Rd.
North Hollywood, CA 91607

Miller's California Ranch Horse and Buggy Display
9425 Yosemite Blvd.
Modesto, CA 95351

N & G Antique Cars
16142 Harbor Blvd.
Fountain Valley, CA 92708

Petersen Automotive Museum
Los Angeles Museum/Natural History
900 Exposition Blvd.
Los Angeles, CA 90007

San Diego Automotive Museum
2080 Pan American Plaza
Balboa Park
San Diego, CA 92112

San Francisco Maritime National Park
Fort Mason Building 201
Hyde Street Pier
San Francisco, CA 94123

Towe Ford Museum
2200 Front St.
Sacramento, CA 95818

Vintage Coach
16593 Arrow Blvd.
Fontana, CA 92335

Vintage Museum and Wildlife Collection
1421 Emerson Ave.
Oxnard, CA 93033

Colorado

Antique Auto House
3312 N. Garfield
Loveland, CO 80538

Dougherty Museum Collection
U.S. 287
Longmont, CO 80501

Forney Transportation Museum
1416 Platte St.
Denver, CO 80202

Pikes Peak Auto Hill Climb Museum
135 Manitou Ave.
Manitou Springs, CO 80829

Connecticut

Connecticut Fire Museum
Route 140
Warehouse Point, CT 06088

Delaware

Delaware Agricultural Museum
866 N. Dupont Highway
Dover, DE 19901

Nemours Mansion and Gardens
Rockland Rd
Wilmington, DE 19899

District of Columbia

National Museum of American History
Smithsonian Institution
4th St. and Constitution Ave. N.W.
Washington, D.C. 20560

Florida

Bellm's Cars/Music of Yesterday
5500 N. Tamiami Trail
Sarasota, FL 34243

Birthplace of Speed Museum
160 E. Granada Blvd.
Ormond Beach, FL 32176

Dezerland Surfside Beach Hotel
8701 Collins Ave.
Miami Beach, FL 33154

Don Garlits Museum of Drag Racing
13700 SW 16th
Ocala, FL 32676

Historical Society of Martin County-Elliott
825 N.E. Ocean Blvd.
Hutchinson Island, FL 34996

Klassix Auto Museum
2909 W. International Speedway Blvd.
Daytona Beach, FL 32124

Georgia

Antique Auto and Music Museum
Stone Mountain Park
Stone Mountain, GA 30083

Little White House Historic Site
Rt. 1
Warm Springs, GA 31830

Museo Abarth
1111 Via Bayless
Marietta, GA 30066-2770

Old Car City
3098 Highway 411
White, GA 30184

SAAB Headquarters Collection
Gwinnett Summit
4405-A International Blvd.
Norcross, GA 30093

Idaho

Idaho State Historical Society
2445 Old Penitentiary Rd.
Boise, ID 83712

Trant's Antique Cars and Museum
5603 Franklin Rd.
Boise, ID 83705

Vintage Wheel Museum
218 Cedar ST.
Sandpoint, ID 83864

Illinois

Byron Lewis Farm Museum
325 W. Lafayette Ave.
Jacksonville, IL 62650

Dale's Classic Cars
Rt. 1
Waltonville Rd.
Mt. Vernon, IL 62684

Grant Hills Antique Auto Museum
Rt. 20E
Galena, IL 61036

Gray's Ride Thru History Museum
1608 E. Main St.
West Fronkfort, IL 62896

Hartung's Automotive Museum
3623 W. Lake St.
Glenview, IL 60025

McDonald's Des Plaines Museum
400 N. Lee Street
Des Plaines, IL 60016

Max Nordeen's Wheels Museum
RR 1
Woodhull, IL 61413

Museum of Science and Industry
57th St. and Lake Shore Dr.
Chicago, IL 60637

Quincippi Auto Museum
Front and Cedar Streets
Quincy, IL 62301

Volo Antique Auto Museum/Village
27582 W. Hwy. 120
Volo, IL 60073

Wheels O' Time Museum
Rt. 88
Peoria, IL 61525

Wheels of Time Museum
11923 N. Knoxville Ave.
Dunlap, IL 61525

Indiana

Door Prairie Museum
2405 South Indiana Avenue
Laporte, IN 46350

Elwood Haynes Museum
1915 S. Webster
Kokomo, IN 46902

Fort Wayne Firefighters Museum
226 W. Washington St.
Fort Wayne, IN 46852

Henry H. Blommel Historic Automotive Data Collection
Rt. 5
Connersville, IN 47331

Indianapolis Motor Speedway Hall of Fame
4790 W. 16th St.
Indianapolis, IN 46222

Maclyn Museum
U.S. Hwy. 52
Metamora, IN 47030

Natmus
1000 Gordon Buehrig Pl.
Auburn, IN 46706

Ruthmere Museum
302 E. Beardsley St.
Elkhart, IN 46514

S. Ray Miller Antique Car Museum
2130 Middlebury St.
Elkhart, IN 46516

Studebaker National Museum
525 S. Main St.
South Bend, IN 46601

Wayne County Historical Museum
1150 North A St.
Richmond, IN 47374

Iowa

Duffy's Collectible Cars
250 Classic Car Court S.W.A.
Cedar Rapids, IA 52404

Kinney Pioneer Museum
U.S. Hwy. 18
Mason City, IA 50401

Schield International Museum
805 W. Bremer Ave.
Waverly, IA 50677

State Historical Society of Iowa
Capitol Complex
Historical Building
Des Moines, IA 50319

Van Horn's Antique Truck Museum
Hwy. 65 N.
Mason City, IA 50401

Kansas

Kansas State Museum of History Annex
6425 S.W. Sixth St.
Topeka, KS 66615

Reo Antique Auto Museum
100 N. Harrison
Lindsborg, KS 67456

Van Arsdale Antique Car Museum
323 W. Broadway
Macksville, KS 67557

Wheels & Spokes Classic Auto Display
383 Mopar Dr.
Hays, KS 67601

Kentucky

National Corvette Museum
350 Corvette Drive
Bowling Green, KY 42101-9134

Rineyville Sandblasting Model A Ford
179 Arvelwise Ln.
Elizabethtown, KY 42701

Thomas Kaiser-Frazer Museum
Rt. 11
Corbin, KY 40701

Maryland

U.S. Army Ordnance Museum
Building 2601
Aberdeen Proving Grounds, MD 21005

Maine

Boothbay Railway Village
Route 27
Boothbay, ME 04537

Cole Land Transportation Museum
405 Perry Rd.
Bangor, ME 04401

Jay Hill Antique Auto Museum
SR 4
Jay, ME 04239

Owls Head Transportation Museum
Rt. 73
Owls Head, ME 04854

Seal Cove Automotive Museum
Pretty Marsh Rd.
Seal Cove ME 04674

Stanley Museum
School St.
Kingfield, ME 04947

Wells Auto Museum
Rt. 1
Wells, ME 04090

Massachusetts

Edaville Railroad
SR 58
South Carver, MA 02366

Heritage Plantation Auto Museum
Grove and Pine Streets
Sandwich, MA 02563

Museum of Transportation
15 Newton St
Larz Anderson Park
Brookline, MA 02146

Michigan

Alfred P. Sloan Jr. Museum
1221 East Kearsley ST.
Flint, MI 48503

Automotive Hall of Fame
3225 Cook Rd.
Midland, MI 48641

Cadillac Historical Collection
2860 Clark
Detroit, MI 48232

Detroit Historical Museum
5401 Woodward Ave.
Detroit, MI 48202

Domino's Classic Cars
44 Frank Lloyd Wright Dr.
Ann Arbor, MI 48106

Gilmore CCCA Car Museum
6865 Hickory Rd.
Hickory Corners, MI 49060

Henry Ford Museum/Greenfield Village
20900 Oakwood Blvd.
Dearborn, MI 48121

Miller Motor Sales
100 E. Cross
Ypsilanti, MI 48198

Motorsports Hall of Fame
43700 Expo Center Dr.
Novi, MI 48375

Poll Museum of Transportation
1715 104th Ave.
Zeeland, MI 49464-1403

R.E. Olds Transportation Museum
240 Museum Dr.
Lansing, MI 48933-1905

Village of Jonesville
103 Evans St.
Jonesville, MI 49250

Ye Olde Carriage Shop
108 Second St.
Jackson, MI 49283

Ypsilanti Antique Auto, Truck & Fire Museum
110 W. Cross
Ypsilanti, MI 48105

Minnesota

Ernie Tuff Museum
Junction I-90 and I-43
Rushford, MN 55971

Missouri

Memoryville, U.S.A.
I-44 and 63 N.
Rolla, MO 65401

National Museum of Transportation
3015 Barrett Station Rd.
St. Louis, MO 63122-3398

Patee House Museum
12th and Penn Streets
St. Joseph, MO 64502

Montana

Oscar's Dreamland
Wise Lane
Rt. 9
Billings, MT 59102

Towe Ford Museum
1106 Main St.
Deer Lodge, MT 59722

Nebraska

Chevyland U.S.A.
Rt. 2
Elm Creek, NE 68836

Harold Wrap Pioneer Village Foundation
Hwys. 6, 34 and 10
Minden, NE 68959

Hastings Museum
1330 N. Burlington Ave.
Hastings, NE 68901

Plainsman Museum
210 16th St.
Aurora, NE 68818

Sawyer's Sandhills Museum
440 Valentine St.
Valentine, NE 69201

Stuhr Museum of the Prairie Pioneer
3133 W. Highway 34
Grand Island, NE 68801

Nevada

Imperial Palace Auto Collection
3535 Las Vegas Blvd. S.
Las Vegas, NV 89109

National Automobile Museum
William F. Harrah Foundation
10 Lake St.
Reno, NV 89501

New Hampshire

Grand Manor Classic Car Museum
Rt. 16 and 302
Glen, NH 03838

New Jersey

Space Farms Zoo & Museum
218 Rt. 519
Beemerville, NJ 07461

New Mexico

Callahan's Auto Museum
410 Cedar St.
Truth or Consequences, NY 87901

New York

American Museum of Firefighting
125 Harry Howard Ave.
Hudon, NY 12534

Auto Memories
County Rt. 38
Arkville, NY 12406

BMW Gallery
320 Park Ave.
New York, NY 10022

Collector Cars Inc.
56 W. Merrick Rd.
Freeport, NY 11520

Hall of Fame/Classic Car Museum
Dirt Motorsports
1 Speedway Dr.
Weedsport, NY 13166

Himes Museum of Racing Nostalgia
15 O'Neil Ave
Bay Shore, NY 11706

Museum of the City of New York
Fifth Ave. at 103rd St.
New York, NY 10029

Old Rhinebeck Aerodrome
42 Stone Church Rd.
Rhinebeck, NY 12572

Wilson Historical Museum
644 Lake St.
Rt. 425
Wilson, NY 14172-0830

North Carolina

Backing Up Classics Auto Museum
4545 Highway 29
Harrisburg, NC 28075

Estes-Winn-Blomberg Antique Car Museum
Biltmore Homespun Shops
Grove Park Inn
Asheville, NC 28804

Greensboro Historical Museum
130 Summit Ave.
Greensboro, NC 27401

Grier Beam Truck Museum
111 N. Mountain St.
Cherryville, NC 28021

North Carolina Transportation Museum
411 S. Salisbury Ave.
Spencer, NC 28159

Rearview Mirror Automotive Center
300 E. Baltic St.
Nags Head, NC 27959

Richard Petty Museum
Branson Mill Rd.
Randleman, NC 27317

North Dakota

Bonanzaville U.S.A.
1351 W. Main Ave.
West Fargo, ND 58078

Ohio

Allen County Museum
620 W. Market St.
Lima, OH 45801

Canton Classic Car Museum
555 Market Ave. S.W.
Canton, OH 44702

Carillion Historical Park
2001 S. Patterson Blvd.
Dayton, OH 45409

Crawford Auto-Aviation Museum
10825 E. Boulevard
University Circle
Cleveland, OH 44106

National Road-Zane Gray Museum
8850 East Pike
Norwich, OH 43767

Professor's Automotive Works
1420 Commerce Park Dr.
Tipp City, OH 45371

Toledo Firefighters Museum
918 Sylvania Ave.
Toledo, OH 43612

Oklahoma

George's Antique Auto Museum
508 S. Grand St.
Enid, OK 73702

Lewis Museum
816 S.E. 1st Street
Lawton, OK 73501

Museum of Special Interest Autos
13700 Hwy. 177
Shawnee, OK 74801

Oklahoma State Firefighters Museum
2716 N.E. 50th St.
Oklahoma City, OK 73111

Oregon

Tillamook County Pioneer Museum
2106 2nd St.
Tillamook, OR 97141

Pennsylvania

Alan Dent Antique Car Museum
Main St.
Lightstreet, PA 17839

Auto's Literature Shoppe
PA Route 522
Fort Littleton, PA 17223

Boyertown Museum of Historic Vehicles
28 Warwick St.
Boyertown, PA 19512

Franklin Mint Museum
Rt. 1
Franklin Center, PA 19091

Gast Classic Motor Cars Museum,
Rt. 896
421 Hartman Bridge Rd.
Strasburg, PA 17579

Holland Automotive Art Collection
111 N. Fourth St.
Allentown, PA 18102

JEM Classic Car Museum
RD 1
Andreas, PA 18211

Kelley Auto Museum
Lehigh Rd.
Boudsboro, PA 18424

Lehigh University College of Engineering
Packard Labs
Packer Ave.
Bethlehem, PA 18015

Reilly Classic Motors
174 Market St.
Kingston, PA 18704

Simpler Times Museum
U.S. Rt. 52
Tidioute, PA 16351

State Museum of Pennsylvania
Third and North Streets
Harrisburg, PA 17108-1026

Station Square Transportation Museum
One Station Square
#450 Bessemer Ct.
Pittsburgh, PA 15219-1170

Swigart Museum
Museum Park
Rt. 22
Huntington, PA 16652

Tee-To-Tum Museum
Rt. 6
Wysox, PA 18848

Thomas' Antique and Classic Cars
214 Willow Valley Lakes Dr.
Willow Street, PA 17584

South Carolina

Calhoun County Museum
303 Butler St.
St. Matthews, SC 29135

Schoolhouse Antiques Museum
517 Flat Rock Road
Liberty, SC 29657

Stock Car Hall of Fame
SR 34 W
Darlington, SC 29532

South Dakota

Friends of the Middle Border
1311 Duff St.
Mitchell, SD 57301

Old West Museum
Hwy. 16
Chamberlain, SD 57325

Pioneer Auto and Antique Town
I-90 and U.S. Hwy. 16 and 83
Murdo, SD 57559-0076

Spearfish Classic Auto Museum
Service Rd. and Heritage Dr.
Spearfish, SD 57783

Telstar Motors
Mustang-Shelby-Cobra Museum
1300 S. Kimball St.
Mitchell, SD 57301

Tennessee

Car Collector Hall of Fame
1534 Demonbreun St.
Nashville, TN 37203

Country Music Hall of Fame
4 Music Square E.
Nashville, TN 37203

Dixie Gun Works
Hwy. 51 S
Union City, TN 38261

Elvis Presley Automobile Museum
Graceland Mansion
3765 Presley Blvd.
Memphis, TN 38116

Hank Williams Jr. Museum
1524 Demonbreun St.
Nashville, TN 37203

Jim Reeves Museum
1023 Joyce Ln.
Nashville, TN 37203

Marathon Village
1305 Clinton St.
Nashville, TN 37203

Music Valley Car Museum
2611 McGavock Pike
Nashville, TN 37214

Smoky Mountain Car Museum
2970 Parkway
Pigeon Forge, TN 37868-1385

Texas

Alamo Classic Car Museum
6401 I-35 South
New Braunfels, TX 78132

Bolin Wildlife & Antique Exhibit
1028 N. McDonald
McKinney, TX 75069

american motor museums

Central Texas Museum of Automotive History
Hwy. 304
Rosanky, TX 78953

David Taylor Classic Car Museum
1918 Mechanic St.
Galveston, TX 77550

GAF Auto Museum
118 Kodak Blvd.
Longview, TX 75607

J.D. Sandefer Oil Annex
113 N. Breckenridge Ave.
Breckenridge, TX 76424

Panhandle-Plains Historical Museum
2401 Fourth Ave.
Canyon, TX 79016

Pate Museum of Transportation
U.S. 377
Cresson, TX 76101

Second Armored Division Museum
27th and Batallion
Fort Hood
Killeen, TX 76544

Utah

Bonneville Speedway Museum
I-80 Business
Wendover, UT 84083

Classic Cars International Museum
355 W. 700 S.
Salt Lake City, UT 84101

Union Station Museum
2501 Wall Ave.
Ogden, Ut 84401

Vermont

Bennington Museum
W. Main St.
Bennington, VT 05201

Virginia

Edgar Rohr Collection Museum
9126 Center St.
Manassas, VA 22110

Glade Mountain Museum
Rt. 615
Atkins, VA 24311

Roaring Twenties Antique Car Museum
Rt. 1
Hood, VA 22723

Staunton Volunteer Fire Department and Jumbo Museum
500 N. Augusta St.
Staunton, VA 24401

U.S. Army Transportation Museum
Building 300
Besson Hall
Fort Eustis, VA 23604-5260

Virginia Museum of Transportation
303 Norfolk Ave.
Roanoke, VA 24016

Washington

Lynden Pioneer Museum
217 W. Front St.
Lynden, WA 98264

Monty Holm's House of Poverty
228 S. Commerce St.
Moses Lake, WA 98837

Whoop-N-Holler Ranch and Museum
1 Whitmore Rd.
Bickleton, WA 99322

Wisconsin

Brooks Stevens Automotive Museum
10325 N. Port Washington Rd.
Mequon, WI 53092

Dells Auto Museum
591 Wisconsin Dells Pkwy.
Wisconsin Dells, WI 53965

Four Wheel Drive Museum
40 E. 11th St.
Clintonville, WI 54929

Hartford Heritage Auto Museum
147 N. Rural St.
Hartford, WI 53027

Midway Auto Museum
U.S. Hwy. 45
Birnamwood, WI 54414

Uihlein Antique Racing Car Museum
Hamilton Rd.
Cedarburg, WI 53012

Zunker's Antique Car Museum
3717 Macarthur Dr.
Manitowoc, WI 54220